A TEXTBOOK
OF ECONOMIC THEORY

By Douglas C. Hague & Alfred W. Stonier

THE ESSENTIALS OF ECONOMICS

A TEXTBOOK OF
ECONOMIC THEORY

BY

ALFRED W. STONIER

Senior Lecturer in Political Economy
University College London

AND

DOUGLAS C. HAGUE

Reader in Political Economy in the
University of London

LONGMANS GREEN AND CO
LONDON · NEW YORK · TORONTO

LONGMANS, GREEN AND CO LTD
6 & 7 CLIFFORD STREET LONDON W I
THIBAULT HOUSE THIBAULT SQUARE CAPE TOWN
605–611 LONSDALE STREET MELBOURNE C I

LONGMANS, GREEN AND CO INC
55 FIFTH AVENUE NEW YORK 3

LONGMANS, GREEN AND CO
20 CRANFIELD ROAD TORONTO 16

ORIENT LONGMANS PRIVATE LTD
CALCUTTA BOMBAY MADRAS
DELHI HYDERABAD DACCA

First published 1953
Second impression 1954
Third impression 1955
Fourth impression 1956
Fifth impression 1956
Second Edition 1957

PRINTED IN GREAT BRITAIN
BY R. & R. CLARK, LTD., EDINBURGH

PREFACE TO THE SECOND EDITION

THE only significant change in this Edition is that we have rewritten the first part of Section 7, on Quasi-rent, in Chapter XIII. We wish to thank Mr. W. E. Armstrong for helping us to redraft this section.

There is, however, one other problem which calls for comment, and this can best be dealt with here. In the discussion of open-market operations (pp. 376-9) we assume that a purchase of, say, £1000 worth of securities by the Central Bank will raise the level of bank deposits by $12\frac{1}{2}$ times this amount—assuming that the cash-deposit ratio is 8 per cent. Various people, including Mr. D. J. Coppock and Mr. J. C. Gilbert, have pointed out that this is an over-simplification. We have ignored the fact that some of the 'cash' created by the Central Bank's purchase of securities is likely to find its way into the hands of the public instead of remaining in the coffers of the banks. There will be what is known as 'the drain of cash' into circulation.

Just how quickly this drain of cash will occur is a matter for debate. Mr. R. G. Hawtrey, who has stressed the importance of this phenomenon, has suggested that it will take place rather slowly so that, in the short run, open-market operations may nevertheless exert the large total effect on bank deposits that we have assumed. On the other hand, bankers may not feel safe in expanding their deposits as much as this, since they will realise that the drain of cash is bound to occur sooner or later. They will consequently not create any more additional deposits than they believe they will be able to sustain in the long run. In practice, then, there is little doubt that the effect of the drain of cash is to reduce the credit-creating powers of open-market operations. In Britain, for example, a given purchase (or sale) of securities by the Central Bank will at present increase (or decrease) total bank deposits by between three and four times the amount of the open-market purchase (or sale). The remaining 'cash' will go into circulation. This qualification to our argument should be borne in mind when reading Section 6 of Chapter XVIII.

We should like to thank the many readers who have pointed out slips and misprints in the text, all of which we have tried to correct.

ALFRED W. STONIER
DOUGLAS C. HAGUE

April 1957

v

PREFACE TO THE FIRST EDITION

THIS book is designed for students with no previous knowledge of economic theory who wish to study the elements of the subject systematically. It is hoped that some parts of the book will also be useful to more advanced students. The method of exposition is similar to that used in lectures on General Economic Theory to first-year students at University College London, who are reading for Part One of the B.Sc. (Economics) degree of London University. The book provides a general introduction to economic theory, but does not deal with the special problems of international trade, public finance and welfare economics.

We wish to thank Professor G. C. Allen for his valuable encouragement and advice. Miss P. A. Nicholson and Mr. A. Kay have helped to check proofs and to compile the Index. Mr. W. J. Corlett has helped in checking the diagrams and with the mathematics. We are especially indebted to Mrs. D. C. Hague for her invaluable secretarial help. Miss E. M. Tompkins and Miss J. C. Wood have also given valuable secretarial assistance.

We also have pleasure in thanking Messrs. Macmillan & Co. Ltd. for giving permission to quote from Alfred Marshall's *Principles of Economics* ; Messrs. Routledge and Kegan Paul for quotations from P. H. Wicksteed's *Commonsense of Political Economy* ; Professor J. R. Hicks for permission to reproduce the proof of the 'Adding-up Problem' from his *Theory of Wages*; and the Editorial Board of *Economica* who gave permission to summarise Professor Oscar Lange's article 'The Rate of Interest and the Optimum Propensity to Consume'.

A. W. STONIER

D. C. HAGUE

LONDON, *July* 1953

CONTENTS

vii

CONTENTS

PART II

EMPLOYMENT THEORY

INTRODUCTION

ECONOMICS can be divided into three parts. These are descriptive economics, economic theory and applied economics. In descriptive economics one collects together all the relevant facts about particular topics ; for example, the agricultural system of Basutoland, or the Indian cotton industry. In economic theory, or economic analysis as it is often called, one gives a simplified explanation of the way in which an economic system works and of the important features of such a system. Applied economics attempts to use the general framework of analysis provided by economic theory to explain the causes and significance of events reported by descriptive economists.

This book is about economic theory and gives an outline of the way in which an economic system works—the kind of outline which applied economists use. Since this is an elementary text-book we shall be forced to discuss our subject in abstract and over-simplified terms. In any case, the real world is a very complex place, and the creation of a theory of economics which tried to take account of all, or even most, of that complexity would be beyond the capacity of any human brain. We shall therefore confine ourselves to building up an analysis which considers only the most important features of the modern economy and which, whilst inevitably abstract and a little unreal, has the virtue of being simple and therefore easily intelligible.

In order to construct a theory of economics one has to undertake two tasks. First, one must make assumptions about conditions in the economy one wishes to analyse. These assumptions, or hypotheses, will be of a broad and general kind, and will be about such things as the way human beings act, their physical environment and their social and economic institutions. Second, one must draw inferences or deductions from such assumptions. It will be useful in this introduction to consider these assumptions and the way in which economic theorists draw conclusions from them in greater detail.

Let us begin by considering the three broad categories of assumptions which we have just mentioned. First, there are assumptions about the behaviour of individual human beings. Economists are most usually concerned with people in two capacities, as consumers and as business men—or *entrepreneurs* as economists often call them. When economists discuss the actions of consumers they assume that consumers behave 'rationally'. For example, they assume that when a consumer goes into a shop and asks for a newspaper, he does not really want a box of chocolates. Again, economists assume that consumers' tastes remain fairly constant and that people do not, for instance, frequently change from being meat eaters to being vegetarians and back again. Economists also assume that consumers always try to get the greatest possible value for their money and do not deliberately spend it on articles which they do not really want.

Similarly, when economic theorists consider the actions of business men, they assume that the main aim of every entrepreneur is to make as much money as possible. This assumption, that consumers seek the greatest satisfaction from spending their money and that entrepreneurs seek maximum money profits, is often referred to as the assumption of 'economic rationality'. So far as consumers are concerned it seems a very reasonable assumption. In the case of business men it may sound a little less plausible. Nevertheless, even there the assumption of economic rationality is probably the most useful one to make. For example, it would be unreasonable to suppose that all business men try to *lose* as much money as possible, so we assume that business men go into business to make money. It may be objected that what business men are really trying to do is something more complicated than simply seeking maximum profits. But to introduce a more realistic assumption would make economic theory very difficult, quite apart from the fact that no-one really knows what the correct assumption would be.

As we shall see later, the assumption that entrepreneurs seek maximum profits does enable us to construct a fairly simple theory of business behaviour. It would, of course, be perfectly possible to construct such a theory on any other conceivable hypothesis. One could, if necessary, construct a theory of business behaviour on the assumption that every business man tries to make profits equal to the square root of his wife's age, or to the number of runs scored by Denis Compton in the previous cricket season, but it would be an extremely intricate theory both to build up and to use. Since it would also be an unrealistic theory, it seems much more sensible to begin by basing the theory of both consumers' and producers' behaviour on a simple and yet plausible hypothesis. And the assumption that both seek the greatest possible benefit for themselves seems better than any other.

The second broad group of assumptions mentioned above is about the physical structure of the world. The assumptions are about geography, biology and climate. Assumptions in this group are usually implicit rather than explicit, but an attempt is made to ensure that economic theory asks nothing which is physically impossible. For example, when economic theorists discuss agricultural problems they acknowledge that harvest time is determined by nature. The economist has to accept this as a fact. Again, no reputable economist would put forward a theory based on the assumption that bananas and grapes grow in profusion in Scotland. Similarly, economic analysis accepts the fact that industrial workers need a given amount of rest each day, and that technical conditions prevent industrial output from being unlimited in amount.

This leads to the basic assumption which economic analysis makes about the physical world. It is assumed that the fundamental feature of the economic world, the feature which gives rise to economic problems at all, is that goods are *scarce*. Very few things in the world, with the exception of air, water and (on occasion) sunshine, are available in unlimited amounts. It is because of this scarcity that goods have to be shared out among individual human beings and it is the job of an economic system to undertake this task of sharing out. If there were no scarcity and no need for goods to be shared out among individuals, there would be no economic system and no economics. Economics is fundamentally a study of scarcity and of the problems to which scarcity gives rise.

The third broad group of assumptions on which economic theory is based relate to social and economic institutions. Two examples of such assumptions used in this book will suffice. We shall assume on the one hand that the analysis relates to a country with a relatively stable political system. For instance, we shall assume that consumers and producers earn their living by exchanging money for goods, and work for wages, in a law-abiding fashion. We shall rule out the possibility that many people might live on the proceeds of smash-and-grab raids or highway robberies.

On the other hand we shall make considerable use of the

concept of a market—an economic institution. By a market economists mean any organisation whereby the buyers and sellers of a particular commodity are kept in close touch with each other and are able to fix its price. Much of the analysis in this book will be based on the assumption that there are numerous 'markets' where the prices of the various goods are determined.

So much for the assumptions which we, in common with other economic theorists, shall make. We must now say something more about the actual process of reasoning by which economic theories, or 'economic laws' as they are sometimes called, are deduced from assumptions of the kind we have just been discussing. Unfortunately it is not easy to illustrate shortly the way in which this is done, but perhaps a simple instance will suffice. When economists discuss the determination of the price of a good in a market, they deduce that one can legitimately expect the price of the commodity traded to tend to a single uniform price throughout the market. For example, economists deduce that if the same kind of fruit is dearer on some stalls in a market than on others, buyers acting 'rationally' will buy only the cheap fruit, and the sellers of the dear fruit will have to lower their prices in order to dispose of their stocks. For since all buyers and sellers in the market are in close touch with each other, everyone will have a shrewd idea what everyone else is doing and thinking. It is only reasonable to draw the conclusion that all buyers and sellers will know all the time what the price of the good traded is.

We have now explained in general terms what economic theory is about. It remains to say a little more explicitly what we shall do in this book. We have seen that one of the economic analyst's interests is in prices ; and rightly so. Everyone is affected when prices rise or fall. The housewife going shopping is seriously interested in whether goods in the shops she visits are dear or cheap. Similarly, every entrepreneur is anxious to find out whether the prices of his products, and of any factors of production he uses, are high or low. Prices are important to everyone. The economist must therefore explain how prices are determined and why they are high when they are high or low when they are low. The first part of this book gives an outline of *Price Theory* and explains the way in which prices, whether of goods or of factors of production, are determined.

Although prices are important in the real world, they are not the only things which matter. In particular, no economist can overlook the importance of knowing what determines the level of employment. For conditions both of unemployment and of inflation cause social unrest. So the second part of this book deals with *Employment Theory* and shows what are the causes of high and low levels of employment and activity.

We turn now to our first topic ; the explanation of how prices are determined.

PART ONE

PRICE THEORY

CHAPTER I

DEMAND AND SUPPLY

1. PRICE

THE price of anything is the rate at which it can be exchanged for anything else. As was shown in the Introduction, one of the main tasks of economic theory is to explain why goods have a price and why some goods are expensive and others cheap. Economic theorists have built up a generalised theory of prices which can be used to analyse the whole range of practical price problems. For all these problems, such as the determination of wage rates, rates of foreign exchange, stock exchange values and the like, exemplify the general principles by which prices are determined.

The fundamental question which price theory sets out to answer is : 'Why is it that goods and factors of production have prices ?' Put quite baldly, the answer is that they have prices because, on the one hand, they are useful, and on the other hand, they are scarce in relation to the uses to which people want to put them. For example, meat could never command a price in an economy composed entirely of vegetarians, however many or few cows and sheep there were. It would not be useful and could not have a price. In addition to being useful, goods must be scarce in relation to the uses to which people want to put them, if they are to be priced. For instance, whilst air is clearly useful to any and every human being, the fact that it is freely available in unlimited amounts ensures that it cannot command a price. It is useful but it is not scarce. Goods like air, which are the gifts of nature and are useful but not scarce, are known as 'free' goods, and do not bear a price, in distinction to 'economic' goods which are scarce and do bear a price.

Goods can be divided into commodities, for example, oranges, socks or sideboards, and services, like haircuts, bus rides or the services of actors and musicians. In order that any such goods may be priced, and may therefore be eligible for consideration in price theory, they must be both useful and scarce.

We have now explained in very broad outline why economic goods have prices, or exchange values as they are sometimes called. It is only because economic goods, whether commodities or services, are useful that they are demanded by buyers, and only because they are scarce that sellers cannot supply them in unlimited quantities. But usefulness and scarcity are only the underlying forces which cause prices to exist. When a price of any good is determined in the market for that good, it is because usefulness and scarcity express themselves concretely in the demand of buyers on the one hand and supply by sellers on the other. This then is the first stage in our argument. Price is determined by the interaction of two sets of influences, those of demand and supply.

2. THE MARKET

We now know that prices are determined by demand and supply, so the next step is to consider the way in which demand and supply interact in the market. The easiest way to do this is by building up a simplified hypothetical model of a market for a commodity. Before doing this, however, it will be useful to say more about the sense in which economic theorists use the word market.

We have seen already that by a market economists mean any organisation whereby buyers and sellers of a good are kept in close touch with each other. It is important to realise that there is no need for a market to be in a single building, as happens, for example, with Smithfield meat market, or the Stock Exchange. It will be just as much a market if buyers and sellers sit beside batteries of telephones, as happens in the foreign exchange market. The only essential for a market is that all buyers and sellers should be in constant touch with each other, either because they are in the same building or because they are able to talk to each other by telephone at a moment's notice.

Let us now build up our hypothetical 'model' of a market for a commodity. We shall call it a cotton market, though, in fact, it is most unlikely that any actual cotton market will correspond exactly to our very simple model. We shall also make several simplifying assumptions about conditions in this 'cotton market', and it is only honest to state them explicitly at the outset. First, we shall assume that every bale of cotton offered for sale is of the same quality, so that there can be no price differences because some bales of cotton are of better or worse quality than others. Second, we shall assume that all the cotton can be bought in either small or large amounts at the same price per bale. This is a reasonable assumption in the case of cotton, but would not be so reasonable when dealing with, for example, motor cars. One could hardly sell motor cars in halves, quarters or eighths. This assumption also implies that there are no rebates of the 'penny each, seven for sixpence' variety, and that when the price changes, it can change by very small steps. Third, we assume that there is a large number of buyers and sellers in the market. Fourth, we assume that the market, whilst not necessarily in a single building, is one in which there are no transport costs between the various parts. We also assume that each buyer and seller in the market knows what other buyers and sellers are doing. Thus, the same price will rule throughout the market, and if price changes in one part of the market, it must change similarly in all parts.

These four assumptions are often made by economists, and technical terms have been coined to describe them. In technical language these assumptions are (1) homogeneity ; (2) divisibility ; (3) pure competition ; and (4) a perfect market. In a word, we are assuming 'competitive' conditions.

Having made these assumptions about general conditions in a competitive market, we must now make some assumptions about the nature of the forces at work in the market—demand and supply. So far as demand by buyers is concerned, it seems reasonable to think that there will be some very high prices at which no buyer will purchase anything, and some very low prices at which all buyers will buy enormous quantities of cotton. Between these limits it seems likely that the lower the price is, the more cotton will be bought. For buyers who were previously unable to afford any cotton will buy gladly when the price falls and *vice versa*. Similarly, it is reasonable to assume that when prices are very high, sellers will be only too keen to sell as much cotton as they can while conditions are good. Again, when prices are low, sellers will tend to hold back their supplies in the hope that prices will rise. At intermediate prices, varying amounts of cotton will be sold, and it is likely that the higher the price is, the greater the amount of cotton offered by sellers will be. For the higher the price, the more anxious sellers will be to dispose of their supplies.

We shall therefore assume that the amounts of cotton supplied and demanded at various hypothetical prices are as shown in Table 1.

TABLE 1

DEMAND AND SUPPLY SCHEDULES

Price per Bale	Demand Schedule (at this price buyers will take (bales))	Supply Schedule (at this price sellers will offer (bales))
130s.	—	120,000
110s.	20,000	100,000
90s.	40,000	80,000
70s.	60,000	60,000
50s.	80,000	40,000
30s.	100,000	20,000
10s.	120,000	—

Assuming that the demand and supply schedules are as shown in Table 1, our assumption that competition is keen means that a price of 70s. a bale will be reached before the market closes. For this is the only price at which the amount demanded is equal to the amount supplied. Only at this price will *all* those wishing to sell and to buy *at any one price* be satisfied.

If the price is above 70s. to begin with, there will be more cotton offered by sellers than is demanded by buyers, and the tendency will be for the price to fall. Those sellers who are unable to dispose of their supplies at the existing price will begin to make price reductions in the hope of attracting custom. As the price falls, demand will increase and supply will decline in the way shown in Table 1, until at the price of 70s. all the sellers who are willing to sell will be able to find purchasers for their cotton. Similarly, if the price is below 70s. a bale, the amount of cotton demanded will exceed the amount supplied and the price of cotton will tend to rise. For there will be many unsatisfied buyers at any price below 70s., and whilst they would be only too glad to buy at a low price if possible, they will be prepared to see the price rise rather than go away empty-handed. When the price has risen to 70s., all the buyers who are prepared to buy at that price will be satisfied.

Only at this price of 70s. a bale will there be no tendency for the price to change. Only at this price will there be no unsatisfied buyers or sellers who are prepared to let prices alter rather than go away without having bought or sold any cotton. Thus it will only be when the price is 70s. a bale that the price will remain stable at a given level. This price at which demand and supply are equal is known in technical language as an *equilibrium price*.

For at this price the forces of demand and supply are balanced, or 'in equilibrium'. Such a price is called an equilibrium price because price settles down, or comes to rest, at such a level as the result of the balancing of the opposing forces of demand and supply.

As a result of this type of analysis, it is said that demand and supply determine price. But it is also often said that price determines demand and supply. These are important generalisations about the relationship between demand, supply and market price. But they are not precise and are at first sight contradictory. The reason why it is difficult to make sense of them is that we have not, so far, made one very important distinction. It is essential in economics to distinguish between the quantity of a good which is demanded or supplied at a particular given price, and the general conditions of demand and supply, which constitute schedules showing the various quantities of the commodity which would be demanded or supplied at many different prices. Only one of these prices can be the actual market price, in our example 70s. It is this market price which determines the amount actually exchanged in the market, in our case 60,000 bales. But this price itself is determined by the interaction of the demand schedule with the supply schedule. It is quite possible that a change in the price at which the market is in equilibrium may occur, and that such a change will alter the amount demanded and supplied. But such a change in the equilibrium price must itself have been brought about by a change in the demand schedule or in the supply schedule or in both. This distinction between demand and supply conditions as shown in schedules and the actual amount demanded or supplied at a single price is important and should always be borne in mind.

There are two other important points relating to the analysis of a market which must be mentioned here. First, it should be obvious that since demand and supply are the two forces which determine price, the analysis will be useless unless demand and supply really are independent of each other. That is to say, one must make the simplifying assumption that buyers do not also appear as sellers and *vice versa*, as happens on the Stock Exchange. Since we are concerned here with a cotton market, it is reasonable to assume that suppliers are not likely to buy their own goods, and that even if occasionally they do, they only buy in negligible quantities. Similarly, if we were dealing with a chocolate manufacturer, we should be entitled to assume that even if he did sometimes eat chocolates, he would never be likely to eat a large proportion of the output of his own factory. We shall assume that, as a rule, buyers and sellers are quite different people, and demand and supply are therefore independent.

Second, it is important not to overlook the relationship between price in one market and price in another. We have seen that in competitive conditions the same price will rule throughout the market for a single good. Naturally there will be less tendency for prices in different markets to bear any particular or close relationship to each other. There will be less connection *between* markets because the dealers in each market will be concerned with a different commodity. Nevertheless there will be some connection even here. For example, if prices in the meat market rise, there is likely to be some rise in prices in the fish market. People will tend to eat fish rather than meat now that meat is dear. The demand for fish will increase and its price will rise. Similarly, a change in the price of cotton may affect the price of wool, since both are used in clothing.

Some markets will be very much less closely related. It is unlikely, for example, that a rise in the price of mustard or of pepper will alter the price of hats. Yet it may have a slight effect. For if people spend more money on mustard, they will have less money to spend on other things, and they may conceivably decide to wear their hats just a little longer. Thus, whilst each market is primarily concerned with determining the price of a single good, every market is related in some degree, sometimes quite great, sometimes very small, to all the other separate markets.

In view of this, it is clear that if we were to take account of all the repercussions of a change in the price of, say, cotton, on the prices of other goods, we should be faced with a very complicated problem, and we are concerned at this stage to make our analysis as simple as possible. We shall therefore confine our attention to analysing only one market at a time, and rule out the possibility of any disturbances from other markets upsetting this analysis. Such an analysis is often used by economists and is known as *particular equilibrium* analysis, since it seeks to explain what happens in one particular market and ignores what is happening in others. Alternatively, it is known as *partial equilibrium* analysis because it seeks to analyse only a part of the economic system. This is in distinction to *general equilibrium* analysis, which we shall undertake later on in this book, where the effects of changes in one market on others are analysed.

What we shall do in this particular equilibrium analysis is to confine our attention to changes in a single market by taking for granted, either that demand and supply in the market isolated for special study are independent of price changes in other markets, or alternatively that such price changes do not occur. It is also important to realise that the demand schedule is constructed on the assumption that consumers have given and constant money incomes. Any change in these incomes would alter the demand schedule, which would have to be completely recalculated.

We therefore assume in particular equilibrium analysis that all prices are given, except the one in which we are interested, and that consumers only have money incomes of a given size to spend. We also assume, as already noted, that demand and supply are completely independent of each other. With such an analytical framework, we shall only be able to give a partial or incomplete picture of the economic system, since the possibility of changes in one market affecting price in another is explicitly ruled out. Nevertheless, this will make our task much simpler whilst enabling us to give a fairly accurate picture of the way in which prices are determined. We can then introduce the complications of general equilibrium when the building of the theoretical system has reached a sufficiently advanced stage.

3. DEMAND

We have shown how the price of any commodity or economic service is determined by the interaction of demand and supply. It is now necessary to see more precisely what demand and supply are. First let us consider demand. What do we mean when we speak of demand ? We have seen that goods are demanded because they are useful, and it might be thought that goods are demanded by everyone who thinks they are useful—by everyone who wants them. In fact, not every want on the part of a consumer expresses itself as a demand in the market. A consumer's desire to buy a good will only affect the market price of the good if this desire can be translated into a money demand for the good in question. Demand in economics means demand backed up by enough money to pay for the good demanded. For example, whilst every Englishman probably wants a country house, very few are able to afford such a home. Only the demand of those who have enough money to buy country houses affects their price. We are concerned in this book only with demand which is effectively backed up by an adequate supply of purchasing power.

We have so far considered the demand for cotton in a hypothetical cotton market. We did so by drawing up a schedule showing the amounts of cotton demanded at various prices, in Table 1. But whilst the use of such arithmetical demand schedules is quite common in economics, the demand for a good is more usually shown graphically by drawing what is called a demand curve for the good in question. A demand curve shows in

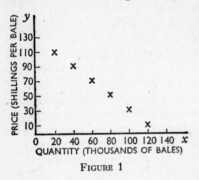

FIGURE 1

visual form the state of affairs on the demand side of the market for a commodity at a given moment. We make the usual assumptions of particular equilibrium, namely, that all prices are constant except that of the good in which we are interested, and that consumers have a fixed money income. On these assumptions we can draw a curve showing how much of the given commodity will be bought at various prices. In the following diagrams we shall show, in stages, how a demand curve is drawn up.

The first stage is shown in Figure 1. Up the vertical axis, known as the y-axis, we measure various hypothetical market prices with which we assume consumers are faced. In fact, what we have done has been to take the prices from Table 1. The prices are therefore measured in shillings per bale. Along the horizontal axis, known as the x-axis, is measured from left to right the increasing total quantity of the good, in this case measured in thousands of bales of cotton, which consumers are assumed to buy at these prices. We can then plot the demand schedule from Table 1 as a series of points. Each point represents the amount of cotton which would be bought at a particular price. We have exactly the same information in Figure 1 as in Table 1, but we have it in a different form.

In Figure 2, perpendiculars are drawn from each of the points shown in Figure 1 to the two axes, forming rectangles. This provides us with more information because the area of each rectangle represents the consumers' total money outlay at the price in question, namely the price per bale multiplied by the number of bales bought.

In Figure 3 we assume that there is complete divisibility so that price and amount demanded can both change by infinitely small steps. This enables us to draw a demand curve joining the points shown in Figure 1 by a continuous line—DD. We also assume that there are no irregularities in demand conditions anywhere between the particular points we have shown in our demand schedule in Figure 1. This makes the demand curve smooth and regular. Finally, we assume, for the sake of sim-

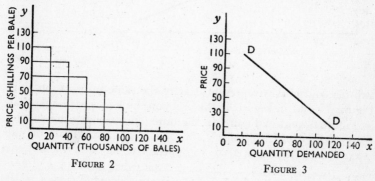

FIGURE 2

FIGURE 3

plicity, that in this particular instance the amount of cotton bought increases by 1000 bales for every fall of 1s. in price. This enables us to draw the demand curve in Figure 3 as a straight line. It follows that a demand curve is a curve showing for each price how much of the good in question consumers would buy at that price. It represents a *functional relationship* between price and amount demanded.

We have drawn this demand curve sloping downwards from left to right. This is the assumption about the general nature of demand curves which economists normally make. One reason for this assumption that demand curves slope downwards from left to right is, as we have seen, that as the price of a good falls, people who were previously unable to buy it will enter the market, and the amount of the good demanded will rise. But there are other reasons. Some people will buy the good, now that its price has fallen, in preference to other goods which they bought before but which are now relatively more expensive. Again, some people who bought some of the good even before its price fell will be able to buy more now that it is cheaper. For these reasons

C

economists assume that demand curves slope downwards to the right.

One fact about demand curves which is worth noting is that their slope depends on the scale used. In Figures 4a and 4b the

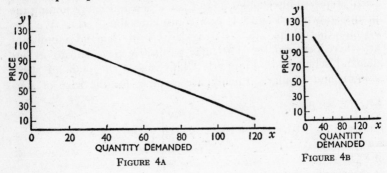

FIGURE 4A

FIGURE 4B

two demand curves represent exactly the same information as in Figure 3. But in Figure 4a the units on the x-axis are larger than in Figure 3, and in Figure 4b the units on the x-axis are smaller than in Figure 3. Similarly, one could alter the units on the y-axis. It is therefore always important to be certain about the scale when drawing or interpreting demand curves.

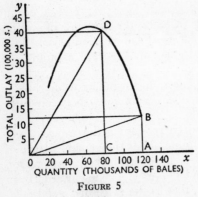

FIGURE 5

Finally, one sometimes finds it useful to show the same information as in Figure 3 on a different type of curve. Instead of showing the amount of the good demanded at each price, we show the total amount of money which consumers are prepared to spend on various hypothetical amounts of the good. This has been done in Figure 5 where we have drawn a *total outlay curve* or *total expenditure curve*. Along the x-axis we measure thousands of bales of cotton. Up the y-axis we measure total outlay in shillings, as given by the rectangles in Figure 2. Thus, the line AB shows that consumers are willing to spend 1,200,000s. on cotton when they buy 120,000 bales. The amount of total outlay can therefore be shown either by the height of a total expenditure curve, as in Figure 5, or by the size of the outlay rectangles as in Figure 2. The total expenditure curve thus expresses a functional relationship between total expenditure on a good and the amount demanded.

It is important to realise that although price is not measured on either axis in Figure 5 it can be discovered from this diagram. For example, in Figure 5 the slope of the straight line OB, *i.e.* $\frac{AB}{OA}$, represents the price buyers will pay for cotton (10*s.* per bale) if OA bales (120,000) are demanded and total expenditure is AB*s.* (1,200,000*s.*). Similarly, the slope of the line OD, *i.e.* $\frac{CD}{OC}$, represents the price paid for cotton (50*s.* per bale) if OC bales are demanded, when total outlay is CD*s.* The fact that the line OB is flatter than the line OD shows that price is lower if OA bales are demanded than if OC are being bought.

4. ELASTICITY OF DEMAND

We have seen that there is a very good case for thinking that demand curves will slope downwards from left to right. This means that the amount of a good which is demanded increases as its price falls. Alternatively, we may say that the demand for the good is 'responsive' to a fall in its price. But although the demand for a good responds to a fall in its price in this way, there will be differences in the degree of responsiveness of different goods to price changes. It is usually agreed that the demand for a good like salt is not very much affected by changes in its price. On the other hand, changes in the prices of goods like radio sets or railway travel do exert a considerable influence on the demand for them.

The reasons for differences in the responsiveness of various goods to changes in their prices are not easy to discover. It is fairly true, however, to say that the main causes of such differences are the presence or absence of competing substitutes. For example, salt is a necessity which fulfils a basic human need in a way in which no other good will. We have to use much the same amount of salt whether it is dear or cheap, for few people will eat meals without salt whatever its price, and pepper and mustard could hardly be used instead. A fall in the price of radio sets, however, is likely to persuade more people to buy them because there are many substitutes for radio entertainment, for example, gramophones, cinemas and theatres. Similarly, a fall in the price of rail travel will attract many travellers from road, air and, perhaps, sea transport. The demand for travel by rail is therefore responsive to a change in its price. The main cause of differences in the responsiveness of the demand for goods to changes in their prices lies in the fact that there are more competing substitutes for some goods than for others.

Economic theory finds it useful to distinguish between those goods which are more responsive to price changes and those which are less responsive. In technical jargon, economists say that the former goods have a demand which is *more elastic* than that for the latter, or that their *elasticity of demand* is greater. *Elasticity of demand is therefore a technical term used by economists to describe the degree of responsiveness of the demand for a good to a fall in its price.*[1] Marshall, who introduced the concept of elasticity of demand into economic theory, says that 'the *elasticity* (or *responsiveness*) *of demand* in a market is great or small according as the amount demanded increases much or little for a given fall in price, and diminishes much or little for a given rise in price'.[2] We shall find that differences in elasticity of demand between goods are very important in economic theory, and that merely to say that the demand for one good is more or less elastic than the demand for another, is not always sufficiently precise. We need a more accurate method of comparing the elasticities of demand for different products.

Marshall provided such a measure of elasticity of demand. He says, 'we may say that the elasticity of demand is one, if a small fall in price will cause an equal proportionate increase in the amount demanded : or as we may say roughly, if a fall of one per cent in price will increase the sales by one per cent; that it is two or a half, if a fall of one per cent in price makes an increase of two or one half per cent respectively in the amount demanded ; and so on. (This statement is rough ; because 98 does not bear exactly the same proportion to 100 that 100 does to 102.)'[3]

We may therefore define elasticity of demand as follows :

[1] Strictly speaking, elasticity of demand refers to the way in which the demand for a good responds to a *change* in its price ; whether a rise or a fall. We talk in this section of responsiveness to a *fall* in price, purely for the sake of convenience. The argument applies equally to the case of a *rise* in price.

[2] Alfred Marshall, *Principles of Economics* (8th Edition), p. 102.

[3] Marshall, *op. cit.* p. 102 (footnote).

Elasticity of Demand

$$= \frac{\text{proportionate change in amount demanded}}{\text{proportionate change in price}}$$

$$= \frac{\dfrac{\text{change in amount demanded}}{\text{amount demanded}}}{\dfrac{\text{change in price}[1]}{\text{price}}}.$$

This formula holds strictly only in the limiting case where the changes in price are infinitesimally small. It should be noted that when elasticity is measured numerically all elasticities will lie between two limits. Where the demand curve is a horizontal straight line elasticity of demand will be infinite; where the demand curve is a vertical straight line elasticity will be zero.

The concept of elasticity of demand is essentially a simple one, but there are one or two important points about elasticity which should be borne in mind. First, it is tempting to imagine that a flat demand curve indicates that the demand for the good to which it relates has a greater elasticity than the demand for a good whose demand curve is steep. It seems natural to think that where the slope of a demand curve is not at all steep the demand for the good is increasing much more rapidly, as price falls, than with a very steep curve. But this is a very dangerous conclusion to draw. If we look again at Figures 4a and 4b, it seems likely that, on this argument, the elasticity of the demand curve in Figure 4b will be less than that of the curve in Figure 4a. Yet we have already seen that the two curves represent precisely the same demand conditions. The only difference between them is that the scales along the x-axes are different. It is therefore clearly dangerous to make any assertions about the relative elasticities of any two demand curves if they are not drawn to the same scale.

If two demand curves are drawn on the same scale and one is steeper than the other, it is true that they do represent different demand schedules. But it is still dangerous to make assertions about their respective elasticities of demand. One can, however, say something. Figure 6 shows two demand curves, AA and BB,

---

[1] This is, of course, the measure of elasticity given by differential calculus. Where p = price and q = quantity demanded, elasticity of demand $= \dfrac{dq}{q} \div \dfrac{-dp}{p}$. What we have written in the text as elasticity = 1, 2 or $\frac{1}{2}$ is thus strictly equal to -1, -2 or $-\frac{1}{2}$. This is because the changes in price and in amount will be in opposite directions. However, we shall for convenience denote elasticities by positive numbers in the text.

relating to two entirely separate hypothetical markets for the same
good (markets A and B), perhaps in different countries. If the
price in both markets falls over exactly the same range, for example

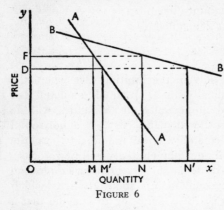

from OF to OD, the
responsiveness of demand
in the market with de-
mand curve BB is greater
than in the market with
demand curve AA. De-
mand increases by NN'
in market B but only by
MM' in market A. There-
fore, so long as one is concerned with a fall in price
*over exactly the same price
range* in each market, it
is possible to say that a

FIGURE 6

flatter curve represents a more elastic demand than a steeper
curve if both are drawn to the same scale—provided that the
initial amounts demanded in each market are much the same.
But one can say no more. One cannot say anything, merely
by looking at the slopes of two curves, about elasticities over
different price ranges on each curve, even if there is the same
absolute change in price in each market. For example, one could

not infer anything about
elasticity of demand,
merely from looking at
the slopes of the two
curves, if price in market
A were to fall by 1s. from
OFs. and price in market
B were to fall also by 1s.
from ODs. This can
easily be seen by study-
ing a single demand
curve.

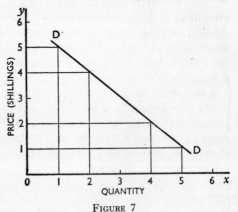

FIGURE 7

In Figure 7 the slope
of the demand curve
DD is constant. If elas-
ticity and slope were closely related, one would naturally expect elasticity to be constant as well. But when price falls by
a shilling, from 5s. to 4s., the amount demanded rises from one

unit to two. Price has fallen by a fifth and the amount demanded has doubled, that is to say the increase in the amount demanded is equal to the original demand. Elasticity of demand is five (*i.e.* $\frac{1}{1} \div \frac{1}{5}$). Yet when price falls from 2*s.* to 1*s.* the amount demanded only rises by one unit, from 4 to 5. Price has fallen by half but demand has only risen by a quarter. Elasticity of demand is one half (*i.e.* $\frac{1}{4} \div \frac{1}{2}$). It is clearly unreasonable to regard the responsiveness of demand to changing price as the same in both cases; and yet the slope of the demand curve is constant, and one might well expect elasticity to be constant as well. If one cannot be dogmatic about the responsiveness of demand on a single demand curve, it is clearly dangerous to make assertions about demand on two different curves, except over the same price range in each case.

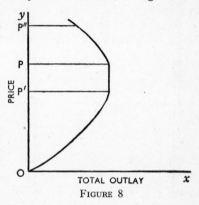

FIGURE 8

If one studies those demand curves which are very elastic and those which are inelastic, it is not long before one notices an important fact. Where elasticity of demand is greater than one, the total amount of money spent on the good in question increases as its price falls. In other words, the total outlay of consumers on the good rises in response to a fall in price. On the other hand, when elasticity of demand is less than one, total consumers' outlay on a good falls as its price is reduced. But where elasticity of demand equals one, outlay by consumers on the good in question is constant whatever the price of the good. As Marshall puts it, 'if the elasticity of demand be equal to unity for all prices of the commodity, any fall in price will cause a proportionate increase in the amount bought, and therefore will make no change in the total outlay which purchasers make for the commodity'.[1]

In Figure 8 we have drawn a curve showing total outlay on a good. As price, measured up the *y*-axis, falls from OP″ as far as OP, total outlay on the good, measured along the *x*-axis, increases. Demand is elastic over this range. Similarly, as price falls below OP′, total outlay diminishes with each fall in price. Demand is inelastic at all prices lower than OP′. But between the prices OP

[1] *Op cit.* p. 839.

and OP′ outlay is constant at all prices. Elasticity of demand
is everywhere unitary and demand is neither very responsive
nor unresponsive to price changes. This situation represents a
dividing line where demand is neither elastic nor inelastic. Let us
now draw an ordinary unit demand curve to show the same
kind of situation as that shown on the total outlay curve in Figure 8
over the range of prices between OP and OP′. This has been done
in Figure 9.

Figure 9 shows two demand curves, on each of which total
outlay is constant at all prices. They both show the same informa-

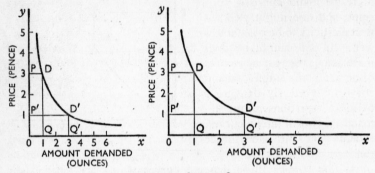

FIGURES 9A AND 9B

tion but are drawn to different scales. In Figure 9a let us consider the two points D and D′. At each point total outlay is the
same. Whether price is 3d. as at D or 1d. as at D′, total outlay
is still 3d. The same situation is shown in Figure 9b but the
scale on the x-axis is larger. In both diagrams total outlay shown
by the rectangles OPDQ and OP′D′Q′ inscribed under the
demand curves at D and D′ respectively, is the same. And this
is true whichever points on the curves one takes. Total outlay is
always constant, and elasticity of demand equals one at all prices.
This type of curve is called a rectangular hyperbola by mathe-
maticians.[1]

We have now seen how one can measure elasticity of demand
numerically. The great advantage of having a method of calculating elasticity of demand in numerical terms is that it does
enable one to classify demands easily into those which are elastic
and those which are inelastic.

Whenever numerical elasticity is less than one, e.g. $\frac{1}{2}$, $\frac{1}{4}$ or $\frac{1}{16}$,

---

[1] It is asymptotic to (i.e. it approaches but never touches) the x- and y-axes.
If it did touch them, the inscribed rectangles would vanish.

demand is inelastic. Demand increases less than proportionately as price falls. It is not very responsive to falls in price. Outlay falls as prices fall. Any demand with numerical elasticity less than one can thus be classified as inelastic. Similarly, when numerical elasticity is greater than one, *e.g.* 2, 5, 7 or 16, demand is elastic. Demand increases more than in proportion to falls in price and total outlay rises as prices fall. One can therefore classify any demand with numerical elasticity greater than one as elastic. Numerical elasticity shows at sight whether demand is elastic or inelastic.

Numerical measures of elasticity of demand thus enable one to tell whether demand on any demand curve is more or less responsive to price changes than on another curve. It is important to remember, however, that there is no particular economic significance in the fact that elasticity is, say, $\frac{1}{2}$ or 2, except that demand is inelastic or elastic respectively, and outlay is thus falling or rising when price falls, as the case may be. Only in three cases is there any important economic significance in the size of elasticity of demand. Elasticity of demand equal to one, with outlay therefore constant, represents the dividing line between elastic and inelastic demands. Infinitely elastic demand implies a horizontal demand curve for the good in question with a small fall in price leading to an infinitely large rise in demand. Again zero elasticity of demand means a vertical demand curve, with exactly the same amount of the good demanded whatever the price.

One further important point to remember is this. Save in exceptional circumstances (*e.g.* where the demand curve is a rectangular hyperbola or a vertical straight line), no demand curve will have *a single elasticity* throughout its length. It will have a different elasticity on each part of it. It is therefore usually incorrect to speak of any demand curve as having *an* elasticity. Usually, each has many elasticities. But, at any given point on any demand curve it will always be possible to discover what the numerical elasticity of demand is.

5. SUPPLY

Supply depends on scarcity, just as demand depends on usefulness. Scarcity is a much more difficult concept to discuss than usefulness, because it is more obviously a relative and not an absolute term. Whilst it is comparatively simple to say whether or not a good is useful, one cannot say whether a good is economically scarce except in relation to the demand for it. Thus while first folios of Shakespeare and genuine Rembrandts are numerically scarce, for their supply is fixed, they may or may not be scarce in the economist's relative sense. If everyone wants them they will be scarce; if no-one wants them they will be plentiful. Scarcity always means scarce in relation to demand.

Why then is it that economic goods are scarce? Why is there a problem of supply? In the case of those few goods the supply of which is fixed absolutely, the position is clear. What of the enormous number of goods which it is possible to produce? The answer is that all these goods can only be produced with the help of factors of production, *e.g.* workers, machines, factories, lorries, fields or entrepreneurs, and these factors are themselves limited in amount. The supply of any commodity is regulated by the fact that in order to produce it, members from two or more of the four broad groups of factors of production, 'land', 'labour', 'capital' and 'enterprise', must be used. Whilst man's wants are many in number, those which he can satisfy at any given time will be comparatively few, because the supply of productive agents is relatively quite small. We shall see later that the process by which equilibrium between demand and supply is brought about determines which of man's wants are satisfied and which are not. For the moment we may note merely that the supply of factors of production is small compared with the demand for them. There are hundreds of goods with prices, and by definition each one is scarce in relation to the demand for it.

We must now lay down a general rule about the shape of supply curves, like the rule that demand curves normally slope downwards. This general rule is that supply curves slope upwards from left to right. In other words, sellers of a commodity are normally willing to sell more of it if its price is high than if it is low. This is a simple principle, but it needs careful interpretation if its implications are to be correctly understood.

(a) Fixed Supply

Let us first consider the supply of the first group of goods, namely those whose quantity is fixed and cannot be increased as a result of economic decisions. Let us assume that a fixed amount of such a good is available. This fixed quantity of the good will be in the possession of certain people. Other people who do not possess any of it at all may be willing to buy some. We can therefore draw a market demand curve sloping downwards, which shows the readiness of these buyers to take various quantities of the good at various hypothetical prices. This demand curve will be faced in the market by a supply curve of the potential sellers. The supply curve will normally slope upwards. This is because, if price is high, sellers can acquire a great deal of money, and thus a lot of other goods, in exchange for the good they are giving up. Therefore, the higher the price of the good in question is, the more worth while its sale will seem. The supply will be greater. The situation in the market will thus determine the price. It will do so by the interaction of the downward-sloping demand curve on the one hand, with the upward-sloping supply curve on the other.

When one considers what are the forces determining the shape of the seller's supply curve, however, one finds that, in this instance, they are of the same type as those which determine the shape of the buyer's demand curve. The buyers decide whether to buy the good in question or to keep their money to purchase other goods. In the same way, the sellers decide whether to keep the good in question for their own use or whether to exchange it for something else. The willingness or reluctance of sellers to sell is therefore determined by the *sellers' demand for their own good*. Unwillingness to sell something one possesses is determined in much the same way as eagerness to buy something one does not possess, if in each case the motive is to satisfy one's wants. One can suppose, if one likes, that sellers actually offer their goods for sale in the market, but 'buy them back' at their reserve price. A decision to sell can then be expressed, without a change of meaning, as a decision not to demand. It is therefore possible and legitimate to represent the supply conditions of a good whose amount is fixed not only by an upward-sloping supply curve, but also alternatively, by a downward-sloping demand curve of sellers for their own good.

In Figure 10 there is a fixed supply, Ox, of a given commodity. The same supply conditions for sellers are represented in Figure 10a by an upward-sloping supply curve SS, and in Figure 10b by a downward-sloping demand curve of sellers for their own good, SOD. In the case of the supply curve in Figure 10a, market price can be deduced from the intersection of this supply curve with the buyers' demand curve, just as in Table 1 we deduced the market price from the intersection of the demand and supply schedules. For example, in Figure 10c the equilibrium price is MPs., the amount bought by buyers and therefore sold by sellers is OM, and the amount not sold is Mx. The same result is obtained in Figure 10d where the sellers' demand is added on sideways to the buyers' demand. Together they constitute the combined demand curve (the broken curve CD) of the market as a whole. This combined demand curve is confronted with a vertical supply curve, xx, representing the fixed stock of the good available. Price is still MP and is determined

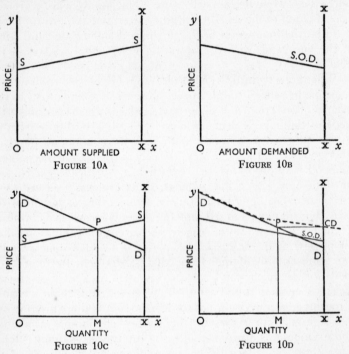

FIGURE 10A

FIGURE 10B

FIGURE 10C

FIGURE 10D

by the intersection of the combined demand curve CD with the curve of fixed supply xx. Amount bought and sold is still OM, and amount not bought (or bought back by sellers) is still Mx. If this situation is represented by a vertical supply curve, it can be regarded as the limiting case of inflexible supply. Similarly, it might conceivably happen that sellers had no demand for their own good. In that case, the ordinary sellers' supply curve would take the shape xx and supply would be inflexible.

This case of fixed supply has been discussed at length, not only because of its analytical importance as a limiting case, but also because of its practical importance. It occurs not only with first editions, etc., but also with the supply of labour. As we shall see later, this can in some contexts be regarded more appropriately as the demand for leisure, since workers are faced with two alternative uses for their (fixed amount of) time. They can either take it as leisure or they can use it to earn income by working. In other words, they can either 'keep' their time for their own use or 'sell' it to someone else and work for him.

(b) Flexible Supply

We now turn to the more usual case of flexible supply. Here the amounts of goods which are produced will alter as price changes. Even in this case, sellers, having produced a good, will naturally have to choose whether to consume it themselves or sell it to others. But they also have to decide whether to produce the good or not produce it at all. We shall assume that it is this latter choice which is important. For whilst shoemakers, for instance, may have a demand for shoes, it is not likely to be quantitatively important in relation to the total supply of shoes. We shall assume throughout our analysis of flexible supply that the main choice facing producers is not between selling their goods to others or using them themselves but between producing goods for sale or not producing them at all. We shall therefore ignore sellers' demand for their own good where supply is flexible. For there is here this much more important problem of deciding how much to produce, which does not exist where supply is completely fixed.

The main factor determining the supply prices of varying outputs of manufactured and agricultural products is the cost of producing them. To put it simply, if consumers want more of a good they have to pay more for it. The reason for this is that it is necessary to attract factors of production away from other industries to the production of the good in question. And it is likely that these factors will be less efficient, or more expensive, or both. This means that costs per unit of output will increase as the output of industry rises. This is an over-simplified explanation of the reason why supply curves slope upwards, but we shall only be able to give a completely accurate one later. We can, however, safely assume for the moment that a greater amount of any good will be supplied if, but only if, its price is higher.

This means that market supply curves normally slope upwards from left to right. There are thus two limiting cases. At one end of the scale a vertical straight line represents totally unresponsive, or 'infinitely inelastic', supply. Supply will not increase at all however much price rises. At the other end of the scale, a horizontal straight line represents very responsive, or 'infinitely elastic', supply, such that a small rise in price evokes an indefinitely large increase in the amount supplied. By analogy with elasticity of demand, the first limiting case of totally unresponsive supply can be defined as zero elasticity of supply, and the second of infinitely responsive supply as infinite elasticity of supply.

Along an upward-sloping supply curve, amount and price both increase together instead of one increasing while the other diminishes, as with a downward-sloping demand curve. The changes in amount and in price are therefore both in the same direction, and elasticities of supply lying between the two limits mentioned above are both positive and finite. There are no problems over minus signs as there are with elasticity of demand. The general measure of the degree of elasticity of supply is

$$\text{Elasticity of Supply} = \frac{\text{increase in amount supplied}}{\text{amount supplied}} \div \frac{\text{increase in price}}{\text{price}}.$$

Thus if the proportionate increase in amount supplied is double the proportionate rise in price, elasticity of supply is 2. The amount supplied changes, proportionately, twice as fast as the price changes. Similarly, if the proportionate change in amount supplied is only half as great as the proportionate change in price, elasticity of supply is $\frac{1}{2}$. On this definition, supply has unitary elasticity if the amount supplied increases in the same proportion as price has changed. Unitary elasticity of supply would be represented graphically by *any* straight line through the origin. Whatever the slope of this straight line through the origin and whatever the scales on the two axes, elasticity of supply will equal one. But it is important to realise that unitary elasticity of supply, unlike unitary elasticity of demand, has no special economic significance.

The distinction between great and small elasticities of supply is important, and we need some measure to show whether one supply curve is more or less elastic than another supply curve over a range, or at a point. But elasticity of supply equal to one, like elasticity of supply of one-half or of two, is only a measure on a scale which divides elasticities greater than zero and less than infinity into arbitrary units. The reason for this asymmetry between supply and demand is that there is no important economic significance like that of constant outlay attaching to any particular degree of elasticity of supply, except for elasticities of zero and infinity. It might be concluded that the concept of elasticity of supply is therefore superfluous. But the idea of the responsiveness of supply to changes in price is so important, that it is useful to keep elasticity of supply as a technical term with a precise definition.

6. EQUILIBRIUM

Having discussed what factors determine demand and supply, we must now discuss how demand and supply interact in the market to determine the price of a good and the amount of it which is bought and sold. We have seen that demand and supply are like two forces pulling in opposite directions. They are balanced, or in equilibrium, at that market price at which the amount demanded equals the amount supplied. This price can be called the *equilibrium price*, and the amount demanded and supplied at this price the equilibrium amount.

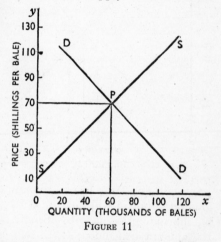

FIGURE 11

These must be distinguished from other hypothetical prices and amounts, which might satisfy the conditions either of demand or of supply separately, but do not satisfy both simultaneously, and therefore cannot be established in the market. Market equilibrium is shown graphically in Figure 11. The demand curve DD intersects the supply curve SS at the point P. In this equilibrium situation, the equilibrium amount of 60,000 bales is exchanged at the equilibrium price of 70*s*.

Our main concern in this part will be to explain how the equilibrium prices, first of goods and later of factors of production, are determined. This means that in Part One we shall spend our time looking into the factors influencing the shape of the demand and supply curves, for goods and factors, for these curves determine their equilibrium prices.

We shall make one important assumption about equilibrium between demand and supply. We shall assume that the demand and supply curves with which we shall be concerned are such that any disturbance of the original equilibrium situation will set in motion forces which cause a return to that equilibrium. The significance of this assumption can be seen from Figure 12.

In Figure 12 are shown a downward-sloping demand curve and an upward-sloping supply curve for a good. The market is

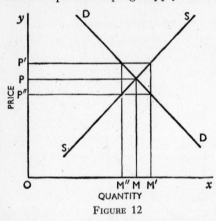

FIGURE 12

in equilibrium when the amount OM of the good is sold at the price of OPs. If now the equilibrium is disturbed and the price rises to OP's. the amount of the good supplied, OM', will exceed the amount demanded, OM". Sellers will be supplying more of the good at the price of OP's. than buyers are prepared to buy at that price and they will therefore have to reduce their price. As

price falls in this way the amount demanded will rise and the amount supplied will fall, until the two amounts coincide at the equilibrium price of OPs. Similarly, if the price falls to OP"s. the amount demanded, OM', will exceed the amount supplied, OM", and competition between buyers will force the price up until once again the equilibrium price of OPs. is reached. The amount exchanged will once again be OM. When the demand and supply conditions are such that a displacement of the equilibrium situation automatically causes a return to it in this way, the equilibrium is said to be *stable*. Equilibrium will be stable when slightly to the left of the equilibrium position the demand price exceeds the supply price, and slightly to the right of it the supply price exceeds the demand price. Equilibrium will also be stable if, at a price slightly above the equilibrium level, the amount demanded falls short of the amount supplied, or if, at a price slightly lower than the equilibrium price, the amount demanded exceeds the amount supplied. If these conditions hold good, any rise in price above the equilibrium level will set in train forces which cause a return to that level, and *vice versa*.

These stability conditions will always be fulfilled if the demand curve slopes downwards and the supply curve slopes upwards. We shall spend a great deal of time in the next few chapters analysing the forces determining the shape of demand and supply curves. This will show why demand curves normally slope downwards and supply curves normally slope upwards, and why equilibrium is therefore usually stable.

SUGGESTED READING

Alfred Marshall, *Principles of Economics* (8th Edition), London, 1920, especially Book III, chapter 4, and Book V, chapters 1, 2 and 3.

P. H. Wicksteed, *The Commonsense of Political Economy*, London, 1933, Volume II, chapter 4.

D

CHAPTER II

CONSUMER'S DEMAND

1. CHOICE BETWEEN ALTERNATIVES

WE have so far given a simple explanation of the way in which supply and demand between them determine equilibrium prices. We must now discuss in greater detail the forces upon which demand and supply depend. Then, at a later stage, we can study more fully the way in which they interact in the market.

We have already seen that market demand curves are likely to slope downwards to the right, but we must provide more adequate justification for that statement. Market demand is the aggregate of the demands of individuals, so we can provide such justification if we first of all analyse these individual demands. In this and the following chapter we shall study the demand of an individual consumer for a consumption good and thereby explain the factors on which both individual and market demand curves depend.

In this chapter we shall give an elementary analysis of consumer demand. We shall assume that:

(1) The consumer's wants remain unchanged throughout.
(2) He has a fixed amount of money available.
(3) He is one of many buyers.
(4) He knows the prices of all goods, each of which is homogeneous.
(5) He can, if he wishes, spend his money in very small amounts.
(6) He acts 'rationally'.

The first question which we need to answer is, 'How does the consumer decide which of the various available commodities to buy?' To answer this let us assume that the consumer, when he makes his purchases, has the sole aim of obtaining the greatest possible satisfaction from his available money resources. In technical language, as we have seen, this means that the consumer obeys the principle of 'economic rationality'. He acts rationally

34

in the sense that he gets the greatest possible satisfaction from his *maxims* money by deliberately planning his purchases and choosing one good in preference to another. This does not necessarily mean that he is behaving selfishly in any moral sense. He may be buying goods for his family and not for himself. He may be buying shoes for a child or a carpet for the sitting-room. But we shall still assume that his decisions about what to buy are taken after deliberate and careful thought.

Basing our argument on these assumptions, we can now discuss the way in which an individual consumer makes his purchases. It will be clear that, since, by definition, all economic goods are *scarcity* scarce, an individual consumer is unable to buy unlimited quantities of them. As we all know only too well from personal experience, this reduces itself in practice to the problem of how to make our money go as far as possible—how to obtain maximum satisfaction from our limited resources. We are constantly compelled to do without this or that good because our incomes are too small to satisfy every desire.

This leads us to an important conclusion. The consumer's *choice* basic problem is that he must choose between alternative satisfactions. Since he is not rich enough to be able to buy everything he would like, he can only buy one thing if he forgoes another. So the problem of choice between alternatives is the important one. The consumer derives maximum satisfaction from his available resources by choosing those goods which are most desirable to him. It is clear then that the terms on which these alternative satisfactions are offered are of crucial importance. The questions which consumers ask are : If we buy this, how much must we pay for it ? Is it worth it ? What alternatives shall we forgo ? And what would be their value to us ?

In practice, consumers invariably make their choices in the *prices* light of existing money prices. A housewife going shopping, who is not certain whether to buy any green peas, will probably allow their price to make up her mind for her. If peas are 2s. 6d. a pound, she will almost certainly refuse to buy any, but at a penny a pound she will take some gladly. Price is the most obvious indicator of the value of the alternative satisfactions which she must forgo if she buys the peas. For the price of peas will determine how many other goods cannot be bought if the peas are bought. And whilst 2s. 6d. less to spend on, say, groceries, will be important, a penny will not.

Yet it is not only the prices of the goods which she is thinking of buying which enter into the housewife's calculations. The price of many other goods which are in the shops will influence her decisions. As Wicksteed says, 'If good sound old potatoes are to be had at a low price the marketer will be less likely to pay a high price for new ones, because there is a good alternative to be had on good terms'.[1]   But, although money prices of other goods in the shops are the most obvious indicators of the alternatives sacrificed, other factors may be supremely important. A decision to buy 1 pound of peas at the high price of 2s. 6d. may well leave the housewife's purchases of other household goods unaffected, but may deprive her of an afternoon at the cinema, mean one less music lesson for her child, leave the local church with half a crown less in the collection plate on Sunday or deprive a charity of a much-needed donation.

The alternative which a consumer finds he must sacrifice may therefore sometimes be the satisfaction of helping a deserving cause. Nor is that all. Instead of deciding to spend half a crown on one good instead of on another, the consumer might decide not to spend it but to save it for spending in the future. Or he could, if he wished, simply decide not to earn it at all. To any consumer at any time the range of possible alternatives from which he will be able to choose will be very great indeed. Nevertheless, on our assumption of economic rationality, any satisfaction which is deliberately chosen from this large set of possible alternative satisfactions will clearly be preferred to each and all of them.

2. SCALES OF PREFERENCE

The first step which the consumer takes when deciding which good or goods will give him the greatest possible satisfaction is therefore to classify these goods in order of preference. He must first of all build up '"a scale of preferences" . . . on which all objects of desire or pursuit (positive or negative) find their place, and which registers the terms on which they would be accepted as equivalents or preferred one to the other'.[2]   Since people do, in fact, decide to buy one good rather than another, they must have such scales of preference in their minds. Of course, despite the fact that people do make choices in a way which suggests that they have scales of preference, it would not be realistic to suppose that people's preference scales are quite complete, completely

---

[1] P. H. Wicksteed, *Commonsense of Political Economy*, p. 21.
[2] *Ibid.* p. 33.

consistent or completely conscious in their minds at all times. But consumer's demand would be much too erratic for us to be able to construct a theory of demand at all unless preference scales were in some degree rational and stable through time, and purchases were made in accordance with them.

One important point must, however, be remembered. Whilst a consumer's purchases at any time are determined by his scale of preferences and his total available resources, which are fixed in amount, the amount of money which he will spend on any one shopping expedition will not itself be fixed in the same way. It will be closely dependent on whether a number of things are available, for example, houses, flats, holidays, entertainments, education, and on their prices, just as, in the same way, expenditure on these things depends on prices in the shops. Nor is it only the absolute quantity of money which the consumer spends on any one shopping expedition which is likely to vary according to the details of the situation. It is equally possible for the 'real' value, or 'purchasing power', of the consumer's money resource to change. For example, it may well be that, when the housewife has finished her morning's shopping, prices have turned out to be higher or lower than she expected, and this may either allow her to buy goods she did not expect to be able to afford, or else force her to do without goods she had hoped to buy. Given her scale of preferences, the housewife will arrange her purchases in the light of the realised purchasing power of her resources.

3. DECISIONS AT THE MARGIN

In order to keep the exposition as simple as possible, we have so far steadfastly avoided discussing the actual quantities of any commodity which a consumer would buy. We have seen that a housewife will decide whether to buy any peas or not when she sees their price and the prices of alternatives, cabbage, carrots, beans, etc. But this only shows whether she will buy any peas at all, and not how many pounds. This is the next problem which must be solved.

Let us imagine a housewife with a husband and five children deciding how many pounds of peas to buy for the Sunday dinner. It is reasonable to suppose that her preference might be such that

If peas cost 1s. a pound, she would buy 3 pounds
  ,,   6d.   ,,   ,,   6 ,,
  ,,   2d.   ,,   ,,   20 ,,

If the price of peas is 1s. a pound, she will just feel willing to take 3 pounds as a treat, hoping that there will be enough for Sunday. If the price is 6d., however, she will just feel willing to take 6 pounds, hoping that there will be more for Sunday and perhaps a few left over for another day. If the price falls to 2d., she will probably buy some for each day of the week, say 20 pounds altogether. The important fact which emerges here is that a pound of peas *as such* does not occupy a definite position in the consumer's scale of preference.

If peas are being sold at 1s. a pound, the housewife is just willing to buy 3 pounds, and this clearly means that she regards the first, second and third pounds of peas as occupying a higher position in her scale of preferences than 1s. But she regards 1s. as being definitely preferable to the fourth pound of peas. Again, when peas are available for 6d., she prefers the fourth, fifth and sixth pounds of peas to 6d., but thinks that 6d. is preferable to the seventh pound of peas. With peas for sale at 2d. a pound, her scale of preferences shows that our housewife regards the seventh to the twentieth pounds of peas (inclusive) as worth more than 2d., but that she regards 2d. as worth more than the twenty-first pound of peas.

We may therefore conclude that our housewife thinks that the fourth pound of peas is worth less than 1s. but more than 6d., that the seventh pound is worth less than 6d. but more than 2d., and so on. But, since we are assuming that the peas are homogeneous, there can be no physical difference between any two or more pounds. This means that the housewife is not deciding whether to buy *a particular* fourth, seventh or twenty-first pound of peas. What she is doing is deciding whether it will pay her to buy 4 pounds of peas in preference to 3, or 7 pounds in preference to 6, taking the current price of peas into account.

This brings us to an extremely important concept in economic theory—the concept of the margin. We must explain what we mean by the margin before we can fully understand the nature of the decision which, as we have just seen, the housewife has to make. We may say that the 'part of the thing which he (the consumer) is only just induced to purchase may be called his *marginal purchase* because he is on the margin of doubt whether it is worth his while to incur the outlay required to obtain it'.[1] Similarly, any unit of a commodity which a consumer is momentarily considering whether to buy—whether he in fact buys it or

[1] Marshall, *Principles of Economics* (8th Edition), p. 93.

not—may be called a marginal unit. Our housewife therefore reviews each unit of the good in turn, and as she does so each unit becomes for the moment a marginal unit. If the housewife buys a unit without much hesitation, it may be regarded as an 'intra-marginal' purchase. If she refuses any unit, it is clearly worth too little for her to buy it at the current price—it is 'extra-marginal'.

It is obvious that when we say that the housewife undertakes this review of the importance of each unit of the good in succession, we are merely repeating in another way what we have already said about the consumer building up a scale of preferences. But we can now state a more useful conclusion. We may say that when the consumer considers if any unit of a good is worth buying, *Marginal* he (or she) is working out the *marginal significance* to him of the *Significan* good he is wondering whether to buy, in terms of the good with which it is to be bought. He is considering what is the value of the marginal unit of the purchased good in terms of the good with which he buys it. Thus, when our housewife was considering whether or not she would buy the sixth pound of peas, that sixth pound had become a marginal pound and the marginal significance of peas in terms of money at that stage would be 6*d*. for a pound of peas. For we know that the housewife was just willing to pay 6*d*. for that pound of peas and therefore 6*d*. must just have been the worth of that pound of peas in terms of money.

In this discussion the careful reader will have seen a clue to *How* the solution of our problem: How does the housewife decide *much?* how many pounds of peas to buy? We may therefore state the answer briefly here and explain it in detail in the next section. Our housewife is considering whether to buy a particular (marginal) pound of peas. She will do so if the marginal significance to her of peas in terms of money is sufficiently high. It may also be said *) diminishing* that, in general, the marginal significance of a good in terms of *(significance* money will decrease the more of that good one has compared with *)* money and other goods.

4. CONSUMER'S EQUILIBRIUM

We can now proceed to explain the way in which the decision on how many peas should be bought is taken. It will be recalled that when peas cost 2*d*. a pound, our imaginary housewife took 20 pounds. She was willing to give up two pennies for a twentieth pound of peas, but not for a twenty-first. It is clear, then, that at this point the housewife preferred the satisfaction which 2d. could give, through its ability to purchase other goods, to the satisfaction given by a twenty-first pound of peas. We shall find that this was because the money price of peas insisted on by greengrocers, namely 2d. for one pound of peas, exceeded the marginal significance in terms of money which the housewife herself attached to this twenty-first pound, perhaps $1\frac{1}{2}d.$ for that one pound of peas.

Let us look at the problem more closely. In our example we have assumed that the housewife is just prepared to take the third pound of peas at 1s. This means that the ruling market price (12 pence for one pound of peas) is just equal to the housewife's own marginal significance of peas in terms of money when the marginal pound is the third pound of peas. With the price reduced to 2d., the marginal significance in terms of money of the third pound of peas (12 pence) can be presumed to remain the same, since scales of preferences are independent of prices. So, since its marginal significance is greater than the current market price of peas, the third pound of peas is bought.

Similarly, it can be seen that the marginal significance to the housewife of the sixth pound of peas in terms of money is just equal to its market price when peas are 6d. a pound. The marginal significance of peas in terms of money is 6d. for the marginal (sixth) pound. If the price of peas now falls to 2d., the marginal significance to the housewife of the sixth pound of peas, namely 6d. for the sixth pound, becomes greater than the market price insisted upon by greengrocers, which is 2d. for 1 pound of peas. So she takes the sixth pound at that price.

We see, then, that if the marginal significance of peas in terms of money to the housewife is greater for any pound of peas than their market price, she will buy that pound. But if (as for the twenty-first pound of peas when peas cost 2d. a pound or more) it is less, she will refuse to buy it. Also, if the marginal significance to the housewife of a particular pound of peas is just equal to the market price of peas (as it is with the twentieth pound of peas when their price is 2d.) she will just be prepared to take that pound.

We can now formulate a vital proposition of consumer demand theory. *A consumer will exchange money for units of any commodity*, A, *up to the point where the last (marginal) unit of A which he buys has for him a marginal significance in terms of money just equal to its money price*. This fundamental proposition enables us to explain how a consumer will reach an equilibrium position where he has no desire to buy any more of a good. If he buys each good until its marginal significance in terms of money is equal to its money price, he cannot then make himself better off by buying any more of the good. If he did buy more he would only become worse off, obtaining units of the good which, as their marginal significances show, are lower on his scale of preference than the units of money which he would have to sacrifice in order to obtain them.

For example, our housewife who can buy peas at $2d.$ a pound is in an equilibrium position when she has bought 20 pounds of peas at $2d.$ a pound. The marginal significance of the twenty-first pound of peas in terms of money is, say, $1\frac{1}{2}d.$ for that 1 pound. That is to say, our housewife regards $1\frac{1}{2}d.$ as being worth only just as much as the twenty-first pound of peas. Yet in order to obtain that twenty-first pound of peas she would have to pay $2d.$ She would have to give up $2d.$, which occupies a higher position on her scale of preferences, to obtain a twenty-first pound of peas which occupies a lower position. She would therefore lessen her total satisfactions if she were to do this. So, on our assumption that all consumers wish to maximise satisfactions, she will not do it, but will remain in the 'optimum' equilibrium position where she gets 20 pounds of peas at $2d.$ a pound. It is not difficult to see that this analysis will hold good for each commodity separately, however many commodities there may be, though, as will be readily appreciated, the limitations of the human mind are such that it becomes extremely difficult to apply it to more than two or three goods at the same time. Nevertheless, it is clear that if consumers are to maximise satisfactions, they must equate the marginal significance of every good in terms of money with its money price. Goods here include consumption goods, capital goods, economic services, articles from which future satisfactions can be obtained, and leisure (the alternative to working and earning money).

When the consumer adjusts expenditure at all margins in this way he is in equilibrium, given his wants on the one hand and his income and the set of market prices on the other. So long as the relative importance of his different wants remains unchanged and his income and market prices remain constant, he will remain 'at rest' in the same equilibrium position. He has no motive for revising his plans, and will continue to buy the same things in the same quantities, until either his wants, or the opportunities of satisfying them, alter. His wants are adjusted to each other and to his environment.

The aim in this chapter has been to give an elementary theory of consumer's demand and the picture which has been given has been one of perfectly rational economic behaviour on the part of the consumer. But this picture is unrealistic in three important ways. In the first place, no sensible consumer really bothers about making minute or very exact adjustments at the margin. Quite naturally, most human beings have not the slightest desire to become calculating machines. Like the Law, normal human nature does not bother about very small things. Even the most careful housewife, with a large family and a very small income, has to draw the line somewhere. The consumer is therefore never completely in equilibrium even if his wants and conditions in the market remain completely stable.

Second, it will usually happen in fact that there are frequent small changes in price (and often in income). The consumer, if he were truly rational, should therefore be continually revising his purchases, making sure that he is using his money all the time in the best possible way. In practice, however, the consumer will tend to have a list of habitual purchases which he will make each week and which he will only revise when conditions change markedly. Many purchases are therefore likely to be based on habit and to be changed only at intervals in order to bring the consumer into line with relatively important changes in market conditions.

In the third place, no-one will ever have worked out in detail beforehand how he would reach a new optimum equilibrium position, with given wants, when there had been a large change in market conditions. A tramp may dream of becoming a millionaire, but he will not have in his mind a detailed scale of preferences between country houses and steam-yachts. The theory of consumer's equilibrium is more useful for interpreting adjustments to small, but not minute, changes than for explaining consumers' behaviour in times of violent economic change.

SUGGESTED READING

P. H. Wicksteed, *The Commonsense of Political Economy*, London, 1933, Volume I, chapters 1, 2 and 3.

CHAPTER III
INDIFFERENCE CURVE ANALYSIS

1. INDIFFERENCE CURVES

WE have seen so far that a consumer makes his purchases in accordance with a *scale of preferences* in which he classifies commodities and services in order of importance. It will be useful to analyse the nature of such a scale of preferences in greater detail. This can be done very conveniently with the aid of diagrams.

As we have seen already, a consumer builds up his scale of preferences quite independently of market prices. He lists commodities in order of importance on the basis of their power to satisfy his wants and before he sees what their prices are. Let us consider a simplified example. A man goes into a greengrocer's shop to buy the week's supplies. Before he makes his purchases we ask him to tell us which combinations of the various commodities that are available would give him greater satisfaction than others, which would give him smaller satisfactions, and which equal satisfactions. Our consumer would be able to provide us with a list of the various available combinations of goods arranged in order of importance. Of course, he would not be able to afford to buy all these combinations of goods. When he learned their prices he would rule out some combinations as not worth the price. But he would be able to say which combinations of the various goods in the greengrocer's shop he would like best, which least, and so on. It would be on the basis of such a list, representing his scale of preferences, that he would ultimately make his purchases. All he has done then is to draw up his scale of preferences in a concrete form instead of drawing it up mentally, and perhaps to some extent subconsciously, as he does when he goes shopping.

Let us now enquire what kind of scale of preferences a consumer would be likely to draw up. In order to simplify the problem, let us assume that there are only two goods on sale— grapes and potatoes. This is not very realistic but we shall find

43

it useful to use a diagrammatic analysis in this chapter, and such an analysis would be very difficult to employ if there were more than two goods to be considered, at least in the early stages. If we confine our attention to a situation where there are only two goods (grapes and potatoes) we can show the combinations of these goods which give various satisfactions to a consumer in a diagram like Figure 13.

In Figure 13 potatoes are measured along the x-axis, the number of pounds of potatoes increasing from left to right.

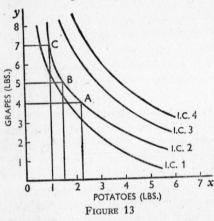

FIGURE 13

Similarly increasing quantities of grapes are measured up the y-axis. The consumer then informs us that if he were at point A with 4 pounds of grapes and $2\frac{1}{4}$ pounds of potatoes, he would be just as satisfied as at point B with 5 pounds of grapes and $1\frac{1}{2}$ pounds of potatoes, or at point C with 7 pounds of grapes and 1 pound of potatoes. These three combinations of grapes and potatoes represent for the consumer the same level of satisfaction—the same position in his scale of preferences.

Now, assuming that the consumer is able to give sufficient information, and that the goods are perfectly divisible, it is possible to draw a continuous line through all points representing the same level of satisfaction as at A, B and C. This has in fact been done in Figure 13. This line shows all those combinations of grapes and potatoes which give the same satisfaction to the consumer. We may say that the consumer is *indifferent* between all those combinations of grapes and potatoes represented by the line passing through A, B and C. This line is therefore known as an *indifference curve*. It shows all those combinations of grapes and potatoes which occupy the same position in the consumer's scale of preferences—which give him the same satisfaction. We have labelled it indifference curve number 2 (I.C.2).

One can draw similar indifference curves showing those combinations of grapes and potatoes which represent higher and lower levels of satisfaction than that shown on indifference curve 2. For example, in Figure 13 all points on indifference curves 3 and 4 represent preferred positions to those on indifference curve 2. All combinations of grapes and potatoes shown on indifference curve 3 represent situations where satisfactions are exactly the same. But at every such point satisfactions are greater than at every point on indifference curve 2. Similarly, the consumer is indifferent between all the combinations of the two goods shown on indifference curve 4, but prefers them all to the combinations on indifference curve 3. Indifference curve 1, on the other hand, represents a lower level of satisfactions than on indifferences curves 2, 3 and 4.

An indifference curve is thus like a contour line on a map, which shows all places the same height above sea-level. Instead of representing height, each indifference curve represents a level of satisfactions. It is, however, quite impossible to *measure* levels of satisfactions in the way that one can measure heights above sea-level. There are obviously no units of measurement. One can say whether one indifference curve represents a higher or lower level of satisfaction than another, but one cannot say *by how much* satisfaction is higher or lower. For this reason we give indifference curves numbers to put them in the right order, 1, 2, 3, 4, etc., but do not attempt to label them in terms of units of satisfaction—since there are no such things.

We have now provided an apparatus which will enable us to represent the consumer's scale of preferences by a set of indifference curves or an *indifference map*. But whilst we have drawn such an indifference map, we have so far made purely arbitrary assumptions about the shape of the indifference curves. In fact, one can make several realistic assumptions about their shape. It will be desirable to see how and why these assumptions are made. The first assumption is that an indifference curve always slopes downwards from left to right. This seems eminently reasonable. If indifference curves did not slope downwards, they would either slope upwards or else be horizontal. If an indifference curve were horizontal it would imply that the consumer would be equally satisfied with, say, 6 pounds of grapes and either 1, 2, 3, 4, 5 or 6 pounds of potatoes. This is obviously not in the least likely to be the case. A combination which includes more of one good and no less of the other will always be preferred to a combination containing less of the one good and the same amount of the other. Nor is an indifference curve likely to slope upwards to the right, for this would mean that the consumer would regard a combination containing a greater amount of both commodities, say 7 pounds of grapes and 3 pounds of potatoes, as giving just the same satisfaction as one containing less of each, say 6 pounds of grapes and 2 pounds of potatoes. This is even less likely to be true. It could only happen if the satisfaction derived from some units of one good were negative. The first assumption therefore appears to be realistic. Indifference curves always slope downwards to the right.

Second, it is assumed that all indifference curves are convex to the origin O, as are all the curves we have drawn so far. This is an important assumption. It can be seen, on reflection, that if one looks at any indifference curve, one can read off the marginal significance of the one good in terms of the other. For example, if the consumer is on indifference curve 2 in Figure 13 and starts off with 4 pounds of grapes and $2\frac{1}{4}$ pounds of potatoes, he would be equally satisfied if he had 5 pounds of grapes and $1\frac{1}{2}$ pounds of potatoes. The marginal significance of a pound of grapes in terms of potatoes is therefore $\frac{3}{4}$ of a pound of potatoes when the fifth pound of grapes is the marginal pound. For the consumer would be prepared to give up $\frac{3}{4}$ of a pound of potatoes for a fifth (marginal) pound of grapes. One can therefore define marginal significance a little more precisely than it was defined in the previous chapter. The marginal significance of a purchased good in terms of the good used to buy it is the amount of the good with which purchases are made (in this case potatoes) which one can give up in order to obtain another marginal unit of the other good (in this case grapes) if one is to remain on the same indifference curve.

This means that the slope of an indifference curve at any point shows marginal significance at that point. The shape of an indifference curve will therefore be important because it will be upon the change of slope of the indifference curve that marginal significance at the various points along it will depend. The assumption that indifference curves are convex to the origin implies something about changes in marginal significance as one proceeds along an indifference curve. It implies that in order to increase his stock of one good, Y, provided he is to become no better (or worse) off by doing so, the consumer will be able to give up less X in order to obtain further units of Y the more Y he has. For example, on indifference curve 2 in order to obtain a fifth pound of grapes and yet be no better off, the consumer can give up $\frac{3}{4}$ of a pound of potatoes; to get the sixth pound he can give up $\frac{1}{5}$ of a pound of potatoes; for the seventh pound he can give up $\frac{1}{6}$ of a pound of potatoes, and so on. Thus, as one moves along an indifference curve, the assumption that it is convex to the origin, that it gets flatter to the right and steeper upwards, implies that the marginal significance of the one good in terms of the other will always diminish progressively as one acquires more of the former good.

This is clearly a very important assumption and it is desirable to discover whether it is a realistic one. Is decreasing marginal significance as one moves along an indifference curve in fact as likely to occur as this assumption suggests? It is clear that marginal significance could not go on *increasing indefinitely* for one good reason. As we saw in the previous chapter, a consumer buys those units of any good for which his marginal significance in terms of money is greater than the price which he has to pay to obtain them. But if there were any commodity for which the consumer's marginal significance were increasing indefinitely and he bought any of it at all at the current (constant) price, he would find that after he had bought some, each succeeding unit which he could buy would have a progressively higher marginal significance. So he would go on buying more and more of the good until he had spent all his money on it. In fact, of course, it is extremely difficult to think of any state of affairs where a consumer does spend all his money on one good in this way. It is therefore not unreasonable to assume that marginal significance does not go on increasing for ever and that indifference curves are therefore more likely to be convex than concave; for concavity would only occur if marginal significance increased indefinitely.[1]

Whilst marginal significance is clearly unlikely to increase indefinitely, is there any reason why there should not be limited regions of a consumer's indifference map where marginal significance increases? Here it is more difficult to give a definite answer. As we have seen, the consumer can never be in equilibrium, buying more than one commodity, if marginal significance is always increasing. At points of equilibrium, therefore, marginal significance must be diminishing. There is no reason, however,

---

[1] It must be remembered, of course, that even if a consumer did spend all his income on one commodity, this would not necessarily mean that the marginal significance of that commodity was increasing. All it might mean would be that the marginal significance of that good, though diminishing, was so high that, even though the consumer bought nothing else, the marginal significance of that good in terms of money remained higher than that of any other good in terms of money.

why there should not be some parts of the consumer's preference scale where he could never be in equilibrium since marginal significance is increasing. This could happen over limited ranges of indifference curves if 'wobbles' or 'bumps of concavity' occurred. An instance of this kind of situation is given in Figure 14.

As one moves along the indifference curve from A to B, the marginal significance of grapes in terms of potatoes is declining. The consumer is prepared to give up progressively fewer potatoes in order to obtain further grapes. Once B is reached, however, a reversal takes place. The consumer suddenly becomes prepared

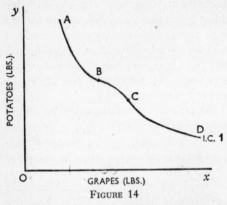

FIGURE 14

to give up increasing amounts of potatoes to obtain each further pound of grapes. This goes on until point C is reached, when conditions again change and the consumer becomes once more willing to give up fewer and fewer potatoes for each additional pound of grapes. The ranges of the indifference curve between A and B and between C and D display normal conditions with diminishing marginal significance of grapes in terms of potatoes. But the range between B and C is abnormal. The marginal significance of grapes in terms of potatoes increases as the consumer has more grapes.

Our assumption, that all indifference curves are convex to the origin, rules out the possibility that there could be increasing marginal significance even over small ranges of indifference curves. This does not seem unreasonable. But in any case, as we have seen already, a consumer can never be in an equilibrium position, buying some of both goods, at any point on an indifference curve which is concave to the origin. Similarly, a consumer will never find it worth while to remain on a *concave range* of an indifference curve, however small that range may be. Since the marginal significance of the good he is buying is increasing, it will pay him to go on buying more and more of it until the indifference curve becomes convex again, marginal significance begins to decrease and finally falls below price. One can therefore take consolation from the fact that even if there are isolated parts of indifference curves where marginal significance is increasing, these can never be possible positions of equilibrium. Our second assumption is that indifference curves are always convex to the origin.

The third assumption is that no two indifference curves can ever cut each other. The real-ism of this assumption can be seen from Figure 15, where two indifference curves do cut each other.

Since point A is on indifference curve 2, it represents a higher level of satisfaction to the consumer than that at point B which is on indifference curve 1. Yet point C lies on both curves. This implies that two levels of satisfaction, A and B, which are by definition

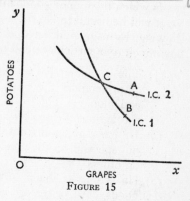

FIGURE 15

unequal, have managed to become equal at point C. This is an unacceptable proposition. Indifference curves can never cut each other.

These are the three basic assumptions about the shape of indifference curves. We shall maintain them throughout this analysis of consumer demand.

2. CONSUMER'S EQUILIBRIUM

We have now outlined a method by which it is possible to show a consumer's scale of preferences for two goods in diagram-matic form. Using this apparatus, one can show how such a consumer will reach an equilibrium position. To do this we shall make one alteration in our indifference map. So far we have assumed that there are only two goods—grapes and potatoes—in existence. But in practice there are other goods, and it will be con-venient if we can include them in our indifference curve diagrams.

We can do this if we draw indifference maps, not for grapes and potatoes, but for grapes and money, or potatoes and money. For money represents command over all other goods and by introducing it into the indifference map we can show the con-sumer's tastes with respect to potatoes on the one hand and money, representing general purchasing power, on the other.

E

We can do this legitimately provided we assume, first, that the prices of all the other goods are given and fixed and, second, that the consumer spends all his money on one good or another and does not save any. On these assumptions the consumer can be represented as choosing between, say, grapes and all the other goods which his money commands.

It will be useful to list the assumptions which will be made in showing, by using indifference curves, how a consumer decides how much of a particular good to buy. The assumptions are :

(1) The consumer has an indifference map showing his scale of preferences for combinations of the good in question and money. This scale of preferences remains the same throughout the analysis.

(2) He has a given amount of money to spend and if he does not spend it on the good we are studying, he will spend it on others.

(3) He is one of many buyers and knows the prices of all goods. All prices are assumed to be given and constant so that money can be shown as representing command over all goods except the one the consumer is buying.

(4) All goods are homogeneous and divisible.

(5) The consumer acts 'rationally' and maximises his satisfactions.

The first step in our attempt to show the equilibrium of a consumer diagrammatically is to find some way of showing on a diagram what his money will buy under given conditions. The consumer's indifference map is shown in Figure 16a. The consumer regards all the combinations of grapes and money on indifference curve 1 in Figure 16a as giving the same satisfactions as each other. Similarly, all the combinations on indifference curve 2 give the same satisfactions, these satisfactions being greater than on indifference curve 1. Indifference curves 3, 4 and 5 represent progressively higher and higher levels of satisfaction. This indifference map shows the consumer's personal tastes.

Figure 16b shows the way in which the size of the consumer's income and the price of grapes influence his purchases. He has a fixed amount of money, OAs. (shown up the y-axis), which he can spend. The market price of grapes is such that if he spends all his money on grapes he can obtain OB pounds. In other words, the price of a pound of grapes is $\frac{OA}{OB}s$. and is shown by the

slope of the line AB. The slope of such a line is thus usually
referred to as the *price slope*.

Now we are assuming that the consumer spends all his income
on one good or another. He must therefore either spend it on
grapes or keep it in money to be spent on other goods. This
means that, given the price of grapes $\left(\dfrac{OA}{OB}s.\text{ per pound}\right)$ the opportunities open to the consumer are shown by the line AB. He can
spend all his money on grapes, whereby he will arrive at point

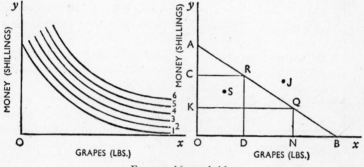

FIGURES 16A and 16B

B with OB pounds of grapes. He can keep all his resources in
cash, which will still leave him with OA*s*. Or he can acquire the
various combinations of grapes and money shown on the line AB.

For example, at point R he could buy OD pounds of grapes
and keep OC*s*. to spend on other goods. At point Q he could
buy ON pounds of grapes and keep OK*s*. to spend on other
goods. Assuming that the grapes are 'completely divisible', he
can acquire any of the combinations of grapes and money shown
on the line AB. This line shows the opportunities of acquiring
grapes which are open to him with grapes at their current price
and is known as a *price-opportunity line* or a *price line*. The consumer cannot go beyond the price line, say to point J, for he is
not rich enough. Nor will he remain inside the price line, say
at point S, for he would not then be spending all his income, and
we are assuming that he spends it on one good or another. The
price line thus represents the opportunities open to the consumer
in the market, given prices and his income ; whereas the indifference curves show his tastes independently of market conditions.
It is extremely important to remember that the indifference map

and the price line are quite independent of one another. The consumer has a scale of preferences which does not depend on prices. Similarly, in competitive conditions prices are given and cannot be affected by the actions of an individual consumer. For there are many other buyers and any individual consumer must take the price of each good as given.

The next step is to show how, given his indifference map on the one hand and market conditions on the other, the consumer reaches an equilibrium position. This is done in Figure 17 where

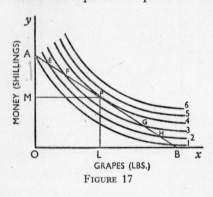

FIGURE 17

we superimpose the price line from Figure 16b on the indifference map from Figure 16a. Since we are assuming that the consumer always aims at obtaining the greatest possible satisfaction, he will naturally attempt to reach the highest possible indifference curve. But in doing this he will have to act within the limits imposed by the fact that he has only a fixed amount of money OA*s*. to spend and that the price of grapes is given. In this case grapes are $\dfrac{OA}{OB}$*s*. a pound.

The consumer begins at point A in Figure 17 with OA*s*. and no grapes. He is on indifference curve 1. He increases his satisfactions by moving to point E, giving up money in exchange for grapes. This increases his satisfactions by putting him on indifference curve 2. If he now moves to point F, exchanging money for grapes, he again becomes better off being now on indifference curve 3. At both E and F the consumer is using all his resources, spending part on grapes and retaining part in the form of money for purchases of other goods. But at F he is better off than at E. He could again increase his satisfactions by moving to P on indifference curve 4. At both F and P he would still be allocating all his money, but at P he would have increased his satisfactions. Having reached P, however, the consumer cannot increase his satisfaction further by substituting more grapes for money. If he did buy more grapes, he would merely find himself back on indifference curve 3 at point G, or on indifference curve 2 at point H. He is not rich enough to be able to reach a position on his scale of preferences higher than indifference curve 4 with grapes as dear as they are. Hence, at point P on indifference curve 4 the consumer is in an optimum equilibrium position, where he is maximising his satisfactions.

At any point on the price line above P (*e.g.* at E or F) the marginal significance of grapes in terms of money to the consumer is greater than the money price of grapes—the indifference curves are steeper than the price line. The consumer therefore increases his satisfactions by giving up money to get more grapes. On the other hand, below P (at G or H) the consumer finds the opposite. The marginal significance to him of grapes in terms of money is now less than the price of grapes. He will therefore buy no more grapes once he has bought OL pounds at a total cost of MA*s*. This leaves him with OM*s*. for other uses. At P the consumer's marginal significance of grapes

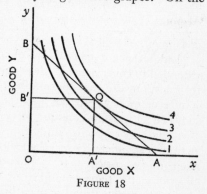

FIGURE 18

in terms of money is equal to the price of grapes in the market, and he is therefore in equilibrium.

This happens because the slope of the price line and the slope of indifference curve 4 are the same at point P. But this position of equilibrium can now be seen visually from the diagram. The consumer in Figure 17 will be in equilibrium where the price line AB is tangent to an indifference curve, for at any such point of tangency the price line and the indifference curve have the same slope and the marginal significance of the good in terms of money (shown on the indifference curve) will equal price (shown on the price line). The consumer will retain the combination of the two 'goods' appropriate to this point on his indifference map.

If we consider two consumption goods instead of one consumption good and money, we must assume that the consumer is paid his income in terms of one of the goods and that their prices in terms of each other are given. Such a case is shown in Figure 18. Here good X is measured on the *x*-axis and good Y on the *y*-axis.

We still assume that the consumer's income, whether paid in X or Y, is fixed, so that he is now able to buy OA of X if he buys nothing but X, or OB of Y if he buys nothing but Y. The price line AB shows all the possible combinations of X and Y which the consumer can buy with his available resources. The steeper the slope of AB, the higher is the price of X in terms of Y, that is, the higher is $\dfrac{\text{Price of X}}{\text{Price of Y}} = \dfrac{\text{OB}}{\text{OA}}$. The slope of AB thus represents the ratio of the money prices of X and Y. The highest indifference curve which the consumer can now reach with his available resources is indifference curve 3. He will be in equilibrium at point Q on this curve, where he buys OA′ of X and OB′ of Y. At point Q the ratio of the prices of X and Y, $\dfrac{\text{OB}}{\text{OA}}$, is equal to the consumer's marginal significance of X in terms of Y.

Indifference curve analysis of the kind outlined above can be extended to cover many kinds of economic problem, and the goods in question can be consumption goods, capital goods, work, leisure or money. In this way the consumer's indifference maps between all possible commodities can be studied. It can be shown that for him to be in equilibrium with respect to all goods the marginal significances of *all* goods in terms of money must equal their money prices. It is important to realise, however, that diagrammatic representations of consumer equilibrium cannot deal adequately with more than three goods. Each good needs one dimension and so two goods need two dimensions, three goods need three dimensions, four goods four dimensions, and so on. On the (two-dimensional) page of a book, three dimensions can only be shown by drawing a diagram in perspective and with more than three goods recourse has to be made to algebra. This is why we shall usually confine our attention to situations where there are only two goods. It is, however, always possible to deal by implication with many goods by putting one good on one axis and money on the other. That is a simple and useful way of making this type of analysis more realistic.

3. THE INCOME EFFECT

We have so far seen how a consumer with given wants and a fixed money income decides which goods to buy and in what amounts. It is now time to discover what will happen if his money income, or the prices of goods, or both, change. On the underlying assumption of 'rationality', the consumer will clearly try to reach a new equilibrium position where he is once again maximising satisfactions. But how will he do this ? Let us answer this question by considering the various ways in which the situation facing the consumer can alter. There are three main ways in which the conditions underlying the equilibrium shown on an indifference curve diagram by the tangency of an indifference curve and a price line can change. First, there is the possibility that the consumer may become better or worse off because his income changes but prices remain constant. The consumer's satisfactions will be either increased or decreased, for he has a larger or smaller income to spend. The result of this type of change is described in technical language as an *income effect*.

Second, it is possible that prices may change, but that the consumer's money income may also change in such a way that he is neither better nor worse off as a result. He will, however, find it worth his while to buy more of those goods whose relative price has fallen. He will substitute the relatively cheaper goods for the relatively dearer ones. The result of this type of change is thus known as a *substitution effect*.

The third possibility is that prices may change, with money income constant, so that the consumer is made either better or worse off. In this situation the consumer will not only have to rearrange his purchases as under the substitution effect, but his 'real' income, his income in terms of goods, will change too. There will thus be an income effect also and this will make the consumer better or worse off, as the case may be. The result of this kind of change in conditions is described as a *price effect* and is a combination of an income effect on the one hand and a substitution effect on the other. In this and the next two sections we must discuss these three effects of changed conditions. First, let us consider the income effect.

The effect of a change in the consumer's income can easily be shown on an indifference curve diagram. It will, however, be convenient to carry out this analysis in terms of two goods rather than in terms of one good and money. Let us assume that a consumer has an increased income to spend, but that the prices of both the goods shown on the indifference diagram remain constant. The effect of a change of this kind can be seen from Figure 19.

Let us assume that the consumer considered in Figure 19 starts with an income of OA in terms of X (OB in terms of Y). He will be in equilibrium at point Q on indifference curve 1. In this position he will have OM of X and ON of Y. If his income now rises to OA' in terms of X or OB' in terms of Y, the consumer

will move from the old equilibrium position to a new position of
equilibrium at Q'. He will now be better off, being on indifference
curve 2, and will have OM' of X and ON' of Y. In other words,
if we assume that the consumer is paid in X, he will exchange
X for Y at the rate of exchange shown by the slope of the price
line until he has acquired ON' of Y, and will retain OM' of X
for his own use. As a result of the rise in his income, the consumer
has increased his purchases of both X and Y and is at a preferred

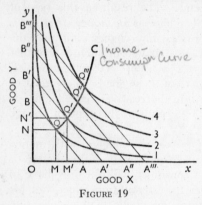

FIGURE 19

position on his indifference
map. If the consumer's income now rises to OA" in
terms of X and then to OA'''
in terms of X, he will be in
equilibrium at Q" and Q'''
respectively.

It is clear that there will
be an infinitely large number
of possible equilibrium positions such as Q, Q', Q", Q''',
one for each possible level of
income. The line Q-Q'''
shows all the possible posi-

tions of equilibrium over the range of income between OA in
terms of X and OA''' in terms of X at the given prices of X and
Y. Any line like O-Q-Q'''-C drawn through the equilibrium
points for all the possible levels of income is known as an
income-consumption curve. It shows how consumption of the two
goods reacts to changing income when prices of both goods are
given and constant. If prices are different, then of course the
income-consumption curve will be different. There is thus a
separate income-consumption curve for each different system of
relative prices for the goods in question. For with each different
set of relative prices the slope of the price line will differ, and so
will the successive points of tangency. An income-consumption
curve thus traces out the income effect as the consumer's income
changes, with given relative prices of the two goods.

It is clearly desirable that we should be able to say what the
shape of an income-consumption curve is likely to be. With most
indifference maps it will be found that all the income-consumption
curves slope upwards to the right, as happens with each of the
three income-consumption curves shown in Figure 20a. This
means that as a rule a rise in a consumer's income will make him

buy more of each of any two goods he is consuming. This will be
the usual shape of the income-consumption curve.

But it is just possible that over some ranges the income- *Inferior
consumption curve might slope upwards to the left, as with the *Goods*
curve ICC′, or downwards to the right, as with the curve ICC″
(in Figure 20b). In these cases the income-consumption curve
shows that, after a point, the consumer, even though he is becoming
richer, consumes less of one of the goods. This can happen if
one of the goods is such that it is consumed in large amounts
only when the consumer is poor and is replaced wholly or partially

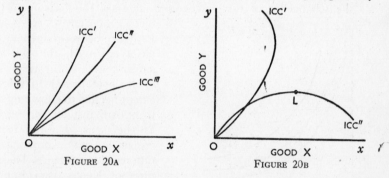

FIGURE 20A   FIGURE 20B

by goods of higher quality when he becomes richer. Such a good
is known in economic jargon as an 'inferior' good. For example,
in Figure 20b if the income-consumption curve is ICC′, X is an
'inferior' good; if it is ICC″, Y is an 'inferior' good. If the
income-consumption curve slopes upwards to the right in the
normal way, we can say that the income effect is *positive* for both
goods. If it slopes backwards or downwards, we can say that
the income effect for one good is *negative*, after a certain point has
been reached. In the case of good Y in Figure 20b the income
effect is negative beyond point L on income-consumption curve
ICC″.

4. THE SUBSTITUTION EFFECT

A substitution effect occurs, it will be remembered, when the
relative prices of goods change in such a way that the consumer
in question is no better or worse off than he was before, but has
to rearrange his purchases in accordance with the new relative
prices.

The substitution effect is shown by Figure 21. Perhaps it can
best be understood if we use a hypothetical illustration. In the

original situation shown in Figure 21 the consumer is in equilibrium at point Q on indifference curve 2, buying ON of Y and keeping OM of good X. Let us assume that in this situation a subsidy is being paid on good Y. The price of Y to the consumer is thus kept down artificially below its true level. Let us now assume that the Chancellor of the Exchequer removes the subsidy. The relative price of Y now rises. Instead of the price of Y in terms of X being $\frac{OA}{OB}$, it is now $\frac{OA'}{OB'}$. But let us further assume that, in order to compensate the consumer for the rise in the price of Y, the Chancellor of the Exchequer increases the consumer's

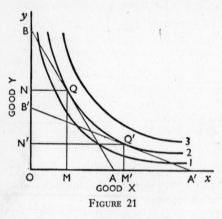

FIGURE 21

income in terms of X. Perhaps because income tax is reduced, the consumer's income in terms of X is increased to the extent needed to allow him to remain just as well off as he was before—to remain on the same indifference curve. The price of Y has risen, but the consumer's income in terms of X has risen also from OA to OA'. This rise in income is just sufficient to compensate the consumer for the rise in the price of Y. There has been what economists call a *compensating variation* in the consumer's income, in terms of X, of AA'. This compensating variation is just large enough to cancel out the change in his circumstances caused by the rise in the relative price of Y. He remains at exactly the same position in his scale of preferences (on the same indifference curve), the rise in the price of Y having been 'compensated for' by the rise in his income.

As a result of these changes, we have a *substitution effect*. The relative prices of X and Y have changed, whilst the compensating variation in income has ensured that the consumer is neither better nor worse off than he was before. Although the consumer remains on the same indifference curve, however, he is on it at a different position. Instead of being at point Q, he is now at point Q'. This move along the indifference curve from Q to Q' represents a substitution effect. The consumer, though neither better nor worse off, moves along an indifference curve, in this case from Q to Q'. He substitutes X which is now relatively cheaper for Y which is now relatively dearer ; but because of the compensating variation in income becomes neither better nor worse off. A substitution effect can always be represented as a movement along an indifference curve, where any change which would have taken place in a consumer's real income because prices have changed, is 'compensated for' by a change in his money income.

5. THE PRICE EFFECT

The most interesting consequence of a change in the situation confronting a consumer is known as the *price effect*. Here the relative prices of the goods in question change but there is no compensating variation in income. The consumer is allowed to become better or worse off. His money gives him greater or smaller satisfaction than it did before because prices have altered —his 'real' income rises or falls. The price effect is shown in Figure 22.

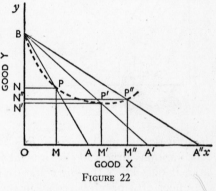

FIGURE 22

The original equilibrium position in Figure 22 is at P where the consumer has OM of X and ON of Y. In this original situation the price of X is such that the consumer could buy OA of X if he spent the whole of his income on it. Let us now assume that the consumer's money income remains constant, but that the price of X falls, so that the same money income will now buy OA' of X instead of OA. Since the price of Y is constant, the consumer's income in terms of Y is OB all the time. The new equilibrium position will be at P' where the consumer has OM' of X and ON' of Y. If the price of X falls again, so that the given income will now buy OA" of X if the consumer buys only X, the resulting equilibrium position will be at P". Each change in the price of X alters the slope of the price line by altering the ratio of the prices of X and Y. The cheaper X becomes compared with Y, the less steep is the slope of the price line and *vice versa*. If we now draw a line connecting P, P', P", etc., we have drawn what is known as a *price-consumption curve*. This shows the price effect. It shows the way in which the consumption of X changes when its price changes, but the consumer's income in terms of Y and the price of Y are unaltered.

Given any consumer's indifference map and given the prices of the two goods shown on it, one can always construct the consumer's income-consumption curve and his price-consumption curve, as we have done in Figure 23. Let us assume that in Figure 23 the consumer begins with an income of OA in terms

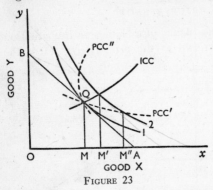

FIGURE 23

of X and with the given price structure is able to reach point Q on indifference curve 1. We can now construct an income consumption curve ICC and a price-consumption curve PCC′ both starting at point Q and showing income and price effects respectively. Whoever the consumer happens to be, it will always be found that

the price-consumption curve PCC′ lies between the income-consumption curve and the original indifference curve 1. Similarly, if one draws the price-consumption curve PCC″, showing the effect of a progressive fall in the price of Y, with the price of X, and income in terms of X, constant, one will find that the curve PCC″ also lies between the income-consumption curve and the original indifference curve, this time to the left and not to the right of the income-consumption curve. This must happen. It follows directly from the fact that the price-consumption curve represents points of tangency between *progressively flatter* price lines and indifference curves which are all convex to the origin, whilst the income-consumption curve represents points of tangency between the same indifference curves and successive price lines all of which have the *same* slope.

At first sight the fact that the price-consumption curve lies between the income-consumption curve and the indifference curve at which the consumer was originally in equilibrium, looks to be a proposition of mere geometrical interest. In fact, it turns out to be of profound economic importance. Let us consider the situation shown in Figure 24. When the price of X falls, the consumer moves from his original equilibrium at P to a new equilibrium position at P'. But it would be correct to look upon this as compounded of a movement on the one hand from P to Q along the income-consumption curve, and of a further movement from Q to P' along indifference curve 2. The movement along the income-consumption curve from P to Q can be regarded as an income effect, and the movement along indifference curve 2 from Q to P' can be looked upon as a substitution effect.

The effect of a price change is thus in reality the resultant of the actions of two separate and different forces, and can be looked at in two parts. First there is an *income effect* which causes a movement along the income-consumption curve and which makes the consumer better off. Now that X is cheaper his money goes further—his 'real' income has risen. Second, there is a *substitution effect* which causes a movement along an indifference curve and makes the consumer buy more of the good X whose price has fallen. X is now relatively cheaper compared with Y. Since in the initial equilibrium the relative prices of X and Y were equal to their marginal significance in terms of each other, this means that the marginal significance of X in terms of Y is now greater than its price in terms of Y. It therefore pays the consumer to substitute X for Y until once again the marginal significance of X in terms of Y equals the price of X in terms of Y. He does this by moving along the new and higher indifference curve. In Figure 24 this means a move from Q to P'.

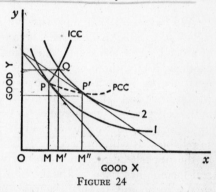

FIGURE 24

It is perfectly reasonable and realistic to look upon the price effect as the net result of an income effect and a substitution effect in this way. In Figure 24 the demand for X rises from OM to OM" as the consumer moves along the price-consumption curve from P to P'. But one can legitimately regard MM' of this increase in demand as the result of an income effect, and the rest —M'M"—as caused by a substitution effect. It is therefore obvious that as the price of any good X falls, the increase in the amount of the good which is demanded depends on the strength and direction of the income effect on the one hand and of the substitution effect on the other. In practice it will usually be found that the amount of every good demanded by an individual consumer will increase as the price of the good falls. This is so because the substitution effect and the income effect are normally both positive. They both act in such a way as to increase the purchases of any good whose price has fallen.

6. 'INFERIOR' GOODS

We have said that normally both the income effect and the substitution effect will be such as to make the consumer buy more of a good whose price has fallen, and we must now see what exceptions, if any, there can be to this rule. The substitution effect must always be such that the consumer will buy more of a good whose price has fallen. This follows directly from the fact that indifference curves are assumed to be convex to the origin. But, unfortunately, as we have already seen, the income effect is not so reliable. It will not necessarily be 'positive' but may well work in the opposite direction. Normally the fact that a consumer's real income has risen will make him buy more of both the goods shown in an indifference diagram, including the one which, by its fall in price, caused the income effect. Where this happens, both the income and the substitution effects are positive and all is well. The consumer buys more of the good which is cheaper, partly because his 'real' income has risen, partly because the good whose price has fallen is now cheaper relatively to other goods. But in certain cases the income effect may be negative, though the substitution effect can never be. A consumer may therefore actually buy *less* of a good when his real income rises as a result of a fall in the price of the good.

We have already seen that there are some inferior goods of which less and not more is bought when the consumer's income rises. Such goods are consumed mainly when the purchaser is poor, and are entirely or partially replaced by goods of superior quality when he becomes better off. The income effect is therefore negative instead of positive. Margarine is usually given as the stock example, for it is normally replaced by butter when consumers become richer—provided there is no rationing. There may well be other goods of the same kind.

It does not necessarily follow, however, that a fall in the price of an inferior good will lead an individual consumer to buy less of it now that his real income has risen. Though the income effect is negative, it may well be too weak to outweigh the positive substitution effect and the consumer's demand curve may well slope downwards to the right in the usual way. This kind of situation is shown in Figure 25. Here we have a fall in the price of X which causes the consumer to move from an equilibrium point at P to a new equilibrium at R. He increases his purchases of X from OM to OM″. But the income effect is negative, and had he merely received an increase in income which took him

from P to Q (which would have made him just as well off as at R) he would have reduced his purchases of X from OM to OM′. It is only because the substitution effect when X becomes relatively cheaper carries the consumer along indifference curve 2 from Q to R that he buys an extra MM″ of it. Only for that reason is there a net increase in his purchases of X. What in

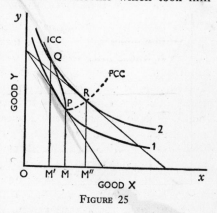

FIGURE 25

fact happens is that when the price of X falls, the negative income effect causes the consumer to buy M′M less of X but the positive substitution effect induces him to buy M′M″ more of X. The net result, which is in some sense a compromise between the income and substitution effects, is that the consumer buys more X, but not so much more X as he would have bought if the income effect had been either zero or positive.

In practice, it is likely that even though there may be many inferior goods, the positive substitution effect will usually outweigh the negative income effect. Only where the negative income effect is very strong, which will usually happen only when the consumer spends a great deal of his income on the good in question, can the demand for a good fall as its price falls.

7. GIFFEN'S PARADOX

It is, of course, conceivable that there may be a few goods for which the negative income effect is so strong that it can outweigh the positive substitution effect. If this happens, individual consumers will buy less of the good when its price falls and more of the good if its price rises. This kind of situation can only exist if the proportion of the consumer's income spent on the good in question is very large. Then a fall in the price of the good will cause a considerable change in the consumer's real income.

A commodity of this kind, which people demand in smaller quantities when it is cheaper than they do when it is dearer, is clearly an inferior good. But it is a rather special kind of inferior good and is often referred to as a 'Giffen good'. It owes this

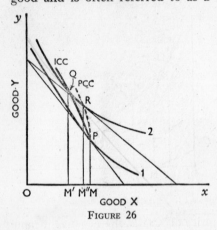

FIGURE 26

name to Sir Robert Giffen,[1] who is said to have claimed during the nineteenth century that a rise in the price of bread often caused such a severe fall in the real incomes of the poorer labouring classes that they were forced to curtail their consumption of meat and other more expensive foods. Bread being still the cheapest food, they consumed more of it, and not less, now that its price was higher. Similarly, if the price of bread fell, people would buy less of it. For their real income would now have risen, and they would curtail their purchases of bread in order to obtain a more varied diet.

The results of a fall in the price of a 'Giffen good' can be seen in Figure 26. When the price of X falls so that the consumer moves from equilibrium at point P to equilibrium at point R, the consumer reduces his purchases of X from OM to OM″. The reduction in purchases of M″M is the net result of a negative income effect which by itself would have caused the consumer to buy M′M less of X, and a positive substitution effect which, alone, would have caused him to buy M′M″ more. The net result is that the consumer buys less X than he did before (OM″ instead of OM), but not so much less as he would have done had there been no substitution effect. The positive substitution effect is swamped by the negative income effect and less X is demanded

---

[1] See Alfred Marshall, *Principles of Economics* (8th Edition), p. 132. See, however, Henry Schultz, *Theory and Measurement of Demand*, pp. 51-2, where the same ideas are attributed to Simon Gray.

now that its price has fallen. Such situations are undoubtedly abnormal but it is possible that they do occasionally occur.

8. THE DERIVATION OF MARKET DEMAND CURVES

A demand curve was defined in Chapter I as a curve showing how much of a good would be bought at various prices—assuming

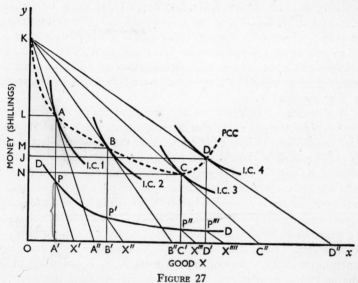

FIGURE 27

all other prices to be constant. If one reflects on the matter, it is clear that an individual's demand curve for a good must be related in some way to his price-consumption curve for the same good. In fact they both represent the same information except that the former gives it in a more directly useful form. It is not difficult to derive the ordinary demand curve of an individual consumer for a good provided only that one knows his indifference map and the size of his income. The way in which this can be done is shown in Figure 27.

In Figure 27 are shown an individual's price-consumption curve KD together with the relevant parts of his indifference map between money (on the y-axis) and good X (on the x-axis). Let us choose at random four points on the price-consumption curve and label them A, B, C and D. At these four positions of equilibrium the consumer buys OA', OB', OC' and OD' units of X

F

respectively. For these same quantities he pays prices per unit of $\frac{KL}{OA'}s$., $\frac{KM}{OB'}s$., $\frac{KN}{OC'}s$. and $\frac{KJ}{OD'}s$., the price of X falling progressively as the consumer moves from K to D. In other words, these prices are given by the slopes of KA″, KB″, KC″ and KD″. Since the consumer has a fixed income of OKs. to spend, when he is at A he spends KLs., keeping OLs. for other purposes. Similarly at B he spends KMs. and keeps OMs., at C he spends KNs. and at D, KJs. One can read off all this information from the y-axis. For, since the consumer's total income is constant at OKs., and since a perpendicular from any point, such as A, to the y-axis tells us how much of his resources the consumer is retaining in money (OLs.), we can also see how much he has spent on X to arrive at A.

A demand curve does not say anything about the size of a consumer's income except that it is constant. Nor does it consider the amount of money left over after the consumer has made his purchases of X. A demand curve only tells us the number of units of X bought at any given price. This can be discovered from the price-consumption curve. As we have seen, the price-consumption curve shows what total expenditure is when any given number of units of X are purchased. We can thus calculate the price of X by dividing total expenditure by the number of units bought. For instance, at K no X is being bought and total expenditure is nil. As one moves from K to B the price of X falls and total expenditure on X increases—as does the amount bought. Beyond C the amount of X bought continues to increase, but total outlay now declines. The price-consumption curve is really only a total outlay curve, like that in Figure 5, but it is upside down.

In order to derive a demand curve, all we need to know is the price per unit of X when any given amount of X is demanded. We can find this most easily by first considering, in Figure 27, the perpendiculars AA′, BB′, CC′ and DD′, from A, B, C and D to the x-axis. If we consider the line AA′, it shows us the amount of X, OA′ units, which is bought at the given unit price of X, $\frac{KL}{OA'} = \frac{OK}{OA''}s$. But what is the price per unit of X? We know it is $\frac{KL}{OA'} = \frac{OK}{OA''}s$., but it is not easy to plot this on a diagram.

In the present context the easiest way to find the unit price of X is to mark off, to the right of AA′ along the x-axis, one unit of X, one pound, one tin, one bottle as the case may be. Let us assume that in this case one unit of X is represented by the distance A′X′. We then draw the line X′P parallel to KA″. The slope of KA″ shows the price of X. Since the slopes of KA″ and X′P are the same, they both represent the same unit price of X. And since A′X′ represents one unit of X, the distance A′P represents the price of one unit of X when OA′ of X is bought. P is therefore a point on the individual's demand curve. It shows how much X he buys when one unit of X costs A′Ps. $\left(= \dfrac{OK}{OA''}s. \right)$.

Similarly, if we mark off one unit of X, B′X″ to the right of B′ and draw X″P′ parallel to KB, we can find the unit price of X when OB′ of X is bought. This price will be B′P′s. $\left(= \dfrac{OK}{OB''}s. \right)$. Point P′ is thus another point on the individual's demand curve, showing how much X he will buy when X is B′P′s. per unit. Similarly we can derive the points P″ and P‴ showing the individual's demand for X when one unit of it costs C′P″s. and D′P‴s. respectively.

We can then draw a demand curve DD showing the amount of X which the individual consumer will buy at various prices of X. It passes through a series of points like P, P′, P″ and P‴ showing price and amount demanded at each price. As we have seen, this demand curve can easily be derived from a consumer's indifference map. In Figure 27 the individual demand curve slopes downwards because, with the indifference map used there, both the income effect and the substitution effect are positive. Individual demand curves will normally be of this general shape. But, as we have seen, there may be some circumstances in which Giffen's paradox holds good and the demand curve does not slope downwards to the right over the whole of its length. An example of this is shown in Figure 28.

In Figure 28 the demand curve begins by sloping downward to the right in the normal way. Over this range of prices the income effect is positive. It is likely that *all* demand curves will slope downwards in the normal way to begin with. For total expenditure on the good in question will usually be relatively small at high prices. The income effect (even if negative) cannot therefore be very important. Once price in Figure 28 has fallen to OP, however, the income effect becomes both negative and strong. It outweighs the positive substitution effect, and the demand curve therefore slopes downwards to the left until price has fallen to OP'. Once this has happened, the demand curve again begins to slope downwards to the right. Prices are so low that total expenditure is very small and the income effect, even if still negative, is once again outweighed by the positive substitution effect. This seems to be the most likely shape of the demand curve for a 'Giffen good'. It is, for example, most unlikely that any demand curve will slope downwards to the left throughout its whole length. It will only be over those price ranges where any negative income effect is extremely strong that the curve will slope downwards to the left.

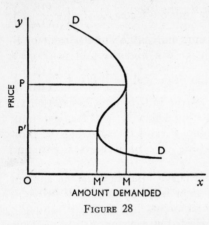

FIGURE 28

We may sum up this discussion on the shape of the demand curves of individuals by saying that in most cases they will slope downwards to the right in the normal way, because as the price of a good falls, the positive substitution effect is reinforced by a positive income effect. But even where the income effect is negative, the demand curve will still slope downwards to the right if the substitution effect is sufficiently strong to outweigh the income effect. Only when the negative income effect is strong enough to offset the substitution effect—a thing which one imagines can only happen over limited ranges of a demand curve—can this curve slope downwards to the left instead of to the right.

All that has been said so far relates to the demand curves of individuals. What can we say about market demand curves? Market demand curves are obtained by adding together the demand curves of all the individuals in the market. How this is done is shown in Figure 29. In Figures 29a and 29b are two individual demand curves. These are added together sideways in Figure 29c. Since both the individuals' curves are identical, and both show no demand for the good at any price at or above OP, the aggregate curve does the same. At each price below OP the aggregate curve shows the sum of the individual demands at the price in question. For example, at the price OP', demand in both Figures 29a and 29b is OA. In Figure 29c demand at the price OP′ is OB, which is twice OA. Because the two individual demand curves are identical, demand on the market curve at any price equals twice the demand on the individual demand curve at that price. It should be noted that *at each price* the *elasticity of demand* on all three demand curves in Figure 29 is the same. Any set of individual demand curves for a good—no matter how many individuals there are—can be added together in this way to give a market demand curve for the good.

Market demand curves will normally slope downwards to the right. For the individual demand curves normally slope down-

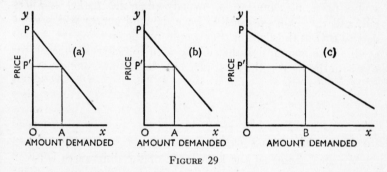

FIGURE 29

wards to the right. Thus, even if the number of buyers in a market does not increase as the price of the good in question falls, the downward slope of the individual demand curves will usually ensure that the market curve also slopes downwards to the right. In practice, however, it is likely that new buyers will enter the market as the price of the good falls, and this will be an added reason why the market demand curve slopes downwards to the right. Even if an individual's demand curve for a good slopes downwards to the left because of Giffen's paradox, it does not follow that the market demand curve will do the same. For one thing, a good which is so 'inferior' to some people so that their demand curves are abnormal, may not be 'inferior' to everyone. There may be enough people buying sufficiently more of the good as its price falls to offset the peculiarities of those who buy less. The market demand curve can still be normal.

Again, even if everyone buys less of a good as its price falls over some ranges, they may not all do so over the same price ranges. It might well happen, therefore, that a good could be a 'Giffen good' to everyone and yet have a normal market demand curve because only a few people regarded it as a 'Giffen good' over the *same* price ranges. Finally, and most plausibly, it is likely that even where a good is of this abnormal 'Giffen' type, new buyers will enter the market as its price falls. They will either not regard it as a Giffen good at all, or else will not do so over the range of prices obtaining just after they first enter the market.

The conditions which have to be fulfilled for a market demand curve to slope downwards to the left are seen to be very stringent. Curves of this type may exist, but they are not likely to do so. For even when all existing buyers have abnormal demand curves, at any price, new buyers will usually enter the market as prices fall, and they will presumably have demand curves which slope downwards to the right or they would not be entering the market at all. The assumption that market demand curves slope downwards to the right is the most plausible assumption one can make.

9. ELASTICITIES

(a) Income-Elasticity of Demand

We shall find that the knowledge of the differences between income, substitution and price effects which we have now acquired will prove very useful in helping us to see more clearly what it is that determines the elasticity of demand for any good. We know that the elasticity of demand for a good depends on the shape of the demand curve for that good. But we have now seen that the demand curve and the price-consumption curve show exactly the same information, though in different ways. Elasticity of demand therefore depends equally on the shape of the price-consumption curve. The shape of the price-consumption curve depends in its turn on the nature of the income effect and of the substitution effect. Thus elasticity of demand depends on two other elasticities. One is the *income-elasticity of demand*. The other is *elasticity of substitution*. Ordinary elasticity of demand, *price-elasticity of demand* as it is often called, is a sort of compromise between income-elasticity of demand and elasticity of substitution, just as the price effect is a compromise between an income effect and a substitution effect. It will be useful to consider these two factors which determine price-elasticity of demand in some detail.

Income-elasticity of demand shows the way in which a consumer's purchases of any good change as a result of a change in his income. It shows the responsiveness of a consumer's purchases of a particular good to a change in his income. More accurately, we may define income-elasticity of demand, e_i of any good, X, as

$$e_i = \frac{\text{proportionate change in purchases of good X}}{\text{proportionate change in income}}.$$

It follows that where the income-elasticity of demand for a good is high, a given proportionate increase in a consumer's income of, say, 1 per cent causes a proportionately much larger increase in the demand for the good of, say, 10 per cent. Here income-elasticity would be $\frac{10}{1} = 10$. Similarly, where a good's income-elasticity is low, a given proportionate increase in income of, say, 1 per cent will cause a much smaller proportionate increase in the demand for the good of, say, $\frac{1}{10}$ per cent. Here income-elasticity will be $\frac{1}{10} \Big/ 1 = \frac{1}{10}$. We are assuming throughout this discussion of income-elasticity of demand that the prices of all goods are given and that it is only the consumer's money income which changes. Now, for all normal goods the income effect will be positive. Income-elasticity of demand will therefore normally be positive too. In other words, changes in a consumer's income and in his expenditure on any single good will usually be in the same direction. All normal income-elasticities therefore have a plus sign in front of them. The actual numerical value of these positive income-elasticities is of course likely to vary considerably.

It is difficult to be certain what are the most important numerical values of income-elasticity of demand, but the following seem to be the more interesting. First, it is useful to distinguish the situation where income-elasticity of demand is zero. This happens when a given increase in income fails to lead to any increase at all in purchases of, and hence of expenditure on, the good whose income-elasticity is being calculated. On one side of the case of zero income-elasticity will be those cases where a rise in income leads to a *fall* in the amount purchased—inferior goods. For all such goods income-elasticity of demand, whether large or small, will be negative. On the other side will be all the goods with positive income-elasticities. More of such goods is bought as income rises. On either side of the dividing line of zero elasticity there will, of course, be finite income-elasticities of varying numerical magnitudes, whether elasticity itself is positive or negative. Zero income-elasticity is thus a useful value to select for special comment for it represents this dividing line.

A second interesting numerical value of income-elasticity of demand is where the whole of any increase in a consumer's income is spent on the good in question. In this situation income-elasticity will be equal to $\frac{1}{KX}$ where KX is the proportion of the consumer's income spent on any good, X, whose income-elasticity is being measured. When income-elasticity $=\frac{1}{KX}$ then the whole of any increase in the consumer's income is spent on increasing his purchases of good X. This also seems a useful case to bear in mind. If *more* than the whole of any increase in income is spent on any good X, income-elasticity of demand will exceed $\frac{1}{KX}$ and *vice versa*.

The third, and perhaps the most interesting value of income-elasticity of demand, is where it equals one. This means that the *proportion* of the consumer's income spent on the good in question is exactly the same both before and after income rises. This too seems to be a useful dividing line. If the income-elasticity of demand for any good is greater than one, it means that an increasing proportion of the consumer's income is spent on the good as he becomes richer. Similarly, if a consumer's income-elasticity of demand for a good is less than one, the proportion of his income spent on that good falls as that income rises. Unitary income-elasticity thus seems to represent an important dividing line. It is surely of some significance if the proportion of a consumer's income spent on any good changes if he becomes richer. It seems reasonable to think that a good with an income-elasticity greater than one, on which a consumer therefore spends a greater proportion of his income as he becomes richer, is in some sense a luxury; and a good with an income-elasticity of less than one, on which the proportion of income spent falls as he becomes richer, is in some sense a necessity. One cannot, of course, give a precise definition of necessities or luxuries in terms of income-elasticities of demand, but the notion that goods with income-elasticities greater and less than one are in a general sense luxuries and necessities respectively seems a useful one.

(b) Elasticity of Substitution

Elasticity of substitution, like the substitution effect upon which it depends, can be measured at any point on any indifference curve. It measures the extent to which one good can be substituted for another if the consumer is to remain on that given indifference curve. The mathematical measure of elasticity of substitution (e_s) between any two goods X and Y, anywhere on any single indifference curve, is given by the following formula:[1]

$$e_s = \frac{\text{Relative increase in the ratio between the two goods possessed X/Y}}{\text{Relative decrease in marginal significance of X in terms of Y}}.$$

There are two limiting cases which are worth considering. First there is the situation where elasticity of substitution is infinite. This occurs wherever the indifference curve in question is a straight line and means that the two goods are perfect substitutes—they are identical. As he moves along an indifference curve, the proportionate change in the ratio between the consumer's holdings of X and Y is indefinitely large compared with the relative change in the marginal significance of X in terms of Y, for this latter change is zero. The marginal significance of X in terms of Y does not change at all. It is most unlikely that in practice one will ever find an indifference curve which is a straight line; for if goods are perfect substitutes, then, economically, they are the same good. Nevertheless, some goods are likely to possess high elasticities of substitution with indifference curves which are nearly straight lines. If two goods are very good substitutes, as, for example, are railway travel and travel by long-distance motor coach, then the elasticity of substitution between them is likely to be extremely high. An indifference curve for goods with very high elasticities of substitution is shown in Figure 30a.

The second limiting case is where elasticity of substitution is zero. In such a situation the two goods cannot be substituted for each other. They must be used in certain proportions to each other or not at all. This again is an unlikely case in practice, but there will be some pairs of commodities which are very bad substitutes and have to be used in practically the same proportions.

---

[1] Algebraically $e_s = -\dfrac{d\left(\dfrac{x}{y}\right)}{\dfrac{x}{y}} \div \dfrac{d\left(\dfrac{dy}{dx}\right)}{\dfrac{dy}{dx}}$. It will be noted that elasticity of substitution should strictly have a minus sign, but for the sake of simplicity we have ignored this in the text.

For example, the elasticity of substitution between shirts and trousers is unlikely to be very high. One will not normally want to have more or less than, say, two or three shirts to each pair of trousers. If this proportion holds good for one's current stock and one has, say, twelve shirts and four pairs of trousers, one will not normally be willing to give up shirts in exchange for trousers

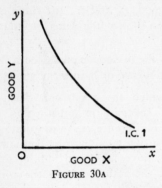

FIGURE 30A

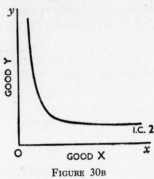

FIGURE 30B

(or trousers for shirts) for very long at anything like the same rate of exchange, without being made better or worse off—without finding oneself on a different indifference curve. If one is to remain on the same indifference curve, one must be offered a large number of pairs of trousers to induce one to part with another shirt, or *vice versa*. Indifference curves between shirts and trousers are likely to take the shape shown in Figure 30b. The numerical elasticity of substitution is there very low.

(c) Price-Elasticity of Demand

Since price-elasticity of demand—the elasticity of demand one normally makes use of in economic theory—depends ultimately on elasticity of substitution on the one hand and income-elasticity of demand on the other, it is possible to show the relationship between these three elasticities in terms of a mathematical formula. The relationship between the three elasticities can be given for the single consumer faced with two goods, X and Y, in a single equation.

Where for good X,

e_p = price-elasticity of demand,

e_i = income-elasticity of demand,

e_s = elasticity of substitution

and $\quad\quad$ KX = the proportion of the consumer's
$\quad\quad\quad\quad\quad\quad$ income spent on good X,

then $\quad\quad$ $e_p = KX \cdot e_i + (1 - KX)e_s.$

This equation holds good in all situations. So, when one knows what any two of the elasticities are, one can always calculate the third.

What the first part of the equation means is that the increase, in response to a fall in price, in the amount demanded of any good depends first on the income effect. This in turn depends, on the one hand, on the proportion of one's income spent on the good because this determines how much of one's income, previously spent on X, is available for new spending now that X is cheaper. The income-elasticity of demand being given, the greater the proportion of one's income spent on the good whose price has fallen, the greater the amount of income set free for new purchases (both of that good and of other goods) and the greater the consequent increase in the purchases of the good in question. The proportionate increase in purchases of a good due to the income effect depends, on the other hand, on the size of the income-elasticity of demand itself. For this determines what proportion of the income set free by the fall in price will be spent on the good whose price has fallen and what proportion will be spent on other goods. The first part of the equation $(KX \cdot e_i)$ thus shows the income effect's influence on price-elasticity of demand. The second part of the formula shows that to the proportionate change in the purchases of X resulting from a change in the consumer's real income must be added the change due to the fact that X is now relatively cheaper than Y. This second factor thus depends in part on the extent to which X can be substituted for Y now that it is relatively cheaper—on the elasticity of substitution. In part, also, it depends on the amount of Y one has and can substitute X for—on the amount of the other good Y, which was being bought before X became cheaper. For, given elasticity of substitution, only to the extent that one was previously buying Y (for which X can now be substituted) will a fall in the price of X result in a switch from the purchase of Y to the purchase of X. The symbols $(1 - KX)$ in the formula therefore show the proportion of income *not* being spent on X—the proportion of one's income within which substitution of X for Y is possible.

Perhaps two numerical illustrations will make the meaning of the formula for price-elasticity of demand clearer. First, let us assume that the income-elasticity of demand for any good, X, is 2, that the elasticity of substitution between X and any (or all) other good(s) Y equals 3, and that the consumer in question is spending $\frac{1}{10}$ of his income on X. The formula $e_p = KX \cdot e_i + (1 - KX)e_s$ then becomes $e_p = \frac{1}{10} \times 2 + \frac{9}{10} \times 3 = \frac{2}{10} + \frac{27}{10} = 2\frac{9}{10}$. Elasticity of demand for good X is therefore $2 \cdot 9$. Second, let us assume that the income- and substitution-elasticities for good X are both equal to one, and that $\frac{1}{4}$ of the consumer's income is being spent on good X. The formula $e_p = KX \, e_i + (1 - KX)e_s$ then becomes $e_p = \frac{1}{4} \times 1 + \frac{3}{4} \times 1 = 1$. Price-elasticity of demand for X equals one. In fact, when both income- and substitution-elasticities are equal to one, price-elasticity must always be equal to one. This should be obvious on reflection, for $KX + (1 - KX)$ always equals one so that $1 \times KX + 1(1 - KX)$ also equals one.

Price-elasticity of demand thus depends both on income-elasticity and on elasticity of substitution, and the formula given above puts the relationship explicitly.

The concepts of income-elasticity of demand and of elasticity of substitution throw light on our previous attempts to discover what determines whether the elasticity of demand for a good is high or low. We saw earlier that the demand for a necessity like salt is very inelastic. We can now say that this is partly because the proportion of income spent on salt is very low so that the income effect of a fall in the price of salt will never be very great. The income-elasticity of demand for salt is likely to be very low too. The demand for salt is inelastic partly, also, because there are no good substitutes for salt, and the elasticity of substitution between salt and other goods is therefore small. The demand for goods like radio sets or motor cars will be much more elastic, because such goods, being expensive, will take a larger proportion of income than salt does, so that the income effect can be great. In addition, the elasticity of substitution between radio sets and other forms of entertainment and between motor cars and other forms of transport will be high.

SUGGESTED READING

J. R. Hicks, *Value and Capital*, Oxford, 1946, chapters i and ii.
J. R. Hicks, 'A Reconsideration of the Theory of Value', *Economica*, 1934 (New Series, No. 1), pp. 52-69.

CHAPTER IV

CONSUMER'S EQUILIBRIUM WITH MORE THAN TWO GOODS

1. SCALES OF PREFERENCE WITH MORE THAN TWO GOODS

IN Chapter II we saw that each consumer will have a scale of preferences on the basis of which he will make his purchases of the various goods which are available. In Chapter III we discussed the individual consumer's behaviour in greater detail and were able to provide diagrammatic representations of scales of preference. It is, however, possible to do this satisfactorily only where there are two goods. We attempted to overcome this difficulty in Chapter III by making money one of the two 'goods' considered. But such an analysis cannot be wholly satisfactory. One can only use it at all by assuming [1] that the prices of all other goods are given and constant. Otherwise one cannot deal with the problem in terms of two-dimensional diagrams. To deal diagrammatically with consumer equilibrium where there are more than two goods one needs to use more than two dimensions, and that is out of the question in a book of this kind. We shall therefore find it best to revert now to the kind of analysis in words used in Chapter II, and see what we can say about the nature of scales of preference where there are more than two goods, drawing wherever possible from the experience gained in Chapter III. We shall thus be able to see what new problems arise where there are more than two goods, which do not arise when there are only two.

Let us see what assumptions are needed. We shall continue to assume that consumers behave rationally. We shall assume that consumers always maximise their satisfactions and that they can do so because they are able to classify and arrange all goods in order of importance—because, that is to say, they can draw up scales of preference. What we must now consider is the nature of such scales of preference. To do this we shall take the

[1] See pp. 49-50.

three assumptions made about indifference curves in Chapter III, and adapt them to a situation where there are more than two goods. First, we shall assume that consumers behave consistently however many different goods there are, and therefore however many possible variations in the physical constitutions of collections of goods there may be. For example, let us assume that a consumer prefers a combination of various amounts of many goods (collection A) to another collection, B. If he also prefers collection B to a third collection, C, then he cannot prefer C to A. In technical language, this is said to mean that the consumer's preferences are *transitive*. The reader will be able to work out the further implications of this assumption for himself. Similarly, we assume that if a consumer is indifferent between two collections of goods X and Y, but prefers Y to Z, then he must also prefer X to Z. We shall assume that a consumer's preference scale is always consistent in this sense of being 'transitive'. This assumption corresponds to the assumption, made in Chapter III, that indifference curves never intersect.

Second, we shall assume that if a consumer is indifferent between two collections of goods, A and B, and if A contains more of any one good than B does, then it must also contain less of at least one other good than B does. Similarly, any collection of goods, A, which contains more of any one good, and no less of any other good than another collection, B, must be preferred to that second collection. This assumption corresponds to the rule laid down in Chapter III that indifference curves always slope downwards from left to right.

Third, we must see what assumption about scales of preference when there are more than two goods corresponds to the assumption that indifference curves are convex to the origin. We have seen that with indifference curves this assumption of convexity means, first, that any point on any indifference curve will be a possible point of stable equilibrium. Whatever the slope or position of an indifference curve it can always be tangential to some price line. Second, the convexity of indifference curves implies that any given combination of goods will be bought in *only one* price-income situation. A given price line can never be tangential to more than one indifference curve, and it cannot be tangential to the same indifference curve at more than one point.

In terms of marginal significance the 'convexity rule' means that as one moves along any indifference curve, increasing the amount of one good and decreasing the amount of the other, the marginal significance of the good whose amount has been increased, in terms of the other good, will always decline.

Where there are more than two goods the corresponding assumptions are as follows. We assume that, for any given consumer who is maximising satisfactions, there is always some level of income and prices at which every possible combination of goods will be bought. It is also assumed that each of these combinations of goods will be bought in *only one* price-income situation. In other words, each collection of goods will be bought by the consumer in *some* price-income situation, but in any given price-income situation only *one* collection of goods will be bought.

It is difficult to formulate this third assumption in terms of marginal significance where there are more than two goods. Where there are only two goods one merely needs to postulate that the marginal significance of the one good, X, in terms of the other good, Y, declines as more and more X is substituted for Y, and yet the consumer remains on the same indifference curve—at the same position in his scale of preferences. Where there are more than two goods one can still accurately consider the marginal significance of one good in terms of another only by discussing what happens when the amount of the good whose marginal significance is being measured is increased in amount, and the consumer becomes neither better nor worse off as a result. But it does not now follow that the amount of *all* other goods must be decreased in order to ensure that the consumer's satisfactions are not increased. If there are three goods X, Y and Z, and the consumer is at a given position in his scale of preferences, it is possible to alter the combination of goods he has, whilst making him neither better nor worse off, in many different ways. For example, if the amount of X is increased, it is possible to keep the consumer at the same position in his scale of preferences by reducing the amounts of both Y and Z; by increasing Y and reducing Z; by keeping Z constant and reducing Y, and so on. And each different change is likely to have a different effect on the marginal significance of X in terms of both Y and Z. We shall in fact need to spend most of this chapter trying to discover how the marginal significances of any three goods are likely to be related. The only general rule we can give is this. If the amount of any one good held by a consumer is increased, and he is kept at the same position in his scale of preferences by a compensating reduction in the amount of at least one of the other goods, then the marginal significance of the good whose amount has been increased must have fallen *in terms of at least one other good*.

Let us study the nature of scales of preference where there are more than two goods in greater detail, considering various possible changes in the equilibrium situation facing a consumer. We shall do this by discussing three goods, X, Y and Z. For in studying three goods one can consider all the important problems which appear once one considers more than two goods—and yet keep the analysis as simple as possible. We begin by assuming that a consumer is in equilibrium with a given income, buying various amounts of X, Y and Z. Let us assume that the price of X now falls, that the prices of Y and Z remain the same, but that there is a 'compensating variation' in the consumer's income just sufficient to offset the fall in the price of X. Now that X is relatively cheaper, the consumer will buy more X because of the substitution effect. But since his total satisfaction is maintained constant, he must now buy less Y or less Z, or both. Otherwise he would be better off. In other words, the compensating variation in income reduces the amount of Y and Z together just far enough to ensure that the new collection of goods (B) which the consumer buys, gives him only the same satisfactions as the old collection (A). We have eliminated any income effect and shall only be concerned with substitution effects.

Now since the price of X has fallen, the substitution effect will cause the consumer to increase the amount of X which he buys, even though he is no better off because there has been compensating reduction in his income. He must therefore have a reduced amount of at least one of the other two goods. In the normal case, the consumer will buy less of both Y and Z now that X is cheaper. He will substitute X for both Y and Z. If this is what happens, then we can say that Y *is competitive with* X *against* Z, and that Z *is competitive with* X *against* Y. If the prices of Y and Z remain constant (as we are assuming), the marginal significance of X both in terms of Y and in terms of Z will diminish. We have already seen in Chapter II that, however many goods there are, a consumer must equate the marginal significance of one good in terms of another with their relative money prices, if he is to maximise his satisfactions. Thus, in our example, only if the marginal significance of X in terms of both Y and Z diminishes, can one account for the increased purchases of X. For, since we are assuming that the prices of Y and Z are constant, the ratio between these prices will also be constant. The consumer could

not be in equilibrium with regard to his purchases of X in the
new position, unless the marginal significance of X had diminished
in terms of both Y and Z. For the money price of X has fallen
relatively to the money prices of both Y and Z. Since we are
assuming that the consumer is still equating relative prices with
marginal significances, the marginal significance of X in terms both
of Y and Z must have fallen.

This method of considering the way in which the marginal
significances of X, Y and Z are affected when X becomes cheaper,
is not entirely satisfactory. For we have assumed that the prices
of Y and Z are given and have thus not discussed the problem
purely in terms of the consumer's preference scale. By implication
we have also been concerned with market prices and it would be
useful to ignore such prices altogether. Let us therefore consider
what will happen if we increase the amount of X which a consumer
has, hold the amount of Y constant, but keep him at the same
level of satisfactions. The amount of Z will clearly have to be
reduced, in accordance with the second rule about scales of
preference given above, to prevent the consumer reaching a
preferred position.

In this case the marginal significance of X in terms of Z must
diminish, for since the amount of Y is constant, we are really
concerned with a two-good situation. But the change in the
amounts of X and Z will also affect the marginal significance of
Y in terms of Z. Since the amount of Z must be reduced, with
Y constant, in order to leave the consumer at the same position
in his scale of preferences, the 'normal' result will be that the
marginal significance of Y in terms of Z will be reduced; the
marginal significance of Z in terms of Y will be increased. For
there is now more Y compared with Z. This is merely a restate-
ment (this time independently of prices) of what was said above.
If the price ratio between Y and Z were maintained, as it was
assumed to be, then if the amount of Z were reduced, the amount
of Y would have to be reduced also. Only thus could the marginal
significance of Y in terms of Z be brought back into line with the
relative price of Y and Z. So, when the amount of Y is held
constant and the amount of Z reduced, as it is here, the marginal
significance of Y in terms of Z must have fallen.

The conclusion we have reached so far is that if the price of X
falls, and the consumer's income is reduced so that his satisfactions
do not increase when he moves to a new equilibrium position
where he has more X, then any other good of which less is bought

G

is *competitive* with X. Alternatively, the good in question can be described as a *substitute* for X. But we have so far ruled out income effects by compensating variations in income. What happens if one takes income effects into account? It is then no longer necessary for the consumer's purchases of Y to fall when X becomes cheaper, even if X and Y are competitive goods in the strict sense as outlined above. If the reduction in the price of X causes a large income effect this may increase the demand for Y (or Z), since the consumer's real income will now be much greater. Similarly, if the income elasticity of demand for Y (or Z) is high, more Y (or Z) may be demanded when X becomes cheaper, even though X and Y (or Z) are competitive. Had there been no income effect, less Y would have been bought. But the 'positive' income effect works in the direction of increasing the consumer's purchases of Y now that his real income has risen. And if this income effect is strong enough it may swamp the substitution effect, which by itself would work to reduce purchases of Y now that X is cheaper. Most goods, however, will be sufficiently competitive with each other to ensure that the purchases of any such good will be reduced if it becomes relatively more expensive—even where there are positive income effects working in the opposite direction. Brown and white bread, woollen and cotton socks, tea and coffee, are all pairs of goods which are usually unambiguously competitive. They will be very strong substitutes and income effects will always be too small to prevent a reduction in the purchases of the good whose price has not fallen. Thus a reduction in the price of, say, tea will always reduce the amount of coffee bought and *vice versa*. It will be realised, of course, that if income effects are *negative* they will merely increase the size of the reduction in purchases of the competitive good whose price has not fallen, over and above that caused by the substitution effect.

2. COMPLEMENTARITY

Let us now consider what happens where, in the case of three goods X, Y and Z, the amount of X held by a consumer increases, and the amount of Y he holds is increased also. Let us first of all consider a situation where the consumer is in an equilibrium position buying some X, some Y and some Z. The price of X now falls, the prices of Y and Z remain constant, but there is a compensating variation in the consumer's income. He will therefore be no better off in the new equilibrium position but he buys more X, less Z and *more* Y. Here, instead of substituting X for both Y *and* Z as in our earlier examples, the consumer actually increases his purchases of Y, whilst reducing his purchases of Z more substantially than before. We may now say that Y *is complementary with* X *against* Z. Similarly, if in the same kind of circumstances an increase in the amount of X held led to a substantial reduction in the amount of Y but an increase in the amount of Z, we could say that Z *was complementary with* X *against* Y. It is, of course, impossible for *both* Y *and* Z to be complementary with X. Whenever there is any number of goods (n) at least one of these goods must be competitive with that in which we are interested. It could conceivably happen, however, that all of the remaining n − 2 goods could be complementary with it, though this is unlikely. On the other hand, of course, it is quite possible for n − 1 of any collection of n goods to be competitive with the remaining good.

Let us now consider what complementarity means in terms of marginal significance by discussing the situation outlined above where X becomes cheaper, the prices of Y and Z remain constant, and more X *and* Y are bought after the compensating change in income. It is clear that since we are assuming that, in the new equilibrium, the price of X has fallen relatively to the prices of both Y and Z, the marginal significance of X in terms of both Y and Z must have fallen also. Only if this has happened can the consumer be again in equilibrium, equating the marginal significances of X, Y and Z with their relative prices.

We have so far defined complementarity, by implication, in terms of market prices, for we have assumed that X becomes cheaper relatively to Y and Z, the prices of Y and Z remaining constant. Let us now see what complementarity means in terms of preference scales. Let us assume that the amount of X is increased, that the amount of Y remains constant, but that the consumer obtains the same satisfactions as before. It follows that the amount of Z must have been reduced. So, as happens when X and Y are competitive, the marginal significance of X in terms of Z must have declined. But the marginal significance of Y in terms of Z will have increased (that of Z in terms of Y will have decreased) even though there is more Y relatively to Z than before. It does so because the consumer uses Y in conjunction with X. He has more X and thus wants more Y to go with it. X and Y supplement or *complement* each other in use. Goods like

bacon and eggs ; tea and sugar ; pipes and tobacco, are examples
of complementary goods. If bacon becomes cheaper and this
causes the consumer to buy more bacon, he may well buy more
eggs to go with the extra bacon, even though his real income is no
greater than before because the amount of at least one other good
has been reduced. If this happens, bacon and eggs will be complementary so far as the consumer in question is concerned.

This definition of complementarity, like our definition of
competitiveness, takes no account of income effects. Fortunately,
however, provided any such income effects are positive they cannot
disturb the conclusions given above. If X and Y are complementary and the price of X falls, more Y is *bound* to be bought.
But some of these increased purchases will be the result of the
positive income effect. The consumer buys more Y partly
because his real income has risen, partly because Y is complementary with X. Therefore, unless the income effect is negative,
a consumer will never buy *less* of a good when the price of its
complement falls. Income effects will cause fewer exceptions
than where goods are competitive.[1]

It will be useful to sum up this discussion. Let us assume
that income effects are positive and are *not* eliminated. Then if
the price of X falls and its purchases rise whilst the amount of Y
purchased falls, X and Y must be competitive in our sense. Had
there been no income effect an even greater reduction in purchases
of Y would have occurred. If the price of X falls and purchases
of Y *rise*, however, we cannot be so certain whether X and Y
are competitive or complementary. It is possible that the goods
may be competitive and yet that the positive income effect is
strong enough to outweigh the reduction in purchases of Y which
would have otherwise occurred. But it is equally possible that
X and Y may be complementary, with the income effect working
in the same direction as the substitution effect. Where the amount
demanded of good Y increases when more X is bought, one can
as a first approximation say that X and Y are goods in *joint
demand*. But it is necessary to eliminate the income effect before
one can say whether X and Y are competitive or complementary.
It follows that whilst (so long as income effects are positive) all
complementary goods will be in joint demand, not all goods in
joint demand will be complementary. Some may be competitive

---

[1] If X and Y are complementary and the income effect is *negative*, more Y
will still be bought when X becomes cheaper, unless this negative income effect
is very strong.

goods for which the positive income effect is strong. The essential preliminary to discovering whether goods are competitive or complementary is therefore the elimination of the income effect.

3. CROSS-ELASTICITY OF DEMAND

It is useful to apply the idea of elasticity of demand to situations where two goods are related in the ways we have been considering, and where a change in the price of one good causes changes in the demand for another. We can do this by discovering whether and to what extent a proportionate change in the price of one good causes a proportionate change in purchases of another good. This gives us a measure of the *cross-elasticity of demand* between the goods. Where there are two goods, X and Y, the cross-elasticity of demand is obtained by considering the change in purchases of Y resulting from a given change in the price of X— the price of Y being held constant. That is to say :

Cross-elasticity of Demand

$$= \frac{\text{proportionate change in purchases of Y}}{\text{proportionate change in price of X}}.$$

It will usually be found that any two goods, X and Y, chosen at random, are sufficiently competitive for the (positive) income effect to be outweighed by the substitution effect. A rise in the price of X (or Y) will therefore cause an increase in the purchases of Y (or X); similarly, a fall in the price of X (or Y) will cause a decline in the purchases of Y (or X). In the 'normal' case then, the changes in the price of X and the quantity of Y will be in the same direction, and the numerical measure of cross-elasticity will be positive. Alternatively, if the goods are in joint demand, a fall in the price of X will cause a rise in the purchases of Y, and *vice versa*. The numerical cross-elasticity of demand between jointly demanded goods will thus be negative.

Whether cross-elasticities are negative or positive, the limiting cases will be where cross-elasticity is infinite and where it is zero. Where two goods are competitive and cross-elasticity is (plus) infinity, a small fall in the price of X will cause an infinitely large reduction in the amount of Y which is bought. If goods are in joint demand and cross-elasticity is (minus) infinity, a small fall in the price of X will cause an infinitely large increase in purchases of Y. Neither of these limiting cases is likely to be found in practice, but cross-elasticities of varying finite magnitude (positive and negative) will be found. The dividing line between these positive and negative elasticities will occur where cross-elasticity is zero and a small fall (or rise) in the price of X has no effect whatever on the purchases of Y.

SUGGESTED READING

J. R. Hicks, *Value and Capital*, Oxford, 1946, chapter iii.
J. R. Hicks, 'A Reconsideration of the Theory of Value', *Economica*, 1934 (New Series, No. 1), pp. 67-73.

CHAPTER V

EQUILIBRIUM OF THE FIRM

1. PROFIT MAXIMISATION

OUR analysis has so far shown how the demand curve for an individual, or for a market, can be derived from the relevant sets of indifference curves. It is now necessary to discuss the way in which the supply curve of a commodity is built up. We can then, at a later stage, discuss the interaction of demand and supply in detail. In order to construct a supply curve, it will be useful first of all to study the equilibrium of the individual productive unit—the firm—just as when we were constructing a demand curve we first studied the equilibrium of the individual consumption unit—the consumer. We shall find, however, that the terminology which we shall have to use now is rather more complicated than it was in the analysis of consumer equilibrium. It will therefore be necessary to spend much of the present chapter in explaining the meaning and uses of the analytical tools which we shall need. This is essential if our discussion is to produce useful results.

At the outset, we must recall the assumption of 'rationality' already mentioned in the Introduction. Until further notice we shall be concerned only with the 'one man' firm. We shall assume that the owner of the individual firm, the entrepreneur as he is called, behaves rationally, in just the same way as we assumed that the individual consumer behaved rationally. But in this context, 'rationality' does not imply maximising satisfaction, as in demand theory. 'Rationality' in the theory of the firm implies that the individual producer aims at earning the greatest possible money profits. Now, no economist believes that all business men do, in fact, always maximise profits, nor does he necessarily believe that they should do so. But every economist wants his analysis of the individual firm to enable him to point to a single position where, in given conditions, the firm will be in equilibrium. It is therefore essential for him to make some assumption of this kind. If no such assumption were made, there would be no single equilibrium position for the firm in any given circumstances. It would be difficult to produce any definite explanation of the way firms fix output and prices at all. This is a similarity between the equilibrium of the consumer and the equilibrium of the firm. But there is one important difference. The satisfaction which the consumer attempts to maximise cannot be measured, for there are no units of measurement. The profits of the entrepreneur can be measured in money. It is objective money profits which the entrepreneur is assumed to maximise.

A further assumption which we shall make throughout our analysis of the firm is that entrepreneurs always produce each output as cheaply as possible, given the technical production conditions. We assume that the entrepreneur always keeps money costs of production as low as he is able. This is an essential assumption, for, here again, it would be impossible to point to an equilibrium position where the firm was at rest if one could not say whether costs had been kept to a minimum or not. One could never know in such conditions what costs really were.

We shall also assume for the sake of simplicity that each firm produces only one product. Our results remain valid however many products a firm makes, but the analysis becomes undesirably complicated if the firm makes two or more. We shall assume, too, unless an explicit statement to the contrary is made, that the price of each factor of production is given and fixed. In technical language, we shall assume that all units of each factor of production are equally efficient and that all the factors are in 'infinitely elastic supply' at their current price. Each entrepreneur can hire as many units of any factor as he wishes at its current price. This is not a very realistic assumption, but it will save us from many difficulties which would otherwise arise. The advantages gained by making it will appear more fully later. For the moment we may notice that it rules out the possibility of higher wages being paid for overtime work, of lower prices being given for bulk purchases of raw materials, and of differences in cost because some units of a factor of production are more or less efficient than others.

Having made these basic assumptions, we can deduce the equilibrium position of any firm from two sets of facts. First, we need to know how much revenue the firm earns from selling various amounts of its product. Second, we must know how much it costs to produce these particular volumes of output. This information can be given in various ways, but let us begin by drawing a firm's total cost curve (TC) showing the total costs of producing various outputs, and its total revenue curve (TR) showing the total receipts earned from selling these same outputs. This is done in Figure 31. The shapes of the curves in Figure 31 are purely arbitrary, but the result is not affected by this. We shall discuss the likely shapes of such curves later.

Now, a firm's profits may be defined as the difference between its total revenue and its total costs. It is clear, therefore, that in Figure 31 the largest profits which the firm could make will be earned when the (vertical) distance between the total cost and total revenue curves is as great as possible. This will in fact be at that output where the slopes of the two curves are the same, that is to say where the tangents YZ and WX to the cost and revenue curves respectively are parallel.

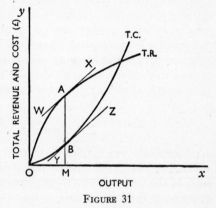

FIGURE 31

In Figure 31 money profits are at a maximum when output is OM units. Profits are then £AB. AB is the longest vertical line one can draw between the total cost and total revenue curves and the tangents to the two curves are parallel at this output. But, whilst it is perfectly reasonable to represent the equilibrium of the firm in this kind of diagram, thus showing at what output profits are maximised, it is a very cumbersome way of doing so. For one thing, the maximum vertical distance between the revenue and cost curves is not always easy to see at a glance. For another, it is impossible to discover price per unit at first sight—only total revenue (*e.g.* £AM when output is OM). Total revenue must be divided by output (in this case OM) in order to discover price per unit.

It is therefore usual to draw diagrams which provide more information at a glance. These diagrams do not use total revenue or total cost at all. They use what are known as average and marginal revenue curves, and average and marginal cost curves. The same kind of equilibrium position as that which was shown in Figure 31 can be found by discovering that level of output at which marginal revenue equals marginal cost. A firm will be in equilibrium when marginal revenue equals marginal cost, for it

will then be earning maximum profits. The 'rational' entrepreneur will therefore fix his output so as to equate marginal
revenue with marginal cost.

We have unfortunately found it necessary to define the
equilibrium of the firm in highly technical language at this very
early stage. We must now explain the terms which have been
used. For though it is a fact that a firm must always be earning
maximum profits when it is equating marginal revenue and marginal
cost, marginal revenue and marginal cost are not terms with which
anyone is automatically familiar. Nor is it immediately apparent
why maximum profits are being earned when they are equal.
We shall therefore proceed to explain, in detail, what marginal
revenue curves and marginal cost curves are, and what shape such
curves will take. We shall then be able to show why profits are
maximised when marginal revenue equals marginal cost.

2. MARGINAL REVENUE

Marginal revenue, at any level of a firm's output, is the
revenue which would be earned from selling another (marginal)
unit of the firm's product. Algebraically, it is the addition to total
revenue earned by selling n units of product instead of $n-1$,
where n is any given number.[1] Marginal revenue is a concept
whose whole importance is derived from the fact that if it is
equated with marginal cost, the firm will be earning maximum
profits, and it is of interest to economic theorists for that reason
alone. Nevertheless, because profit maximisation is the fundamental assumption in the theory of the firm, marginal revenue is
a very important concept. We shall have to devote some space
to a discussion of its meaning.

Since marginal revenue can mean the revenue which is earned
by selling *any* (marginal) unit of output, it is possible to draw a
marginal revenue curve showing the (marginal) revenue earned
by each individual unit of output which the firm produces. In
order to discover the marginal revenue curve of any firm, it is
desirable to start from the total revenue curve for its product,
like the curve TR in Figure 31. This total revenue curve shows
the total amount of money earned by the firm when output (sales)
is at various levels. It is therefore the same thing, from the
firm's point of view, as the curve showing consumers' total ex-

---

[1] Alternatively, one could denote it as the addition to total revenue earned by
selling n +1 units instead of n.

penditure on the product of the firm. From this total revenue curve we can derive the average revenue curve of the firm. For average revenue (or receipts (price) per unit of output) is $\frac{\text{Total Revenue}}{\text{Output}}$ at each level of output. Average revenue at each level of output can therefore be discovered from the total revenue curve. The average revenue curve shows the price of the firm's product at each level of output. Marginal revenue at the same outputs can also be derived from the total revenue curve. For example, if the total revenue curve shows that two units of output can be sold for 19s. and one can be sold for 10s., the sale of the second (marginal) unit earns an extra 9s. of revenue for the firm. Marginal revenue is 9s. at this level of output. A marginal revenue curve can then be drawn showing the addition to total revenue earned by selling a further (marginal) unit of output, when output is at the various levels for which total revenue is known.

Let us consider the relationship between marginal, average and total revenue at each level of output more fully by using schedules instead of curves. Let us assume that the situation in an imaginary firm is that shown in Table 2.

TABLE 2

TOTAL, AVERAGE AND MARGINAL REVENUE SCHEDULES

Output	Total Revenue	Average Revenue (total revenue ÷ output)	Marginal Revenue (addition to total revenue)
1	10s.	10s.	10s.
2	19s.	9s. 6d.	9s.
3	27s.	9s.	8s.
4	34s.	8s. 6d.	7s.
5	40s.	8s.	6s.
6	45s.	7s. 6d.	5s.
7	49s.	7s.	4s.
8	52s.	6s. 6d.	3s.
9	54s.	6s.	2s.
10	55s.	5s. 6d.	1s.

Exactly the same information is shown by the total (TR), average (AR) and marginal revenue (MR) curves in Figure 32, the curves in Figure 32 having all been plotted from the figures given in Table 2. It is not difficult to derive average and marginal revenue curves geometrically from the corresponding total revenue curves. As we have already seen, the slope of a line from the origin to any point on a total revenue (or expenditure) curve shows price per unit, or average revenue, for the output in question.

In Figure 32 the slope of the line OA $\left(i.e. \dfrac{BA}{OB}\right)$ shows the price of the good in question when output is OB (5) units. Alternatively one can discover average revenue by marking off one unit

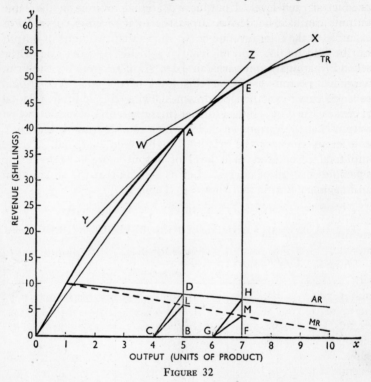

FIGURE 32

along the x-axis to the left of B, shown in this case by the length CB. If one then draws CD parallel to OA, one finds price per unit. For since the slope of OA shows price per unit, so does the slope of CD. And since CB represents one unit, BDs. (8s.) represents the price of one unit, just as BAs. represents the 'price' of OB units. D is therefore a point on the firm's average revenue curve showing price per unit when output is OB. One can derive all the other points on the average revenue curve (AR) in a similar way. For example, when output is OF (7 units) and GF represents one unit of the good in question, average revenue is FH*s.* (7*s.*). OE would be here parallel to GH.

Similarly, marginal revenue at any output is shown by the slope of a tangent to the point on the total revenue curve appropriate to that output. For example, in Figure 32 YZ is a tangent to the total revenue curve at A. The slope of YZ represents the rate at which total revenue is changing at the output OB. In other words, it shows the net addition to revenue caused by the last unit produced—it shows marginal revenue. Thus, if we draw CL parallel to YZ we obtain the revenue added by the unit CB. In this instance marginal revenue is BL*s.* (6*s.*). Similarly, if WX is tangent to the total revenue curve at E, its slope represents marginal revenue when output is OF. Here GM is parallel to WX and marginal revenue is FM*s.* (4*s.*). We can thus construct the marginal revenue curve for any firm by drawing all the tangents to its total revenue curve, and finding their slope.

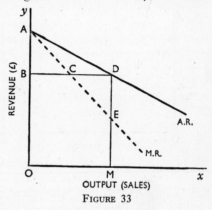

FIGURE 33

In most of the following analysis we shall only be concerned with average and marginal revenue curves, so we can ignore total revenue curves for the moment. It can be shown that there are definite geometrical relationships between any average revenue curve and the corresponding marginal revenue curve. We shall find it useful to state the main principles of these relationships. So long as the average revenue curve is falling, marginal revenue will be less than average revenue. The marginal revenue curve itself may be rising, falling or horizontal according to circumstances, but normally it will fall too. The simplest relationship occurs where both the average and the marginal curves are straight lines. Where this happens the marginal revenue curve will cut any line perpendicular to the y-axis half-way to the average revenue curve. This can be seen from Figure 33.

Figure 33 shows a straight-line average revenue curve AR and the corresponding straight-line marginal revenue curve MR. In order to prove that the marginal curve always lies half-way between the average revenue curve and the y-axis, let us draw in

DB and DM, perpendicular to the y- and x-axes respectively, from the arbitrarily chosen point D on the average revenue curve. DB then cuts the marginal curve at C, and DM cuts it at E. We need to prove that BC = CD. Now the area BDMO equals the area AEMO, because each equals the total revenue earned from selling the output OM.[1] But the rectangle BDMO is equal to the area BCEMO plus the triangle CDE. Similarly, area AEMO is equal to the area BCEMO plus the triangle ABC. It follows that the triangle CDE is equal in area to triangle ABC. But angle

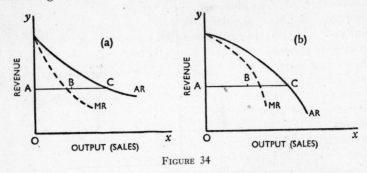

FIGURE 34

ABC = angle CDE, for both are right angles. And angle ACB = angle DCE (vertically opposite). Thus the triangles ABC and CDE are equal in all respects, having equal areas and equal angles. Thus BC = CD. The perpendicular BD to the y-axis from point D on the average revenue curve is therefore bisected at C by the marginal revenue curve, MR. This also means, of course, that the slope of the straight-line marginal curve $\dfrac{AB}{BC}$ is equal to twice the slope of the straight-line average curve $\dfrac{AB}{BD}$; for

$$\frac{AB}{BC} = \frac{AB}{CD} = 2\frac{AB}{BD}.$$

These relationships hold generally for straight-line average and marginal revenue curves.

In a similar way, where the average revenue curve is *concave upwards*, as in Figure 34a, the marginal revenue curve cuts any

[1] The rectangle BDMO shows average revenue times output, *i.e.* total revenue. The area AEMO sums the marginal revenues over the range of output between O and M. That is to say, it sums all the additions to outlay over this range and thus gives total revenue for output OM.

line perpendicular to the y-axis less than half-way to the average revenue curve. Again, where the average revenue curve is *convex upwards*, the marginal curve cuts any line perpendicular to the y-axis more than half-way to the average revenue curve. For instance, in both Figure 34a and Figure 34b, B is the midpoint of a perpendicular to the y-axis from the average revenue curve.

We have now discussed the relationships between the average and marginal revenue curves along a perpendicular to the y-axis. These relationships are important. But from an economic point of view it is even more useful to analyse the relationships between average and marginal revenue on any perpendicular to the x-axis. In other words, it is useful to consider the relationship between marginal and average revenue *at any output*. This can be done in terms of elasticity of demand.

First, however, we must clear up a rather important matter of terminology. It will be apparent that the average revenue curve of a firm is really the same thing as the demand curve of consumers for the firm's product. There is therefore a temptation to call the firm's average revenue curve its 'demand curve'. For it shows how much of the firm's product will be demanded at various prices. But a consumer's demand curve shows the demand of the consumer for a commodity. So it is only reasonable to expect that the firm's demand curve would show the demand of the firm for something or other. In fact, we shall discover later that the firm has a demand curve—for factors of production. We shall therefore try to avoid confusion by speaking in our present context of the firm's *average revenue curve* and not of its 'demand curve'. Some economists use the alternative term *sales curve*. We shall reserve the term 'firm's demand curve' for use in the more specialised sense of a demand curve for factors of production later in this book.

In order to discuss the relationships between average and marginal revenue and the elasticity of demand on the firm's average revenue curve, we need to extend our definition of elasticity of demand. For the sake of simplicity we have so far assumed that all demand curves are straight lines. Now, since the average revenue curve of the firm is the same thing, looked at from another aspect, as the demand curve by consumers for the firm's product, the measure of elasticity of demand which we have already given is perfectly applicable to finding the elasticity of demand on a firm's average revenue curve. But it is unlikely that in practice all average revenue curves (or for that matter demand curves) will be straight lines. We must therefore consider what will happen if average revenue curves really are curves.

We have so far measured elasticity in terms of mathematical formulae, but there are simpler measures. In Figure 35, for example, one can measure elasticity of demand on the average revenue curve AR at the point R, by drawing a tangent to the curve at R. Numerical point elasticity of demand is then given by

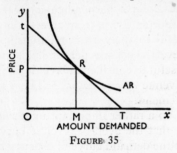

FIGURE 35

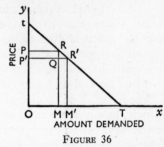

FIGURE 36

dividing the portion of the tangent above R (Rt) into the portion below R (RT). That is to say, elasticity of demand at point $R = \dfrac{RT}{Rt}$.[1] This can be proved in Figure 36, where for simplicity's sake we once again draw a straight-line demand curve.

We know that provided RR′ is very small (as is the case here), we can define elasticity of demand as

$$\frac{\text{change in amount demanded}}{\text{original amount demanded}} \div \frac{\text{change in price}}{\text{original price}}.$$

Thus elasticity $= \dfrac{MM'}{OM} \div \dfrac{PP'}{OP}$, or alternatively

$$= \frac{QR'}{OM} \div \frac{QR}{RM} = \frac{QR'}{OM} \times \frac{RM}{QR} = \frac{QR'}{QR} \times \frac{RM}{OM}.$$

But since the triangles RQR′ and RMT are similar, we can write $\dfrac{QR'}{QR}$ as $\dfrac{TM}{RM}$. The equation $\dfrac{QR'}{QR} \times \dfrac{RM}{OM}$ thus becomes $\dfrac{TM}{RM} \times \dfrac{RM}{OM}$. Cancelling out, we get elasticity $= \dfrac{TM}{OM}$. But, since triangles MTR and PRt are similar, $\dfrac{TM}{OM} = \dfrac{RT}{Rt}$. Point elasticity of demand on a demand curve can thus always be found by drawing any tangent

[1] See Marshall, *Principles of Economics*, pp. 102-3.

tT to the curve at any point R and calculating $\frac{RT}{Rt}$. With this measure of point elasticity of demand we can study the relationships between average and marginal revenue curves at any output. Let us consider the situation shown in Figure 37.

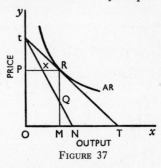

FIGURE 37

We know that elasticity of demand at point R on the average revenue curve in Figure 37 $=\frac{R'T}{Rt}$. Now the triangles PtR and MRT have equal angles. Therefore $\frac{RT}{Rt}$ can be written alternatively as $\frac{RM}{tP}$.

We now draw a line from t which bisects PR at X and then passes through Q. This line will in fact be 'marginal' to the tangent tT because it cuts the perpendicular PR, from P to the tangent, at its mid-point X.

Thus, in the triangles PtX and XRQ,
$$PX = RX,$$
$$\angle PXt = \angle RXQ \text{ (vertically opposite)}$$
and $\qquad \angle tPX = \angle XRQ \text{ (right angles).}$

Therefore triangles PtX and XRQ are equal in all respects, and tP equals RQ. So instead of writing elasticity at R as $\frac{TR}{tR} = \frac{RM}{tP}$ we may write it as $\frac{RM}{RQ} = \frac{RM}{RM - QM}$. So, at the output OM, elasticity $= \frac{RM}{RM - QM}$. But at this output, RM = average revenue, and QM = marginal revenue. We can thus write elasticity as $\frac{\text{average revenue}}{\text{average revenue} - \text{marginal revenue}}$. Symbolically, where at any output

$\qquad$ A = average revenue,
$\qquad$ M = marginal revenue
and $\qquad$ e = point elasticity on the average revenue curve,

$\qquad e = \frac{A}{A - M}$. It follows from this that $eA - eM = A$;

$$\therefore \ -eM = A - eA,$$
$$\therefore \ M = \frac{eA - A}{e} = A\frac{e - 1}{e}.$$

H

Similarly, since eA – eM = A, it follows that eA – A = eM;

$$\therefore A(e - 1) = eM,$$

$$\therefore A = \frac{Me}{e - 1},$$

$$\therefore A = M\frac{e}{e - 1}.$$

The general rule therefore is : At any output Average Revenue = Marginal Revenue × $\frac{e}{e - 1}$; and Marginal Revenue = Average Revenue × $\frac{e - 1}{e}$, where e = point elasticity of demand on the average revenue curve.

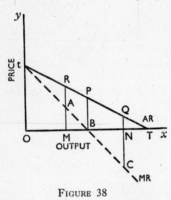

FIGURE 38

If the elasticity of a firm's average revenue curve at a given output is equal to one, marginal revenue equals average revenue

$$\times \frac{1 - 1}{1} = \text{average revenue} \times 0 = 0.$$

Therefore where the elasticity of the average revenue curve equals 1, marginal revenue equals 0. This can also be seen from Figure 38.

In Figure 38 elasticity on the average revenue curve is equal to one at point P where output is OB. For PT = Pt and therefore $\frac{PT}{Pt} = 1$. At this output marginal revenue is zero. Similarly, when elasticity of demand equals 2 (at point R in Figure 38), where RT = 2Rt,

$$M = A\frac{2 - 1}{2} = \tfrac{1}{2}A.$$

In other words AM = $\frac{1}{2}$RM. Marginal revenue equals half average revenue. Marginal revenue is, in fact, *always* positive at any output where the elasticity of the average revenue curve is greater than one. This happens in Figure 38 over the range of the average revenue curve between t and P. Similarly, over the range between P and T where elasticity is less than one, marginal revenue is *always* negative. This can be seen from our formula by taking an elasticity less than one, say $\frac{1}{4}$—at point Q. Here QT = $\frac{1}{4}$Qt and

$$M = A \times \frac{\frac{1}{4} - 1}{\frac{1}{4}} = A \times \frac{-\frac{3}{4}}{\frac{1}{4}} = -3A.$$

Marginal revenue is negative and is three times average revenue—in Figure 38 CN =3QN. So, marginal revenue is always positive where the average revenue curve is elastic and always negative where it is inelastic. With the aid of these formulae, it is possible to discover marginal revenue *at any output* from average revenue at the same output, provided one knows point elasticity of demand on the average revenue curve.[1]

3. MARGINAL COST

Marginal cost is the cost of producing a marginal unit of a firm's product. It is parallel on the supply side to marginal revenue on the demand side. It is therefore possible to derive average and marginal cost curves from a total cost curve of the type shown in Figure 31. Let us first of all construct a table showing total, average and marginal cost in a hypothetical firm at various outputs.

TABLE 3

TOTAL, AVERAGE AND MARGINAL COST SCHEDULES

Output	*Total Cost*	*Average Cost*	*Marginal Cost*
1	30s.	30s.	30s.
2	40s.	20s.	10s.
3	45s.	15s.	5s.
4	48s.	12s.	3s.
5	50s.	10s.	2s.
6	72s.	12s.	22s.
7	105s.	15s.	33s.
8	160s.	20s.	55s.
9	270s.	30s.	110s.
10	450s.	45s.	180s.

One can plot the values shown in Table 3 on curves in just the same way as one can plot total, average and marginal revenue. We shall not do this here. But there are one or two points about the figures which should be noted. First, average cost at any output $= \dfrac{\text{Total Cost}}{\text{Output}}$. Second, marginal cost is the total cost of n units of output minus the total cost of n – 1 units.[2] Thus, if

---

[1] These formulae were given by Mrs. Joan Robinson in *The Economics of Imperfect Competition*, p. 36.

[2] Or the total cost of n +1 units minus the total cost of n.

one starts from any total cost curve, average cost, at any output shown on that curve, is given by the slope of a straight line from the origin through the point in question. Similarly, marginal cost is given by the slope of a tangent to the total cost curve at any given output.

Again, since marginal and average cost are concepts similar to average and marginal revenue, the relationships which we set out in the previous section hold equally for marginal and average cost. The fundamental difference between average revenue and

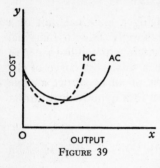
FIGURE 39

average cost curves is this. The average revenue curve for a firm represents the demand for the product of the firm. It follows that average revenue curves (like demand curves) will not normally slope upwards at any point. Average cost curves, on the other hand, can, and usually do, both rise and fall. We shall have to discuss the likely shape of average cost curves in detail soon.

For the moment, we can safely assume (as we did in fact assume in Table 3) that average and marginal cost curves are always U-shaped like the curves shown in Figure 39. We can now deduce the relationships between such curves.

It will be seen from Figure 39 that so long as the average cost curve (AC) is falling, marginal cost (MC) is less than average cost. Similarly, if average cost is rising, marginal cost is greater than average cost. But one cannot deduce anything about the *direction* in which marginal cost is moving from the way average cost is changing. If average cost is falling, marginal cost may be either rising or falling. If average cost is rising, marginal cost may be falling or rising. But if average cost is constant, marginal cost must be constant. The relationship between marginal and average cost is therefore sometimes found difficult to understand. It is often most easily understood if explained in terms of batting averages.

Let us assume that Hutton's batting average is 60. If in his next innings he scores less than 60, say 52, his average will fall because his marginal score is less than his average score. But this latest marginal score may well be higher than his previous marginal score. He might, for example, have had a 'duck' in his previous innings, so that his marginal score has, in fact, risen considerably.

But so long as his marginal score, whether rising or falling, is less than his average score, that average score will fall. On the other hand, if the average curve is horizontal, the corresponding marginal curve will be identical with it. This can also be illustrated by batting averages. If Hutton's average is 60 and he now plays an innings in which he scores just 60, then his average and marginal scores will be equal. His average score will neither rise nor fall.

Some people find it easiest to remember this relationship between average and marginal values with the aid of Figure 40.

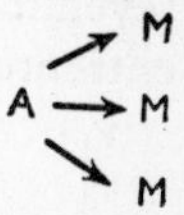

$$A \longrightarrow \begin{array}{c} \nearrow M \\ \to M \\ \searrow M \end{array}$$

FIGURE 40

In Figure 40, where marginal value is above (greater than) average value, average value rises. It is as though marginal value were pulling average value up towards itself. Similarly, where marginal value is below average value, average value falls, as though marginal value were pulling average value downwards. When marginal value is the same as average value, average value remains constant, as though marginal value were pulling average value along horizontally. But we must stress again that one can make no generalisations of this kind about whether marginal cost will be rising or falling when average cost is rising or falling. This relationship between marginal and average values is only a 'one way' relationship.

Finally, it is most important to remember that when we draw

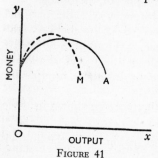

FIGURE 41

average cost curves, or (if it were possible) average revenue curves, which are U-shaped, the corresponding marginal curve will always cut the average curve at its lowest point. This was shown in Figure 39. As we have seen, when average cost is falling, marginal cost is below average cost. Similarly, when average cost is rising, marginal cost is greater than average cost. So at the moment when average cost stops falling but has not yet begun to rise, the marginal cost curve passes through the average cost curve in order to be above it when average cost starts to rise again. If, on the other hand, as in Figure 41, any average curve (A) is shaped like an inverted U, the corresponding marginal curve (M) will always cut the average curve at its highest point.

4. EQUILIBRIUM OF THE FIRM

On our assumption of 'rationality', a firm will be in equilibrium when it is earning maximum money profits. But the money profits of a firm will always be maximised when its marginal revenue equals its marginal cost. So, on the assumption that the entrepreneur desires maximum money profits, he will fix his output at that level which equates marginal revenue with marginal cost.

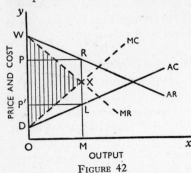

FIGURE 42

In the firm shown in Figure 42 marginal revenue equals marginal cost, and the firm's money profits are therefore maximised, when the output OM is produced. The price which the firm can charge for this output, shown on its average revenue curve, will be MR, which is the same thing as OP. The amount of profits will be shown by the area of the rectangle PRLP'. This is the largest rectangle which it is possible to draw between the average revenue curve, the average cost curve and the y-axis. The area of rectangle PRLP' will also be equal to the shaded area WXD which lies between the marginal revenue curve, the marginal cost curve and the y-axis. For, any vertical line between the marginal cost and revenue curves represents the addition to profits resulting from the production and sale of the marginal unit of output in question. Area WXD merely sums these receipts for all units of output.

Profits at any level of output can therefore be shown in three different ways, as below :

Profits = Total Revenue – Total Cost (as shown by the line AB in Figure 31)

= Average Revenue × Output – Average Cost × Output (as shown by rectangle PRLP' in Figure 42)

= Σ[1] Marginal Revenues – Σ Marginal Costs (as shown by the area WXD in Figure 42).

It must here be stressed that the equation of marginal revenue with marginal cost is of no particular significance in itself. But

---

[1] The Greek capital 'sigma', meaning 'the sum of'.

it does provide an easy and convenient method of discovering that output at which profits will be maximised. It therefore obviates the need for discovering where the largest possible profit-maximising rectangle can be drawn. In Figure 31 we discovered the profit maximising output by finding the position where the tangents to the total cost and revenue curves were parallel. But, as we have seen, these tangents merely showed marginal revenue and marginal cost, which are equal when the tangents are parallel. Figure 31 merely provided a rather cumbersome method of doing what we have now done in Figure 42.

It is desirable that we should see more clearly why profits will be maximised when marginal revenue equals marginal cost. A little reflection shows that this must always happen. For example, if, in the circumstances shown in Figure 42, output were increased beyond OM, marginal cost would exceed marginal revenue. Each additional unit of output in excess of OM could only add an amount of money to the firm's revenue smaller than the cost of making it. An increase in output would therefore reduce profits. Similarly, if output were reduced below OM, marginal revenue would be greater than marginal cost. Units of output which could have added more money to the firm's revenue than to its costs, would not have been produced. Profits would be smaller than they could have been. It is clear, therefore, that profits are at a maximum when marginal revenue equals marginal cost. In Figure 42 profits are maximised when output OM is sold at price OP.

We have now succeeded, by assuming that entrepreneurs always fix output so as to maximise money profits, in giving a determinate solution to the main problem of the individual entrepreneur. The fundamental question he has to answer is, 'How much of my product shall I produce and what price shall I charge for it?'

It is, of course, perfectly reasonable at this stage to ask, 'Do business men really equate marginal cost and marginal revenue?' The answer usually is: 'Not as such'. Entrepreneurs usually fix their output on the basis of either total cost and total revenue, or, more usually, of average cost and average revenue. For example, they may try to find that output at which the excess of total revenue over total cost is at a maximum. But provided we feel that it is reasonable to assume that business men seek maximum profits—provided we agree to stand by the assumption of 'rationality'—it makes no difference at all to the actual output produced

whether profits are calculated on the basis of total, average or
marginal costs and revenues. As we have already seen, it is
perfectly possible to show the equilibrium position of a firm in
several different ways. We have merely chosen the most convenient way of showing at what output the difference between
total revenue and total cost will be at a maximum. Our method
has, however, one advantage. When we draw our type of diagram
we can always see the equilibrium position of the firm at a glance.
We can therefore accept this particular kind of diagram as providing a very useful weapon of analysis.[1]

5. THE FIRM'S AVERAGE REVENUE CURVE

It will be readily appreciated from the analysis of the previous
section that, if we are to produce a theory of the individual firm
which bears some resemblance to reality, it is extremely important
to discover what shape the various curves used in the analysis are
likely to take in the real world. In the next two sections we shall
attempt to do this.

Our first task is to find what will be the shape of the individual
firm's average revenue curve. The shape of the average revenue
curve of the individual firm will depend on conditions in the market
in which the firm sells its product. Broadly speaking, the keener
the competition of its rivals and the greater the number of fairly
close substitutes for its product, the more elastic will a firm's
average revenue curve be. As usual, it is possible to be precise
about limiting cases. One limiting case will occur when there are
so many competitors producing such close substitutes that the
demand for the product of each individual firm is infinitely elastic
and its average revenue curve is a horizontal straight line. This
will mean that the firm can sell as much of its product as it wishes
at the ruling market price. If the firm raises its price, then, owing
to the ease with which the same, or a very similar, product can
be bought from competitors, it will lose all its customers. If the
firm were to lower its price, it would be swamped by orders from
customers wishing to take advantage of its price reduction. The
demand—and the elasticity of demand—for its product would be
infinite.

This situation is illustrated in Figure 43. Figure 43a shows

---

[1] Readers who are interested in the relation between economic theory and
business practice will find a useful summary in F. Machlup, 'Marginal Analysis
and Empirical Research', *American Economic Review*, 1946, p. 519.

the demand and supply curves for the product made by an industry of highly competitive firms. The equilibrium price is OP and the equilibrium amount OM is sold at this price. This equilibrium price holds good throughout the market and all the firms making the product have to accept it. The individual firm has to accept the price OP but can sell as much as it wants at that price. Average revenue is thus constant at the price OP, so PL (in Figure 43b) represents the average revenue curve of an individual firm. Because average revenue is constant, marginal revenue will

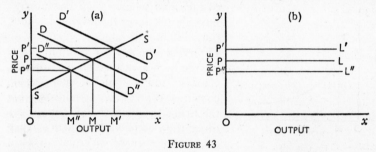

FIGURE 43

also be constant and will be equal to average revenue. The line PL therefore represents both the average and the marginal revenue curves of the firm.

If the demand for the industry's product increases and market price rises to P', the average revenue curve of each individual firm rises to P'L'. If demand decreases, price falls to P" and the average revenue curve of the individual firm falls to P"L". It is important to realise that whilst the vertical scales in both Figures 43a and 43b are the same, the horizontal scale is very many times greater in Figure 43b than in Figure 43a. This is because the output of the industry will be many times greater than that of the firm. Each individual firm produces only a minute part of the total output (OM) of the industry and is unable to influence the price (OP) of the industry's product by its own actions. This case of a horizontal demand curve is known as representing the limiting case of 'pure' competition.

The other limiting case will be where competition, far from being keen, is absent—where there is monopoly. Now it might be thought that where a single entrepreneur was the only supplier of a particular product, the demand curve for his product would be a vertical straight line, and that for any given amount of his product he could extort just as much money as he wished. But this is not realistic. However necessary the product of any firm may be, and however few the competitive substitutes, there must always be some limit to a producer's power to raise his prices. Consumers have only a limited income, and even if a single producer were able to force the consumers to pay as much as they could, he could never do more than take the whole of their incomes whatever his output.

The limiting case of 'pure' monopoly, as we may call it, will occur when a producer is so powerful that he is always able

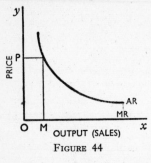

FIGURE 44

to take the whole of *all* consumers' incomes whatever the level of his output. This will happen when, as in Figure 44, the average revenue curve for the monopolist's firm has unitary elasticity and is at such a level that all consumers spend all their income on the firm's product whatever its price. Since the elasticity of the firm's average revenue curve is equal to one, total outlay on the firm's product will be the same at every price. The pure monopolist takes all consumers' incomes all the time.[1]

But it will be seen that even the 'pure' monopolist cannot control both the price of his product and the amount which will be demanded. He can fix *either* price *or* output. If he fixes his price, say at OP, then the amount which will be demanded (OM) is decided for him by what consumers will take at that price. If he fixes his output, then price is decided in a similar way by what his customers will pay when output is at the given level. Even a 'pure' monopolist can never fix both price and output at the same time. Within these limits, however, the 'pure' monopolist's power is complete. It should be noted that since total revenue is constant at all levels of output, marginal revenue is always zero. The marginal revenue curve coincides with the x-axis.

Pure monopoly has so far never existed, and presumably never will. Pure competition probably does exist, especially in the world markets for foodstuffs and raw materials. But these two types of situation are of importance rather as limiting cases than as practical possibilities, and the great majority of actual firms will be found to be producing in the region of *imperfect* (a better word

[1] Cf. Piero Sraffa, 'Laws of Returns under Competitive Conditions', *Economic Journal*, 1926, p. 545.

than 'impure') *competition* lying between these two limits. We shall discuss imperfect competition at great length later on, but for the moment we may say that the smaller the number of producers making any product, and the smaller the range of close substitutes for it, the less elastic will be the average revenue curve of any firm producing in these conditions.

In the real world, the average revenue curves of individual firms are likely to range all the way from those depicting almost pure competition, which are almost horizontal, to those denoting very imperfect competition, which are much steeper. The actual shape of these average revenue curves will depend on the presence or absence of competing substitutes for the product of the firm in question. Alternatively, we may say that the less elastic the average revenue curve of a firm is, the more 'imperfect' is competition in the market to which it sells, and the more elastic the demand curve, the more nearly 'pure' competition is.

We have now given a general classification of average revenue curves. This will provide a useful basis for our later analysis. But we have so far steadfastly ignored one very important factor— time. The implication throughout our analysis has been that we were studying the firm's average revenue curve in a period of time during which conditions did not alter. What difference will it make if we remove this assumption and allow for the passage of time? So far as average revenue curves are concerned, it is difficult to make satisfactory generalisations. There is no reason why demand should change in any particular way over time. We shall therefore assume, for the moment, that demand conditions are the same in the short and the long run. If we make this assumption, we shall be able to concentrate attention on changes in *cost* over time, in response to a *once-for-all* change in demand. As we shall see later, this is a much more interesting and important economic problem.

6. THE FIRM'S SHORT-RUN AVERAGE COST CURVE

The firm's average cost curve is rather more difficult to discuss than is its average revenue curve. There are two reasons for this difficulty. First, one cannot now avoid discussing explicitly the problems which arise from the passage of time. This means that we must first discuss short-run cost curves and then long-run cost curves. Second, it is possible for an average cost curve to slope both upwards and downwards, whereas an average revenue curve is only likely to slope downwards to the right. This adds to our problems. It has already been suggested, as a first approximation, that average cost curves are likely to be U-shaped. It is now time for us to justify this statement.

We shall devote this section to a discussion of short-run cost curves. The short run will be more carefully defined later. For the moment, we may take it to mean a period of time within which the firm can only increase output by hiring more labour and buying more raw materials. We shall assume that such items as the capital equipment of the firm cannot be altered or added to within this short period of time. It is on this basis that we must now try to explain why cost curves, or more accurately, short-run average cost curves, are likely to be U-shaped.

It is possible to discuss this problem either at a simple level or at a more advanced and complicated one. It will probably be most useful to give both kinds of explanation in turn. In order to give the more simple explanation, it is necessary to divide the costs of the firm into two broad categories, which, when added together, make up total costs. First, every firm has what are known as *fixed* or *overhead* costs. That is to say, it has those costs which are independent of output, those costs which must be incurred whether output is large or small. Such 'fixed' costs cannot be avoided if the firm is to remain in business at all, and include such payments as rent, rates, insurance, maintenance costs, debenture interest, many administrative expenses, and the like. These costs will all, broadly speaking, *have* to be met even if only a very small output is produced, and in the short period the amount of these fixed costs will not increase or decrease when the volume of output rises or falls. In terms of our definition of the short period, fixed costs are the costs of all those factors of production whose amount cannot be altered quickly.

Thus, the total fixed costs of any firm are not likely to fluctuate in the short run, except within very narrow margins, whatever the level of output. This is very important, for it means that if the fixed costs of a firm are shared equally between the various units of output, if, that is to say, we calculate average fixed cost, or fixed cost per unit of output, each of those units of output will bear a greater amount of fixed cost when output is small than when it is large. For instance, in the firm shown in Figure 45, total fixed cost is £60,000 whatever the output. The curve showing average fixed cost per unit at the various levels of output is the curve AFC. When output is 1000 units, average fixed costs are

£60 per unit. When it is 2000 units, they fall to £30 and so on. Average fixed costs fall continuously as output rises, and the average fixed cost curve is a rectangular hyperbola.

This gives us an inkling of the reason why a firm's average cost curve falls as output rises from low levels to higher ones. But we must go more deeply into the problem if we are to explain why cost curves are U-shaped.

The costs of the firm which are not 'fixed' costs are known as *variable* costs. These are the costs of all those factors of production whose amount can be altered in the short run. Such costs include, for example, payments for wages, raw materials, fuel and power, transport and the like. The total variable costs of a firm therefore vary with output in the short run. Now, if total variable costs always changed in proportion with every change in output, average variable cost (*i.e.* total variable cost ÷ output)

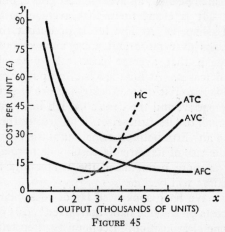

FIGURE 45

would always remain constant. This is not likely to happen in practice. It is, of course, quite reasonable to assume that as output rises from zero to the normal 'capacity' output, average variable costs will not change very greatly. Since we are assuming that all factors of production are available at a constant and known price, no increase in factor prices can occur as output changes. It is likely, however, that the variable factors will produce somewhat more efficiently near a firm's capacity output than at very low levels of output, though there is no reason to expect great variations.

But once normal capacity output is being produced, a further increase in output will undoubtedly increase average variable costs quite sharply. Greater output can be obtained but only at much greater cost. Increased output can come only from the use of more of those factors of production whose amount can be altered in the short run, or from obtaining harder work from existing ones. The fact that more and more workers have to be used will lead to overcrowding and bad organisation. The fact that existing factors have to be used more intensively will mean that workers tend to suffer from overstrain and that machines tend to break down more frequently. Even though we are assuming that overtime rates are not paid when more work is demanded, it is likely that costs will rise. The average variable cost curve will thus take a shape like that of the curve AVC in Figure 45. If the curves AFC and AVC in Figure 45 are now added together, we obtain an average total cost [1] curve ATC, or, as it is more usually called, an average cost curve, pure and simple.[2]

It is clear, then, that average cost curves are likely to be U-shaped. At low levels of output the spreading of the fixed costs over more and more units of output as output rises, will mean that average costs fall quite sharply when production increases. At high levels of output, average variable costs will be likely to rise quite quickly because of strong pressure on the firm's capacity, and the continued fall in average fixed costs will be too small to offset this rise. The greater the importance of fixed costs in any firm before normal output is reached, and the more speedy the rise of its variable costs once normal output has been passed, the more pronounced the U-shape of its short-run average cost curve will become.

We have spoken so far of costs being divided into 'variable' costs on the one hand and 'fixed' costs on the other. This is only one classification. Economists often talk instead of 'direct' costs and 'overhead' costs, or of 'prime' and 'supplementary' costs. These distinctions amount to the same thing in the end. 'Variable', 'prime' and 'direct' costs represent all those costs which can be altered in the short run as output alters. 'Fixed', 'overhead' or 'supplementary' costs are those costs which in the short run remain the same in total whatever output is.

This simple explanation of the reasons why short-run average cost curves are U-shaped is quite realistic. But it *is* only a simple explanation, and we must now provide a more detailed and adequate one. In order to do this, we need to discuss what Marshall has called the 'internal economies' of the firm. These are those economies in production—those reductions in production costs—which can be created within the firm itself when

---

[1] Average total cost sounds rather like a contradiction in terms, but it should be fairly clear what it means.

[2] It should be noted that the marginal cost curve in Figure 45 is marginal to both the average variable and the average total cost curves. It therefore cuts both these curves at their minimum points.

output increases. It seems certain that in all firms, average cost falls to some extent over low ranges of output as output rises. We may discuss the reasons for the 'internal economies' so obtained under four heads.

(a) Labour Economies

Since the earliest days of economics, great stress has been laid on the principle of the 'division of labour'. Adam Smith, an early economist, in *The Wealth of Nations*, published in 1776, explained[1] that, if each worker concentrated on a small operation in the manufacture of an article, instead of performing every operation in its construction, production would be greatly increased, and greater efficiency obtained. He attributed these results to three facts. 'First, to the increase of dexterity in every particular workman; secondly, to the saving of the time which is commonly lost in passing from one species of work to another; and lastly, to the invention of a great many machines which facilitate labour, and enable one man to do the work of many.'[2]

But it was one of Adam Smith's most important contentions that the economies to be reaped from this division of labour were 'limited by the extent of the market'. 'When the market is very small, no person can have any encouragement to dedicate himself entirely to one employment, for want of the power to exchange all that surplus part of the produce of his own labour, which is over and above his own consumption, for such parts of the produce of other men's labour as he has occasion for.'[3]

Now all this is clearly important for the individual firm. It is obviously possible for a firm to reap economies by dividing up the production of an article into a large number of relatively small operations. But the extent to which such division of labour will be worth undertaking will depend on the scale of output. If only a very small number of articles is produced, it will not be worth giving each man one very small job on which to concentrate entirely. If this were done, he would not be working at all for much of his time.

We have here, in the advantages of the division of labour, a clue to one of the reasons why average cost curves will fall over the earlier parts of their length. As output increases, division of labour, and the greater efficiency it brings with it, will become more and more profitable.

[1] *The Wealth of Nations*, chapters ii and iii.
[2] *Ibid*. chapter i.   [3] *Ibid*. chapter iii.

(b) Technical Economies

Internal economies of a similar kind can be found in the technical sphere. A large electro-plating plant, for example, costs a great deal to keep in operation, and the cost per unit will clearly be smaller when output is greater. Again, in modern industry, large machines cost a great deal to 'tool up'. A machine pressing out, say, the side of a motor car will take a week or more to be put ready to produce a particular design. The greater the output of this particular car, therefore, the lower the *unit* cost of 'tooling up'. Similarly, if a die is being made to mould a particular product, the cost *per unit* of output of having the die made will depend on the output of the product.

(c) Marketing Economies

Similar internal economies are yielded in marketing. Within very broad limits, the cost of marketing does not vary in proportion with output. We are in this chapter assuming that a firm makes only one product, but only for the sake of simplicity. We may note here that when more than one product is made, and especially when the products are closely related, it is not ten times as hard to sell ten different products as to sell one. But even if there is only one product, it can be advertised widely almost as easily as it can be advertised locally.

(d) Managerial Economies

In just the same way, the cost per unit of management will almost certainly fall as output increases. A good manager can organise a large output just as efficiently as a small one, and he will do so, in general, for the same wage. In addition, if the scale of production rises, it may pay to take on a first-rate manager who is well worth his pay now that profits are greater and the job of management more complicated.

We see, then, that there are good reasons for expecting average costs to fall as output rises. But a little reflection will show that there is often no real difference between the reasons for which average costs fall and the reasons for which average fixed costs fall, in response to an increased output. Average fixed costs fall because they are spread over larger volumes of output— because the fixed charges (mainly for buildings and machinery) are being spread more economically. But it is just the same with other factors. Management costs fall because they can be spread over more units of output. Advertising costs do not rise in proportion to a rise in output.

All this boils down to the fact that most factors of production can be most efficiently employed at a fairly large output, but work less efficiently at small outputs because they cannot be divided into smaller units—they are *indivisible*. A manager cannot be chopped in half and asked to produce half the current output. Similarly, plant cannot be used less fully without being used less economically. It also is indivisible. The reason for these internal economies can therefore usually be found in what technical economic jargon terms 'indivisible factors of production' or, more shortly, but in a monstrosity of English—'indivisibilities'. The only important exception occurs in the case of the division of labour. Whilst it is certainly true that because of the division of labour, labour efficiency changes as output rises, it is not reasonable to suggest that labour is 'indivisible'.

It will usually be found that for a time the short-run average cost curve of a firm will fall as output rises, since better use is being made of indivisible factors of production and other economies are being reaped. But there will usually be a limit to the range of output over which average cost will fall. There will usually be some output where all the factors used by the firm are being employed as efficiently as possible and where average cost is therefore at a minimum. It will happen at the output where all factors are being used in the 'right' or 'optimum' proportions with each other. This output is known as the 'optimum' output since optimum use is being made of all the factors of production. The firm will be producing the optimum output when its average cost is at a minimum.

Once the optimum output has been exceeded, cost will rise, mainly because indivisible factors are now being used *too* fully, or, to put it another way, they are being used in the wrong proportions compared with the variable factors. Just as average cost fell when better and better use was being made of the indivisible factors, so average cost rises when they are being worked too hard. For example, as output exceeds the optimum, management problems will increase and managerial efficiency will decline. The entrepreneur will be unable to deal with the very large output, and management problems will get out of hand. There will be too many workers per machine for really efficient production. This leads to the conclusion that there are very good reasons for feeling that the firm's short-run average cost curve will be U-shaped.

I

But this is really only one aspect of a fundamental principle of economics known as the *Law of Variable Proportions*. We shall have occasion to discuss this 'law' more fully in Chapter X, but something must be said about it now. Economists have always based their analyses on a belief that the production of a given factory cannot be increased very far without average cost rising. This idea, which early economists described as the 'law' of diminishing returns, was made the basis of their economic theory. We still retain this 'law' or 'statement of tendency' as a basis of modern economics. Its full usefulness will be seen later. For the moment we may see that it does at least enable us to generalise about the shape of short-run cost curves.

The law of diminishing returns, or law of variable proportions as it is usually called nowadays, shows what happens if successive units of a 'variable' factor (a factor of which the amount employed can be varied) are added to a given quantity of a 'fixed' factor whose amount cannot be altered. The addition of more and more units of the 'variable' factor will in the end lead to a decline in the increment of output produced by each additional unit of the variable factor. This theory is advanced only on the assumption that the state of technical knowledge is given and that no new inventions are developed during the period to which the 'law' relates. The validity of the law is usually upheld on a basis of empirical observation. Because the world's food supply cannot be grown on a football pitch by adding an infinite number of farm labourers, the law seems realistic. We have ourselves given similar justification for our belief in it.

The relevance of this 'law' to the shape of the short-run average cost curve is obvious. In the short run one factor of supreme importance—capital—is fixed in amount for the individual firm. So is management both in the sense of general management and, say, supervision of the workers. The combination of different amounts of variable factors with the fixed factors of capital and management means that beyond a certain point returns will fall off as output increases—costs will rise. Both capital and management will be worked too hard for efficient production. It should be borne in mind, however, on what assumptions this contention is made. First, it is completely independent of any variations in factor prices as more of any factors are used. We are assuming that prices of all factors, wages, raw material prices and the like, are constant whatever the amounts used by the firm.

Second, the law of variable proportions does not imply that some units of a factor of production are less efficient than others. We are deliberately assuming that all units of a factor are equally efficient. This may not be really true but it is a convenient simplifying assumption. It follows that if a firm employs fifty-one workers where it previously employed fifty, each one of the fifty-one workers produces exactly as much as each other one. But output per man will nevertheless be smaller than it was when only fifty men were employed. Because the plant is of fixed size each worker will have less elbow-room as the total number of workers increases, and the productivity of each, though the same as that of every other worker, will fall off. Since we are assuming that wages per man are constant, it follows that average variable costs must rise since output per man is falling. Economists therefore maintain that once a certain point has been reached, average variable costs will rise because productivity per man falls off whilst wages remain constant. But it must be stressed that one can only say that this will happen *after a certain stage*. When only a small number of men is being employed there is the likelihood that productivity per man will rise as output increases. For example, if our hypothetical firm were employing only twenty men, progressively greater specialisation and division of labour might be feasible as employment rose—say to forty men. Output per man might be higher when forty were employed than when twenty were working. Average variable costs would then fall as employment rose from twenty to forty men. The 'law' of diminishing returns states that with given technological conditions there will be *a point beyond which* the addition of more variable factors to a fixed factor will bring falling returns per unit of variable factor, and with constant factor prices will cause average variable costs to rise. Before this point is reached it is possible for productivity to increase as variable factors are added to a fixed factor. In the end, however, returns must diminish.

We have now seen why economists assume that short-run average cost curves are U-shaped. We shall be able to give a more complete explanation of the underlying physical production conditions at a later stage, but for our present purposes the analysis given above will suffice. It seems desirable to say explicitly at this point that once one has decided what shape the average cost curve of a firm is, it is always quite easy to draw the corresponding marginal cost curve, whose relationship to the average cost curve we have already discussed. The fundamental

conclusion of this section is that short-run average cost curves
are U-shaped.

7. LONG-RUN AVERAGE COST CURVES

One can safely make the generalisation that long-run average
cost curves will normally be U-shaped just as short-run ones will,
but that they will invariably be flatter than short-run ones. The
U-shape of a cost curve will be less pronounced the longer the
period to which the curve relates.

This question, like that of the shape of short-run curves, can
be dealt with either simply or in a more complicated way. The
simple explanation is again in terms of fixed and variable costs.
It is clear, on reflection, that the longer the period one is considering, the fewer costs will be fixed and the more will be variable.
Over a long period of time there are very few costs which are just
as great if output is small as they are if it is large. For in economics we define the long period as that period during which the
size and organisation of the firm can be altered to meet changed
conditions.

Over a long period, unwanted buildings can be sold or let to
sub-tenants, insurance policies can be varied in size according
to changing conditions, and administrative and marketing staff
decreased or increased in order to deal efficiently with smaller or
larger outputs and sales. As a result, total fixed cost can vary to
a considerable extent over long periods, whereas in the short run
its amount is fixed absolutely. In other words, the longer the
period under consideration, the fewer costs are 'fixed' and the
more costs become 'variable'. This means that in the long run
the firm is able to adapt the 'scale' of its operations to produce any
required output in the most efficient possible way. In the short
run a reduction in output will raise average costs because fixed
costs will represent a larger amount per unit of output. In the
long period, however, fixed costs can be reduced somewhat if
output continues at a low level. Average fixed cost will therefore
be lower in the long than in the short run.

In the short run also average variable costs will rise sharply
when output exceeds the normal maximum. In the long run the
size of the firm can be increased to deal with an increased output
more adequately, overcrowding can be dealt with and management
can cope with other problems of high output. Variable costs will
rise less sharply in the long run than in the short run.

In terms of our more detailed argument, we may say that in the long run the indivisible factors of production can be used more economically, because in the long run they are in fact, to some extent, divisible. In the short run the shape of the cost curve of the firm depends on the action of the law of variable proportions, with capital and management as fixed (indivisible) factors. In the long run the cost curve of the firm depends on what are known as *returns to scale*. In the long run the amount of capital can be altered and the management can be arranged differently if neces-sary. They are no longer com-pletely indivisible.

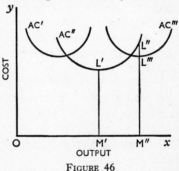

FIGURE 46

When all factors of pro-duction can be used in differing proportions in this way, the scale of operations in the firm can be altered. We are now dealing with 'returns to scale'. Each time the scale of opera-tions changes we must draw a new short-run cost curve for the firm. For example, in Figure 46 let us assume that the firm has the short-run cost curve AC″. The optimum output will then be OM′. In the short run, an increase in output to, say, OM″ can be achieved, but only by allowing cost to rise to M″L″, for in the short run the 'scale' of operations is fixed. In the long run, however, a new plant can be built. Let us assume that the firm now has the short-run cost curve AC‴. This means that by increasing the scale of its opera-tions the firm can produce the output OM″ at a cost of M″L‴ instead of M″L″.

The individual short-run average cost curves thus retain their U-shape. At any given scale of operations the firm will encounter regions of rising and falling costs. But in the long run the firm can produce on a completely different cost curve to the left or right of the original one. For each different scale at which the firm can operate there will, of course, be an output where average cost is at a minimum (*i.e.* a lowest point on the relevant short-run average cost curve). At this output the firm is said to be pro-ducing at its technical 'optimum', given its scale of operations. Output is 'optimum' in the sense that average cost is at a minimum.

In the long run, therefore, the firm will be able to adjust its scale of operations so that it is producing any given output at lowest cost. For instance, in Figure 47, if the firm in question wishes to produce output OM', it will find it best to produce at that scale which has the average cost curve SAC'. If it wishes to produce OM" it will be best to produce on the curve SAC", and if it wants to produce OM''' it will produce on SAC'''. In each case it will be producing the output concerned at the lowest possible cost. It is important to remember, however, that only in the long run can the scale of operations be increased or diminished. In the short run the scale of operations will be fixed, and

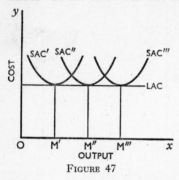

if output moves below or above the optimum level, average costs will inevitably rise along the short-run curve in question, for example SAC', SAC" or SAC'''.

FIGURE 47

It is therefore possible to draw a long-run average cost curve showing what the long-run cost of producing each output would be. In the long run the scale of operations can be completely adjusted to any new output as cheaply as is practicable, and the long-run average cost curve will show what it will cost to produce any given output when all possible adjustments have been made.

What shape will such a curve take ? The answer depends on the assumptions made. We are assuming that factor prices are constant. No change in costs can be caused by changes in factor prices. But we can make various assumptions about the divisibility of factors. The simplest case is to assume, as we have done in Figure 47, that all factors are infinitely divisible and that there are no economies to be reaped from, for example, the division of labour. This means that in the long run all factors can be adjusted so that the proportions between them are the optimum ones, and production can take place at the lowest point on the relevant short-run average cost curve.

It will be seen from Figure 47 that on this assumption the long-run cost curve of the firm, LAC, is a horizontal straight line. Returns to scale are constant, even though returns *at a given scale* are variable. This is not, however, a very reasonable assumption. It is unlikely that all factors are infinitely divisible, even in the long run. And there will almost certainly be some economies to be reaped from the division of labour as output is raised.

It is far more probable that some factors of production will be indivisible. Management in particular is likely to be incompletely divisible. An entrepreneur will be unlikely to produce twice a given output as efficiently as he produces that given output, however long he is given to get used to the idea of having to do so. It is therefore reasonable to think that firms will still produce more cheaply at some scales of output than at others, even in the long run, if only because beyond a certain point management is difficult. Certain combinations of factors will thus produce at

lower costs per unit than others. This means that in such conditions, which are likely to be found in practice, the short-run average cost curves of the firm will have different minimum points. For example, in Figure 48 it will be seen that the short-run

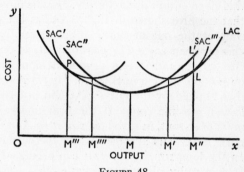

FIGURE 48

average cost curve SAC″ has a lower minimum point than either the curve SAC′ or SAC‴. Its optimum output is obtained at lower cost. The long-run average cost curve which is a tangent to all the short-run curves will be the curve LAC. It will therefore be U-shaped itself. But it will be flatter than the short-run cost curves—the U shape will be less pronounced. Such a curve is known as an 'envelope' since it envelops all the short-run curves. In a sense the term 'envelope' is misleading. An envelope is physically distinct from the letter which it contains. But every point on an 'envelope' long-run cost curve is also a point on one of the short-run cost curves which it 'envelops'.

The relationship between the short-run average cost curves and the long-run average cost curve, when these are of the type shown in Figure 48, needs further explanation. It is clear that, for any given output, average cost cannot be higher in the long run than in the short run. This is because any adjustment which will reduce costs, and which it is possible to make in the short run, must also be possible in the long run. On the other hand, it is not always possible in the short run to produce a given output in the cheapest possible way. If output changes, it is impossible to change the amounts used of all factors in the short run, but they can all be altered—if they ever can be altered—in the long run. The long-run average cost curve can never cut a short-run average cost curve—though they may be tangential to each other.

It is quite possible for the long-run average cost curve to lie below any *one* short-run cost curve for many outputs. But at any given output, the long-run average cost curve must be tangent to some point on one short-run curve. It is tangential to the short-run cost curve relating to that size of plant which produces this given output most cheaply. Let us illustrate this by supposing that the firm shown in Figure 48 has been producing for a long time at the output OM. This output can be produced more cheaply than any other possible output on the long-run average cost curve, and is also produced more cheaply than any other output on the curve SAC″. The firm has adapted its scale to that implied by the curve SAC″ in order to produce OM at the lowest possible cost. If the firm now wants to produce OM″ units of output, in the short run it has to expand output along the curve SAC″ and average cost for the output OM″ will be £M″L′. In the long run, however, it can produce this output for £M″L. It does so by adjusting the scale of its plant so as to produce the output OM″ as efficiently as possible. This happens if it builds a plant of that size which has the cost curve SAC‴ and produces output OM″ with it. The short-run curve SAC″ now ceases to be relevant. If the firm wishes to change output again, it can only do so in the short run along the curve SAC‴. At any one moment a firm can only produce on a single short-run cost curve because its plant is of a fixed size. But in the long run it will choose the most suitable point on the most suitable short-run average cost curve, and this will be a point on the long-run average cost curve as well.

Two further points are of interest. First, it should be borne in mind that the long-run average cost curve is not tangent to any short-run average cost curve at the short-run curve's minimum point except in the case of that short-run curve which is tangent to the long-run curve at the latter's lowest point. In Figure 48 this happens at the output OM when the short-run curve SAC″ is tangential to the lowest point of the long-run curve. Careful examination of Figure 48 shows that for all outputs smaller than OM the lowest long-period costs occur on the falling portion of the short-term average cost curves. For example, the output OM‴ is best produced in the long run by producing at point P on the short-run curve SAC′. But this output is smaller than the optimum output for a plant of this size, which in this case would be at OM″″. In the long run any output *less* than OM is produced most cheaply by building a plant with a given optimum output and using it to produce at less than this optimum output. Similarly, any output *greater* than OM can be produced more cheaply by using a smaller plant working to more than optimum (short run) capacity than it can by building a larger plant and using it to produce its optimum output.

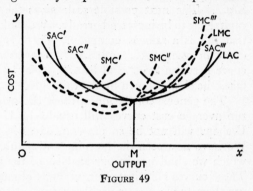

FIGURE 49

Second, if, as in Figure 49, we draw all the short-run marginal cost curves corresponding to the short-run average cost curves, and if we draw the long-run marginal cost curve to the long-run average cost curve, we can generalise about the relationships between the various marginal curves. Each short-run marginal curve (SMC) cuts the corresponding short-run average curve at the latter's lowest point. Similarly, the long-run marginal cost curve (LMC) cuts the long-run average cost curve at its lowest point. It is clear from Figure 49 that the long-run marginal cost curve is flatter than the short-run marginal cost curves. This is what one would expect, for the U shape of the long-run average cost curves is less pronounced than that of the short-run average cost curves. Thus, if one starts from the long-run optimum output OM,

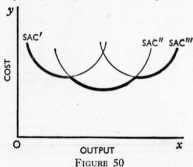

FIGURE 50

and output increases, marginal costs rise more sharply in the short run than in the long run. Similarly, if output falls from OM, marginal costs fall more substantially in the short run than in the long run.

One less usual type of cost curve is shown in Figure 50. Here the capital equipment is only capable of alteration discontinuously. The original scale of output gives the short-run average cost curve SAC′. The next possible scale gives the curve SAC″, because capital has to be increased greatly. We could assume, for example, that this is a railway company. There is no possible short-run curve between SAC′ and SAC″. Similarly, there is no possible curve between SAC″ and SAC‴. The long-run curve therefore takes the shape shown by the thick black line in Figure 50.

The general conclusion of these last two sections is that long-run average cost curves will usually be U-shaped, but that this U shape will not be so pronounced as in the short-run curves. We have now seen the meaning and nature of the various curves which we shall use in our analysis of the problems of the firm. These curves constitute our weapons of analysis. We must now use them to attack our problems.

SUGGESTED READING

Alfred Marshall, *Principles of Economics* (8th Edition), London, 1920, Book IV, chapters 8, 9, 11, 12 and 13 ; Book V, chapter 4.
Joan Robinson, *Economics of Imperfect Competition*, London, 1933, chapters i and ii.

CHAPTER VI

COMPETITIVE INDUSTRY

1. DEFINITION OF PURE AND PERFECT COMPETITION

IN the previous chapter we discussed the meaning and structure of the various types of curves which we shall need to use in discussing the conditions under which the firm and the industry will be in equilibrium. So far, however, we have merely discussed the various possible shapes of such cost and revenue curves. It is now time to see, using these curves, how the firm reaches equilibrium in various conditions. The simplest case with which to begin is that where there is keen competition. We shall therefore proceed now to analyse conditions for the equilibrium of the firm in a competitive industry. This will not only enable us to see what conditions in such an industry will be like, but will also bring to light in a simple context most of the fundamental features of the equilibrium of the firm. For however competitive or monopolistic the conditions facing a firm happen to be, the main features of the equilibrium of the firm remain essentially the same.

It will be useful, at the outset, to define competitive conditions more carefully than we have done so far. We spoke in Chapter V of *pure competition* where demand for the product of the individual firm was infinitely elastic, so that the firm could sell all it wished at the existing market price, but was unable to alter the price by its own actions. We saw that in such conditions the average revenue curve of the firm would be a horizontal straight line. There are three fundamental prerequisites for the existence of pure competition between producers. These are as follows.

(a) Large Numbers

The first condition for pure competition in an industry is that there must be a large number of firms in the industry. This is essential, because only when there are many firms in an industry can each firm be sure that any action on its own part will have no noticeable effects on the price and output of the whole industry.

123

If there are many firms in an industry, any one of them can increase or decrease its own output quite substantially without needing to fear that there may be a violent change in the price of the product of the industry as a result. The firm will be producing such a small proportion of the total output of the commodity that even a large change in its own output will have a negligible effect on the output and the price of the industry as a whole. The individual firm has to take the price of the product as given and unalterable.

(b) Homogeneous Products

Second, each of the firms in a 'purely' competitive industry must be making a product which is accepted by customers as being identical, or *homogeneous*, with that made by all the other producers in the industry. This ensures that no entrepreneur can put his price up above the general level. If he did do so, consumers could buy the same good from other producers at a lower price. Best-grade cotton is best-grade cotton whichever planter grows it, and one does not find individual cotton planters advertising their product as better than that grown by their next-door neighbour if both are of equal quality. When the goods are homogeneous in this way a uniform price must rule throughout the market.

It is, however, important to realise that it is the consumer who decides whether or not two products are homogeneous. It is only if *buyers* agree that two producers are making exactly the same good that their prices will be the same. If buyers find real or imagined differences between the two products, their prices are bound to differ, however alike the two articles really are. For example, if a customer wrongly believes that the 'Co-op' sells goods which are inferior to those supplied by 'Quality Groceries', he may pay the latter 3s. 6d. for a good which he could have got from the former for 2s., even though the goods are identical. Again, Mr. Smith may prefer to buy his gardening implements from Mr. Jones, because they both belong to the same club or go to the same church, even though Mr. Jones charges higher prices for the same goods than Mr. Williams farther down the street. If buyers behave in this way, competition cannot be pure, for the products are not homogeneous in the eyes of the consumers.

These two assumptions between them ensure that the firm's average revenue curve shall be horizontal. The fact that there are many producers prevents the individual firm from exerting any influence on price. The fact that products are homogeneous means that buyers do not regard one producer's product as 'better' than another's and prevents price differences from emerging.

It is probably worth pointing out here that we have so far assumed, and shall continue to assume until further notice, that there is always pure competition *between buyers*. We have taken it for granted that the total number of buyers is very large, and that each one takes so small a proportion of the total sales of any good that no one buyer can alter the price of a good by his own actions. Buyers must therefore take prices as given, even where a monopolistic seller can alter prices to suit himself. The fact that in this chapter we are assuming perfect competition between *both* buyers *and* sellers is important and should be borne in mind.

(c) Free Entry

The third fundamental condition which must be fulfilled if there is to be pure competition in an industry is that anyone who wishes to enter the industry must be allowed to do so. It is difficult, however, to be quite sure what is and what is not a restriction on entry into an industry. For example, in the road passenger transport industry it is desirable that every omnibus or coach should measure up to certain required standards of safety. A refusal to allow unsafe buses into the industry would not usually be regarded as a restriction on entry. Rather would it be accepted as an essential condition for the well-being of passengers, transport workers and other road users.

Nevertheless, whilst border-line cases of this kind may well be important in some circumstances, it will, as a rule, be possible to decide quite quickly whether or not there is restriction on entry into any industry. A monopolistic association, for example, will refuse entry into an industry to anyone whom it does not wish to allow into the industry. If it is able to enforce its decisions, this will mean that the number of firms in an industry can be kept at the existing number, or even reduced if some firms leave the industry, while prices are maintained at a high level. Our third prerequisite for pure competition thus ensures that the number of firms in the competitive industry can always remain large because new blood is always allowed to enter.

These three conditions, large numbers of firms, homogeneous products and free entry, between them ensure that there is pure competition in the sense that there is competition which is completely free from any monopoly elements. Between them they ensure that the average revenue curve of each of the individual firms in the competitive industry is a horizontal straight line. One can, however, distinguish also between pure competition, which we have just defined, and 'perfect' competition—a concept frequently used by economists. For there to be 'perfect' competition, it is necessary to make some additional assumptions. In particular, it is necessary to assume that there is perfect knowledge on the part of all buyers and of all sellers about conditions in the market. In addition it is usual to assume complete mobility of factors of production between industries. It is also convenient when discussing perfect competition to make the assumption that all producers work sufficiently close to each other for there to be no transport costs. Strictly speaking, two identical goods are not homogeneous in the economic sense if they are not in the same place. For example, I may have the choice between buying identical kettles from Smith in my village or from Brown in the next village. But if the bus fare is 6d. each way, Smith may charge me 1s. extra because he knows it would cost me 1s. to fetch the same sort of kettle from the next village. We shall assume that differences caused by transport costs do not exist, otherwise prices for the same physical good would differ. These additional assumptions are not essential if one merely desires to show what conditions must be fulfilled if monopoly on the selling side is to be absent. But they are useful in building up a hypothetical model of a competitive industry. We shall therefore discuss the conditions in an industry where there is 'perfect' rather than 'pure' competition. This is our next task.

2. NORMAL PROFIT

Two essential conditions must be fulfilled if there is to be equilibrium in a perfectly competitive industry. First, each and every individual firm must be in equilibrium. This will happen when each firm in the industry is earning maximum profits, by equating marginal revenue with marginal cost. Second, the industry as a whole must be in equilibrium. This will occur when there is no tendency for firms either to enter or to leave the industry, which will only happen when all the entrepreneurs in the industry are earning enough money to induce them to stay in the industry, and when no entrepreneur outside the industry thinks that he could earn enough money, were he to enter it, to make the move worth while.

If these conditions are fulfilled, and there is no movement of firms either into or out of the industry, it is clear that the entrepreneurs of all the firms which are in the industry must be earning at least enough money to induce them to remain in it. In technical economic language, we describe this situation by saying that every entrepreneur in the industry is at least earning 'normal' profits. 'Normal' profits, for an entrepreneur in any industry, are those profits which are just sufficient to induce him to stay in the industry. It follows, on the other hand, that if an industry is in equilibrium, with no movement in or out, no-one outside the industry foresees the possibility of being able to earn 'normal' profits if he were to enter the industry.

We shall need to make considerable use of the idea of 'normal' profits, and it will be useful, in this chapter, to simplify the problem by making two not entirely realistic assumptions about it. Let us assume that all the entrepreneurs in the industry we are studying would all prove to be of identical efficiency if they left it and went to another industry. On this assumption, 'normal' profits will be identical for every entrepreneur in the industry we are studying. But let us also assume (unless an explicit statement to the contrary is made) that the entrepreneurs are not all of equal efficiency *within* the industry and that some can therefore earn more money than others. Some may earn 'supernormal' profits. These assumptions imply that there is a general rate of 'normal' profits for the whole industry—that all entrepreneurs' earnings must fall to exactly the same level before they will leave the industry—but that within the industry some entrepreneurs earn more than others. These two assumptions are not entirely consistent but they will enable us to simplify the analysis in this chapter. They will be abandoned in a later chapter.[1]

It follows from the foregoing analysis that if, for any reason, profits of all entrepreneurs in any industry rise above 'normal' (if they are 'supernormal'), there will be a tendency for the number of firms in that industry to increase. For we may assume that entrepreneurs outside the industry will expect to be able to earn at least 'normal' profits if they enter. If, on the other hand, profits for everyone fall below 'normal' (if they are 'subnormal'), there will be a fall in the number of firms in the industry. Some firms will be forced out by bankruptcy and their entrepreneurs will go in search of 'normal' profits elsewhere. We can say, therefore, that the industry as a whole and all the individual firms

[1] See Chapter XV, p. 326.

in it will be in equilibrium—in 'full equilibrium' as it is often
called—when all firms are maximising profits and when there is no
tendency for firms to enter or leave the industry. In such conditions all the firms in the industry will be earning at least normal
profits.

The fact that we have introduced normal profits into our
analysis means that we must make a slight alteration in the
content of our average cost curve. If a firm is to remain in the
industry, its decision to do so will depend, not on whether it is
covering average total cost as we have hitherto defined it, but on
whether it is also earning at
least normal profits. So, in
order to be able to construct
an analysis which enables us
to decide easily whether or
not firms will be willing to
stay in an industry at their
current level of earnings, it
will be useful to include
'normal' profits in average
costs. In future, the average
cost curves which we shall
draw will include such 'nor-
mal' profits. This should be remembered, because it will not be
convenient to point it out specifically on every occasion when an
average cost curve is drawn. The introduction of normal profits
gives an additional reason for us to expect average cost curves to
slope downwards over low ranges of output. We shall assume that
each entrepreneur must earn a certain amount of money if he is to
stay in the industry, and it is usual to assume that this sum of
money representing normal profits is independent of output. We
shall assume that an entrepreneur must earn a fixed sum of money if
he is to stay in the industry, and that he wants that fixed amount of
money whatever output he is to produce. Because normal profits
represent a fixed amount of money, it follows that, as output rises,
normal profits calculated per unit of output fall. For the fixed
sum of money representing normal profits is spread over a progressively larger number of units of output as production rises.
Here is our additional reason for expecting average cost curves to
fall over low ranges of output.

In Figure 51 we have drawn an average cost curve excluding
normal profits (AC) and another including them (AC + NP). It

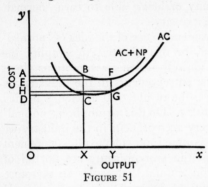

FIGURE 51

will be seen that as output rises, the vertical distance between the two curves steadily falls. Normal profits per unit of output decline progressively. For example, when output is OX, normal profit per unit of output is BC, when output is OY it is FG. It should be noted that the areas of any rectangles showing normal profits such as the rectangles ABCD and EFGH are the same. This is inevitable if, as we are assuming, normal profits represent a given sum of money.

If average cost includes normal profits in this way, it is clear that a firm will be earning normal profits when average cost (including normal profits) is equal to price. Now, we have seen in Chapter V that it is reasonable to assume that all average cost curves are roughly U-shaped. We also know that in perfect competition each firm's average revenue curve is a horizontal straight line. Thus, in perfect competition the only situation

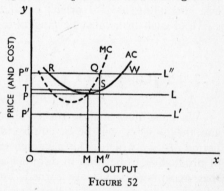

FIGURE 52

in which the firm can be in equilibrium *and* earning normal profits is when the average cost curve is tangential to the average revenue curve. Only then can average revenue equal price, and the firm cover all its costs and just earn normal profits. This is shown in Figure 52.

In Figure 52 it is clear that the firm cannot *both* be in equilibrium *and* be earning normal profits for any position of the average revenue curve below PL. For example, with the average revenue curve P'L' the firm must earn less than normal profits whatever its output, for at no output is average cost (including normal profits) equal to price. On the other hand, if the average revenue curve is above PL, as with P"L", it is possible for average cost to equal price (in this case at R and W). But at neither R nor W would the firm be in equilibrium. For the firm will only be in equilibrium when it is equating marginal revenue and marginal cost. With the average revenue curve P"L", this will happen when the firm produces the output OM" and sells it at the price OP". At this level of output it will be in equilibrium but will be earning 'supernormal' profits, equal to the area P"QST.

K

The only position where the firm can be in equilibrium and only earn normal profits occurs where it is producing the output OM. This will happen when the price of the industry's product is OP. Then marginal revenue will be equal to marginal cost but average cost will also equal price (average revenue). Since competition is perfect, average revenue will, of course, equal marginal revenue. It therefore follows that if a perfectly competitive industry is to be in full equilibrium, with all firms not only earning maximum profits (equating marginal revenue with marginal cost) but in fact earning normal profits with average cost (including normal profit) equal to price, the average cost curve of each firm must be tangent to its average revenue curve.

3. EQUILIBRIUM OF THE FIRM AND THE INDUSTRY IN THE SHORT RUN

We must now analyse the conditions under which the firm and the industry will be in equilibrium in the short run—in a period of time which is long enough to allow the variable factors of production to be used in different amounts in order to ensure that maximum profits are earned, but during which the fixed factors cannot be altered in amount.

We shall find it useful, in this analysis of the short-run equilibrium conditions in any industry, to be quite explicit about the cost conditions of the various firms. If costs differ between firms, the equilibrium position of the industry will not be the same as it would be if all firms had identical cost curves. We shall therefore consider the short-run equilibrium of the firm and of the industry in three different situations. First, we shall assume that all factors of production are homogeneous. This means that, assuming that perfect competition in the market for factors guarantees identical factor prices for all producers buying the same factors, all firms will have identical cost curves. For, since all units of all factors, including entrepreneurs, are identical, each entrepreneur will be able to combine the same factors in the same way. And since we are assuming that every firm produces each output at the minimum possible cost, we may conclude that all firms will have identical cost curves when all factors are homogeneous.

Second, we shall see what difference it makes if we assume that all factors of production except entrepreneurs are homogeneous, but that entrepreneurship is heterogeneous. This means that costs will differ between firms because some entrepreneurs, being more efficiênt than others, can use exactly the same factors to produce a given output more cheaply. Third, we shall see what happens when all factors are assumed to be heterogeneous. In this situation cost differences between firms will be even greater, because all factors will be of differing efficiencies and not merely entrepreneurs. Let us now consider the short-run equilibrium of the industry under these three conditions.

(a) All Factors Homogeneous

Figure 53 shows the short-run position in two firms using homogeneous factors in conditions where there is perfect competition in the factor market and where the prices of all factors are given (and constant). The two firms have identical cost curves, for it is assumed that each produces every output at the lowest possible cost.

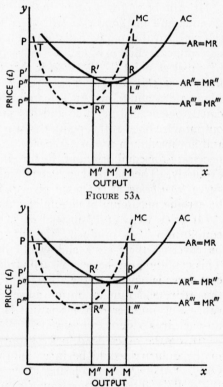

FIGURE 53A

FIGURE 53B

Let us assume, to begin with, that price, in the perfectly competitive market for the product of the firms, is £OP. All firms have to take this price of £OP as given, and will adapt their output so as to maximise profits. The horizontal straight line PL therefore represents the average revenue curve of the firms, and since competition is perfect it is also the marginal revenue curve.

All firms have identical costs, so each will maximise profits if it produces the output OM and sells it at the perfectly competitive price of £OP. Since average cost is only £MR at the output OM, and price is £OP, each firm earns £PLRP' of 'supernormal' profits. Both firms in Figure 53 are in equilibrium, since both are earning maximum profits. But the industry is not in equilibrium, for all firms have identical cost curves. They will thus all be producing the same output and earning the same 'supernormal' profits—£PLRP'. Since no firm can create new fixed equipment in the short run, no new firms can enter the industry, except in the long run. In the long run new firms will enter the industry and, having identical costs with the existing firms, will compete away the supernormal profits. In the short run, however, the number of firms in the industry is too small for there to be 'full equilibrium', and all firms earn supernormal profits.

It will be noted that in both firms in Figure 53 marginal revenue and marginal cost will be equal at L, and that it is by reference to this point that the profit-maximising output will be determined. But marginal revenue and marginal cost will also be equal at point T. Why is it that the firms are not in equilibrium at this level? This becomes clear on examination of Figures 53a and 53b. At T marginal cost has only just become equal to marginal revenue and has previously been greater. If output were fixed at this point, the firm would be earning *minimum* and not maximum profits. We may therefore state the conditions necessary for equilibrium of the firm in perfect competition more explicitly. The marginal cost curve must cut the marginal revenue curve *from below* at the point of equilibrium. A firm can never be earning maximum profits unless this happens.

If price were £OP″ instead of £OP, the firms would be in equilibrium when producing the output OM′. They would just be covering their costs and would be earning normal profits. This condition can be seen visually from the fact that the average cost curve is tangent to the average revenue curve. The situation thus represents full equilibrium in the industry, even in the short run. The number of firms is just large enough to ensure that no-one earns supernormal profits.

If, on the other hand, price happened to be OP‴, the firms in the industry would be in equilibrium producing the output OM″. All would be losing money, losses being equal to P′R′R″P‴. Thus the 'maximum' profit a firm can earn is a loss of £P′R′R″P‴. This is the smallest loss the firms can make if they are to produce at all. It follows that whilst the firms can be in short-run equilibrium, they will not be in long-run equilibrium.

In the long run firms will leave the industry until those remaining just earn normal profits.

The obvious question to ask therefore is : 'Does it pay a firm which is losing money to stay in the industry ?' The answer is that it all depends on the length of time which is being considered. In the long run, if the efficiency of the firm remains unaltered, it should leave the industry altogether. By definition, if the entrepreneur is not earning normal profits he will prefer to leave the industry in the long run.

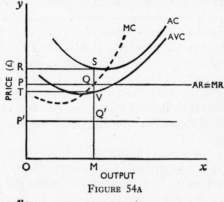

FIGURE 54A

In the short run he may prefer to stay in business. For by our definition of the short period he cannot, within such a period, alter the fixed capital of his firm, and this fact will influence his decision. Since the 'fixed' costs of the firm *must* be met in the short run, even if the firm closes (unless it is to go bankrupt alto-

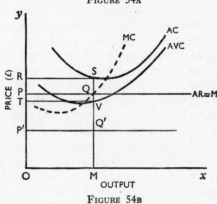

FIGURE 54B

gether), it will pay the entrepreneur to remain in production if by doing so he earns anything which will help him to cover his 'fixed' costs. This can be seen from the firms in Figure 54. We still assume identical costs. The firms will remain in business so long as they can cover their variable costs. Since variable costs can be avoided, even in the short run, the firms can refuse to employ any variable factors if they do not wish to do so. It will therefore pay entrepreneurs to take on variable factors only if they can pay for them and still have something left over to help to meet fixed costs. This will, however, be no more than making the best of a bad job in the short run, and will not provide a long-run solution to their troubles. That can only come from a reduction in costs or a rise in price.

Looking at the short-run problem in greater detail, we can see that in each firm in Figure 54 the 'loss minimising' output is OM, for price is £OP per unit of output. Price (average revenue) therefore exceeds average variable cost MV (as shown on the average variable cost curve AVC) by QV. This means that it will be worth while for the firm to continue running in the short run. For some fixed costs can be covered after variable costs have been met. In this case, for example, £PQVT is available to meet fixed costs. The firm is losing £PRSQ, which is less than it would have lost if it had closed down altogether, but had to go on meeting fixed costs. It would then have lost £RSVT.

If short-run price were only OP', losses would still be met with at every output. For example, if output were OM, average cost would be £OR (= MS) and losses per unit £RP'. In this case, however, average variable cost is not covered. At no output can variable costs be covered by revenue, and far from helping to meet fixed costs, the fact that the firm remains in production is merely making things worse. For example, at output OM the firm is losing an additional £P'Q'VT by refusing to close down altogether. It will therefore pay the firm to stop producing anything at all, even in the short run, though it may be possible to reopen later.

What can we conclude from this analysis ? We can see that, in the short run, it is possible for firms to bring themselves into a position of equilibrium where they are producing that output which maximises profits or minimises losses, even though in some cases this may mean that production stops altogether. One is entitled to assume that it will not be difficult for the firm to do this even in a short period of time. But it will be very much less likely that the industry will be able to bring itself into a 'full' equilibrium in the short run. For such a 'full' equilibrium can only occur when all firms are earning normal profits. A little reflection will be sufficient to convince one that it is only by accident—only if there happens to be just the right number of firms—that the whole industry will be in equilibrium in the short run. It is much more probable that there will have to be a long-run adjustment before the number of firms in the industry can change and full equilibrium be brought about. It is important to realise that we have shown two firms only in our diagrams, simply

for the sake of convenience For, since all factors are homogeneous, the situation will be the same in every firm in the industry.
But it should not be forgotten that the analysis only applies to
an industry where there is a large number of firms producing a
homogeneous product.

(b) *Entrepreneurs Heterogeneous, other Factors Homogeneous*

If entrepreneurs are not all identical in efficiency, then costs
can differ between firms even though all factor prices are the

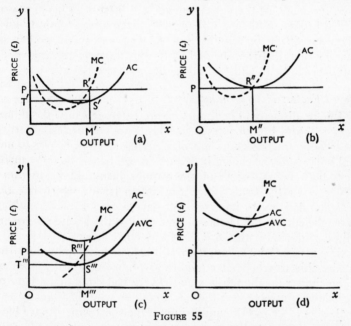

FIGURE 55

same to all firms and all factors except entrepreneurs are homogeneous. The more efficient entrepreneurs will be able to produce
more efficiently than the others, and their firms' costs will therefore be lower. Different firms will be producing different outputs
at different cost, even though all firms make the same product
and sell it at the same price. The kind of situation which is
likely to exist in the short run is shown in Figure 55.

Firm A has the most efficient entrepreneur of the four firms
shown, and it is in short-run equilibrium producing the output
OM' and earning supernormal profits of PR'S'T'. Firm B, with
a somewhat less efficient entrepreneur, produces an equilibrium

output of OM″ and earns only normal profits. Firm C has a still less efficient entrepreneur and loses money. But since firm C is covering its variable costs, it pays it to go on producing the output OM‴ in the short run, for losses are thereby minimised. Finally, firm D has the least efficient entrepreneur of the four firms, and even in the short run cannot cover variable costs at any output. It pays it to close down.

This diagram shows, in miniature, the situation in a perfectly competitive industry when entrepreneurs differ in ability. In the short run some of the entrepreneurs will be making large supernormal profits. Others will be making large losses. In each case the firm will be in equilibrium earning maximum profits by equating marginal revenue and cost. But the industry as a whole is unlikely to be in 'full' equilibrium in the short run.

(c) *All Factors Heterogeneous*

Where all factors of production are heterogeneous, the differences in costs between firms are likely to be even larger than where only entrepreneurs are of differing efficiency. The same kind of situation as shown in Figure 55 will occur, but the differences between the costs of the various firms are likely to be greater. For the firms which can obtain labour which is more efficient relatively to its wage will have a cost advantage. The more efficient are the factors a firm is using, the greater its profits will be compared with those earned by other firms.

The general conclusion, then, still holds. Each individual firm will be able to reach an equilibrium profit-maximising position in the short run, though it may (in very bad conditions) have to close down entirely. But there is no reason why the industry as a whole should be in full equilibrium in the short run. As we have seen, most firms will usually be earning either supernormal or subnormal profits in the short run. Only in the long run is equilibrium in the industry as a whole likely to come about—by an increase or a decrease in the number of firms in the industry.

4. LONG-RUN EQUILIBRIUM OF THE FIRM AND INDUSTRY

What, then, is likely to happen in a perfectly competitive industry in the long run? Because we are assuming that there is perfect competition, there will be no restrictions on entry into the industry and all factors of production will be perfectly mobile. It is therefore reasonable to argue that in the long run firms will enter or leave the industry until no firm outside the industry thinks it could earn normal profits if it were to enter the industry. Let us again consider what will happen in our three sets of conditions. We shall now need to use long-run cost curves instead of short-run ones, but this is the only difference in the analysis.

(a) All Factors of Production Homogeneous

Where all factors of production are homogeneous and each factor has a given and uniform price, it is not difficult to see that the industry will be in 'full' equilibrium in the long run. Each firm will adjust its output so as to equate marginal revenue with marginal cost. But in the long run each firm will also be in the position shown in Figure 56b, where average cost, average revenue, marginal cost and marginal revenue are all equal to each other and to price. This is the 'full equilibrium' position. It will be reached because, since all firms have identical cost curves and since there is free entry and perfect mobility, firms will enter or leave the industry until all are earning normal profits. And because costs are identical, if any one firm is earning normal profits all firms will be. In perfect competition, with all factors homogeneous, each firm and the industry as a whole will be in full equilibrium where marginal revenue = marginal cost = average cost = average revenue (price).

It is interesting to note that in full equilibrium each firm will be producing the 'optimum' output where average cost is at a minimum. This is advantageous to consumers since the product in question is being produced in the cheapest possible way without any firm making a loss. But *all* firms can only be producing the optimum output if all have the same minimum point to their cost curves, and this is unlikely to happen if all factors are not homogeneous. So we must now turn to the second situation where not all factors are homogeneous.

(b) Entrepreneurs Heterogeneous, all other Factors Homogeneous

As we have seen, where entrepreneurs are heterogeneous, some firms will be able to produce the same output at lower cost than others. This means that even in the long run it is conceivable that some firms will be able to earn 'supernormal' profits. Let us consider the two firms shown in Figure 56, firm A in Figure 56a and firm B in 56b.

Firm A has a more efficient entrepreneur, and therefore has lower costs than firm B. Let us assume that in the long run firm B

is just efficient enough to remain in the industry and to earn
normal profits. We could describe it as a 'marginal' firm. It is
'on the margin of profitability' because any fall in price would, in
the long run, send it out of the industry. Since firm A has a more
efficient entrepreneur, it is able to earn supernormal profits of
£PRST even in the long run. It can therefore be described as
an 'intra-marginal' firm. The only way in which firm A could be
forced to earn normal profits in the long run would be for there

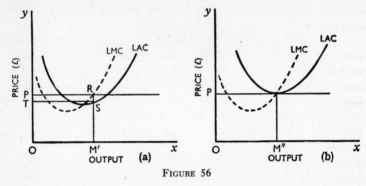

FIGURE 56

to be an influx of very efficient producers able to compete more
effectively with firm A than firms like B. This eventuality is, of
course, a possible one, but it is not necessarily a likely one, and
it would, of course, drive B out of the industry. It therefore
follows that even in the long run some firms will be able to earn
supernormal profits if they have more efficient entrepreneurs than
other firms.

(c) *All Factors Heterogeneous*

The same result will occur where all factors are heterogeneous.
The firms with the most efficient factors will be able to earn
supernormal profits even when 'marginal' firms are only just
earning normal profits. It is important to bear in mind that this
whole analysis is based on the assumption that normal profits
are the same for *all* entrepreneurs—and this need not be the case.

5. EXTERNAL ECONOMIES AND DISECONOMIES

We have now almost reached a stage where we can construct
the short- and long-run supply curves of a perfectly competitive
industry. First, however, we must discuss external economies

and diseconomies of production. In the previous chapter we discussed those economies of production obtained by changing the internal organisation of the firm as output changes, *internal economies and diseconomies*—economies and diseconomies resulting from its own internal organisation which enable the firm to produce more or less efficiently at some outputs than at others. We must now discuss *external economies and diseconomies*. These are those economies and diseconomies in production which depend on increases in the output of the whole industry rather than on increases in the output of the individual firm.

External economies occur where an increase in the size of an industry leads to lower costs for the individual firms composing the industry. For example, in the coal-mining industry, the fact that, in pumping water from its own workings, a mine also pumps water from the workings of other mines, means that the more pits there are in the area, the drier each pit will be. Another very important type of external economy is to be found where the efficient development of the industry depends greatly on the interchange of technical information between firms. In such a case it is obvious that the larger the industry is, the more feasible and worthwhile it will be to set up large-scale information services and to publish such things as trade newspapers and magazines.

On the other hand, it is perfectly possible for a growth in the size of an industry to lead to external diseconomies—to rises in costs. For example, it may well happen that if an industry expands it needs more workers skilled in a particular kind of work. In such conditions, if workers are not all equally efficient, it may be necessary to attract less efficient workers away from other industries. Thus, even if money wages remain constant, wage costs will rise as less and less efficient labour is taken on. But it is quite possible that, in order to attract labour away from other industries, wages may have to be raised for the particular type of labour needed. This will be a diseconomy of increased production which is external to the individual firm—the increased size of the industry as a whole has raised the costs of the individual firm.

External economies and diseconomies need to be brought into our analysis because we are about to consider the nature of the supply curve of the perfectly competitive industry. The shape of such a supply curve will depend, in part at least, on whether external economies or diseconomies arise as an industry increases or decreases the scale of its operations.

6. THE SUPPLY CURVE OF THE PERFECTLY COMPETITIVE INDUSTRY

Our main aim in this chapter and the preceding one has been to bring us to a position where we can build up a supply curve for a perfectly competitive industry. This is an essential step before we return to a discussion of the relationships between demand and supply, outlined in Chapter I. The shape of a competitive supply curve will not, however, always be the same. It will depend on the production conditions underlying it. Let

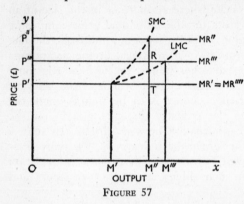

FIGURE 57

us therefore consider what the shape of the supply curve will be, with various different assumptions about these underlying conditions. The simplest assumption we can make is that all factors of production are homogeneous and are in perfectly elastic supply to the industry. We shall continue to assume throughout that there is perfect competition in the factor market so that the prices of all units of each factor are the same.

We can consider the supply curve of the industry in three different situations. First, we may see what it will be in the short run when not only is the number of firms given, but also the size of the individual firm cannot be altered. Second, we shall consider a long-run situation where we shall assume that the individual firm is able to alter the scale of its operations, but where, for the moment, we shall assume that the number of firms remains constant. Third, we shall consider a long-run situation where we shall assume that both the number of firms and the scale of operations in the individual firm are able to change.

Let us now assume that the initial situation is one where both the industry and firm are in full equilibrium with each firm producing at the minimum point of both its short- and long-run cost curve. This situation can be seen in Figure 57.

All firms in the industry will have identical cost curves because factors are homogeneous, and will therefore originally be in long-run equilibrium, where they are producing an output of OM′ and selling it at a price of £OP′. Marginal revenue, shown by the curve P′ – MR′, is equal to both short- and long-run marginal cost for all firms in the industry, and all these firms are earning normal profits. Since competition is perfect, marginal revenue will equal average revenue (price).

In order to discover what the shape of the industry's supply curve is, let us assume that the price of the product rises to OP″ and the marginal revenue curve rises to P″ – MR″. In the short

run it is apparent that the supply curve of the individual firm is, in perfect competition, its short-run marginal cost curve SMC. The only way in which any firm can produce more in the short run is by expanding output along its short-run marginal cost curve. In fact, if price rises, as in Figure 57, to OP″, marginal revenue

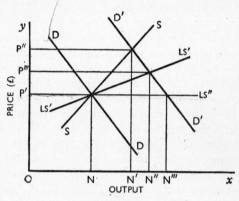

FIGURE 58

will equal marginal cost at the output OM″. Since all firms are identical (on our present assumption), the total increase in the output of the industry as price rises to OP″ will be M′M″ multiplied by the number of firms in the industry. Or, to put it another way, the supply curve of the industry will be a lateral summation of the supply curves of the individual firms. In Figure 58 it has been assumed that the industry consists of ten identical firms with the cost curves shown in Figure 57. The short-run supply curve of the industry is the curve SS. It shows that when price rises from OP′ to OP″, because the demand curve shifts from DD to D′D′, output rises from ON to ON′—by NN′—which is ten times M′M″ in Figure 57. (The distance M′M″ in Figure 57 is not one-tenth of the distance NN′ in Figure 58, because the scale on the x-axis is greater in Figure 57 than in Figure 58.)

It is clear that the short-run supply curve of a competitive industry will always slope upwards, since the short-run marginal cost curves of the individual firms will always slope upwards too. The steepness of the industry's short-run supply curve will depend on the slope of the cost curves of the individual firms. Where the cost structures of all the individual firms in the industry are identical, the elasticity of the industry's supply curve will be equal to the elasticity of the separate firms' marginal cost curves. The only general rule one can lay down is that the industry's short-run supply curve must slope upwards to the right.

We must now consider what will be the industry's long-run supply curve, assuming first of all that the number of firms remains constant. If this happens, the long-run equilibrium situation in Figure 57 will be where output is OM‴ and price OP‴. The long-run marginal cost curve of the individual firm (LMC in Figure 57) will be less steep than the short-run one, and output will be able to expand more than in the short run (by M′M‴ instead of by M′M″). Because output is able to expand, price falls—to OP‴. The long-period supply curve of the industry (with the number of firms fixed) will be the curve LS′ in Figure 58. The increase in the output of the industry is now NN″ compared with the original output of ON. NN″ is ten times M′M‴ in Figure 57. This particular type of long-run supply curve thus slopes upwards to the right—though less steeply than the short-run supply curve. It slopes upwards because the long-run marginal cost curves of the individual firms on which it depends, will also slope upwards. It may be noted that in this new long-run situation, with price OP‴, all the firms in the industry will be earning abnormal profits, as shown in Figure 57. This can happen, even in the long run, because the number of firms in the industry is assumed to be constant.

Finally, we must consider the more usual long-run situation where not only can the *size* of all firms in the industry alter, but it is also assumed that the *number* of firms can change. We assume, in fact, that there is free entry into the industry, and that new firms continue to enter until no abnormal profits are being earned. In the short run a firm in this condition will produce, in Figure 57, the output OM″ at the price OP″. But in the long run the individual firm, shown in Figure 57, will be in exactly the same position as in the original equilibrium. Output will be OM′ and price OP′. Marginal revenue will be shown by the curve P′ – MR⁗ which is identical with the curve P′ – MR′. New firms will have entered the industry and all abnormal profits will have been competed away. The output of each firm is once again OM′, but, because there are now more firms, the output of the industry has increased. This can be seen from Figure 58. The long-run supply curve, where the number of firms can alter, is the curve $P' - LS''$, and it will be seen that, in equilibrium, the output of the industry is now ON'''. This long-run supply curve is horizontal because new firms have entered the industry—firms which are identical with those already there—and marginal cost in each firm has returned to the original level. Provided that all factors are homogeneous, the long-run supply curve of the industry (with free entry) will be a horizontal straight line and supply price will be the same whatever the output. This is the simplest possible kind of 'free entry' long-run supply curve, and represents a first approximation to reality.

It is unlikely that in practice all factors will be homogeneous. It is much more likely that entrepreneurs, at least, will be heterogeneous. If factors other than entrepreneurs are heterogeneous, it is reasonable to look upon this as an external diseconomy of the industry. All firms may have to hire some less efficient factors if the size of the industry increases. The increased size of the industry will raise the costs of all firms. For even if all units of factors continue to earn the same money reward, the less efficient will produce a smaller output than the more efficient, and the cost of such output will rise. If entrepreneurs are heterogeneous, however, there will be no effect on the costs of firms previously in the industry if an expansion brings in new entrepreneurs. It will only be the new firms which have higher costs. This situation is therefore not the same as where heterogeneity of other factors causes external diseconomies. Let us now consider what will be the shape of the supply curve of the industry where entrepreneurs are heterogeneous, but all other factors are homogeneous.

So far as the short-run supply curve is concerned, the fact that entrepreneurs are heterogeneous will make little difference. It will still represent a lateral summation of the short-run marginal cost curves of the individual firms. These marginal cost curves will, of course, now be different for each firm, so that the process of summing them will be more complicated than where factors are homogeneous. But, since the number of firms is fixed in the short run, and since the short-run marginal cost curve of the firm always rises fairly steeply, the short-run supply curve of the industry will always rise too. Whether or not factors of production are homogeneous, the short-run supply curve is bound to slope upwards to the right, but with heterogeneous factors it will slope upwards rather more steeply.

In the long run the number of firms will be able to increase, assuming that there is free entry. But since the new firms which enter the industry in the long run, in order to raise output, will be run by less efficient entrepreneurs, their costs will be higher at each level of output than in existing firms. For long-run equilibrium to occur at a greater output, the price of the industry's product must have risen. Only in that way can less efficient firms be attracted into the industry (and be maintained there). The rise in price needed to produce a given increase in output will be smaller than in the short run. This is partly because in the long run firms will be able to produce an increased output more efficiently than in the short run. Partly, however, it is because in the long run, as the number of firms increases, existing individual firms will be able to reduce their output again and so reduce their marginal costs. The supply curve of the industry, with heterogeneous entrepreneurs and all other factors homogeneous, will therefore slope upwards, whilst with all factors homogeneous it will be horizontal. But it is likely to slope upwards rather less steeply in the long run than it does in the short run.

Finally, we must consider what will be the shape of the industry's supply curve where there are external economies and diseconomies. We may here confine our attention to the long-run supply curve. External economies and diseconomies can only be important in the long run, for only in the long run can the size of the industry alter and any repercussions of this on costs of production occur.

We have seen that if all factors of production are homogeneous and in perfectly elastic supply, the long-run supply curve of the industry will be horizontal. If in such conditions there are external economies, the long-run supply curve will slope downwards. If, on the other hand, there are external diseconomies, the supply curve will slope upwards. We have also seen that where entrepreneurship is not homogeneous in a perfectly competitive industry, but all other factors are homogeneous, the long-run supply curve will slope upwards. In this case, the existence of external diseconomies will accentuate the upward slope of the supply curve. External economies, however, will offset to some extent, and perhaps, if strong enough, even reverse, the upward slope of the supply curve. The long-run supply curve could thus slope either upwards or downwards or be horizontal, depending on how strong the external economies are.

To sum up, then, in the short run the supply curve of the perfectly competitive industry will always slope upwards to the right. In the long run, assuming that there is free entry, it is likely to slope upwards unless all factors are homogeneous, but it may conceivably slope downwards if there are sufficiently great external economies as the industry expands.

We have now seen how a supply curve is built up. Our next main task is to analyse the relationship between demand curves and supply curves. In particular we shall be able to study with greater precision the differences between short- and long-run supply curves. First, however, it will be useful to say something about elasticity of supply, where supply curves are real curves and not straight lines as we assumed in our discussion of elasticity of supply in Chapter I.

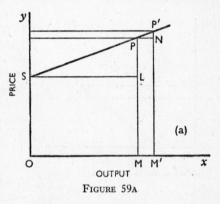

FIGURE 59A

We saw there that any supply curve which is a straight line passing through the origin, whatever its slope, will possess unitary elasticity of supply. We may now add that any straight-line supply curve which cuts the (vertical) y-axis (or whose projection cuts the y-axis) will have an elasticity greater than one. Any straight-line supply curve which cuts the x-axis (or whose projection cuts the x-axis) will have an elasticity which is less than one. This can be proved with the aid of Figures 59a and 59b.

In Figures 59a and 59b SP′ is a supply curve and SL, PN and OM′ are all parallel. Now, we saw in Chapter I that elasticity of supply equals

$$\frac{\text{Increase in amount supplied}}{\text{Amount supplied}} \div \frac{\text{Increase in price}}{\text{Price}}.$$

Therefore over the range PP′ on the supply curve SP′ in Figure 59a, elasticity of supply $= \dfrac{MM'}{OM} \div \dfrac{NP'}{MP}$. This can, however, be written alternatively as $\dfrac{PN}{OM} \div \dfrac{NP'}{MP} = \dfrac{PN}{P'N} \times \dfrac{MP}{SL\,(=OM)}$. But since

L

the triangles SLP and PNP' are similar, $\dfrac{PN}{P'N}$ is equal to $\dfrac{SL}{PL}$. The formula can therefore be written $\dfrac{SL}{PL} \times \dfrac{MP}{SL} = \dfrac{MP}{PL}$. In Figure 59a MP is greater than PL, so that elasticity is greater than one. It is clear, in fact, that elasticity of supply will always be greater than one, if the supply curve (or its projection) cuts the y-axis. For, whenever this happens, MP will be greater than PL and $\dfrac{MP}{PL}$ will be greater than one. In some cases, as in Figure 59b, the supply curve cuts the x-axis. In Figure 59b the distance PL is now

between P and the point L where a perpendicular SL from the y-axis cuts PM projected below the x-axis. The y-axis has been projected below O to meet the supply curve projected below the x-axis. In such cases PL will exceed MP. Elasticity of supply $\dfrac{MP}{PL}$ will always be less than one, when the supply curve cuts the x-axis. Finally, whenever the supply curve passes through the origin, PL and MP will always be of equal lengths. Elasticity of supply will always be one.

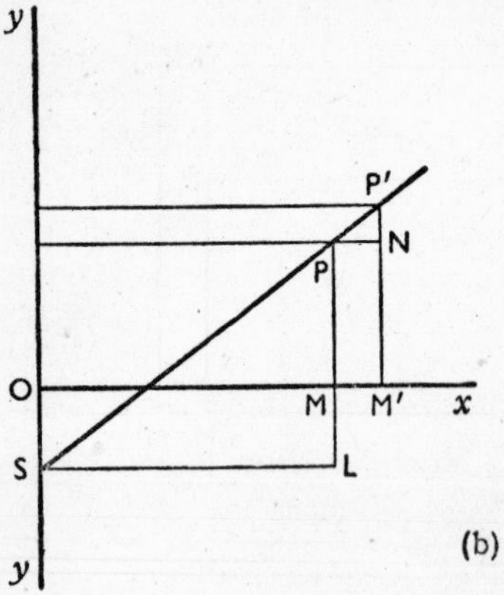

(b)

FIGURE 59B

It is simple enough to apply this analysis to finding the elasticity of supply curves which are true curves. If one draws a tangent to any point on such a curve, the position at which the tangent cuts an axis will indicate whether elasticity at the point of tangency is greater or less than or equal to one. If the tangent to a supply curve cuts the y-axis, the supply curve has an elasticity greater than one at the point to which the tangent is drawn. If the tangent cuts the x-axis, the supply curve has a point elasticity of less than one. If the tangent passes through the origin, point elasticity is equal to one where the tangent touches the supply curve. This provides a simple rule for discovering whether elasticity of supply is greater than, less than, or equal to one. The precise numerical elasticity can, of course, be calculated in the usual way from the formula for elasticity of supply.

SUGGESTED READING

Alfred Marshall, *Principles of Economics* (8th Edition), London, 1920, Book IV, chapters 9 and 13, Book V *passim*.

Joan Robinson, *Economics of Imperfect Competition*, London, 1933, chapters vi and vii.

E. H. Chamberlin, *The Theory of Monopolistic Competition* (5th Edition), Cambridge, Mass., 1946, chapter i.

CHAPTER VII

COMPETITIVE EQUILIBRIUM

1. EQUILIBRIUM AND CHANGE

WE have seen how the demand and supply curves for a product made by a perfectly competitive industry are determined. We must now use these curves to see in greater detail how equilibrium between demand and supply is brought about. We touched on this problem at the end of Chapter I and showed how, with given demand and supply curves, the equilibrium price of a good would be determined by the intersection of these curves. The amount demanded at this price would equal the amount supplied, and the market would be in equilibrium.

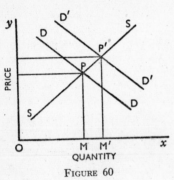
FIGURE 60

Equilibrium in the market is therefore a situation depending on and satisfying the existing conditions of demand and supply at any given moment of time. But, in addition, equilibrium implies a situation of rest, or absence of change, over a period of time. In this sense, the market is said to remain in a state of equilibrium only so long as demand and supply conditions are unchanged. If either demand conditions or supply conditions, or both of them, alter, the market passes from the old to a new equilibrium.

Such a change can be shown in a diagram. For example, in Figure 60 the demand curve shifts upwards and to the right from DD to D′D′, whilst supply conditions remain exactly the same. For the sake of simplicity, it is assumed that the new demand curve is parallel to the old. The new equilibrium price is higher and the new equilibrium amount demanded and supplied is larger than the old. This shows itself in the fact that P′ is above and to the right of P. This change can be called for short a rise in demand price or an increase of demand. Consumers are now

148

willing to buy any given amount of the good at a higher price than before. Similarly, at any given price they are now willing to buy a larger amount than in the old equilibrium situation. The effect of an increase in demand is to raise price and to increase sales.

In Figure 61 it is the supply curve which shifts to the right and downwards from SS to S'S', while demand conditions remain constant. This diagram shows an 'increased supply' or a

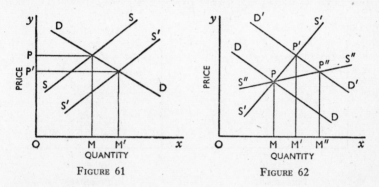

FIGURE 61   FIGURE 62

'fall in supply price'. At each price sellers will supply a larger amount than before. The result is that sales increase from OM to OM' and price falls from OP to OP'.

It is not necessarily the case, however, that a given change in demand or supply conditions always causes the same change in price or amount demanded. With a given increase of demand, price rises more and sales increase less the steeper the supply curve is. For example, in Figure 62 the supply curve S'S' is steeper than the curve S"S". P' is above and to the left of P", showing that price would rise more and sales increase less with the supply curve S'S' than with the curve S"S", when a given increase in demand took place. Since the slope of both supply curves relates to the same units on the x-axis and y-axis, the steeper curve is less elastic, at each price, than the flatter curve. With inelastic supply, a given increase in demand raises price more than with elastic supply. Similarly, with a given increase of supply, price will fall more with an inelastic demand curve than with an elastic one.

If both demand and supply increase, sales are bound to increase. But price may or may not rise. It will rise if the amount which would now be demanded at the old price exceeds the amount which would now be supplied at that price. But it will fall if the amount which would now be supplied at the old price exceeds the amount which would now be demanded at that price. And if the amount demanded at the old price still equals the amount supplied, price will not change. The first case may be called a smaller increase of supply than of demand, the second case a greater increase of supply than of demand, and the third an equal increase of demand and supply. These first two cases are illustrated in Figure 63, where price rises from OP to OP' when

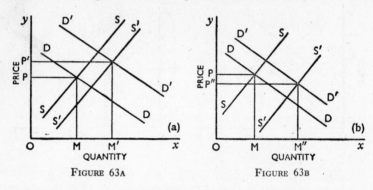

FIGURE 63A   FIGURE 63B

demand increases more than supply (Figure 63a), but falls from OP to OP" when supply increases more than demand (Figure 63b). The amount of the good exchanged rises from OM to OM' in the first case and from OM to OM" in the second.

In just the same way, an increase of demand with a simultaneous decrease of supply will raise price and *increase* sales if the new demand price for the old equilibrium amount is higher than its new supply price. Similarly, sales will *diminish* and price will rise if the new supply price for the old amount is higher than its new demand price. In the first case the increase of demand is greater than, and in the second case smaller than, the decrease of supply. Both cases are illustrated in Figure 64, where sales increase from OM to OM' in Figure 64a, but diminish from OM to OM' in Figure 64b. In Figures 64a and 64b OM and OP represent the old, and OM' and OP' the new, prices and amounts.

It is the function of the market to bring about equilibrium at every moment of time between the forces of demand and supply at that moment. But since one or other of these forces is continually changing, at any rate in respect of some goods, one or more market prices will be changing at every moment. These price changes may be due to changes in consumers' tastes or incomes on the demand side, or to changes in technical knowledge, or the relative scarcity of factors of production on the supply side. All such changes can be represented in the way we have shown by shifts of the demand and the supply curves respectively. Such changes may take the form of a gradual increase of demand or supply, or a gradual diminution of them, when they will be accompanied by a corresponding gradual change in price. Again, they may take the form of alternating increase and diminution of

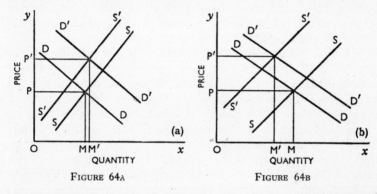

FIGURE 64A   FIGURE 64B

demand or supply. In this latter case, market price will fluctuate through time. Price changes of these types can be adequately explained by the kind of analysis we have discussed in this section.

2. EQUILIBRIUM AND TIME

There is one other type of change in demand and supply conditions which is important enough to merit special study. We have already seen that supply conditions will be different the longer the period of time which one takes into consideration. For example, if demand suddenly increases, price is likely to rise sharply in the short run because firms will be expanding output along fairly steep short-run marginal cost curves. But in the long run firms will be reorganised so as to produce the new and higher output more efficiently. For firms will now be producing along their rather flatter long-run marginal cost curves. In addition, new firms will have been able to enter the industry. The initial change in equilibrium prices is caused by the changed conditions of demand, but the succeeding changes in price over time depend on the response of conditions of supply to the new demand situation. And the magnitude of such changes in supply will usually differ according to the length of time being considered.

Economists find it important to discuss the way in which supply responds to any once-and-for-all change in demand conditions. The reason why such a study is necessary is to be found in the nature of technical conditions of production. It will always take time to make those adjustments in the size and the organisation of a factory which are necessary if it is to work as efficiently as possible at any new scale of output. Once demand has increased (or decreased) a series of adjustments will be put in motion in every firm in the industry, and these adjustments will bear fruit one after the other as time passes.

Now, it will usually be found that economists carrying out this type of analysis concentrate their attention on the response of supply through time to a sudden and permanent change in demand conditions. There is an important reason for this. As we have seen, the reason why changes in supply conditions can only be made after a period of time has elapsed, is that technical factors prohibit instantaneous adjustment to changed demand conditions. But there is nothing on the demand side to correspond to this slow process of adjustment on the supply side. There is no reason why, if supply conditions change, demand conditions should change as well, or, if they do, why they should change differently in the short run and the long run. Changes in consumers' tastes are not dependent on technology in the way that supply conditions are. Admittedly consumers' tastes may, and probably will, change as time goes on. But this will be a change of data and not a change induced by changed supply conditions. There is no necessary reason why the long-run demand curve should differ from the short-run demand curve, however odd the behaviour of supply has been.

This asymmetry between demand and supply is important because it explains the apparent preoccupation of economists with adjustments of supply over time to once-and-for-all changes in demand and not *vice versa*. It does not mean that either demand or supply is more important as a factor determining price. Both are equally important. But demand and supply do not respond either equally, or equally quickly, to changed conditions. We must expect that the longer is the period during which demand and supply are coming into equilibrium, the more changes will have time to take place. If we were to study the changes in demand and supply which would take place, in response to any change of data, during many successive very short periods of time, we should find that we had introduced unnecessary and intolerable detail into the analysis.

To avoid this problem, it is now usual to follow the method of analysis used by Marshall. He found that all the most important problems raised by the introduction of time into economic analysis of this kind could be dealt with by considering the way in which, and the extent to which, equilibrium between demand and supply was brought about in three periods of time : the market period, the short period, and the long period. The properties of these three types of time period can be summarised as follows :

(a) The Market Period

Marshall conceived of the market period as being only a single day, or a very few days. The fundamental feature of the market period is that it will be so short that supplies of the commodity in question will be limited to existing stocks, or, at most, to supplies which are 'in sight'. On the basis of this 'market' supply and of the existing 'market' demand for the commodity, a temporary equilibrium will be brought about between demand and supply. With perfect competition between buyers and between sellers, an equilibrium price will be determined. This 'market' equilibrium price will, however, only exist temporarily and it will not be reasonable to expect that the market equilibrium price will be similar to prices in preceding or succeeding 'market periods'.

(b) The Short Period

The short period, Marshall defined as a period which was long enough for supplies of a commodity to be altered by increases or decreases in current output, but not long enough for the fixed equipment producing this output to be adapted to produce larger or smaller outputs. In the terminology of the theory of the firm, we may say that output can be altered in the short period only by producing at a different point on a given short-run marginal cost curve. The size and kind of the individual plant would be taken as unalterable. No change in the scale of operations would be possible, nor could new firms enter the industry, in the short run.

Equilibrium brought about in this period will represent a 'short-period equilibrium' and supply will be able to adapt itself, at any rate partially, to a change in demand. It can therefore be expected that in the short period, a *short-period equilibrium price* will be brought about. Variations or oscillations in market price caused by conditions special to each separate market period will still occur, but these will tend to range round a fairly well-defined position of short-run equilibrium.

(c) The Long Period

In the long period, as defined by Marshall, there is time for firms' fixed equipment to be altered so that output is capable of adapting itself more fully to changes in demand conditions than it was in the short period. There is time to build new machines and factories, and old ones can be closed down or allowed to fall to pieces. A 'long-period equilibrium' between demand and supply will be brought about and in this equilibrium position supply will be able to adapt itself fully to any change in demand. Market equilibrium will now tend to show oscillations round, and variations from, a fairly clearly defined long-period equilibrium position.

For the sake of completeness, it may be added that Marshall also talked of a secular [1] or very long period, during which not only might all the changes which occur in the ordinary long period take place, but all the underlying economic factors, such as the size of population, supplies of raw materials, general conditions of capital supply and the like, would have time to alter. We shall not consider the secular period in any detail, since it is much too long to provide any really satisfactory generalisations for economic theory. In any case, the technique of analysis needed to study 'secular equilibrium' is the same as for ordinary long-period equilibrium.

3. 'NORMAL' PRICE

We must now introduce the concept of 'normal' price. Marshall defines 'normal action' as that which one expects to be taken by a person or group of persons under given conditions.[2] Similarly, 'normal results' are defined as those results which may reasonably be expected as the outcome of a given situation. 'Normal prices' are therefore those prices which may reasonably be expected in given conditions of demand and supply. But time is very im-

---

[1] Derived from Latin *saecula* and meaning age-long.
[2] *Principles of Economics*, p. 34.

portant here.   A different price will be 'normal' in the long period
from that which is 'normal' in the short period.   In our discussion
of equilibrium prices in short and long periods we shall really be
concerned with short- and long-period 'normal' prices—those
prices which one may reasonably expect to occur in the short
and long runs respectively.

An important reason for introducing Marshall's periods of
time is that it is thereby possible to throw light on the disputes
which have often raged between economists on whether demand
or supply is more important in determining price.   Marshall
likens this dispute to an argument about whether the upper or
lower blade of a pair of scissors really cuts a piece of paper.[1]
He says that if the upper blade is held still and the lower blade
moved, it is reasonable, provided one does not wish to be completely accurate, to say that the lower blade does the cutting.
Alternatively, if the lower blade is fixed and the upper moved, it
is reasonable, provided again that one makes no claim to scientific
accuracy, to say that the upper blade is cutting the paper.   Similarly, in certain circumstances, it is possible to say, with some
justification, that either demand or supply determines price.

For example, in a fish market where there is a given stock of
fish on hand, and where, owing to the danger that it will go bad
if kept for long, that stock must be quickly disposed of, it is not
unreasonable to say that price is governed by demand.   Since
supply is fixed, it is demand which determines price.   For the
sake of brevity, one may use this simplified argument, but one
cannot claim strict scientific accuracy.   At the other extreme, in
the long run when supply and demand changes have worked
themselves out fully, the 'normal' long-period price will be the
long-run money cost of production (including normal profits).
Ignoring the oscillations of market price, the long-period 'normal
price' around which such oscillations will occur can be roughly
described as determined by supply—by costs of production.
Again this is not strictly accurate, but has some truth in it.

The only really accurate answer to the question whether it is
supply or demand which determines price is that it is both.   At
times it will seem that one is more important than the other, for
one will be active and the other passive.   For example, if demand
remains constant but supply conditions vary, it is demand which
is passive and supply active.   But neither is more or less important
than the other in determining price.   It is, of course, important

---

[1] *Ibid.* p. 348.

to realise that, in practice, a long-period normal price will never be arrived at. There will usually be a change in some of the conditions underlying the long-period equilibrium before it has had time to come into being. The long run—like tomorrow—never comes.

We may now discuss the way in which prices are determined in these various time periods. We shall use the usual method of economic theory and proceed step by step. We shall concentrate our attention on those things which seem most important, by assuming that all other things, except the ones in which we are interested, are equal. As Marshall put it, 'He (the economist) segregates those disturbing causes, whose wanderings happen to be inconvenient, for the time in a pound called *Ceteris Paribus*'.[1] It should always be remembered that whilst in this way it is possible to construct a simple theory, it will not be a fully accurate theory. The more simple a theory is, the less accurate it must inevitably be. As Marshall says, 'A man is likely to be a better economist if he trusts to his common sense and practical instincts, than if he professes to study the theory of value and is resolved to find it easy'.[2]

4. MARKET EQUILIBRIUM

In order to explain the importance of Marshall's time periods for price theory, we shall study the way in which the supply of a commodity adapts itself through time to a once-and-for-all change in the demand for it.

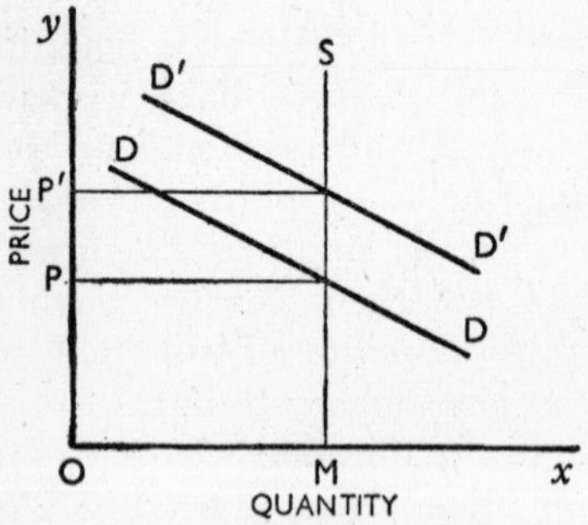

FIGURE 65

Let us imagine a fish market with a given supply of fish. We assume that the fish cannot be kept overnight and that the whole supply must therefore be sold quickly, since none of it can be kept back. Competition between buyers and sellers will mean that the equilibrium price is established where demand is equal to supply. This position is shown in Figure 65 where the supply curve is the vertical straight line MS. This implies that sellers are determined to sell the whole supply of fish, OM, whatever its price—that

[1] *Op. cit.* p. 366.   [2] *Op. cit.* p. 368.

sellers have no demand for their own fish. This is the assumption which we are making throughout Part One, and it seems a fairly reasonable one. If the sellers did demand their own fish, the supply curve would slope upwards to the right in the normal fashion.

In this market, with demand conditions shown in the curve DD, the equilibrium price of OP will be reached, and the whole supply of fish will be disposed of. If, however, there is a sudden and permanent rise in the demand for fish to D'D', perhaps because of the sudden advent of a serious cattle disease, the price of fish would rise to OP'. There would be no increase in the supply of fish, since the only available supplies are already in existence and cannot be increased except after a day or two. The whole supply of fish would still be sold, but the price would rise. Owing to the fact that supply is fixed, demand exerts its full influence on the price of fish, which rises considerably.

5. SHORT-PERIOD EQUILIBRIUM

In the short period, the supply would begin to react to the change in the demand for fish, which we are assuming to be permanent. In this short-period analysis we shall ignore factors like changes in the weather which would cause daily fluctuations in the number of fish caught and therefore affect prices from day to day. The influence of the weather can only be seen in periods which are too short to affect our analysis at this stage. Similarly, we shall ignore changes which can only occur over very long periods of time. We shall, for instance, assume that there is not enough time for low wages in the fishing industry to persuade sailors to become bank clerks or farmers instead. Such influences affecting the supply of sailors can only enter our analysis if it relates to long periods of time. We therefore abstract from these problems by 'impounding them' for the moment in *ceteris paribus*.

The problem which has to be faced in the short run is, 'How can we attract sailors into the fishing industry until more of them have been trained? And how can we renovate, or otherwise put into service, more boats?' The answer will usually be, 'By offering wages to sailors which are high enough to attract them from jobs on passenger and cargo boats and by ensuring that the owners of old and not very efficient boats earn enough to make it worth while using them'. By definition, no new firms can enter the fishing industry in the short run but those already in it can use their existing equipment more intensively.

The price which will solve this short-run problem, the 'short-period normal price' of fish, will be that price for fish which will rapidly ensure that enough sailors and boats go out fishing for all of them to earn the minimum amount of money they are prepared to accept for an average day's work. The market price will still oscillate round this 'normal' price, but the normal price itself will be high enough to ensure that the additional factors of production persuaded to work in the fishing industry find it worth remaining there. This short-run 'normal' price must inevitably be higher than the original market price, for sailors can only be attracted away from other ships by higher wages, and old boats can only be enticed back to sea by higher returns.

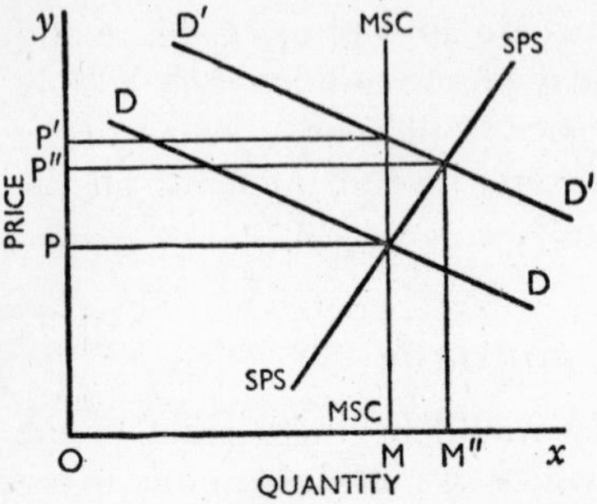

FIGURE 66

In Figure 66 the curve MSC —the market supply curve— shows that in the new demand conditions (given by the demand curve D'D') the market price rises from OP to OP' when demand changes. The short-period supply curve SPS shows that, in the short period, supply is able to adapt itself somewhat to the changed demand conditions. The short-run normal price will be OP" which is higher than the original market price OP, but not so high as the second market price of OP'. The supply of fish has also increased slightly from OM to OM". More fish is sold and price is not quite so high as in the market period.

6. LONG-PERIOD EQUILIBRIUM

In the long period, supply conditions are fully adapted to meet the new demand conditions. The problems and changes which have to be considered in the long period are rather different from those which arise in the short period. For example, new fishermen would have to be attracted from other jobs, and new firms set up. But it is not likely that the new workers in the industry would be noticeably more or less competent fishermen than the original ones. New boats, nets and other equipment would be produced, and this might well affect the industry producing them. For example, the increased demand for such equipment might enable it to be produced more cheaply if the industry making it were able to expand and to reap external economies. It is therefore not easy to decide what the shape of the long-period supply curve of the fishing industry will be.

In Figure 67 the long-period supply curve (LPS) slopes upwards to the right, though less steeply than does the short-period curve shown in Figures 66 and 67. The long-period 'normal' price is OP‴, as compared with the short-run price of OP″, which

is higher, and the original market price OP, which is lower. In the long run it is possible to obtain fish more cheaply and in larger quantities than in the short run, but only at a rather higher price than in the original situation. In the long run, therefore, supply is able to adapt itself as fully as possible to the changed conditions of demand. The extent to

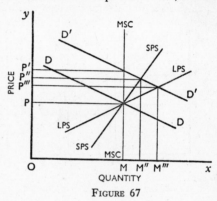

FIGURE 67

which the long-run price differs from the original price thus depends on the ease with which additional supplies can be acquired in the long run. Market prices will still oscillate and fluctuate but they will do so in the long run round a long-period 'normal' price.

It is, however, possible that the long-run supply curve may be horizontal—if the fishing industry is a constant cost industry—or even falling—if there are external economies as the industry expands in the long run. These cases are shown in Figure 68.

In Figures 68a and 68b the original market price is OP, which rises initially to OP′ when the change in demand takes place. The market supply is OM. In the long run, price falls again to OP, since the industry has a horizontal supply curve (LPS). The amount OM′ is now sold. With constant long-run costs, the long-run normal price is therefore the same as the original price. In Figure 68b the long-run normal price is OP″, which is lower than the original price because of external economies. The amount sold is OM″.

It follows, therefore, that the long-run normal price can be higher than, lower than, or the same as, the original market price, depending on supply conditions in the industry in question. The

short-period normal price, however, will invariably be higher than
the long-period normal price.   It is highly improbable that there
will be any change in the organisation of the industry, which will
increase the efficiency of the industry, which could be made in the
short period but could not be made in the long period.

It is probably worth pointing out that 'normal' prices are not
the same thing as 'average' prices unless prices are constant.
Normal prices are those prices to which one may expect actual
prices to tend ; average prices will be an arithmetical average of all

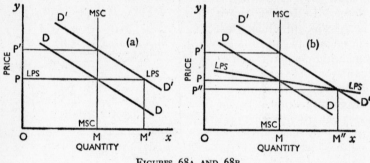

FIGURES 68A AND 68B

actual prices.   They will not only be influenced by fortuitous
fluctuations and oscillations, but will also take account of the
general trend towards the 'normal' price.

This analysis by means of time periods has enabled us to show,
in an elementary way, how prices vary over time.   It has enabled
us to drop the assumption, made practically throughout the previous chapters, that demand and supply conditions are given.   It
has allowed us to assume that both can, and often will, change.   In
technical economic language, we have proceeded from a static
analysis, where demand and supply conditions are given, to an
analysis of *comparative statics*, where demand and supply conditions are allowed to change and the new equilibrium is compared
with the old.

The construction of a truly dynamic theory of economics,
where more continuous changes in demand and supply conditions,
like those which occur in the real world, are analysed, is the ultimate goal of most theories of economics.   But such theories are
usually very complicated, and mean that a great deal of algebra
is needed.   We shall find it simpler in this book to confine
the analysis of the problems of time to a discussion which uses

the more easily manageable concept of Marshall's three different periods to study only comparative statics. After all, these give us the basis for quite a useful analysis.

SUGGESTED READING

Alfred Marshall, *Principles of Economics* (8th Edition), London, 1920, Book V, chapters 5-13.

Ragnar Frisch, 'Alfred Marshall's Theory of Value', *Quarterly Journal of Economics*, November 1950, p. 495.

M

CHAPTER VIII

MONOPOLY

1. THE ASSUMPTIONS

HAVING seen how prices and output are determined in a perfectly competitive industry, we must now see how they are arrived at when competition is not perfect. As we saw in Chapter V, the two limiting types of market situation, those of pure competition and pure monopoly, are not likely to be found very often in practice. In the real world it is the region of 'imperfect' competition lying between these limits in which one is interested. We turn now, therefore, to a study of the way in which prices and output are determined in conditions of imperfect competition. In making this transition from perfect to imperfect competition, we shall find it useful to keep some of the assumptions we have made so far, but others will be dropped. We shall now say explicitly which of the assumptions will be retained in this discussion of imperfect competition.

We shall continue to assume that there is perfect competition *between buyers*. We shall assume that there are many consumers buying each product, so that no one consumer is sufficiently important in the market to be able to have any influence on the price of the product by his own actions. So far as the individual consumer is concerned, the prices of all goods must be taken as given. We shall also continue to assume that each consumer is 'rational', that he bases his purchases on a scale of preferences which enables him to draw up indifference maps, and that from the indifference maps of such consumers it is possible to derive demand curves showing how much of each commodity they will buy at various prices. These individual demand curves can then be added together to give a market demand curve. The demand curve for the product of an individual *industry* therefore means exactly the same thing under imperfect competition as it does under perfect competition.

So far as the individual firm is concerned we shall continue to assume that the sole aim of its entrepreneur is to earn maximum profits. In other words, we keep the fundamental assumption of 'economic rationality'. Therefore, when diagrams are drawn showing the equilibrium position of the firm, such an equilibrium will always occur when marginal revenue equals marginal cost, whether competition is perfect or imperfect. There is, however, one important difference between the equilibrium position of the individual firm in perfect competition and its equilibrium position in imperfect competition. When competition is imperfect, there are no longer sufficient firms in the industry for a change in the output of any one of them to have a negligible effect on the output of the industry as a whole. Thus, whilst it is true that the nature of the demand curve for the product of the industry as a whole is not affected by the fact that competition is now imperfect, it will be found that the average revenue curve of the individual firm does have a different shape when competition is not perfect. We can no longer assume that the average revenue curve of the firm is a horizontal straight line when competition is imperfect. In conditions of perfect competition, where each individual firm has to take the price of the industry's product, once given, as fixed and unalterable, the firm's average revenue curve is a horizontal straight line. In imperfect competition this is no longer the case.

As has been stated earlier, when there is imperfect competition the average revenue curve of the individual firm slopes downwards throughout its length. This implies an important corollary. In perfect competition, since the firm's average revenue curve is a horizontal straight line, marginal revenue and average revenue are always equal. In imperfect competition, however, average revenue is always falling, and therefore marginal revenue falls as well, but even more swiftly. In geometrical terms, the marginal revenue curve always lies below the average revenue curve and normally slopes downwards more steeply. It will also be remembered that when, in perfect competition, the industry as a whole is in 'full' equilibrium, not only does marginal cost equal marginal revenue, but these are themselves equal both to average revenue and to average cost. In imperfect competition this is not the case. In equilibrium marginal revenue still equals marginal cost, but since marginal revenue is less than average revenue, marginal cost is also less than average revenue—than price.

These, then, are the main differences between the assumptions made in analysing perfect and imperfect competition. They are not very great differences. Unfortunately, however, there is no single representative case of imperfect competition as there is of perfect competition. Though the fundamental distinguishing characteristic of imperfect competition is that average revenue curves slope downwards throughout their length, they may well slope downwards at very different rates. Instead of having one single case of imperfect competition to compare with the single case of perfect competition, we can find some instances where the firm's average revenue curve slopes downwards only very gently and where competition is almost perfect, and other cases where that slope is very steep and competition is extremely imperfect. There is no single case of imperfect competition, but a whole range or series of cases representing progressively more and more imperfect competition.

Since the general term, imperfect competition, covers all situations where there is neither 'pure' competition nor 'pure' monopoly, it is usual to distinguish several separate and different smaller categories within the broad field of imperfect competition. We shall discuss these various narrower types of imperfect competition in turn. We shall begin with a type of market form which has always attracted the attention of economists—that of *monopoly*. Strictly interpreted, a 'monopolist' is the sole producer of his product, and the distinction between the firm and the industry, both producing the same product, so important in perfect competition, goes. The firm of the monopolist is not only a firm, it is an industry. It is the only firm producing the product in question. The firm, that is to say, takes on the characteristics of the industry, and has an average revenue curve which slopes downwards just as the demand curve for the product of an industry slopes downwards.

2. PURE MONOPOLY

Before embarking on the analysis of monopoly, where, although each firm is the only producer of a given good, this good has to compete indirectly with other goods all of which are competing for the same consumers' incomes, it will be useful to look for a time at the limiting case of 'pure' or 'perfect' monopoly, where competition even in this limited form is completely absent. We have already given a definition of 'pure' monopoly, and have shown that it will occur when the average revenue curve of the firm is a rectangular hyperbola with an elasticity of demand equal to one, and when the monopolist takes the whole of the community's income all the time.[1] It is important to remember, however, that

[1] See pp. 105-6.

unlike perfect competition, which is a reasonable approximation to reality in certain industries, pure monopoly is merely a theoretical limiting case.

No-one is a complete monopolist because in the end all producers must be competing for the limited resources of consumers. Ultimately all goods are competitive with each other, however imperfectly. This means that the only way to be a perfect monopolist would be to produce *all* goods. It is therefore useful to distinguish between 'monopoly' where one has competition but not very close competition, and 'pure monopoly' where one has no competition at all. For a real world monopolist is an imperfect competitor rather than the sole and absolute controller of all commodities.

The explanation of the way in which a 'pure' monopolist would fix his output and price need not detain us long, for the answer is very simple. Since a 'pure' monopolist earns a fixed and constant amount of money (the whole of all consumers' incomes), his profits will be at a maximum when his total costs are as low as possible. This will presumably happen when he is producing a very small output (perhaps only one unit) and selling it for an extremely high price. It could never pay a pure monopolist to produce more than a very small output so long as his costs were positive.

One merely has to state the kind of price-output policy a pure monopolist would follow to see how unrealistic the idea of pure monopoly is. No one producer in any country is in such a powerful position that he can sell a minute amount of his product for a fantastically high price taking the whole of consumers' incomes in the process. Pure monopoly is merely a theoretical limit. We must turn for a more realistic analysis to the producer who is called a 'monopolist' in the real world; to the producer who controls the whole supply of a single commodity which has no close substitutes. The question of how such a producer will fix his price and his output is much more important.

3. MONOPOLY AND PERFECT COMPETITION COMPARED

If we define a monopolist as the sole producer of a product which has no closely competing substitutes, it is possible to generalise about his price-output policy and to compare the equilibrium of the firm under monopoly with the equilibrium under perfect competition. It is important to remember at the outset that under monopoly, since this is an extreme form of imperfect competition, the average revenue curve of the firm will slope downwards throughout its length. One can then say first of all that no monopolist will ever fix the output of his product at any level where the elasticity of his average revenue curve is less than one. For if he were to do so, it would always be possible to increase his total receipts by restricting output. We have already seen that when elasticity on any average revenue curve is less than one, total receipts will be always falling as output increases—marginal revenue will be negative. It follows that total revenue will rise if output is decreased. So, provided that a monopolist's marginal costs are not negative (which is most unlikely), he will always be able to earn larger profits by reducing his output, if he is producing an output at which the elasticity of demand for his product is less than one. For, since marginal costs are invariably positive, a reduction in output will reduce total costs. At the same time, since elasticity of demand is less than one, a reduction in output will raise total revenue. Profits will therefore rise as output is reduced. Only if a monopolist has negative marginal costs, which seems impossible, will it pay him to produce an output where the elasticity of demand for his product is less than one.

If the elasticity of a monopolist's average revenue curve were equal to one over a small range of outputs, he would be completely indifferent which of those outputs he produced—so long as marginal cost was zero. If marginal cost were positive, a much more probable situation, it would always pay the monopolist to reduce his output until the elasticity of demand for his product became greater than one. For any reduction in output would reduce total costs, but since elasticity is equal to one, it would leave total revenue at exactly the same level as before. We are assuming here that, with all normal average revenue curves, a range where elasticity is equal to one will have elasticity greater than one at all points to the left of that range. A monopolist's equilibrium position will always be where the elasticity of demand for his product is greater than one. For only in such conditions will it be possible for a monopolist with positive marginal costs to find an output where, if he decreases production, revenue falls by more than costs fall. If elasticity were not greater than one, a reduction in output would always raise profits.

Figure 69 shows an extreme situation where a monopolist has no costs of production, the time-honoured case of a mineral spring, for example. The equilibrium position will be where the monopolist produces the output OM and sells it at OP*s*. per unit. This will maximise his receipts. Point R on the average revenue curve will have an elasticity equal to one and total receipts will be at a maximum. Marginal revenue will thus be zero and will equal marginal cost.

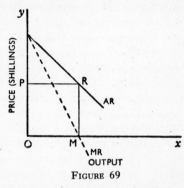

FIGURE 69

Figure 70 shows the more usual situation where the monopolist has positive marginal costs. We have, however, assumed that these costs are constant, but only in order to simplify the analysis. Here the monopolist is not interested in any part of his average revenue curve beyond point R, because beyond R elasticity of demand is less than one. Between R and R′ the curve has an elasticity equal to one and, since his marginal costs are positive, it will pay the monopolist to reduce output at least as far as R′. If the producer's average revenue curve had an elasticity of demand equal to one at all points to the left of R, it would pay him to reduce his output until he was selling as little as possible (presumably one unit) for an extremely high price. This would not, of course, mean that the producer was a 'pure' monopolist. As we have seen, such a producer must not only have an average revenue curve of unit elasticity, he must also take all consumers' incomes all the time. Even so, it is likely that all monopolists will have ranges of their average revenue curves (in Figure 70 this is to the left of point R′) where the elasticities of demand for their products are greater than one. A monopolist like the one in Figure 70 will therefore produce where output is OM and marginal revenue equals marginal cost, and the elasticity of the average

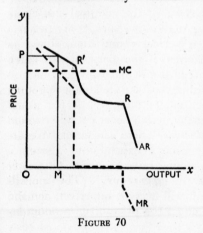

FIGURE 70

revenue curve at this output will be greater than one. Since demand curves with unit elasticity throughout are unlikely to occur, the real world monopolist (unless he has zero marginal costs) will normally produce where elasticity of demand is greater than one.

As we have seen, the very large range of situations covered by the collective term, monopoly, means that it is not possible to find any single case of monopoly or to generalise about monopoly in such a way as to allow it to be compared simply with perfect competition. Nevertheless it is possible to say something about the differences between monopoly and perfect competition. The only really general feature which is common to both is that, in both perfect competition and monopoly, equilibrium is given by the equation of marginal revenue with marginal cost. But even here there are differences between the two cases. In particular, where there is perfect competition the marginal cost curve must always be rising at and near the output where the firm is in equilibrium. This follows from the fact that there are many firms in a perfectly competitive industry.

In any perfectly competitive industry the average revenue curve and the marginal revenue curve of the firm are both horizontal. But, as has been shown earlier,[1] the perfectly competitive firm is only in equilibrium when the marginal cost curve cuts the marginal revenue curve from below. If the marginal cost curve cuts the marginal revenue curve from above, profits are not at a maximum. This means that in perfect competition, since the marginal revenue curve is horizontal, if the marginal cost curve is to cut it from below, then marginal cost must be rising at and near the equilibrium output. Falling cost curves are incompatible with equilibrium under perfect competition, for if the firm's marginal cost curve falls continually, it can never cut a horizontal marginal revenue curve from below. There can never be equilibrium. In such conditions the firm will expand until it becomes so large that its average and marginal revenue curves ultimately begin to fall in order to cut the marginal cost curve. The firm will become so large that competition will become imperfect, and the individual firm will be able to affect the price of its product by altering its own output.

The first difference between perfect and imperfect competition, then, is that whilst in perfect competition the marginal cost curve of the firm must be rising at or near the equilibrium output, in imperfect competition this need not be the case. A monopolistic

[1] See p. 132.

firm can be in equilibrium with rising, falling or constant marginal costs. The only conditions which must be satisfied if there is to be equilibrium are that marginal revenue shall equal marginal

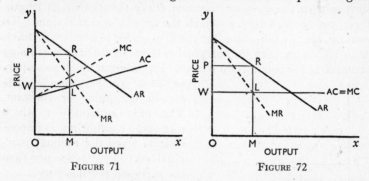

FIGURE 71　　　　　　　　　　　　FIGURE 72

cost, and that the marginal cost curve shall cut the marginal revenue curve *from below*. Let us analyse monopoly equilibrium by means of diagrams.

In Figure 71 marginal cost is rising. This ensures that there will be equilibrium in monopoly as in perfect competition. The equilibrium output in Figure 71 is OM and the monopoly price OP. 'Supernormal' or 'monopoly' profits are shown by the rectangle PRLW.

In Figure 72 marginal costs are constant and are equal to average costs. This condition is incompatible with equilibrium under perfect competition, since, if a firm could afford to produce at all, there would be no limit to its size unless competition became imperfect. The monopolist in Figure 72, however, is in equilibrium; equilibrium output is OM, monopoly price is OP and monopoly profits are shown by the area PRLW.

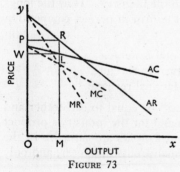

FIGURE 73

Monopoly equilibrium is also possible with falling marginal costs, as in Figure 73. Here monopoly output is OM, monopoly price OP and monopoly profits PRLW. The marginal cost curve must cut the marginal revenue curve from below or from the left, but so long as it does so there can be equilibrium. If marginal costs are falling more rapidly than marginal revenue, equilibrium

is clearly impossible. The only situation incompatible with monopoly equilibrium is thus one where marginal costs are falling more
swiftly than marginal revenue. If the marginal cost curve is
steeper than the marginal revenue curve throughout its length,
there can be no output at which the firm is in equilibrium. To
sum up, then, equilibrium for the firm under perfect competition
can only occur when the marginal cost curve of the firm is rising
at and near the equilibrium output. Equilibrium under monopoly
can occur whether marginal costs
are rising, falling or constant.
The only situation in which
monopoly equilibrium is impossible is when the (falling) marginal cost curve is steeper than
the marginal revenue curve.

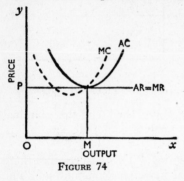

FIGURE 74

The second major difference
between equilibrium under perfect competition and under
monopoly lies in the size of
profits. We have seen that in
perfect competition the entrepreneur will, in the long run, be
unable to earn supernormal profits.[1]

In Figure 74 the perfectly competitive firm is in long-run
equilibrium, earning only normal profits. Supernormal profits
can be earned in the short run, but in the long run they will be
competed away by new entrants into the industry. Thus the long-
run conditions of equilibrium for the firm in perfect competition
can be summarised as follows :

Total cost = Total revenue.
Average cost = Average revenue.
Marginal cost = Marginal revenue.

In addition, these last four items will be equal to each other and
to price. If, in the short run, demand for the industry's product
increases, price rises and supernormal profits are earned. In the
long run, however, these supernormal profits disappear, and only
normal profits are earned.

In monopoly it is quite possible for the firm to earn supernormal profits in the long run. The firms shown in Figures 71,
72 and 73 were in short-run equilibrium and were earning supernormal profits. But it is not necessary to assume that such

[1] See p. 137. We assume homogeneous entrepreneurs.

profits will be competed away even in the long run. Free entry is often not possible in monopoly situations for either institutional or technical reasons, and if free entry is absent then the monopolist may be able to protect himself against competition for a very long time. Of course, if there is freedom of entry and competitive firms begin to produce close substitutes for the monopolist's good, the firm ceases to be a monopolist. The second difference between competition and monopoly is therefore that monopoly profits can be maintained even in the long run.

This does not mean, however, that a firm cannot, even under monopoly, be earning only normal profits.

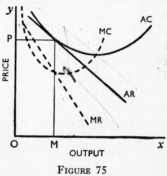

In Figure 75 we have the interesting case of a firm producing with a downward-sloping average revenue curve denoting imperfect competition, but earning only normal profits—for its average cost curve is tangent to its average revenue curve. It will be noted,

FIGURE 75

however, that such a firm must be producing at less than optimum size. In other words, it will not be producing at minimum average cost. A downward-sloping average revenue curve can never be tangent to a U-shaped average cost curve at or beyond its lowest point. Thus the second difference between competition and monopoly is that in the long run a competitor can never earn abnormal profits whilst a monopolist can do and usually does, though it is conceivable that he may not.

4. DEGREES OF MONOPOLY

We have seen that in monopoly the firm's average revenue curve will always slope downwards. This means that its marginal revenue curve will always lie below its average revenue curve. So, since the firm is in equilibrium where marginal revenue equals marginal cost, it follows that in equilibrium marginal cost is less than average revenue. In other words, marginal cost is less than price. The size of this difference between marginal cost and price is sometimes used to measure the extent of the firm's monopoly power. In perfect competition, when a firm is in long-run equilibrium, marginal cost equals price. When a firm is in a very monopolistic position, marginal cost is considerably less than price. Economists therefore refer to the difference between marginal cost and price as measuring the *degree of monopoly*. The larger the difference between marginal cost and price, the greater is the firm's monopoly power.

This gap between marginal cost and price will depend ultimately on the elasticity of demand for the firm's product—on the elasticity of its average revenue curve. This follows from the equations which we gave on p. 98 to show the relationship between marginal and average revenue. The lower the numerical elasticity of demand, the farther does marginal revenue at any output lie below average revenue—the farther, when the firm is in an equilibrium position, does marginal cost fall short of price. Differing elasticities of demand, shown by varying differences between price and marginal cost, are useful measures of the degree of monopoly. The lower is elasticity of demand, the greater is the 'degree of monopoly'.

A second indication of the strength of a monopoly is the size of the supernormal profits the firm is able to earn. In perfect competition firms will be unable for long to earn more than normal profits, because if they do, competitors will enter the industry. With monopoly, new entrants will not normally compete monopoly profits away in this manner. But there will usually be some level of profits at which new firms will find it worth taking the risk of trying to break the monopoly. The stronger the monopolist's position, the greater the profits he will be able to earn without attracting rivals. The size of monopoly profits is thus another (perhaps more reliable) measure of the monopoly power possessed by any firm.

5. DISCRIMINATING MONOPOLY

'Discriminating monopoly' or 'price discrimination' occurs when a monopolist charges different prices for different units of a commodity, even though these units are in fact homogeneous so far as their physical nature is concerned. The extent to which discrimination can occur will obviously depend on the circumstances. In the most favourable situations, it is just conceivable that the price charged could be different for every individual unit of a commodity. Such a situation could be described as 'perfectly discriminating monopoly'. It is more usual, however, to find that it is different individual consumers who are charged different prices. It would be most unusual to find a single consumer being offered several identical units of a good at different prices. Discrimination between buyers is more usual than discrimination between units of a homogeneous good.

It should be clear that discrimination between customers is incompatible with perfect competition. If there are many sellers of a homogeneous good, it is quite a simple matter for a consumer who feels that he is badly treated by one supplier to go to another one. It would be impossible in perfect competition for some sellers to charge 6d. for an article and others 1s. The people who were charged 1s. could easily go to other producers and get the good for 6d. Price discrimination can only occur when there is imperfect competition. But the relationship is not reversible. Price discrimination does not always occur whenever there is imperfect competition.

It is, of course, possible for a number of imperfectly competing sellers to carry out a jointly agreed policy of price discrimination. In this analysis of discriminating monopoly, however, we shall assume that it is a single monopolist in whose policy we are interested. The results hold good without serious qualification if discrimination occurs with other types of imperfect competition. We shall assume throughout this analysis that every monopolist always maximises his profits. It is important to decide first in what conditions discrimination is possible at all. We have seen that it is impossible under perfect competition. It may also be impossible even under monopoly. The fundamental condition which must be fulfilled if discrimination is to take place is that there can be no possibility of resale from one consumer to another. If the same commodity is supplied to Brown at 1s. and to Smith at 6d., and if Brown and Smith can exchange goods freely, the discrimination will break down. For Smith will buy the good for both of them. So, if price discrimination is to succeed, communication between buyers in different sectors of the monopolist's market must be impossible, or at any rate extremely difficult. In technical language there must be no 'seepage' between the discriminating monopolist's different markets.

6. CONDITIONS FOR PRICE DISCRIMINATION

It follows that if price discrimination is to succeed there must always be a special reason why consumers in different parts of the monopolist's market cannot communicate with each other. This limits the possibilities of price discrimination fairly narrowly.

There are three main types of situation where price discrimination can occur even though there is no fundamental difference between the goods offered to each customer. These are as follows :

(a) *Discrimination owing to Consumers' Peculiarities*

Discrimination in this type of case can occur for three main reasons :

(i) It can happen where consumer A is unaware that consumer B gets the same good more cheaply. Or, to put it more generally, it can happen when consumers in one part of the market do not know that prices are lower in another.

(ii) It can exist where the consumer has an irrational feeling that though he is paying a higher price he is paying it for a better good. For instance, it is probably irrational to think that one gets a better view of a film from the front row of the 2s. 3d. seats than from the back row of the 1s. 9d. seats.

(iii) Discrimination can occur if price differences are so small that it does not seem worth worrying about them.

(b) *Discrimination based on the Nature of the Good*

This type of case occurs particularly when the good in question is a direct service. Whilst it is possible for matches to be resold by a customer who is only charged a low price to one who pays a high price, it is impossible to do this with haircuts or 'perms'. Since resale of such direct services is impossible, differences between their prices can exist for different consumers. It is, of course, likely that in some cases the homogeneity of the good is not really complete. For example, it is not entirely realistic to think that a film is quite as enjoyable seen from the front row of a cinema as it would be from farther back. The service provided to the consumer is not the same.

It may be noticed in passing that in the past the most usual example of this type of discrimination was of the doctor who charged a poor man £1 for removing his tonsils, whilst he charged a rich man £100. The advent of the National Health Service seems to have robbed us in Britain of this practical illustration. But in any case it has defects. In particular, it is not wholly reasonable to think that doctors are quite as anxious to maximise profits as are many business men. Kindness of heart is probably more usual with doctors than with manufacturers.

(c) Discrimination because of Distances and Frontier Barriers

Discrimination often occurs where consumers are separated by distances or where the fact that a national frontier separates two markets means that tariffs can be levied. In such cases prices can diverge. A good may be sold in one town for 6d. and in another for 1s., and so long as the cost of transport is not less than 6d. per unit, resale will not be profitable. Again, where a monopolist serves two different markets, say, a home market with a tariff and a world market without a tariff, he can clearly hope to take advantage of the tariff barrier and raise his prices in the protected market. Similarly, an import prohibition at home would be very effective in allowing a monopolist to keep up the price in his home market. Such market features are clearly not inherent in the nature of the good sold but are a result of artificial or geographical barriers between one state and another.

It should be noted that all these forms of price discrimination depend ultimately on the monopolist's power to ensure that no-one else sells his product to everyone at a lower price. In most cases monopoly power will depend on the monopolist's ability to retain his customers, even if rivals enter his market, because they prefer to patronise his firm. In some cases, however, there are other restraints on competition. In the case of doctors, for example, the practice of charging higher prices to rich people depends ultimately on everyone in the profession accepting this as a convention. In other cases there may be legal sanction for price discrimination—as with the sale of electricity at different rates for lighting and heating. In this case the customer is liable to penalties if he tries to save money by using electricity for lighting instead of heating.

7. THE ANALYSIS OF PRICE DISCRIMINATION

We have now seen in what conditions price discrimination is possible. When will it be profitable? This question can be answered by applying the ordinary theory of the firm to a case where there are two markets (or even more) instead of only one. This complicates the analysis needed but does not affect the fundamentals of that analysis at all. We can still base the theory on the assumption that the monopolist seeks maximum profits and therefore fixes his output so as to equate marginal revenue with marginal cost. Now, however, the firm has two separate markets, so that marginal revenue and marginal cost must be equal in both markets. We shall assume that there are many buyers in each market so that there is perfect competition between buyers within each market. We shall also assume that buyers in the one market are unable to communicate with buyers in the other.

On the sellers' side we shall assume to begin with that the monopolist is a monopolist in both markets. This means that his average revenue curve will slope downwards in each market. We shall also assume that price discrimination is physically *possible*. It will only be *profitable* if elasticity of demand in the one market is different from elasticity of demand in the other. It will only pay a monopolist to discriminate between two markets provided that the elasticities of demand are different in the two markets. Let us examine the two possible cases.

(a) *Elasticity of Demand the same in each Market*

Let us assume that the elasticity of demand in each market is the same at each price as elasticity of demand in the other. This means that the two average revenue curves slope downwards, each changing its elasticity at the same rate as the other. The fact that the two markets are unable to communicate with each other does not matter, for the demand in each is of the same quality.

(b) *Elasticity of Demand different in each Market*

If the elasticities of demand in the two markets at all the relevant prices are different, the monopolist will be able to profit from price discrimination. And provided he wants to earn maximum profits he will in fact discriminate. It is possible, of course, that the monopolist might be legally forbidden to pursue a policy of price discrimination. Assuming that this is so, he would fix that single monopoly price which would maximise profits by equating marginal cost with marginal revenue for the two markets added together.

We shall assume here, however, that discrimination is not prevented by law. The question which the monopolist now asks is, 'Is elasticity of demand the same in both markets at the single monopoly price?' If elasticity *is* the same in each market at that price, the monopolist will not discriminate, even though the elasticities may be different at *all other* prices. For if elasticity at the single monopoly price is the same in each market, marginal

revenues will also be the same. This follows from the formula
Marginal Revenue = Average Revenue $\times \dfrac{e-1}{e}$, where e is point
elasticity of demand. If average revenue (single monopoly price)
is the same in each market and elasticity of demand is also the same,
then one can see immediately from the formula that marginal
revenues in the two markets will be equal. This means that if
output is transferred from one market to another, there will be no
gain in total revenue. What is gained in one market will be lost to
the other. There is thus no motive for discrimination here.

Let us now assume that at the single monopoly price the
elasticity of demand is different in each market. If elasticity of
demand at the single monopoly price is smaller in one market than
in the other, discrimination will pay. If the elasticity of demand
is very low in one market (market A), the price will be raised
even above the single monopoly price. For, since the demand
in market A is very inelastic, it is very insensitive to price changes
and a rise in price will not cause much fall in demand. Similarly,
if elasticity of demand is very great in the other market (market B),
demand will there be very responsive to price changes. It will
therefore pay to lower the price of the good in market B below
the single monopoly price. For, since elasticity of demand is very
low in market A, a decrease in sales will decrease revenue only very
slightly, whilst, in market B, elasticity is high and a reduction in
price will add a great deal to revenue. It will pay the monopolist,
who is charging the single monopoly price to transfer goods from
market A with the inelastic demand to market B with the elastic
demand. The loss of revenue from reducing sales by one (marginal)
unit in market A which has inelastic demand will be smaller than
the gain in revenue from expanding sales by one (marginal) unit
in the market B which has elastic demand, for prices will rise more
sharply in market A than they fall in market B. This follows
from the formula cited above. When average revenue is given,
marginal revenue will be greater the greater is elasticity of demand.
So where average revenue (single monopoly price) is the same in
each market, marginal revenue will be greater where elasticity is
greater (market B) and *vice versa*. But how long will it be worth
while continuing this process of transferring units of the good
from the market with the low elasticity of demand to the one
with the high elasticity? Let us analyse this problem in two
stages.

Let us first assume that the monopolist has a given output

N

already produced and merely wants to distribute it in the most profitable way between the two markets. Let us consider a situation where the elasticities of demand in the two markets are different and where marginal revenues in the two markets are therefore different also, but where the monopolist begins by distributing his output between the two markets in such a way that the single monopoly price obtains in each. In order to maximise profits the monopolist will restrict his output in the market with the inelastic demand (market A), and expand it in the market with the elastic demand (market B). He will do this because he is adding more to his revenue in market B than he is taking away from his revenue in market A. Since to begin with, price (single monopoly price) is the same in each market, marginal revenue is greater in market B than in market A. This follows from the formula given above. Thus the discriminating monopolist would move up the marginal revenue curve in market A (by restricting sales and raising price) and down the marginal revenue curve in market B (by expanding sales and lowering price) until the marginal revenues in each market were equal.

It should be noted that in this equilibrium position, prices will be different in the two markets and the elasticities of demand in the two markets will be unequal also. It follows from our formulae that if marginal revenue in each market is to be the same but prices are different, elasticities of demand will be different too. Price will be higher in the market with the less elastic demand and *vice versa*. We see therefore that if the output to be distributed between his two markets is fixed in amount, it will be most profitable for a discriminating monopolist to divide it between the markets in such a way that the marginal revenues are equal when the whole output is just being disposed of to one market or to the other. Only if marginal revenues in the two markets are equal will it be unprofitable to shift output from one market to the other.

Let us now assume that total output is not fixed in this way but can be varied. Once again marginal revenues in the two markets must be equal if profits are to be maximised. But it is essential now not only that marginal revenue should be the same in each market, but that this marginal revenue should also be equal to the marginal cost of producing the whole output. This is the condition of equilibrium in discriminating monopoly. The position may be shown in a rather complicated diagram, Figure 76.

Figure 76 refers to a producer selling in two different markets.

For the sake of simplicity we assume for the moment that he is a monopolist in only one of the markets and that the other is perfectly competitive. In market H, the home market, the producer is a monopolist and the elasticity of demand for his product is not very great, so his average revenue curve AR^H slopes downwards. So does the marginal revenue curve MR^H. In the world market, W, there is perfect competition, and elasticity of demand for the monopolist's product is infinitely great. The average revenue curve AR^W is a horizontal straight line and coincides with the marginal revenue curve for the world market MR^W.

In Figure 76 the marginal cost curve for the monopolist's output is shown by the curve MC. In order to discover how much output it is worth producing altogether, the monopolist must find where this marginal cost curve intersects the combined marginal revenue curve. Once the size of the total output has been determined, the shares which should go to each market can be decided by allocating the output in such a way that marginal revenues are equal in each market. In Figure 76 the combined marginal revenue curve is given by the composite curve ARTD. On this curve, marginal revenue in the world market is added on sideways to marginal revenue at home. The intersection of the monopolist's marginal cost curve with the combined marginal revenue curve (at T) gives an output of OM as that total output which maximises profits.

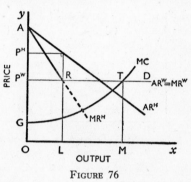

FIGURE 76

This output OM must now be shared between the two markets. It is clear from Figure 76 that the only way in which the marginal revenues in each market can be equal to each other and to marginal cost MT is for OL to be sold in the home market at a price of OP^H and a marginal revenue of RL. This leaves an amount of LM to be sold in the world market at a price of OP^W and with a marginal revenue MT equal to OP^W. MT is also the same as RL. Price is thus higher (OP^H) in the monopolistic home market than in the competitive world market (OP^W). The monopolist's total profits are equal to the area ARTG. These profits are at a maximum and are contributed to by both markets.

When both markets are monopolistic it is still possible to
show, by drawing diagrams, what the monopolist's price-output
policy will be, as in Figure 77. Figures 77a and 77b show the
average and marginal revenue curves of the firm in question for
two separate markets (markets 1 and 2). These markets have
different elasticities of demand at each price. In Figure 77c the
profit maximising output is shown to be determined by the intersection of the marginal cost curve for the monopolist's whole
output (MC), with the curve showing the combined marginal

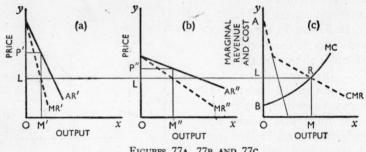

FIGURES 77A, 77B AND 77C

revenue earned from the two markets (CMR). The curve CMR
is obtained by adding the curves MR' and MR" together sideways.
In this equilibrium situation output is OM, and marginal revenue
is OL = MR. The output OM has therefore to be distributed
between the two separate markets in such a way that marginal
revenue in each is OL. This means that OM' must be sold in
market 1. For with sales at that level marginal revenue in market 1
is OL. Price is OP'. Similarly, OM" must be sold in market 2, at
a price of OP". Marginal revenue is OL here too. The monopolist's profit is shown by the area ARB in Figure 77c and is at a
maximum. This same solution in terms of marginal and average
revenues and costs can also be shown by combining Figures 77a,
77b and 77c in a single diagram, but naturally this diagram is
somewhat complicated.[1]

We have seen that if a discriminating monopolist is to be in
equilibrium, two separate conditions have to be fulfilled. First,
marginal revenue in both (or all) markets must be the same.
Second, these marginal revenues must also equal the marginal
cost of the monopolist's output. These two conditions have been

---

[1] Readers will find such a diagram in Joan Robinson, *Economics of Imperfect
Competition*, p. 183.

analysed separately but it is important to remember that they must hold simultaneously. In other words, $MR' = MR'' = MC$ is nothing more than an application of the general principle 'in equilibrium marginal revenue equals marginal cost' to the special case where discrimination between different parts of the market is possible.

SUGGESTED READING

Joan Robinson, *Economics of Imperfect Competition*, London, 1933, especially chapters iii, iv, v, xv and xvi.
E. A. G. Robinson, *Monopoly*, London, 1948, *passim*.

CHAPTER IX

MONOPOLISTIC COMPETITION

1. MONOPOLISTIC COMPETITION

WE have so far concerned ourselves, in our analysis of imperfect competition, with the problems of firms run by individual monopolists, and producing products which do not compete closely with any other goods. We have seen that in such firms the extent of monopoly power will depend mainly on the shape of the average revenue curve. We have assumed, however, that the shape of such an average revenue curve is given to us. We have said nothing about the way in which it will be determined, apart from showing that it depends ultimately on consumers' tastes and on the number of rival goods competing indirectly for consumers' incomes.

In the real world, however, imperfect competition does not usually mean only one producer who has no closely related goods competing with his own—as we suggest when we talk of a monopolist. The great majority of imperfectly competitive producers in the real world produce goods which are very similar to those made by their rivals. It follows that such producers must always be very concerned about the way in which the actions of these rivals affect their own profits. This kind of situation is dealt with in economic theory by the analysis of what is called *monopolistic competition*, or *group equilibrium*. Here, there is competition which is keen, though not perfect, between many firms making very similar products. The concept of monopolistic competition was introduced into economic analysis by Professor E. H. Chamberlin.[1]

It is reasonable to suppose that in these circumstances the shape of the firm's average revenue curve will be determined not only by the tastes and whims of consumers, but also by the price-

[1] Professor E. H. Chamberlin in *The Theory of Monopolistic Competition* uses this term in the sense in which we have used 'imperfect competition' in this book. (See *op. cit*. p. 9 (footnote).) We shall, however, use the term *monopolistic competition* to mean the large group of firms making very similar products. Since this is the main type of market situation which Professor Chamberlin analyses, this seems a justifiable procedure.

output decisions of rival producers. The problems of monopolistic competition are therefore more complicated than those of
perfect competition. In perfect competition there is at any rate
only one homogeneous commodity. In monopolistic competition
there is differentiation of products. Products are not homogeneous, as in perfect competition, but neither are they only remote
substitutes, as in monopoly. What this really means is that in
monopolistic competition there are various 'monopolists' competing with each other. These competing 'monopolists' do not
produce identical goods. Neither do they produce goods which
are completely different. Product differentiation means that
products are different in some ways, but not altogether so.
'Branding', the use of attractive packets and wrappers, and the
use of trade-marks and of trade-names will be the most usual
methods by which products are differentiated, even if physically
they are identical, or almost so. In addition, of course, it will be
possible to make slight improvements or alterations in the physical
constitution of a product to persuade consumers that it is rather
superior to other similar products.

To analyse monopolistic competition, then, we must discuss
the kind of market situation where imperfectly competitive producers meet serious competition from many close rivals. It is
reasonable to doubt whether the monopoly analysis given so far is
applicable to this kind of imperfect competitor who has to worry
seriously about the price-output policies of his rivals. Apart from
the fact that the demand curve is different in monopolistic competition, the cost curve poses a problem too. In monopoly we
could assume that the firm's cost curve was given, since we were
studying only one individual firm. In monopolistic competition,
however, since many rival firms are producing rather similar
products, they will all be using rather similar factors of production.
The firms' cost curves therefore must bear some relation to each
other. For example, an increased demand for factors of production because the number of firms in the monopolistic group
increases, may well raise the prices of these factors to other firms
in the group. The idea of independent cost curves, even if it
seems satisfactory under conditions of monopoly, can never be
completely satisfactory in monopolistic competition. In order to
simplify the analysis, however, we shall assume that all firms in
the same 'group' of monopolistically competitive firms have
identical cost curves and that these curves remain at exactly the
same level whatever the number of firms in the group. In other

words, we assume that all factors of production are homogeneous
and in perfect elastic supply to the monopolistic group. We also
assume that there are no external economies or diseconomies of
production when the number of firms in the group increases.
Professor Chamberlin makes this same assumption [1]—an 'heroic'
assumption as he calls it—though he later relaxes it.

The reason why we shall find it useful to spend much time
discussing the meaning and the problems of monopolistic competition, is that in the real world this is probably the predominant
type of market situation. Before we begin this analysis of monopolistic competition, however, there is something to be said for
trying to discover in what conditions the notion of a single and
independent monopolist, as outlined in the previous chapter, is
realistic. The fundamental feature of monopolistic competition
is that all goods do compete with each other to some extent, and
this seems to suggest that the idea of a single monopolist can never
be wholly realistic. Yet there must be some situations where the
idea of monopoly as outlined above is useful. Let us see what
these are.

2. THE VALIDITY OF THE IDEA OF MONOPOLY TODAY

The idea of monopoly as we have discussed it in Chapter VIII
is quite appropriate where there are several monopolists (let us
call them A, B and C) whose products are not at all closely
related—whose products are only very bad substitutes for each
other. In such a situation there is clearly no close competition
between the three producers. It is therefore perfectly legitimate
to regard the average revenue curve of each firm as independent
and given. Each such average revenue curve will be downward-
sloping and its shape will depend on the tastes of consumers and
on the action of *all* other producers in the economy, whatever their
products, when price is changed. It is the behaviour of *all*
other producers *taken together* which guides the action of the
simple monopolist.

Now it is obvious that, in this particular case, where there are
no close substitutes for the monopolist's product, he will only
need to consider the large range of very distant competitors,
including other monopolists. So far as A, for example, is concerned, the other monopolists, B and C, are no more serious rivals

[1] *Theory of Monopolistic Competition*, p. 85.

than other, perhaps perfectly competitive, producers. Since his competitors are so distant (and so many in number), it is impossible for the monopolist to isolate the influence of any one of them separately. The monopolist can therefore regard his average revenue curve as entirely dependent on consumer demand. He will not find it worth his while to probe into the way in which the actions of other firms determine its shape.

What happens, then, if a monopolist in such a situation makes monopoly profits? Since all other goods are only very distant competitors with his own, there is no real likelihood that large earnings on the part of any one monopolist will cause his rivals to change their policies. There is very little reason to suppose that they will alter their own plans merely because he happens to be earning monopoly profits. By definition, they do not produce the same product. They do not even produce close substitutes. The monopolist's profits are therefore safe. He can justifiably look upon his average revenue curve as unaffected by the actions of his rivals, and he has no reason to think that they will compete away his monopoly profits.

In a case like this the idea of a single monopolist is realistic. Such a notion is not realistic, however, when the monopolist faces a large number of rivals each producing very close substitutes for his own product. It is then impossible to obtain a realistic analysis if one looks at individual producers in isolation. Here, as in perfect competition, we are concerned not only with the firm but also with the industry. The problem of a group of closely competitive rivals—a monopolistic 'group' or 'industry', as we might call it—must now be faced. This is much more relevant for practical purposes than the idea of an independent monopolist. In the real world it is very usual to find competition between a number of producers each making something a little different from each of the others. And where there is a range of competing substitutes of this kind, the elasticity of demand for each individual product will be much higher than it would be where competition was with more remote rivals. The actions of rivals will be more important and the analysis needed will be different.

3. GROUP EQUILIBRIUM

We may begin our discussion of monopolistic competition by considering the nature of the monopolistic group or industry. Whilst it is clear that here we have competition between a group of producers who are all making fairly similar products, it is also clear that the limits of the industry will not be so easy to define as they were under perfect competition. Since the fundamental feature of monopolistic competition is differentiation of the product, the simple task of discovering where is the border-line between an industry making homogeneous products and the rest of the economy—the task with perfect competition—disappears. In monopolistic competition there are bound to be many border-line cases where firms could legitimately be classed in two or more industries.   Nevertheless, if it is possible to discover situations where there is a number of firms making very close substitutes, all competing with each other, and then there is a large gap in the chain of substitutes, it is reasonable to regard the closely competitive producers as forming an 'industry' or 'group' of monopolistic competitors.

For example, let us assume that each motor-car firm produces only one product each (which is, of course, untrue). It is then reasonable to regard the rather similar products of the various motor firms as competing fairly closely with each other. But it would not be reasonable to think that there was equally close competition between cars and, say, tractors or delivery vans. Thus, whilst tractors and vans are technically in the same industry as motor cars, they are not regarded by consumers as closely competitive goods. So far as consumers are concerned, competition between cars on the one hand, and the products of other monopolistic 'groups', bicycles, scooters, hansom cabs and tube-trains on the other, is not much greater than competition with cinemas, clothing, houses and the like.

Each firm in the monopolistic 'group' composing the 'motor industry' has a downward-sloping average revenue curve. This is, first, because the motor cars will not be identical as they would in perfect competition, and second, because there will presumably not be as many firms in the 'industry' as there would if competition were perfect. But the shape of each firm's average revenue curve will now be determined not only by the competition of distant rivals in other 'industries', about whose actions the individual firm need not worry ; it will also be determined by the actions of the very close rivals inside the same monopolistic group, whose actions will need to be carefully watched.

In monopolistic competition, the firm earning monopoly profits will need to be very alert if it is to safeguard them. If one firm is making large monopolistic profits by producing a new and popular product, there will clearly be a temptation for other firms in the same group to undertake the manufacture of products which are as closely competitive with the products of the successful firm as it is possible to make them. The more directly other firms can compete with the firm making large profits, the more money they will be able to earn for themselves. And since all firms in the group are making similar products, they will all be in a position, should they wish to do so, to compete away these large monopolistic profits by making their product more similar to that of the innovating firm.

It is therefore reasonable to assume that all products made by a group of monopolistic competitors can, if necessary, be made more like each other, even though they cannot be made identical. One can also assume that any very profitable type of product made by one member of the group will soon be made by all, though with slight variations in design. If the products of the group are, say, motor cars, and one firm starts to make a fortune by introducing streamlining, all firms will naturally follow suit. It follows that in monopolistic competition any large profits earned by firms will tend to be competed away in the long run. If the goods made by all firms in the industry are not identical it is unlikely that abnormal profits will be eliminated completely, but the fact that the goods are very similar, taken in conjunction with our 'heroic' assumption of identical cost curves, means that such profits are bound to be eaten into. Again, if all existing firms are making large profits, then, unless the industry is protected by legal restrictions on entry, new firms will be able to enter the group and compete these profits away by producing yet more rather similar products.

The conclusion to be drawn from this analysis is thus that in the short run, when there is monopolistic competition in an industry but the number of firms is fixed, they can all earn abnormal profits or losses. In the long run, however, the position will be similar to the long-run position in a perfectly competitive industry. Large abnormal profits will be competed away. The result will be that in monopolistic competition the long-run equilibrium position will be one where the individual firm is earning only 'normal' profits, or, more likely, only very small abnormal profits. Different firms will probably earn different profits, these profits being larger the more popular the firm's own product is.

The process by which the short- and long-run equilibrium

positions are reached by a firm in monopolistic competition is
shown in Figure 78.

Figure 78 shows a firm producing in monopolistic competition.
We assume that the average and marginal cost curves (AC and
MC) for its own particular product (like those of all other firms)
remain the same in both the short and the long runs.   In the short
run (Figure 78a) the firm finds that marginal revenue equals
marginal cost at the output OM and is able to earn abnormal

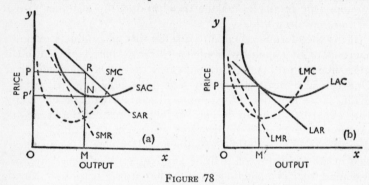

FIGURE 78

profits of PRNP′ in this equilibrium situation.   The firm is in
short - run equilibrium and is able to make abnormal profits
because there are not enough closely competitive substitutes made
by other firms to compete these profits away.

In the long run (Figure 78b), at that level of output where
marginal cost equals marginal revenue (OM′), the average revenue
curve has become tangent to the average cost curve and the firm
is earning only 'normal' profits.   Competitors (both old and new)
are producing similar products, and the firm's abnormal short-run
profits have been competed away.   This situation is similar to
that of long-run equilibrium in perfect competition.   The main
difference is that whereas in perfect competition the average
revenue curve of the firm is a horizontal straight line, in monopolistic competition it slopes downwards.   It follows therefore
that, so long as cost curves are U-shaped, the long-run equilibrium
of a firm producing in monopolistic competition must inevitably
occur at a smaller output than in perfect competition.   For it is
impossible for a downward-sloping average revenue curve to be
tangent to a given U-shaped cost curve except to the left of the
position where a horizontal average revenue curve would be
tangent to it.   This means that, in long-run equilibrium in

monopolistic competition, output must always be smaller than at the 'optimum' perfect competition output.

It is clearly desirable that we should separate those features of Figure 78 which are of purely geometrical significance from those which are economically important. First, it should be noted that the only reason why the average revenue curve is a straight line is that this simplifies the diagram. The equilibrium conditions would hold equally if it were a real curve. Second, it is

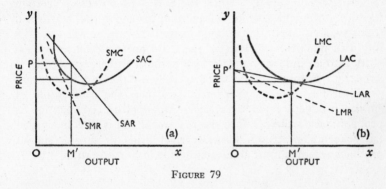

FIGURE 79

important to note that, again for the sake of simplicity, the long-run average revenue curve has been drawn parallel to the short-run one. This again will not necessarily happen in practice.

It is, in fact, quite possible that the average revenue curve of a firm producing in monopolistic competition will be more elastic in the long run than in the short run, as in Figure 79. The firm shown in Figure 79 has a short-run average revenue curve (SAR) which is less elastic than its long-run average revenue curve (LAR). It seems realistic to think that in the long run the average revenue curve in monopolistically competitive firms will in fact be more elastic than in the short run. For all products made by a monopolistic group or industry will, as we have seen, tend to become more similar as time goes on. Everyone will naturally be looking for the most profitable type of article and all will try to make it. Similarly, if new producers enter the industry, this is likely to mean that instead of, say, twenty similar cars being produced, there will now be, say, forty. This again means that each of the cars is likely to be more similar to each of the others than it was previously. And the more closely competitive substitutes there are, the more elastic the demand for the product of any one firm in the 'group' will be.

It can be seen, therefore, that since monopolistic competition means considerable competition between many firms producing slightly different goods, it is really more like perfect competition than monopoly. For practical purposes this is important. To use perfect competition as anything more than an artificial limiting case is unrealistic, since it is unreasonable to think that most firms in a real-world industry make products which are homogeneous, or that in any such real-world industry abnormal profits are completely eliminated. Since there is undoubtedly a certain measure of imperfection of competition throughout all real-world industry, it is likely that monopolistic competition will often be found in practice. So long as there are no legal restrictions on entry into an industry, and so long as most firms produce goods similar to those of other firms already in the industry, every producer must always be prepared to meet the competition of similar products made by rivals. Monopolistic competition is probably very widespread in the real world. It is thus likely that fairly keen competition between rival firms producing similar products removes most abnormal profits in the long run.

4. ADVERTISING

As we have seen, the concept of monopolistic competition takes as its main feature the assumption that products are differentiated. Everyone tries to make a product which is just a little different from everyone else's. This inevitably means that producers working in such conditions do their best to ensure that their own products are superior in some way or another to those of their rivals. This is how abnormal profits are competed away. In some cases it may be possible to produce such competition by altering the physical nature of the product. But whether or not the product is altered, it is usually found worth while to try to persuade consumers that one's own product is different from others—even though physically it may be identical. We must therefore discuss the problems which arise when advertisement is undertaken with a view to persuading consumers that one product is preferable to another. For it is undoubtedly true that producers of many goods, toothpaste and cigarettes, for example, spend much time and energy in convincing consumers that their own brand is better than other brands.

We have already implied that a producer who is working in conditions of monopolistic competition has to make two important decisions. First, he has to decide how much of his product to produce, and at what price to sell it. This is a decision common to all producers whatever sort of market they are producing in. Second, he has to decide whether to produce one good with one set of physical characteristics or another good with a slightly different set. For example, a producer might have to decide whether to streamline the bonnet of his brand of car or not. This sort of decision is only important in monopolistic competition. In perfect competition, all the products of the industry are identical in any case. In monopoly, on the other hand, there are no closely competing products at all and the design of the monopolist's good will not be of such crucial importance. Only where there is monopolistic competition will changes in design be a vital factor in causing competition.

Similarly, the producer in monopolistic competition must decide whether or not to spend money on advertising to persuade people to buy his good and, if so, how much money. This problem, again, is one which is not important for the producer in perfect competition or for the monopolist. The monopolist, since there are no close substitutes for his product, need not worry very much about whether he can convince people that his good is different from other goods, since they know that it is. On the other hand, advertisement of this kind is incompatible with perfect competition. Since in perfect competition all producers are making identical goods it is not usual to try to persuade consumers that one firm's product is different from another's. If this were done and consumers *did* become convinced that, say, Williams's wheat was better than Jones's, even though they were homogeneous, that would immediately destroy perfect competition. It must be pointed out, however, that there can be advertising of a kind in perfect competition. It is advertisement undertaken by all the producers together—by the whole industry—to persuade consumers to take their product instead of that of other industries. The exhortation to 'eat more fruit' and the advice that 'there is *no* substitute for wool' are examples. But competitive advertising *within* an industry is incompatible with perfect competition in the industry.

It is now time to discuss the costs of advertising, or *selling costs* as they are more usually called, in a monopolistically competitive group. There are, of course, two kinds of advertisement. First, there are those advertisements which give the consumer information that he would not have had if the producer had not provided it. For example, most public announcements in important newspapers merely give information without attempting to persuade. Again, technical information about the uses of particular products is often given purely for the benefit of consumers by independent bodies, for example by Government Departments.

Second, there are those advertisements which do not give information but which merely try to persuade the consumer to change his attitude to the good in question. We all know what toothpaste is and what it does, but the various producers try to persuade us that their own brand is better than all the rest. And this type of advertising is often successful. It follows that if a producer can persuade people to buy his product by producing appealing posters, our assumption that the demand curve is an objective fact given by consumers' tastes on the one hand and by the number and activity of rivals on the other, is no longer realistic. Where successful advertisement is undertaken it must be replaced by a demand curve which can be altered or shifted by the producer's own efforts—if only he is prepared to spend money and effort on advertising.

We can now discuss these two types of advertising in rather greater detail. The first type of announcement, that which merely gives information, is not incompatible with the analysis which we have so far used. We have assumed that there is perfect competition between buyers. This really means that we have assumed that all buyers are in possession of all relevant information about all the products which are available. This is likely to be the case in the capital goods markets and in the markets for some finished products where the consumers are business men with wide knowledge. It is less likely to be the case for the ordinary consumer buying the finished product. Here, there is great scope for informative advertising. For example, as it has become possible to view television broadcasts in areas of Britain outside London it has been necessary to give technical information to potential viewers. Advertising has been needed merely to enable people to discover the possibilities and limitations of television. This type of advertising is desirable since it enables a rational choice between goods of the kind we have continually assumed to be made. This kind of advertising will help to increase the sales of all firms in the 'group' because it will make consumers more aware of the potentialities of the product made by the 'group'.

Much advertising, however, is not of this kind. It is of the second kind. It is not informative advertising but persuasive advertising. The aim is merely to persuade consumers that X's product is better than all other similar products. In this analysis we are not concerned with moral judgments and it does not concern us whether the advertisements are strictly truthful or not. The important thing from our point of view is the effect of advertising, and we can justifiably say in this respect that the fundamental aim of all 'persuasive' advertising is to attract the consumer's attention and imprint the name of a particular product on his mind. The aim is always to persuade the consumer to put his hand in his pocket and buy the product in question. Advertising of this kind can help to increase the sales of all firms in the 'group' if it brings the product of the whole group to the notice of consumers. But the main aim is to increase the sales of one firm at the expense of others, and not to increase the sales of the 'group' as a whole.

5. THE ANALYSIS OF SELLING COSTS

It is thus obvious that the whole aim of 'persuasive' advertisement is to induce consumers to buy more of a particular entrepreneur's product. The producer who is deciding whether to advertise is therefore making a decision of fundamentally the same kind as that which he makes when he decides what price to charge for his product or how large an output to produce. It is not really very important to him whether his firm maximises its profits by changing the price-output of its products, by altering the physical constitution of its products ; or by spending money on advertising.[1] These are all examples of maximisation decisions. It is therefore possible to analyse the problem of how much selling cost to incur in just the same way as one can analyse the problem of which price-output policy a firm ought to pursue. In the case of advertising decisions a two-dimensional diagram is rather clumsy but it does show the fundamental features of the problem, from the point of view of the individual firm.

In Figure 80 sales of a given good, which we call good X, are measured along the horizontal x-axis and price up the vertical y-axis. We shall assume that the nature of good X does not change throughout the analysis. In practice, of course, as we have

---

[1] We have not shown in detail how a firm will adapt the nature of its product —'differentiate' its product—in order to maximise profits. For a fuller analysis of this problem, the reader should consult Chamberlin, *op. cit.* pp. 94-7.

O

seen, the fundamental reason why advertising is undertaken at all is that it changes the nature of the good so far as the consumer is concerned. This assumption is therefore not entirely realistic. Provided, however, that the physical make-up of the good is given and its costs therefore constant, this problem is not of very great importance. But it is desirable to bear this assumption in mind throughout the following analysis.

In Figure 80 the original situation is one where the firm is in equilibrium. The average revenue curve for the firm's product is

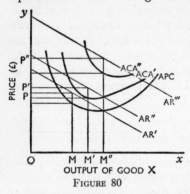

FIGURE 80

AR'. This is the basic average revenue curve before any advertisements are undertaken. Similarly, APC is the basic cost curve. This represents only average *production* costs, and is the curve we are assuming to be identical in all firms in the 'group'. It does not include any advertising costs. We assume throughout this analysis of selling costs that the firm desires to earn maximum profits so that the original equilibrium position in Figure 80 is where output is OM and price is £OP. In this position maximum profits are being earned.

If advertisement is now undertaken a new equilibrium position will be reached. Let us assume that £1000 is spent on advertising. The cost of advertising per unit of output will depend on the size of that output. Advertising cost per unit of output will be £1000 with an output of one unit and £1 with an output of 1000 units. This means that the average cost curve including £1000 spent on advertising (ACA') gradually curves closer to the average production cost curve APC as output increases. The effect of spending the £1000 on advertising is, however, to increase demand. At every price a larger quantity of the good can be sold than before and the new average revenue curve AR" is therefore to the right of the original one. The equilibrium position of the firm will now be where output is OM', price is £OP', and profits are maximised. In the firm depicted in Figure 80, this new equilibrium position will be one where output is greater and price higher than in the original equilibrium. The important question, however, is not what happens to price or output but whether or not profits are larger than they were in the original equilibrium. This depends on whether net revenue rises when the selling costs of £1000 are incurred. If this happens and profits are greater, then the advertising has proved worth while. If the profits are not greater, the move was unwise.

If profits have risen because of advertising this means that further advertising expenditure might well increase them still more. The firm might therefore decide to spend £2000 on advertisements instead of £1000. It would pay the firm to continue to increase selling costs in this way so long as the advertising in question added more to revenue than to costs. Only when the additional revenue from a marginal unit of advertising expenditure equalled this (marginal) selling cost, would profits be at the highest possible level. This would happen in Figure 80 with selling costs of £5000. The cost curve would now be the curve ACA″, and the revenue curve AR‴. Output is then OM″, and price OP″. After this point it would be found that profits began to decline again as a result of any further expansion of advertising outlay. An extra pound added to selling costs would not yield an equal increase in revenue. There is therefore for each firm producing in 'monopolistic competition' a whole set of average revenue curves and average cost curves, each pair of curves corresponding to a different level of selling costs. The producer's problem is to decide which pair of curves represent the position where money profits are maximised, and at which point on this pair of curves output should be fixed.

It will be useful to consider more carefully the way in which, and the extent to which, the firm's average revenue curve is likely to be affected by advertising expenditure. It can be seen that in drawing Figure 80 we have made two assumptions. First, we have assumed that demand increases when advertising is inaugurated. This is a reasonable assumption but it is not inevitably true. A bad artist might conceivably alienate consumers, but this is not often likely to happen in practice. We can legitimately assume that advertising will never reduce demand. The question is, by how much, if at all, will demand increase ? A small increase may not be worth the cost incurred in obtaining it ; and it is by no means axiomatic that increased selling costs are always worth while.

The second assumption which we have made is more dubious. Whilst we have assumed that the average revenue curves are straight lines only for the sake of simplicity, we have also assumed that the new average revenue curve is parallel to the old. This also is an assumption made solely on the grounds of convenience. The implications of this assumption should, however, be carefully considered. It implies that elasticity of demand is lower at each price on the new curve than on the old one. This seems reasonable. If a producer's advertisements succeed in their intention they will clearly make people look upon his product as rather different from other products. The most reasonable result to expect from this will be for the elasticity of demand for the good to fall. Consumers will now regard the commodity in question as being more desirable, even if its price is rather higher than the prices of close substitutes, for consumers have been persuaded that the good in question is rather different from other goods. They now believe that these other goods are not nearly such good substitutes for it as they had hitherto supposed. It is thus highly probable that the elasticity of demand for the advertised product will, in fact, decline. The extent to which elasticity of demand is likely to decline is, of course, uncertain. In practice, the producer is not so much interested in his ability to reduce the elasticity of demand for his product as in his ability to raise its sales. Increases in sales caused by shifts of the whole demand curve cause the most obvious and significant changes in profits. Changes in elasticity of demand are of only secondary importance.

The effects of advertising on prices and output are equally uncertain. It is possible that, by inaugurating an advertising campaign, the producer may be able to increase the sales of his product and yet not lower its elasticity of demand. This will mean that if he now lowers the price of his good he can increase his output considerably. On the other hand, if, as seems more likely, elasticity of demand falls as a result of advertising, it may pay the producer to raise his price and decrease his sales. The most reasonable result to expect will be that elasticity of demand will fall, that the volume of demand will increase somewhat at each price and that price and output will therefore both increase as a result of the advertising campaign.

We have so far assumed that advertising takes place in an industry already producing under conditions of monopolistic competition. It must be remembered, however, that monopolistic competition with product differentiation may well be the result and not the cause of advertising. There are, of course, endless practical possibilities, but two limiting cases are apparent. On the one hand, if there is a monopoly, this means that there are no firms producing closely competitive substitutes. If in such circumstances the monopolist feels that he is not earning enough money, the only way for him to increase his sales is to persuade consumers that his product is in fact a good substitute for some distant rival's products.   In other words, the monopolist will try to increase both the volume and the elasticity of the demand for his products.   On the other hand, if there is perfect competition in an industry, so that all firms' products are homogeneous, an individual producer may try to persuade consumers that his product is not, in fact, identical with those of other firms.   Here the aim is to lower the elasticity of demand for the product in question.   Between these limits there are endless possible situations and one cannot say *a priori* which are more likely to occur.

One final point is interesting.   In practice, advertising of the kind envisaged in this second limiting case may have been fairly widespread in recent years.   Producers in perfectly competitive industries may well be dissatisfied with the prospect of earning increased profits.   For such profits can only result from an increased demand for the output of the whole perfectly competitive industry.   Entrepreneurs producing in such conditions will sometimes find it possible to increase their own incomes by persuading consumers that their particular product has some special characteristic which distinguishes it from the other products made by the industry.   A case in point seems to be tea. Over the last forty years or so, tea, which had hitherto been regarded as a more or less homogeneous product, has been packed in various different-coloured packets with the intention of persuading consumers that, since the packets are different, so is the tea, and there is reason to think that other previously homogeneous products have been differentiated in the same way.   Flour seems to be another example.   If it is true that this kind of change has taken place, then it is reasonable to conclude that in practice the aim of many advertising campaigns is to reduce elasticity of demand, as well as to shift the firm's average revenue curve bodily to the right.

6. OLIGOPOLY

We have been concerned in this chapter and in the previous one with a discussion of the different types of imperfect competition which are likely to occur.   Such a discussion is often referred to as study of 'market forms'.   The final type of market form—the final species of imperfect competition—which needs to be analysed here, is known by the word *oligopoly*.   This specimen of economic jargon is derived by analogy from the more respectable term, monopoly. A monopolist is a single seller. Oligopoly therefore occurs where there are only a few sellers. It differs both from monopoly, where there is only one seller, and from perfect and monopolistic competition, where there are many. In other words, we now introduce the notion of a small group of producers in distinction to the large group which we studied in the three previous sections.

The simplest case of oligopoly occurs when there are only two sellers and is known as *duopoly*. Duopoly analysis raises all the fundamental problems of oligopoly. These are basically different from the problems of monopoly, of perfect competition and of monopolistic competition. The analysis of duopoly, moreover, provides a simplified model for an explicit statement of the problems of oligopoly. Duopoly itself is not likely to be met with very often in practice but the conclusions to be drawn from a study of duopoly can easily be extended to cover situations where there are three, four, five or more sellers. We shall assume to begin with that the products made by the various oligopolists are identical. Where products are homogeneous in this way, one can speak of *oligopoly without product differentiation*. At a later stage, the analysis will be extended to study oligopoly situations where the products of the firms concerned are not identical but are differentiated, being only close and not perfect substitutes for each other.

We can therefore divide this study of duopoly into two main parts—the study of oligopoly with and without product differentiation. It will be readily appreciated that oligopoly with product differentiation is in reality only a rather special case of monopolistic competition. The important difference is that, since the number of producers is smaller, the actions of rival firms need more careful and individual attention. In the large group of monopolistic competition the many rivals can legitimately be looked at *en masse*. But since the numbers of competitors in oligopoly with product differentiation are small, the reactions of individual producers are both much more easily discernible and much more important than in monopolistic competition.

7. OLIGOPOLY WITHOUT PRODUCT DIFFERENTIATION

The analysis of oligopoly without product differentiation is most easily approached through an analysis of duopoly without product differentiation. For, as we have seen, duopoly is merely a particular example of oligopoly. The important feature of duopoly, with or without product differentiation, is that the individual producer has to consider very carefully what the indirect effects of his own decision to change price or output will be. Since, in duopoly without product differentiation, there are only two producers of identical goods, any price or output change by the first producer is bound to affect the second, whose reactions will in turn change the position of the first, and so on. The individual producer therefore has to acknowledge that he may change the whole situation in which he is producing in this indirect way if he changes his own price-output policy.

Such a chain of reactions does not occur either with monopoly or with perfect competition. The monopolist will fix his price and output so as to maximise his profits and is able to ignore the effect on his rivals as he does so. For all these rivals are producing extremely distant substitutes for the monopolist's own good, so, even if a monopolist's actions may conceivably affect his rivals' prices and profits to some extent, any backwash on the demand for his goods resulting from their reaction to his own actions will be so small that he can ignore it entirely. Similarly, in perfect competition, the producer adjusts his output to fit in with given market conditions. He can do nothing himself to alter these conditions. For the basic assumption of perfect competition is that the number of firms is very large. Any change in the output of a single producer will therefore have a negligible effect on the profits or prices of other producers. Thus both in monopoly and in perfect competition it is possible to regard the individual producer's revenue and cost curves as given independently of his own actions. The profit-maximising output of the individual producer can then be read off from these curves without difficulty.

In duopoly without product differentiation the position is quite different. It would be extremely dangerous to assume that with identical products and with only two producers (let us call them A and B) A can ignore the policy of B. It would also be dangerous to assume that A could ignore the indirect effect on his own price and profits of changes made by B in response to his own (A's) decisions. A must always have at least one eye on B. The position may well be likened to that in a game of cards. It is impossible to say beforehand what is the best way of playing any given hand, since one does not know in advance which cards the other players hold. The best way of playing the hand will not

depend entirely on how likely it is that particular cards will be
played. It also depends on how anxious and able you are to keep
your opponents guessing about which cards you have and which
you have not.

It will be clear from this analogy that there is no simple
solution to the question. How will a duopolist, where products
are identical, fix his output and price ? The answer will depend
on the assumptions which are made about the two producers.
There is no single determinate solution as in monopoly, perfect
competition or monopolistic competition, but a whole series of
different possible solutions, each depending on different assumptions. In particular, the solution depends on whether A thinks
that he can persuade B to make a foolish response to any change
which he makes. The key to any solution of the problem of
duopoly lies in the kind of assumptions which are made about B's
reactions to a change of price and output by A, and *vice versa*.
It is not surprising, therefore, that economists have produced
many different explanations of duopoly, each based on different
hypotheses about what A might expect B to do. There is no
need, here, to give a list of these different solutions.[1] The more
useful procedure will be to find which are the most realistic
solutions.

The search for plausible assumptions about duopoly without
product differentiation is not an easy one. A simplified model is
indeed so simple that it is difficult to illustrate it from practical
experience. It is, however, possible to make certain reasonable
assumptions. We shall assume first of all that the two producers
are of equal intelligence. We shall also assume that the costs of
each firm are the same, or at any rate not very different. The
simplest assumption to make is, of course, that each producer
has no costs at all, as was done in the traditional analysis by
Cournot,[2] of duopoly between the owners of mineral springs.
But this is not very realistic. It is, however, quite sensible to
think that the only two producers of an identical good will have
similar costs.

It is more difficult to make assumptions about demand conditions in oligopoly. In perfect competition this is easy, since the

[1] Readers who are interested in these solutions of the duopoly problem will
find a survey of them in E. H. Chamberlin, *Theory of Monopolistic Competition*,
chapter iii, and in William Fellner, *Competition among the Few*, chapter ii.

[2] *Recherches sur les principes mathématiques de la théorie des richesses*,
chapter vii.

price is given to each individual producer as an objective fact, determined for him by the equilibrium between market demand and market supply. In monopoly again, the average revenue curve is an objective fact, given quite independently of the monopolist's own actions. In duopoly without product differentiation there is no such objective average revenue curve for the individual producer. Both firms are producing identical goods. So, if we continue to assume (as we must) that consumers are indifferent which producer they patronise when prices are the same for each firm's good, we cannot say how many consumers will go to A except on some assumption about what B's price is. If the consumers are in fact indifferent whether they buy from A or B at a given price, we may reasonably assume that, when both firms charge the same price, half the consumers will buy from A and half from B. It will be a matter of pure accident whether *individual* consumers go to A or to B.

On this assumption that when both firms charge the same price each producer will sell the same amount, where will the price actually be fixed ? Since consumers are indifferent between the two producers, each must in the long run charge the same price. If this were not the case, the producer charging the higher price would be unable to sell any output at all. Nevertheless it is difficult to say what this single price will be. A cannot necessarily be assumed to begin by charging the same price as B, since B will also be attempting to charge the same price as A, and there is no reason why one producer should fix his price before the other does.

What, then, are we to assume about the 'equilibrium' price which two duopolists will charge, perhaps as a result of bitter experience in a price-war, perhaps by independent decisions or perhaps by actual (or tacit) agreement and discussion ? The simplest solution, which will satisfy both the duopolist and the economic theorist, is that the single monopoly price will be charged by both firms either as a result of consultation or of independent experiment.

Both parties will be wise to fix on that price which would be charged if there were only a single monopolist producing both their outputs. This price could be charged, either as a result of actual or tacit agreement between the duopolists or as a result of each deciding, quite independently, that this would be the best price to fix. It would clearly not pay the duopolists to fix their price at any other price than that charged by a monopolist. For the monopolist is assumed to fix his price at that level which will maximise his profits. The joint profits of the duopolists would therefore also be at a maximum at this level. We are assuming, of course, that the total costs of the monopolist would be the same as the total costs of the two monopolists for the same output. This need not be the case. The best that the duopolists can do is therefore either to make an actual monopoly agreement, or else to behave independently in the same way as they would if there were one.

If the duopolists were to raise their price above this monopoly level they would lose money. If it did not pay the monopolist to charge a higher price it would not pay them to do so. On the other hand, it would not pay them to lower their price. If A lowered his price, B would have to follow suit or lose all his customers, and any price below the monopoly price must be one at which the combined profits were reduced below the maximum monopoly level—or the monopolist would have chosen it himself. If there is an actual or tacit agreement between the duopolists it does not seem likely that they will pursue a policy of price reduction. By so doing they will merely both lose money. This, then, is one solution to the problem of what happens where there is duopoly without product differentiation. If both producers want to make as much money as possible, assuming that the market is shared equally between them, they will fix the same price (and output) as would have been fixed by a single monopolist. This gives us a determinate solution showing an optimum equilibrium position.

The solution does, of course, depend ultimately on our assumption that the cost curves of the two producers are identical. It also assumes that the monopolist's total cost at the equilibrium output is equal to the sum of the costs of the duopolists. This is not an entirely reasonable assumption, and the solution is to that extent unrealistic. We have assumed, in fact, that the joint problem of the duopolists is the same as that of a single monopolist. They will therefore simultaneously fix the same price as the monopolist and will share the market and the profits equally.

We must now consider what will happen if one duopolist tries to earn more than the other by raising or lowering his price. If both duopolists are intelligent they will not try to do this, since they will see that they are both bound to lose. They will merely take equal shares in a smaller pool of profits. It is possible, however, that if both duopolists are unintelligent each will attempt to gain at the expense of the other in this way. If A cuts his price, B, having lost all his customers, may decide to respond by cutting his price even further. A will reply with yet a further price cut and so on, each duopolist cutting prices in an attempt to regain the market.

If, on the other hand, the duopolists were of unequal intelligence, A, the less intelligent, might make a series of price cuts to each of which B would be forced to reply. Being more intelligent, B would realise that the best thing to do would be to make an identical cut, hoping that A would then realise that a further cut would not pay. But in any case, whether both duopolists were determined to cut each other's throats, or only one of them was unwise enough to reduce his price, the effect would be to reduce profits below the maximum. It is difficult to say where equilibrium would be reached. All one can say is that the price would hardly be likely to fall below the point at which both duopolists were only earning normal profits. In the long run, at any rate, it would not be possible for them to remain in the industry if price fell below this level. The least satisfactory of the possible equilibrium positions for such duopolists is thus where each is earning only normal profits.

This second solution is one where the follies of the duopolists artificially create a position similar to that of equilibrium in perfect competition. It is not an optimum equilibrium position but it is nevertheless a possible equilibrium position. The difference between this situation and that of equilibrium in perfect competition is this. In perfect competition it is as a result of inexorable market forces that a long-run equilibrium situation is brought about where only normal profits are being earned. In the case of duopoly it is artificially created as a result of an unnecessary price-war between the duopolists. It may be noted once again that our result depends upon the assumption of identical costs in the two firms. If, in fact, the costs or the normal profits (or both) are different for the two duopolists, the firm with lower costs may be able to undercut the other and, by making it earn less than normal profits, force it out of existence in the long run. Thus duopoly might become monopoly.

We have seen already that the best course for the duopolists will be to fix the monopoly price and to share the market. It may be noted, however, that this does not necessarily imply a formal agreement between the two firms. There is likely to be such an agreement (provided the law does not prevent it), but the same result could come about if each producer independently worked out the best possible solution, assumed that his competitor had done the same, and then put the policy into effect. To sum up then, it is possible that the duopoly price, in the long run, will settle at any level between the monopoly price and the perfectly competitive price. In the short run the duopoly price might even fall below the competitive price with both firms failing to earn even normal profits. The most sensible, and probably the most likely solution, however, is the optimum one where the monopoly price is charged, and the monopoly profits are divided between the two producers.

The solution to the problem of what happens in oligopoly without product differentiation where three, four, etc., producers make identical goods is equally uncertain. With three producers the monopoly solution is rather less probable. Agreement between three producers will usually be harder to obtain than with only two producers, and it will be rather less likely that each of the three will decide independently to charge the monopoly price. With four producers the same arguments hold, and the likelihood that they will fix a monopoly price is still more remote. As the numbers of firms increase they must sooner or later become sufficiently numerous for perfect competition to be inevitable unless there is some strong personality able to form a monopoly even from a larger number of firms. The price which will be fixed in oligopoly without product differentiation is thus indeterminate, but is likely, in general, to be lower the larger the number of producers, until in the end there are enough for a perfectly competitive equilibrium to be reached.

8. OLIGOPOLY WITH PRODUCT DIFFERENTIATION

Where there is oligopoly *with* product differentiation in any market, not only is the number of firms small but their products are also differentiated. The main generalisation which can be made about this type of oligopoly is that, in general, monopoly agreements are likely to be more unusual than in oligopoly without product differentiation. Since the products of the various firms are not identical, a monopoly arrangement would probably be harder to arrive at. It would be more difficult to merge the two firms, and even a price policy would be harder to agree upon. For now that products are differentiated each firm will have its own clientele, and will almost certainly be anxious to go on producing for these customers as an independent firm. Where there is anti-monopoly legislation such collusion will, of course, also be illegal.

Let us consider the simplest case first. What happens in duopoly with product differentiation ? It is clear that in such a situation it will always pay the two producers to refrain from undercutting each other in such a way as to cause a price-war. It is, however, no longer so certain that a change in price on the part of one producer will provoke an immediate retaliatory change by the other. In oligopoly *without* product differentiation the fact that products are identical means that if one producer raises his price he loses all his customers. He will therefore never do this. On the other hand, if a producer lowers his price his rival will

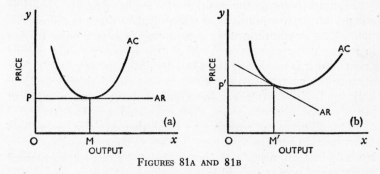

FIGURES 81A AND 81B

immediately lose all *his* custom and will make a price cut of his own. But in oligopoly *with* product differentiation the fact that products are somewhat different means that it may be possible for one producer to raise or lower his price without needing to fear either the loss of all his customers on the one hand, or an immediate response by his rival on the other.

In such a situation it is possible for consumers to be attached more or less firmly to one product rather than the other. So, the assumption that the producers will share the market equally, which we could make for duopoly without product differentiation, need no longer hold. The simple monopoly solution is, as we have seen, less probable, for we are now dealing with two products and not one. On the other hand, there seems to be less danger of a price-war since the producers will not respond quite so readily to price cuts as where there is no product differentiation.

If there are three, four or five producers of differentiated goods the monopoly solution becomes progressively less probable. The difficulties of forming a monopoly organisation, already considerable where there are so many firms, will be further complicated by product differentiation. As we noted above, each firm will have its own clientele and its own goodwill.   On the other hand, it is possible that there will be cut-throat competition with a final solution analogous to that of monopolistic competition.

For example, Figure 81a shows the equilibrium of a single firm producing in conditions of oligopoly *without* product differentiation.   A price-war has forced price down to OP.   At this price the firm can sell an output of OM, just earning normal profits by so doing.   If it were to raise its price it would lose all its customers, assuming its rivals did nothing. If it were to lower its price it would go out of business in the long run.

Figure 81b shows the position of a similar firm but this time one producing in conditions of oligopoly *with* product differentiation.   The equilibrium after a price-war is here similar to that in monopolistic competition.   The firm is earning only normal profits but it is producing less than the optimum output.   This is because the average revenue curve is downward-sloping and not horizontal.   The price-war has eliminated abnormal profits but the final equilibrium is not that associated with perfect competition.   This is not surprising.   Conditions are similar to those under monopolistic competition.   In fact, of course, since products are not identical, firms with 'better' products can still earn small supernormal profits even in this situation.

The few producers, though they could have agreed to band together and protect each other's profits, may therefore deliberately decide to create conditions of monopolistic competition by their keen rivalry.   Profits are then bound to be smaller than they need have been with a monopoly agreement—unless one or more firms retire, or are forced to retire, from the competitive struggle. It is only too obvious that the best interests of all the oligopolists lie in making an agreement to ensure that there is no price-war. As we have seen, however, the problems which would arise in doing this are often great, especially where monopoly is frowned on by the law.   In addition, now that products are not identical each producer will have an interest in keeping his own particular customers ; and he may find that a price other than the monopoly price enables him to do this.   It is therefore likely that the final price will be one which is intermediate between the monopoly price and the cut-throat competition price.   The actual price will depend on the conditions prevailing, and will differ from case to case.

What, then, is the equilibrium situation in oligopoly with product differentiation likely to be ?   Let us assume that there are three firms producing similar, but not identical products, and that the prices of these products have been fixed for some time at a given level where each was making fairly large profits. Let us also assume that the firms are producing in different regions but that the cost of transport between these regions, previously high, falls, so that the three markets become closely competitive. What will happen? The price charged by each firm may now be either higher or lower than the most profitable price. But it is extremely improbable that any price change will be made. If each producer continues to earn good profits, he may argue that to lower his price would be to start a price-war and to bring ruin. On the other hand, he may well feel that if he were to raise his price he would lose also. For he is not sure how closely competitive with his own his rivals' products are. He is therefore not very keen to experiment with changes in prices and output in order to discover what the optimum price is. This type of experimenting may be suitable for a monopolist, who need not fear the reactions of his rivals. For the oligopolist, however, it may well mean a catastrophic fall in sales if he raises his price and alienates consumers, or a serious price-war if he lowers price very far and incurs the displeasure of his rivals. Oligopolists producing differentiated goods might therefore be content, so long as they are making a reasonable amount of money, to leave price and output exactly as they are for the sake of a quiet life.

This type of situation is not likely to occur in oligopoly without product differentiation since the individual producer must always immediately follow any price cuts by his rivals, otherwise he would lose *all* custom. In oligopoly with product differentiation, however, the idea that, above all, oligopolists want to avoid trouble seems an attractive one. It would mean that, in oligopoly of this kind, no-one changed prices except at infrequent intervals. Whilst occasional price-wars might occur, prices would soon return to the old levels when the rivals saw that they were merely cutting each other's throats.

This notion is, in fact, a most interesting one because it is one which throws doubt on our basic assumption of profit maximisation. It may well be that in this picture of oligopoly with product differentiation, where producers prefer a quiet life to the hazards of always seeking maximum profits in conditions where the results of any price change are most uncertain, we have a realistic picture of what frequently actually happens in the real world. The real-world entrepreneur, especially if he is an oligopolist, often seems to be much more anxious to avoid the perils of price-wars than he is to earn maximum profits.

The various different market situations which we have discussed in the last few chapters can be conveniently summarised in the following table.

TABLE 4

A CLASSIFICATION OF MARKET SITUATIONS

Number of Firms	Type of Market Situation	
	Homogeneous Products	Differentiated Products
Many firms	Perfect competition	Monopolistic competition
Few firms	Oligopoly without product differentiation	Oligopoly with product differentiation
One firm	Monopoly	—

Table 4 should explain itself, but perhaps one or two comments on it would be useful. First, it is important to note that apart from perfect competition all other types of market situation can be grouped under the general heading of imperfect competition. Monopolistic competition is then the 'least imperfect' or 'most nearly perfect' type of competition. Monopoly is the 'most imperfect' type of market situation. Second, we have ignored 'pure' monopoly in this classification since it is only a theoretical limiting case. Third, it will be noted that the situation where a single firm produces differentiated products does not seem to have any meaning at all—especially since we are assuming that each firm produces only one product.

Finally, it is worth noting that one can distinguish between these various types of market situation by considering cross-elasticities of demand. In perfect competition the cross-elasticity of demand for the product of a single firm with respect to a change in the price of the rest of the industry will be infinite. That is to say, the proportionate fall in the demand for the product of a single firm will be infinitely large compared with any given proportionate fall in the price of the product of the whole industry. Similarly, in monopolistic competition the cross-elasticity of demand for the product of a single firm with respect to a change in the price of the other products made in the monopolistic 'group' will be very high. The cross-elasticity of demand for the product of a monopolist with respect to a fall in the price of other products in the economy will be very low. A given proportionate change in the price of other goods will cause only an extremely small proportionate change—if indeed it causes any change at all—in the demand for the product of a monopolist.

SUGGESTED READING

E. H. Chamberlin, *Theory of Monopolistic Competition*, Cambridge, Mass., 1946, especially chapters iv-vii.

William Fellner, *Competition among the Few*, New York, 1949, especially chapters i and iv-vii.

Robert Triffin, *Monopolistic Competition and General Equilibrium Theory*, Cambridge, Mass., 1940, *passim*.

K. W. Rothschild, 'Price Theory and Oligopoly', *Economic Journal*, September 1947, p. 299.

CHAPTER X

LAWS OF RETURNS

1. THE THEORY OF FACTOR PRICES

WE have now reached an important stage in our analysis. So far we have only been concerned with showing how the prices of goods are determined in conditions both of perfect and imperfect competition. We now come to another broad field of economic theory. We shall discuss how the prices of factors of production are determined. In the past, ideas about the determination of factor prices were often referred to as the *Theory of Distribution*. Nineteenth-century economists were extremely interested in the problem of how much of the receipts of industry and agriculture went to the various factors of production. For political and social reasons they felt it important to know how the relative incomes of the various social groups were likely to be determined. Nowadays, in pure economic analysis at least, the centre of interest has shifted. Economic theory is more concerned with what determines the prices of the factors of production than with what determines their respective shares of the national income. What we are about to embark on therefore is a study of the way in which factors of production are priced, and not a study of their respective shares in the income of the community. We shall not therefore use the older title of the 'Theory of Distribution' to describe this part of our study.

Our analysis of the pricing of factors of production will in fact be exactly parallel to the analysis of the pricing of commodities and services, which we have already undertaken. For although on social and political grounds one may feel some qualms about saying so, all the broad groups of factors of production—land, labour, capital and entrepreneurship—have 'prices' in the form of rent, wages, interest and profits respectively. This chapter is in a sense a digression from the main line of argument. We shall here be entirely concerned with a discussion of production conditions. But this discussion will enable us to look both backwards and forwards. It will enable us to say more about the technical production conditions underlying the shape of cost curves—a problem already touched on in Chapter V—and determining the returns to factors of production in various circumstances—the subject of the next few chapters.

2. EQUAL PRODUCT CURVES

We shall find that the easiest way to discuss the laws of returns is to use an analysis of the same kind as we used in Chapter III. In Figure 82 we assume that two factors of production, X and Y, are being used to produce a given product. Amounts of factor X are measured along the x-axis and amounts of factor Y along the y-axis. Technical conditions are such that if OL units of factor Y and OM units of factor X are being used, 20 units of the product are produced. Again, if OL′ units of factor Y and OM′ units of factor X are being used, 20 units of product are produced. Similarly, the co-ordinates of any other point on the curve AC besides B and B′, show the quantities of the two factors X and Y

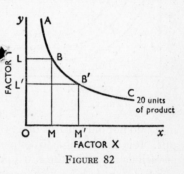

FIGURE 82

needed to produce 20 units of product. The curve AC, that is to say, shows all those combinations of the two factors which, in given technical conditions, will produce 20 units of output. We do, of course, assume throughout this analysis that technical production conditions are given and constant, and that the factors used are being combined as efficiently as possible in these given production conditions. The curve AC thus shows the smallest combinations of the two factors needed, in the existing state of technology, to produce any given output. Curves like AC have been variously described as equal product curves, iso-product curves and iso-quants. We shall call them equal product curves since this is the clearest and simplest term.

The equal product curve AC in Figure 82 is similar to an indifference curve. It shows all those combinations of factors which yield a certain product, just as an indifference curve shows all those combinations of goods which provide a certain level of satisfaction. But there are important differences between equal product curves and indifference curves which we may note.

First, and most obvious, there is the fact that whilst it is impossible to find any units in which to label indifference curves, one can label equal product curves in terms of amounts of product made. Whilst there is no way of measuring satisfaction in physical units, one can measure output of a homogeneous product in physical terms without any difficulty. Similarly, if one draws 'higher' and 'lower' equal product curves, as in Figure 83,—if we draw equal product 'maps'—it is possible to say by how much production is greater or less on one equal product curve than on another.

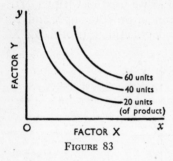

FIGURE 83

For example, the second equal product curve in Figure 83 shows an output of 40 units, an output 20 units greater than on the first equal product curve. The third equal product curve represents an output twenty units greater than on the second—60 units instead of 40—and so on. Thus equal product maps do not only enable one to measure physical quantities of output. It is also possible to compare the sizes of such physical outputs at various points on the equal product maps. One can see by how much output is higher or lower at one point than at another, in a way which one cannot do with the satisfactions considered on indifference maps. We can label equal product curves in units of the product without difficulty, and do not have to content ourselves with the non-commital numbers 1, 2, 3, 4, etc., as with indifference maps. This is an advantage.

We now need to know the probable shape of equal product curves, just as in Chapter III we needed to know the probable shape of indifference curves. In fact they will be of the same general shape and for the same kind of reasons. First, equal product curves will slope downwards to the right. This must be the case so long as additional units of any factor of production do not produce *negative* amounts of product. Now this is not an impossibility. One can imagine situations where, with two factors, say land and labour, so many men might be employed that they would all get in each other's way. The result of adding more men would be actually to reduce the total physical product. An increase in the other factor of production, land, would be needed to maintain the product constant.

But whilst this might happen, it would never pay an entrepreneur to produce in such a situation. Factors must cost something if they are to be eligible for consideration in economic analysis at all. Thus, whenever a given product is obtainable with less of both factors, as it would be if equal product curves sloped upwards, it can be obtained with less expense. Any entrepreneur who was maximising profits would never use a combination of factors shown on an upward-sloping portion of an equal product curve. So, whilst it is certainly not inconceivable that, over certain ranges, equal product curves might slope upwards, such ranges could never contain equilibrium positions. We can therefore ignore this possibility. Similarly, a horizontal range of an equal product curve, though it could conceivably exist, could never include a possible position of equilibrium. The given output could always be obtained with less expense from a factor combination shown on a downward-sloping portion of the same curve. We can therefore safely assume that, over those ranges in which we shall be interested, equal product curves slope downwards to the right.

The second assumption about equal product curves is that they are convex to the origin. This is an important assumption, but it is not immediately apparent why equal product curves should be of this shape. This assumption clearly implies something about the marginal significance of one factor in terms of another. Let us be quite clear first of all what marginal significance means in this context. In terms of ordinary indifference curves, the marginal significance of one good in terms of the other means the amount of the one good which a consumer can give up in exchange for more of the other, and yet remain on the same indifference curve. With equal product curves the marginal significance of one factor, X, in terms of another factor, Y, is the amount of the factor Y which it is possible to give up in exchange for one more unit of factor X without altering the amount of product made—whilst remaining on the same equal product curve.

For example, let us imagine a situation where one unit of factor X and ten units of factor Y are being used to produce twenty units of product. What is the marginal significance of factor X in terms of factor Y ? If the product is to be kept constant whilst one unit of factor X is added to the factor combination already being used, a certain quantity of factor Y must be dispensed with. Otherwise the total product would increase. It might, for example, be necessary to dispense with two units of factor Y, now that an additional unit of factor X had been taken on, if the amount of product were to be kept constant. In this situation, the marginal significance of X in terms of Y is $X = 2Y$. In this way, one can calculate the marginal significance of one factor in terms of the other at any point on any equal product curve. But this marginal significance of one factor in terms of the other will always depend on the slope of the equal product curve. And the way in which the slope of an equal product curve changes, as one moves along it, will determine the way in which the marginal significance of one factor in terms of the other changes.

What, then, does the assumption that equal product curves are convex to the origin imply about the marginal significance of one factor in terms of the other? It means that the marginal significance of one factor in terms of the other will always diminish along any equal product curve. On any equal product curve, that is to say, the more of factor X is being used, the less of factor Y will it be possible to give up in exchange for a further unit of X if product is to be kept constant. Similarly, of course, the more units of Y are being used, the less X will it be possible to give up in exchange for yet one more unit of Y. This assumption that equal product curves are convex to the origin and that the marginal significance of one factor in terms of the other therefore always diminishes along an equal product curve, is useful and important. We must now see whether diminishing marginal significance of one factor in terms of the other when the amount of the first factor is increased is in fact likely to occur as a general rule, for our fundamental assumption about production conditions is that it does.

This assumption that equal product curves are convex to the origin—that marginal significance always diminishes—can be justified in exactly the same way as can the convexity of indifference curves—so long as competition between buyers of factors is perfect. When we discussed consumer's equilibrium in terms of indifference curves we assumed that the prices of all goods were given, and that all price lines were therefore straight lines. Any volume of purchases made by a single consumer was assumed to leave the relative prices of the goods he bought unaltered. By making this assumption, we were able to show that convexity of indifference curves was an essential condition for equilibrium of the consumer.

As we shall see in a moment, the 'perfectly competitive' buyer of factors makes his purchases in accordance with an equal product map just as a consumer does with an indifference map. He is in equilibrium where his (straight line) price line is tangential to a convex equal product curve. For in this way he just reaches the highest possible equal product curve. But this means that at the point of equilibrium the relative prices of factors equal the marginal significance of one factor in terms of the other. In consequence, the purchaser buys each factor until its marginal significance in terms of money is just equal to its money price. If, however, the marginal significance of a factor *increased* as one hired more of it, as it would on a concave equal product curve, and it was worth buying any of the factor at all, it would be worth spending the whole of one's outlay on it. For each succeeding unit of the factor would have a progressively higher marginal significance and would be correspondingly more worth hiring— given the relative factor prices shown on the (straight) price line. Concave equal product curves would make it worth hiring only one of the factors. It follows from this that, since in practice one does not often find large numbers of men or large areas of land producing output on their own and without any co-operating factors, it is reasonable to think that concave equal product curves are unrealistic so long as competition between buyers of factors is perfect.

This does not, of course, rule out the possibility of 'bumps' or 'wobbles' on an equal product curve. On the other hand, it is clear that a producer would never be in equilibrium on such a range of an equal product curve. Only where marginal significance is diminishing can he be in equilibrium. And since economists are not interested in situations where equilibrium is impossible, we can ignore such unusual portions of equal product curves. The fundamental assumption of diminishing marginal significance along an equal product curve is therefore reasonable in conditions of perfect competition between buyers of factors.

It is, however, possible that competition between the buyers of factors may not be perfect. This is more likely to happen with buyers of factors than with buyers of ordinary consumption goods. It is reasonable when dealing with consumers to assume that there are large numbers of them—that competition between them is perfect. But there may be only a few, or even only one firm, buying factors. If there is, say, only one purchaser of certain factors of production, the prices of these factors will almost certainly be influenced by his own purchases of them. This means that the price line need not be a straight line, but may be concave to the origin. The more of one factor the firm buys compared with the other factor, the higher the former factor's relative price will be and *vice versa*. It follows that such a producer could be in equilibrium, with the price line tangent to a *concave* equal product curve, provided only that the concavity of the price line is greater than that of the equal product curve. The concave price line would show that relative prices were varying and not constant. We shall assume here, however, that though a single monopolistic firm buying two factors might be in an equilibrium on a concave equal product curve, all such equal product curves are in fact convex to the origin. This is our second assumption about equal product curves. But it is an *assumption* and cannot be justified on *a priori* grounds.

Finally, equal product curves, like indifference curves, can never cut each other. If they did so, there would be a logical contradiction.

3. RETURNS TO SCALE

We can now use equal product curves to discover how returns to factors of production will change as the amounts of factors used are altered in certain ways. First, however, there is a point which needs discussing. The equal product maps we have used so far show only two factors. This is not altogether realistic. The idea that labour and capital can produce a product with no-one to supervise them is a little unreasonable. It would therefore be desirable to use an analysis where there were three or four factors of production, with the entrepreneur as one of them. The others could then be labour, land or capital, as one wished. Unfortunately this would complicate the diagrams needed. Strictly, one would need to draw diagrams in three (or more) dimensions, one for each factor, if one used this type of analysis. If one did use three dimensions, the third factor would have to be measured up the third axis and the product, instead of being shown on two-dimensional equal product curves, would have to be shown on equal product surfaces in three dimensions. This is very difficult on the two-dimensional page of a book. In addition, since entrepreneurship is not a factor of production which can be varied (in the single firm) or even measured (since there are no units of measurement), it would not be useful to try to do this. Instead, we shall carry out a formal analysis in terms of two factors, extending our results to apply to more than two factors where this is appropriate. This will enable us to see the general relationships between input of factors and output of product, which is all that is really needed at this stage of the analysis.

We shall analyse the laws of returns in two stages. In this section we shall consider returns to two factors of production where both can vary—returns with two variable factors. In the next section, we shall consider returns to two factors where only one factor can vary and the other is in fixed amount. This is the case of returns to one variable factor, considered in the 'law of variable proportions'.[1] We shall assume throughout that competition between buyers of factors is perfect—that all *price lines* are straight lines.

Let us discover how a firm will change its output in the long run in response to a change in the demand for its product, assuming that it can alter the amounts of both factors. To do this we must introduce the prices of the factors in question into the analysis, for the amounts of factors hired by the firm, in a given situation, will depend on

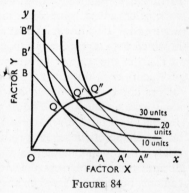

FIGURE 84

the relative prices of these factors as well as on the technical conditions shown on the firm's equal product map. Let us assume that the firm has the equal product map shown in Figure 84, and that in the existing situation the price of factor X divided by the price of factor Y is equal to $\dfrac{OB}{OA} = \dfrac{OB'}{OA'} = \dfrac{OB''}{OA''}$.

We shall also continue to assume that the firm wishes to produce each output as cheaply as possible. If this is so, and if the firm wishes to produce twenty units of product, it will be in equilibrium at point Q' on the equal product curve representing twenty units of output. Here the price line A'B' is tangential to the equal product curve. Only at point Q' will the firm be producing the twenty units of output as cheaply as possible. For to reach any point other than Q' on the equal product curve representing twenty units of output, the firm will have to spend more than OA' in terms of X, or OB' in terms of Y, to obtain the appropriate combination of factors. Similarly, if the firm wishes to produce thirty units of the product, it will only be in equi-

[1] See p. 114.

librium at point Q″. OA″ in terms of X or OB″ in terms of Y represents the lowest cost at which thirty units of output can be produced. It will be noted that at all points such as Q, Q′ and Q″ the marginal significance of X in terms of Y is equal to the relative money prices of factors X and Y. This is shown by the fact that the equal product curves are tangential to the respective price lines. Such equilibrium positions are therefore analogous to those shown in consumers' indifference maps.

Given the relative price of factors X and Y, a firm which is able to vary the amounts of both these factors at will always fixes its scale of output at some point along a line like O – Q – Q′ – Q″ in Figure 84. This line is known as a *scale line*, for it shows the way in which the entrepreneur adjusts the scale of his operations when he changes the scale of his output. It shows the cheapest way of producing each output, given relative factor prices. Where both factors are variable, the firm will always produce at some point along such a scale line. The slope of the scale line in question will depend both on the relative prices of the factors concerned and on the shape of the equal product curves. One cannot say precisely where on any such scale line a firm will in fact be in equilibrium until one knows the output it wishes to produce. This can only be deduced from an analysis of the product market. One can, however, be certain that where both factors are variable the entrepreneur will be producing somewhere or other on a scale line like the one shown. A scale line, therefore, shows the way in which factor combinations will alter, where both factors can be varied in response to changes in the output which the firm is producing, given the relative prices of the factors. It must be remembered, of course, that on every equal product map there will be a different scale line for *every* different relative price of the factors.

From such an equal product map we can find two things. First, having obtained the scale line corresponding to any particular ratio of the prices of the factors, we can tell whether *returns to scale* (returns along the scale line) will increase, diminish or remain constant as output varies. Second, we can tell whether the proportion between the amounts of the two factors of production used will remain the same or will vary as one moves along any one scale line. These two problems should not be confused, for they are in essence quite separate.

Let us consider the way in which these two influences affect the nature of scale lines by studying first a relatively simple type of equal product map. Let us assume that if we start from any given combination of two factors and double the amount of each factor, this doubles the product. Similarly, let us assume that if we treble the amount of each factor, we treble the product, and so on. In other words we assume that, with this equal product map, whenever we change the amounts of both factors in a given proportion, we change the product in that same proportion. In this case *all* the scale lines on the equal product map will be straight lines through the origin. Similarly, *returns to scale* along every scale line on the equal product map will be constant. An equal product map with constant returns to scale on *every* scale line is shown in Figure 85. The constancy of returns to scale is displayed by the fact that the distance between successive equal product curves along any one scale line such as OABCD or OA″B″C″D″ is always the same. For example, in Figure 85 OA = AB = CD ; OA′ = A′B′ = B′C′ = C′D′ ; and OA″ = A″B″

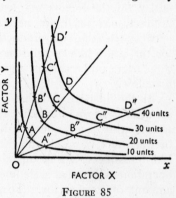

FACTOR X

FIGURE 85

= B″C″ = C″D″, etc. One can say alternatively that with given relative factor prices, and therefore with a constant price slope, *returns to outlay* are constant. For if factor prices are constant and one doubles the amount of each factor, one will clearly double outlay on the two factors together. Thus, with this particular type of equal product map, one can use the terms returns to scale and returns to outlay interchangeably. As we shall see later, with other kinds of equal product map it is more correct to speak of returns to outlay rather than of returns to scale.

With the equal product map shown in Figure 85 it is said that the production function, the function which relates the amount of output to the amounts of the factors needed to produce it, is homogeneous of the first degree. We can write any production function in the general form $P = f(X, Y)$, where P = amount of product and X and Y are factors of production. That is to say, the product P is a function of, or depends on, the quantities of the two factors X and Y which are used to produce it. The production function giving the relationship between factors used and product produced in the conditions shown in Figure 85 will be such that if the factors X and Y are both changed in any given proportion, the product P will also change in that same proportion.

A homogeneous production function of the first degree is a useful one to study first because it is a simple one. But, as we have seen, it implies that with given and constant relative factor prices, the proportion between the two factors always remains the same whatever output is being produced. Is this a correct assumption? It need not necessarily be. Even if there are constant returns to outlay along a scale line, so that by doubling the outlay on the factors at given relative prices one doubles the product, one need not necessarily keep a constant proportion between the factors of production. It would be perfectly possible for the scales line to bend in one direction or the other, even if there were still constant returns to outlay along an individual scale line.

It should be noted that it is necessary to talk of returns to *outlay* instead of returns to *scale*, when the proportions between factors vary as output changes. For when the proportions between factors on any one scale line vary as output changes, it is impossible to speak unambiguously of doubling the scale of operations along that scale line in the usual sense of doubling the amount of each factor. To increase the amounts of both the factors in the same proportion would mean moving to a different scale line. One can, however, still unambiguously compare changes in *outlay on factors* with the changes in output to which they give rise. For example, if outlay on the factors is doubled and the product doubles also, one can say that returns to outlay are constant.

Now it is quite possible that although returns to outlay are constant along any scale line, the *proportions* between the factors along that same scale line may alter. Constant returns to outlay and constant proportions between the two factors are not the same thing. Nor is there any good reason why constant proportions between factors at all levels of output should often be found in practice. In this chapter it will be convenient to assume, for the sake of simplicity, that the proportion between the two factors remains the same whatever the scale of output is. This will enable us to use the terms returns to scale and returns to outlay interchangeably. But it should always be borne in mind that this is only a convenient simplification. No-one would suggest that constant proportions between factors always occur, or that returns to scale and returns to outlay always mean the same thing.

It is not difficult to think of instances where the proportions between factors will vary as the scale of activity changes. For example, the output of a single-storey factory could be doubled by adding a second storey. This would change the proportion between land and capital. Similarly, an increase in the output of a particular type of clothing might well make it possible to cut out the pieces of the garment with less waste of cloth. Constant proportions between factors will not necessarily occur but we shall assume here that they do.

So much for the problem of whether the proportions between factors must always remain the same or not as the scale of operations changes. Let us now return to the question of whether returns to outlay are likely to be constant in practice. It does not really seem very sensible to assume that this will always happen even where, as we are assuming, there are only two factors of production. It seems quite plausible to suppose that a change in the scale of operations can often mean increasing or decreasing returns to outlay. Over relatively low levels of output it is likely that increasing returns to outlay will occur, because with the larger output there are economies of scale to be reaped. It is likely, for example, that division of labour would increase output as the number of men employed rose. There is thus a likelihood of increasing returns to outlay whether or not the scale lines themselves are straight lines. Similarly, one would expect diminishing returns to outlay over other ranges of output. The type of equal product map which will occur when this happens is shown in Figure 86. Here we have drawn the scale line as a straight line purely to simplify the construction of the diagram.

Up to the point R on the scale line shown in Figure 86 returns to outlay increase as output rises. Beyond R, however, returns decrease as outlay continues to increase. As we have already explained, we have assumed only for the sake of simplicity that all scale lines are straight lines. This is not really likely to be the case. But it *is* justifiable to assume that returns to outlay will vary. It is not intuitively obvious, however, why returns to outlay should vary in any particular way when both (all) factors can vary. All one can say is that there seems to be more likelihood that returns will vary than that they will be constant. We know from observation of the world that, for example, division of labour often enables production to be carried on more efficiently as output rises. We also know that diseconomies of production can arise when output becomes very large.

It will, of course, be clear that there are similarities between scale lines on equal product maps and income-consumption curves on indifference maps. They both represent points of tangency between successive price lines of constant slope and successive equal product and indifference curves respectively.

So far we have seen that returns to outlay may either vary or remain constant as output changes, with two variable factors.

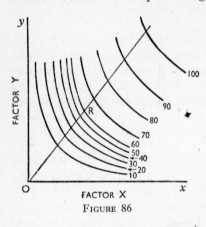

FACTOR Y

R

100
90
80
70
60
50
40
30
20
10

O   FACTOR X   x
FIGURE 86

But this kind of analysis is of limited use in economics. For in practice, at least one factor of production is usually fixed in amount. In Chapter V, for example, what we spoke of as 'returns to scale' were, strictly speaking, returns to more than one variable factor. For we then assumed that, even in the long run, entrepreneurship was a fixed factor of production. True 'returns to scale' in the sense of returns where *all* factors vary will very rarely be found in the real world. It will therefore be more realistic to study now the case of only one variable factor and discover what can be said about the way physical returns to that factor will alter. For, so long as one factor at least is fixed and one is variable, the results will be the same in essence as where several are fixed and one (or more) is variable.

4. MARGINAL PHYSICAL PRODUCTIVITY

We now assume that the firm uses a fixed amount of the factor Y in conjunction with varying amounts of factor X. In Figure 87a there is OM of the fixed factor Y, which is used in conjunction with varying amounts of factor X. The way in which returns to factor X change as the amounts of factor X vary can be discovered by studying conditions along the horizontal line MM in Figure 87a. For at each point on this line there is a fixed amount (OM) of factor Y being used with different amounts of the variable factor X. We can, however, represent the physical returns to the variable factor in several ways. Just as we can represent costs and revenues by total, average and marginal cost curves, so we can portray the

physical productivity of a variable factor of production by drawing
total, average or marginal physical productivity curves to show
returns to this variable factor. It is the shapes of such physical
productivity curves—especially marginal physical productivity
curves—which we must consider now. A marginal physical
productivity curve shows the changes in the marginal physical
productivity of a variable factor as the amount of it which is added

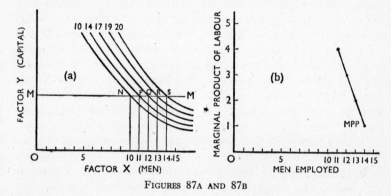

FIGURES 87A AND 87B

to a fixed factor alters. This marginal productivity curve will
form the basis of our analysis of the pricing of factors of production.

We can discover the marginal physical productivity of any
variable factor from any equal product map in the way shown in
Figure 87a.

In Figure 87a a fixed amount of OM of factor Y, say, capital,
is used in conjunction with varying amounts of factor X, say,
labour. As employment increases from ten men to eleven men,
four additional units of output are produced. Total production
rises from ten units to fourteen units. The marginal physical
productivity of labour is thus four units of output. This is shown
by the intersection of the horizontal line MM with the equal
product curve representing fourteen units of output at point P,
which is opposite eleven men marked off along the x-axis. The
twelfth man adds three units of output to the product. Total
output rises from fourteen units to seventeen units as one moves
from P to Q. The thirteenth man adds two units (from Q to R),
the fourteenth one unit (from R to S), and so on. We can now
construct Figure 87b to show the marginal physical productivity
of factor X (labour) on a marginal physical productivity curve.

The marginal physical productivity curve in Figure 87b shows how physical productivity, measured up the y-axis, changes as the numbers of men employed, measured along the x-axis, change. In this particular instance, the marginal physical productivity curve of labour (MPP) slopes downwards. We shall assume that this is the usual shape. As we shall see later, the marginal physical productivity of any variable factor is usually assumed to diminish as more of this variable factor is added to a fixed factor (or factors). It is also possible to draw an average physical productivity curve (derived from the equal product map by dividing total output at each level of employment by numbers of men employed) which bears the usual average-marginal relationship to the marginal physical productivity curve. The total physical productivity curve could also easily be derived either from the equal product map or from the average and marginal physical productivity curves.

This assumption that the marginal physical productivity of a variable factor used with one or several fixed factors will diminish, is important because such an idea has always held a place in economics. In the past it has usually been known as the 'law of diminishing returns', or, more recently, the 'law of variable proportions'. One can state the 'law of diminishing returns' thus: An increase in the amount of a variable factor added to a fixed factor causes, in general, a less than proportionate increase in the amount of product, given technical conditions.[1]

The 'law of diminishing returns' is thus not couched directly in terms of diminishing marginal productivity, though it comes to the same thing. We shall see, however, that diminishing marginal productivity is probably not so ubiquitous as some earlier economists seem to have thought. There may be ranges of marginal physical productivity curves where marginal physical productivity is increasing and not diminishing. Instead of falling throughout, as in Figure 87, the marginal physical productivity curve may rise for a short time before it ultimately falls. Diminishing marginal physical productivity does not always occur. Some modern economists therefore speak of *eventually* diminishing marginal productivity. This, it turns out, is a much more general condition. For, whilst it is conceivable that, before diminishing, marginal physical productivity may rise, in the end it is likely to fall. But it is not inevitable that this will happen.

In order to see more fully under what conditions marginal

[1] Cf. Alfred Marshall, *Principles of Economics*, p. 150.

physical productivity will diminish and in what conditions it will increase, let us first consider a situation where the production function is homogeneous of the first degree. Here, there will *always* be diminishing marginal physical productivity along any horizontal or vertical line like MM in Figure 87a. That is to say, whenever there are varying proportions between factors, with one fixed and the other variable, marginal physical productivity will always diminish. This must be the case, but perhaps it will be useful to prove why it must be so. Before we do this, however,

it will be convenient to derive the marginal physical productivity of a variable factor from an equal product map in rather a different way from the way in which we did it in Figure 87. In Figure 87 equal increments of a variable factor were added to a given amount of a fixed factor, and we saw that the resulting increments of product showed the marginal physical productivity of the variable factor. In Figure 88,

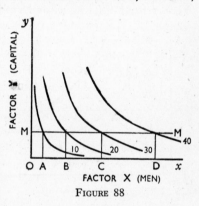

FIGURE 88

with a homogeneous production function of the first degree, we instead consider several equal successive increases in production along any horizontal, such as MM, and see how many men are needed to cause these equal increments of output. If this is done, we can see that to increase output from ten to twenty units along MM in Figure 88 requires the addition of AB more men to the fixed amount of capital OM and the OA men who are already employed. To increase production from twenty to thirty units needs BC more men, and so on. The number of units of the variable factor (labour) needed to raise output by the same absolute amount, here ten units, increases as we move along the horizontal MM from left to right. In other words, the marginal physical productivity of labour diminishes. For, if progressively more men have to be taken on to give the same absolute increase in output as employment rises, then clearly the product of each additional man (marginal productivity) is falling. Now with a homogeneous production function of the first degree, the distance between two successive equal product curves along a horizontal such as MM, like the distance BC, is

Q

always greater than a similar distance immediately to the left of it, in this case AB. This means that as more of a variable factor is added to a fixed factor, the marginal physical productivity of the variable factor falls progressively—with this type of equal product map. That this will always be the case with a homogeneous production function of the first degree can be proved from Figure 89.

In Figure 89 there are three equal product curves, showing ten, twenty and thirty units of output respectively. Along the x-axis are measured differing amounts of the variable factor X, applied to

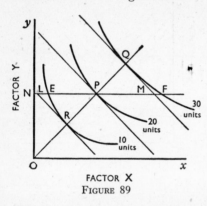

FACTOR X
FIGURE 89

a fixed amount (ON) of factor Y shown on the y-axis. A scale line showing constant returns to outlay (because the production function is homogeneous of the first degree) passes from the origin through point P. Tangents have been drawn to the equal product curves at the points R, P and Q where the equal product curves and the scale line intersect. Since these tangents all touch the equal product curves where the scale lines cut them, they must be parallel to each other; for all equal product curves have the same slope on the same scale line. We wish to prove that the intercept PF, between the equal product curves representing 20 and 30 units of output, is greater than the intercept EP between those representing 10 and 20 units. Since the production function is homogeneous of the first degree, $RP = PQ$; for, as we saw earlier, with this type of production function, returns to scale are always constant. Because $RP = PQ$ and because the tangents are parallel to each other, the intercepts LP and PM on the horizontal line NF are also equal to each other. Now LP is obviously greater than EP, because the equal product curve representing ten units of output is convex to the origin, whilst the tangent to it is a straight line. But EP is consequently less than PM, because $PM = LP$. Similarly, PF is greater than PM and is therefore also greater than EP. This proof holds with any equal product map representing a homogeneous production of the first degree. On any such equal product map the marginal physical productivity of a variable factor always falls as more of it is added to a fixed factor. So, if production functions were always homogeneous of the first degree and if returns to scale (and outlay) were always

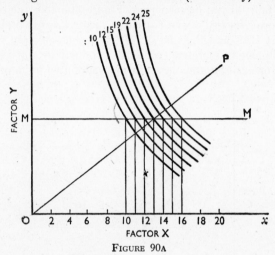

FIGURE 90A

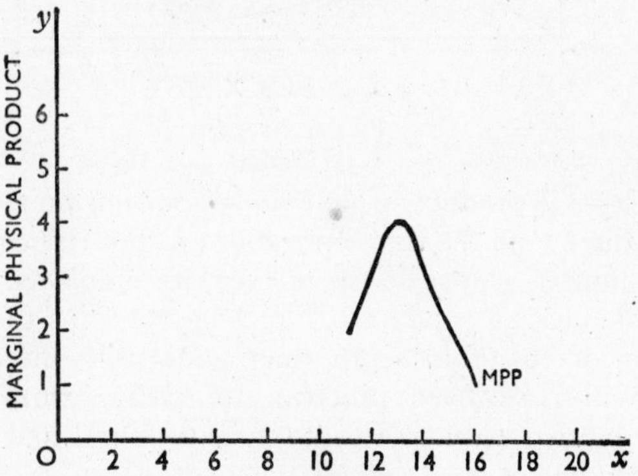

FIGURE 90B

constant, marginal physical productivity would always fall. But if returns to outlay are not always constant, marginal physical productivity to the variable factor may rise over some ranges of employment.

Figure 90a shows an equal product map on which the horizontal line MM shows returns to differing amounts of a variable factor X, used in conjunction with OM of a fixed factor Y. Figure

90b shows the marginal productivity curve of the variable factor X. In Figure 90a returns to outlay clearly rise to begin with as one moves up the scale line OP ; if output exceeds 19 units returns to outlay fall. It can be seen from Figure 90b that the marginal physical productivity of the (variable) factor measured along the *x*-axis first rises and then falls. If fewer than thirteen men are being employed, marginal physical productivity of labour is rising. For example, the eleventh man adds two units of output

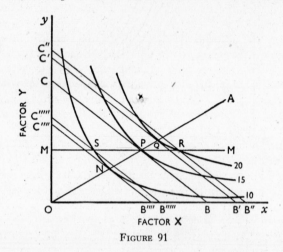

FIGURE 91

to the firm's total product, which rises from ten units to twelve, the twelfth three, and the thirteenth four (output rises from fifteen to nineteen units). Once fourteen men are employed, however, the marginal physical productivity of labour begins to fall. The employment of this fourteenth man adds only three units of output (which rises from nineteen to twenty-two), that of a fifteenth only two (twenty-two to twenty-four), and that of a sixteenth only one.

It will probably be valuable if we can show in a more general way under what circumstances returns to a variable factor (marginal productivity) can increase as more of that factor is employed in conjunction with a fixed factor. This has been done in Figure 91 where there are three equal product curves representing ten, fifteen and twenty units of output respectively. All scale lines (like OA) are straight lines through the origin, and it is along such scale lines that the firm will expand output (given the relative prices of factors) so long as both factors can be freely varied in amount as output is increased. Returns to outlay (scale) are clearly increasing along the one scale line shown (OA). For since NP is much greater than PQ, a much smaller increase in outlay on factors is required to raise output from fifteen to twenty units than to raise output from ten units to fifteen. Similarly, marginal productivity is increasing along MM since SP is greater than PR.

Let us assume that the relative factor prices are such that the firm is producing fifteen units of output at point P. If the firm now wished to produce twenty units of output, it would proceed, if both factors could be freely varied in amount, to produce at point Q on the scale line OA. This would require an outlay of OB′ in terms of factor X (or OC′ in terms of factor Y). If, in fact, factor Y is fixed in amount at OM and factor X only can be varied, the firm could only produce twenty units of output by producing at point R. And this would require a greater additional expenditure (BB″ in terms of X or CC″ in terms of Y) than would be needed to produce at Q (only BB′ in terms of X, CC′ in terms of Y). But since returns are increasing strongly along the scale line, the additional outlay needed to raise output along the scale line from fifteen to twenty units (BB′) is smaller than the outlay needed to raise output from ten units to fifteen (B′′′′B). Similarly, to increase output from ten to fifteen units along MM (from S to P) requires an additional outlay of B′′′′′B, whilst to raise it from fifteen to twenty units (from P to R) costs only an additional BB″. In other words, returns to outlay do not increase so rapidly along MM as along OA. The excess of B′′′′B over BB′ is greater than the excess of B′′′′′B over BB″. But returns to outlay do still increase along MM.

To put the point more generally, since the move from P to Q is along a scale line, the proportion between the factors which is appropriate to the existing ratio between the factor prices can be maintained. But the move from P to R is one which disturbs this 'optimum' proportion between factors. Production therefore increases less rapidly along MM than it would have done if output could have been increased along the scale line OA. But since returns to scale are *increasing very strongly*, this departure from the 'optimum' proportion between the factors does not cause an actual decrease in marginal product as output expands along MM.

One can sum up thus. *Whenever all the scale lines on an equal product map are straight lines through the origin*, the following conditions will hold. If returns to scale (outlay) are *constant*, the marginal productivity of a variable factor used in conjunction with a fixed factor will always diminish as more of the variable factor is used. If returns to scale (outlay) are *decreasing*, marginal productivity will likewise always diminish ; and when returns to scale (outlay) are *increasing*, marginal productivity will still diminish unless the returns to scale are increasing sufficiently strongly.

Even if the scale lines are not all straight lines through the origin, the above rules will always hold (though now for returns to *outlay*) provided that all scale lines slope upwards to the right. If scale lines take any other shape (*e.g.* are horizontal, or slope downwards to the right), there will be exceptions to the above rules. It is impossible to say intuitively whether such exceptions will be numerous, but one must allow for the possibility that they will be found.

It follows from the above discussion that the 'law of diminishing returns' does not hold with all types of production function. In some situations marginal productivity may rise before it ultimately falls. But there is no *a priori* reason for assuming that marginal productivity must ultimately fall. The 'law of eventually diminishing marginal productivity' need not always hold either. One cannot, therefore, make any definite statement about the way marginal productivity will behave. It need not always diminish. It seems reasonable to think that, in the end, the addition of more and more units of a variable factor to a fixed factor will cause marginal productivity to decrease. The field will ultimately be overcrowded with farm labourers and the factory with workers. But this might easily happen at an output *larger* than that at which the firm has already reached equilibrium. Diminishing marginal productivity is by no means an inevitable and certain feature of real-world production conditions.

The foregoing discussion may seem somewhat inconclusive, but that appears to be inevitable. One can, however, say quite definitely that so long as there is perfect competition in the markets for factors and products, marginal physical productivity must begin to diminish at some level of employment if firms are to be in equilibrium at all—as we shall see later. But since in practice there is often imperfect competition, firms can easily be in equilibrium so far as their purchases of factors are concerned, even though the marginal productivity of these factors is increasing. For the sake of convenience, however, we shall assume for the remainder of this book that marginal productivity curves are shaped roughly like an inverted U—that eventually the marginal physical productivity of any variable factor applied to a fixed factor diminishes.

The argument of this chapter has been throughout in terms of only two factors. But the results can easily be extended to cover situations where there are more than two factors. We shall be mainly concerned in the rest of Part One with the way in which returns to a single variable factor behave if this factor is used in combination with one or more fixed factors. And the results we have obtained in the present section hold equally however many fixed factors there are—provided that one factor only is variable.

SUGGESTED READING

Sune Carlson, *The Theory of Production*, London, 1939. (For readers with a fairly good knowledge of calculus.)

A. P. Lerner, *The Economics of Control*, New York, 1946, chapters xii and xiii.

CHAPTER XI

MARGINAL PRODUCTIVITY

1. THE PRICING OF FACTORS OF PRODUCTION

ARMED with the information obtained in the previous chapter, we may now return to the main trend of our argument and analyse the way in which factor prices are determined. We shall discover that the key to the pricing of factors of production lies in marginal productivity—that the reward of a factor of production depends, in the end, on what it produces, but before turning to the detailed analysis it will be useful to explain its basic principles of the analysis.

We simplified our analysis of the pricing of goods by taking the prices of all factors needed to make them as given. In analysing the determination of factor prices we shall allow explicitly for the fact that the price of a factor of production is not only determined by conditions in the market for that factor, but is also determined by conditions in the market where the product made by the factor is sold. We shall also allow for differing degrees of perfection of competition in both the factor and the product markets.

It is clear, therefore, that it would be possible to undertake a lengthy and intricate analysis of factor prices by assuming many different combinations of conditions in the markets for factors on the one hand, and for the products they make on the other. In order to simplify the analysis, we shall confine our attention to situations where there is either perfect competition or monopoly in one or both markets. The curious reader will no doubt be able to extend the analysis for himself to cover cases of oligopoly and monopolistic competition.

One final point is important. We have seen that monopoly in the market for a product means that the monopolist is the only seller of a particular article, and that he does not need to worry about the reactions of rivals to changes in his price-output policy because they produce only very remote substitutes for his own product. We must now envisage the possibility that in the market for a factor of production, where the buyers are firms, there may be one firm which is large enough and important enough to have a unique position on the buying side. To describe such a situation, Mrs. Joan Robinson has suggested the word *monopsony*.[1] A monopsonist is the only firm on the buyers' side of a market just as a monopolist is the only firm on the sellers' side. A monopsonistic firm is the only firm demanding a particular factor of production.

In this chapter we shall complicate our discussion of factor prices just sufficiently to allow for conditions of monopoly or perfect competition in the product market and of monopsony or perfect competition in the factor market. In each case we shall find that our answer to the question, 'What determines the prices of factors of production?' can be explained in terms of marginal productivity. The essence of our theory is that the price of any factor of production depends on its marginal productivity. What precisely we mean by marginal productivity—a concept already met with in the previous chapter—is the next topic which we must discuss.

2. MARGINAL PRODUCTIVITY

It seems best to divide this explanation of the meaning of marginal productivity into two parts. First, let us discover why we are interested in productivity at all. The productivity of factors of production is important since factors of production are not hired or bought because they are *directly* useful in the way that consumption goods are. They are only useful indirectly. If set to work they can produce goods which do satisfy wants directly. It is for this reason that the demand for factors of production depends on what they can produce—on their productivity.

For example, let us consider labour because it is largely in connection with wage theory that this idea of productivity as the fundamental determinant of factor prices has been worked out. The economist finds the basis of his analysis of wages in labour productivity. He assumes that if the wage paid to one man is greater than that paid to another, then the first man produces more. This does not, of course, provide a complete solution to the way in which wages are fixed. The theory which we shall build up in the next few chapters is more complicated than this. But productivity does provide a convenient starting-point for a theory of factor prices.

[1] *The Economics of Imperfect Competition*, p. 215.

One important point must always be borne in mind. So far as economic theory is concerned, it is assumed that the relation between productivity and wages is a one-way relation. That is to say, it is assumed that wages depend on productivity, but that productivity does not depend on wages. Yet the relationship is by no means so simple as this in practice. It is perfectly reasonable to look upon low wages in poor countries as the cause as well as the effect of low productivity. Malnutrition among workers is clearly one cause of low output. Nevertheless it would be difficult to build up a theory of factor prices if *wages* depended on productivity but *productivity* also depended on wages. We shall therefore (justifiably) look upon wages as determined by productivity and not *vice versa*.

We have seen why productivity is important in determining factor prices. What we must now see is why it is *marginal* productivity that concerns us. Why not average productivity? Why not productivity per head or per unit? The answer to this is the same as to the question 'Why do we study marginal revenue and marginal cost in the theory of the firm?' Just as an entrepreneur is maximising his profits when he equates marginal revenue and marginal cost, he is also maximising profits if he equates the marginal productivity of each factor with its marginal cost. This will be seen more clearly as we proceed. Let us now build up an analytical scheme, based on marginal productivity, by which the theory of factor prices can be outlined. We must first make several assumptions about this theoretical model. We shall begin by assuming that there is perfect competition in the market for a factor of production, say, labour—that there is a very large number of buyers and sellers of labour, none of whom is important in relation to the total of buyers and sellers. We also assume, for the moment, that there is perfect competition in the market for the product which the labour is making. We shall assume that the labour is homogeneous in the sense that all workers are equally efficient. This is not an entirely reasonable assumption, but it will simplify our analysis greatly. A further assumption we shall make is that the number of hours which will be worked each week by any one man is given, and that problems of overtime can be ignored. This will enable us to measure amounts of labour in terms of numbers of men each working a fixed number of hours per week. In this way we can ensure that additional labour only comes onto the market in the form of more men and not in the form of longer hours worked by each man. We thus have a standard of homogeneous labour which will enable us to measure amounts of the factor in the same way as we measured output in terms of a homogeneous product in value theory. Finally, we shall for the present only concern ourselves with explaining what determines the price of *a single variable factor* which is applied to a given amount of one or more fixed factors. This last fact must be borne in mind throughout.

On the basis of these assumptions let us begin by considering the marginal physical productivity of labour for a single firm. This marginal productivity can be derived from the firm's equal product map, as we saw in the previous chapter. Let us assume that the firm with which we are concerned produced potatoes and that as the number of men employed increases from one to ten, the weekly product of the firm changes as follows :

TABLE 5

SCHEDULES OF TOTAL AND MARGINAL
PHYSICAL PRODUCTIVITY

Men Employed	Total Product (cwts. of potatoes)	Marginal Physical Product (cwts. of potatoes)
1	6	6
2	13	7
3	25	12
4	45	20
5	70	25
6	100	30
7	127	27
8	152	25
9	170	18
10	180	10

The important feature of these schedules is that the marginal physical product of labour—the increase in the total product of the firm as additional men are taken on—rises when these additional men are taken on, until there are six men. Once six men are employed, however, the marginal physical productivity of labour begins to decline again. This type of situation is the same as that which we discussed in our analysis of the 'law' of variable proportions in the previous chapter. As different amounts of the variable factor (labour) are applied to given and fixed amounts of other factors, the marginal product of labour increases up to a point (here where six men are employed) and then declines again. It will be remembered that we are assuming that all marginal physical productivity curves are of this shape.

If more men are employed after the point of maximum marginal productivity has been reached, the marginal physical productivity of labour begins to decrease. We have here simply another instance of the 'eventually diminishing returns' discussed in Chapter X. After a certain stage has been reached, it must therefore become unprofitable to go on applying more and more men to a given amount of, say, land and entrepreneurship, though what that stage will be we cannot yet say. One important point must, however, be remembered. The seventh man is assumed to be just as efficient as the sixth although marginal physical productivity begins to fall when he is taken on. Seven equally efficient men produce just as much as each other, but each produces a little less than each of six equally efficient men had been able to produce. This is a result of physical production conditions and has nothing to do with inefficiency on the part of any of the workers. Perhaps each of seven men has less 'elbow-room' than each of six men and marginal productivity falls off because of this.

Having produced this hypothetical schedule of the marginal physical productivity of labour, showing how the marginal physical productivity of labour changes in response to changes in the numbers of men employed, it would be quite simple to turn this schedule into a diagram of the kind we drew in the previous chapter. But for our analysis we do not need a diagram showing the marginal productivity of a factor in terms of physical units—in this case hundredweights of potatoes. We are not interested in marginal physical productivity so much as in the money which a firm earns from the sale of this physical output. The entrepreneur does not usually pay his worker in potatoes but in cash. What interests him most is how much he can add to the *revenue* of his firm when he progressively increases the size of his labour force. He has to compare what the employment of each additional (marginal) unit of each factor (in this case labour) adds to the revenue of the firm with what it costs him when he hires such an additional unit of the factor.

We shall therefore find it more useful to draw what is called a *marginal revenue productivity curve*. This shows the addition to the total revenue of the firm caused when successive marginal units of labour are added to the fixed amounts of the other factors which it employs. Such a curve can easily be constructed from a marginal physical productivity schedule like that in Table 5, if one knows the price of the firm's product. Let us assume that potatoes are 5s. per cwt. Now, since we are assuming that competition in the potato market is perfect, we can take this price of 5s. as given and unalterable, whatever the output of the firm we are studying is. Thus marginal revenue product, in perfect competition, is simply marginal physical product multiplied by price. The marginal revenue productivity schedule of the firm in question is therefore as follows :

TABLE 6

A MARGINAL REVENUE PRODUCTIVITY SCHEDULE

Number of Men	Marginal Physical Productivity (cwts. of potatoes)	Marginal Revenue Productivity (physical product × price (5s. per cwt.))
1	6	30s.
2	7	35s.
3	12	60s.
4	20	100s.
5	25	125s.
6	30	150s.
7	27	135s.
8	25	125s.
9	18	90s.
10	10	50s.

This marginal revenue productivity schedule can be shown alternatively, on a diagram like Figure 92 where a marginal revenue productivity curve (MRP) shows the addition to total revenue when successive additional marginal units of labour are employed by the firm in question. Numbers of men are measured along the x-axis and marginal revenue product (in shillings) up the y-axis. Marginal revenue productivity curves like the one in Figure 92 will form the basis of our analysis of factor prices. One can, of course, draw an average revenue productivity curve bearing the usual average-marginal relationship to the marginal revenue productivity curve, like the curve (ARP) in Figure 92. Such a curve shows, for any level of employment shown on the x-axis, the average amount of revenue earned for the firm by each man. That is to say, the average revenue productivity of labour at any level of employment is total revenue ÷ number of men employed. Since the marginal revenue productivity curve is shaped like an inverted U it cuts the average revenue productivity curve at its highest point.[1]

One important problem has so far been ignored. We have already seen that a factor of production can only produce output when used in conjunction with other factors. The output of any firm is not the result of a *single* variable factor being used in isolation. It is produced by that factor when combined with other fixed factors. The average revenue productivity curve we have drawn in Figure 92 shows total amount of revenue ÷ number

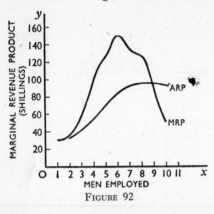

FIGURE 92

of men. It does not take account of the fact that some of the revenue earned by the firm is due to the productivity of the other factors—land, capital or enterprise—used in conjunction with labour. We therefore need to distinguish between the *gross* and the *net* product of a factor. Average *gross* revenue productivity of a factor shows total revenue of the firm at any level of employment ÷ the number of men employed. The average *net* revenue productivity of, say labour, shows the *total revenue attributable to labour* ÷ the number of men employed. We shall therefore need to ensure that the revenue productivity curves we draw show only the productivity of the factor whose price we are interested in. If we are concerned with labour we need to draw curves showing the *net* and not the *gross* revenue product of labour, as we have done so far.

There are two possible ways of discovering the *net* productivity of a factor. It would be perfectly legitimate, in an elementary analysis, to assume that only a negligible amount of the co-operating factors was being used. If this were the case, their contribution to the gross revenue of the firm would be so small that it could be ignored. One could justifiably regard labour as the only factor producing revenue. Gross and net revenue productivity would amount to the same things. But this is rather an unrealistic procedure. There is a rather more satisfactory method. We can discover the net productivity of, say, labour

[1] See p. 101.

from its gross productivity, if we assume that the rewards of the other co-operating factors are independently known. At each level of employment of labour we can deduct from the total *gross* revenue of a firm a sum of money equal to the rewards of all the other factors except the one we are considering. This gives total *net* revenue of the factor under consideration. We can then obtain average and marginal *net* revenue productivity from this information in the usual way. This reduction of gross to net revenue is not an easy matter when the amounts of more than one factor are

variable, as they can be, but we shall postpone these difficulties until a later stage.[1] In the case of a single variable factor the task of translating gross into net revenue productivity is fairly simple.

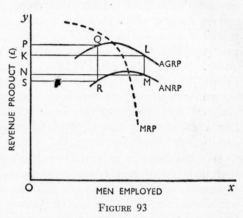

FIGURE 93

We always assume for the present that the amount of capital and entrepreneurship used by each firm is fixed. Thus, if we know the 'prices' of capital and entrepreneurship, we can deduct a fixed amount of money representing the 'normal' profits of entrepreneurship and the 'price' of the given amount of capital from the total *gross* revenue of the firm at each level of output and can discover total *net* revenue at these levels of output. It is then not difficult to derive the average gross and average net revenue productivity curves by dividing total gross and total net revenue at each level of employment by the number of men employed.

In Figure 93 the curves AGRP and ANRP represent the gross and net average revenue productivity curves of labour (the single variable factor). Since the factors other than labour are fixed in amount, any rectangles in Figure 93 like KLMN and PQRS will have the same area. The same fixed sum of money representing the given costs of capital and entrepreneurship together, is used with a progressively larger volume of labour as output rises. We have not shown marginal *net* and *gross* revenue productivity separately

[1] In Chapter XVI.

in Figure 93 because with only one variable factor there is no difficulty in calculating marginal revenue productivity. When only one factor is variable, marginal revenue productivity is the same whether one is considering net or gross revenue productivity. Until further notice, we shall refer to marginal revenue productivity curves and not to marginal *net* revenue productivity curves since the two are in fact identical when one is studying a single variable factor. Since the amounts of the other factors are the same whatever the level of output, it is only by changing the amount of the variable factor that the revenue earned by the firm can be altered. This is essentially the same problem as with the marginal costs of the firm. In the short run, the costs of entrepreneurship and capital do not enter into the firm's marginal cost curve. We shall therefore be able to carry out an analysis of the pricing of a single variable factor with the productivity curves shown in Figure 93, where labour is the only variable factor, and shall not need to complicate our analysis further until a much later stage when we have to allow for more than one factor being used in varying amounts.

We have spent a great deal of time explaining the meaning of marginal and average revenue productivity curves because they represent the chief weapon of analysis which we shall need in our discussion of the pricing of factors of production. In fact, the marginal revenue productivity curve of a factor to the firm, which we have been discussing, is really *the firm's demand curve for that factor of production*. In this analysis we shall consider the marginal revenue productivity curve of labour because labour seems to be the factor which is most likely to be variable, but what we have to say applies in principle to the other variable factors of production as well. The marginal revenue productivity curve of labour to the firm is the firm's demand curve for labour. It is often said that the demand for labour is a *derived demand* because labour is only demanded for what it will produce. So, in Figure 94 the marginal revenue productivity curve (MRP) shows the 'derived' demand curve for labour of a hypothetical firm. The demand for labour is 'derived' from the demand for the product it is helping to make.

In this instance, since we are at present assuming perfect competition between firms demanding labour, the supply side of the entrepreneur's problem is simple. The supply conditions confronting the firm are represented by the horizontal straight line WW. This shows the supply curve of labour to the individual firm. Since there is perfect competition in the labour market, the firm is able to hire as much labour as it wishes at the ruling wage of £OW per man. Just as a perfectly competitive firm can take the price of its product as given, so it can take the wage per man as given too. The firm's demand for labour is so small compared with the total demand for labour that any change in this demand, even a proportionally large one, does not affect the price of labour. This is a perfectly legitimate assumption since we are only concerned with the problems of a single competitive firm.

In these circumstances the firm can regard the curve WW as representing both the average and the marginal wage (AW and MW). The average amount of money paid to such a worker is £OW. Similarly, the addition of every marginal unit of

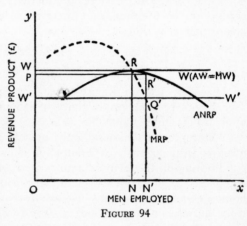

FIGURE 94

labour increases the wage bill by £OW too. *The firm will be in equilibrium—profits will be maximised—when the marginal revenue productivity of the factor (in this case £NR) is equal to the marginal cost of the factor—the marginal wage.* In Figure 94 this happens when ON men are employed. If fewer men were employed the firm could add more to its receipts than to its costs by increasing the employment it offered, for labour's marginal revenue productivity would then exceed its marginal cost. Similarly, if more than ON men were employed, the marginal cost of labour—the marginal wage—would exceed its marginal revenue productivity and the firm would be paying more to its marginal employees than their employment was adding to its revenue. The firm is thus in equilibrium, in Figure 94, when ON men are employed. At that level of employment profits are at a maximum. It should be noted that, with perfect competition between buyers of labour, equilibrium is only possible if the marginal revenue productivity curve of labour is falling at and near the equilibrium position. This explains why economists have been so anxious to show that

R

marginal physical productivity must eventually diminish. Otherwise equilibrium would be impossible.

We can therefore say that, since we shall continue to assume 'rationality' on the part of the entrepreneur, a firm will be in equilibrium when the marginal revenue productivity of any factor to the firm equals its marginal cost. Profits will then be maximised. With perfect competition between firms buying in the factor market, this means that the average cost of the factor will also equal its marginal revenue productivity. The condition for equilibrium of the *firm* when there is perfect competition in the labour market is thus:

Marginal revenue productivity of labour
= Marginal wage = Average wage.

It will be seen in Figure 94 that, with wages at £OW, the average net revenue productivity of labour is also equal to the wage. This implies that the *industry* is also in full equilibrium, with entrepreneurs earning only normal profits. In fact, the position is analogous to the situation shown in diagrams where equilibrium of the firm is represented in terms of costs and revenues. In a competitive industry where entrepreneurs are homogeneous, every firm's average revenue productivity curve will, in full equilibrium, be tangent to the 'wage-line', as in Figure 94. In the short run, the 'wage-line' might be below or above WW, in which case greater or less than normal profits respectively would be earned. But in the long run firms will enter or leave the industry until normal profits only are being earned.

For example, if the wage-line is below WW, as at W'W', employment will be ON' and abnormal profits of W'Q'R'P will be earned. The firm is in equilibrium but the industry is not. In the long run, then, assuming that entrepreneurs are homogeneous, firms will enter the industry until only normal profits are again being earned. For the entry of new entrepreneurs into the industry will lower the price of its product and this will lower the marginal and average net revenue productivity curves. Similarly, the increased demand for labour by the expanding industry may raise wages. The average revenue productivity curve will fall and the 'wage-line' may rise until they are tangential to each other. In the same way, if firms are earning less than normal profits, entrepreneurs will leave the industry until equilibrium is reached.

It should be apparent on reflection that Figure 94 is closely related to the sort of diagrams we used in analysing the firm's price-output policy in Chapters V and VI. It will therefore be useful to study the similarities and differences between these two kinds of diagram.

In Figure 95a we have reproduced the essential parts of Figure 94. In Figure 95c we have shown the cost and revenue

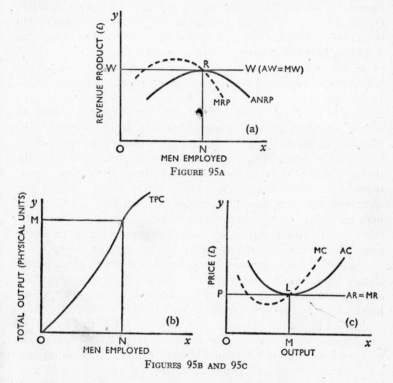

FIGURE 95A

FIGURES 95B AND 95C

curves of the same firm whose demand and supply for labour are shown in Figure 94. To simplify the analysis, let us assume that instead of paying a fixed amount of money for entrepreneurship and capital the firm pays nothing. This makes the interpretation of the diagrams simpler, but makes no difference in principle. The productivity and cost curves thus represent labour productivity and cost only. Figure 95b shows the production conditions for the good in question and provides a link between Figures 95a and 95c. The total product curve TPC shows how the total output of the good made by the firm changes as employment is increased.[1]

In Figures 95a and 95c it is assumed that the firm is in equilibrium, maximising profits, and also that the industry is in equilibrium with each individual firm earning normal profits. The two diagrams show us that the firm is in equilibrium when OM units of output are produced and ON men are employed. Figure 95b shows that production conditions are such that when ON men are employed a total output of OM units of output will in fact be produced. What the entrepreneur is doing in Figure 95c is finding how many units of output he must produce to maximise profits by looking at his cost and revenue curves. The size of the labour force needed to produce this output is shown by Figure 95b. In Figure 95a the entrepreneur is deciding how many men to employ to maximise his profits, taking the number of units of output produced by varying labour forces as given by Figure 95b. The two diagrams 95a and 95c thus show alternative methods of representing the same equilibrium position for the firm. But since the two diagrams each show different items on the two axes, there is no direct and obvious link between them. Figure 95a shows what the revenue productivity and the cost of labour per man is. Figure 95c, however, shows labour cost (there being no other costs) and revenue per unit of output. It is therefore impossible to translate one diagram directly into the other.

Nevertheless, since we are assuming that there are no costs except labour costs, one can make some simple generalisations about the relationship between the two diagrams. On the one hand, the number of men employed in Figure 95a (ON men) multiplied by output per man, equals output (OM) in Figure 95c. Similarly, average cost in Figure 95c (ML) equals average net revenue productivity (RN) in Figure 95a divided by output per man. These diagrams therefore represent the same equilibrium position but they do so in different ways.

To sum up, an entrepreneur will take on more units of any variable factor of production until its marginal revenue productivity is just equal to its marginal cost—until, if the factor is labour, the marginal worker adds to the firm's revenue just as much as he adds to its wage bill. The firm is in equilibrium in its purchases of labour when the marginal wage equals the marginal revenue productivity of labour. In perfect competition, with full equi-

---

[1] It will be noted that the scale on the y-axis in Figure 95b is larger than on the x-axis in Figure 95c.

librium, this also means that wages equal the average (net) revenue productivity of labour.

As the first step in our theory of the pricing of factors we have shown that a firm will act in a determinate way to maximise its profits. It will hire factors until the marginal revenue productivity of each such factor equals the marginal cost of the same factor. But this has been a very simplified analysis. We have ignored the problem of how to price more than one factor at a time and have assumed that there is perfect competition. These are assumptions which we must keep for the moment. But it is now time to find out what happens in the industry as distinct from the firm.

We have so far taken wages as given, and have shown that the volume of employment offered by the firm depends on the marginal revenue productivity of labour. We now want to find how the wage of labour itself is determined. We can do this only by looking at all entrepreneurs on the one hand and all workers on the other. It is impossible for the level of wages to be affected by the action of a single entrepreneur when there is perfect competition. We are therefore justified in assuming the level of wages to be constant when we are dealing with the single firm. But wages can only be taken as given by the individual firm. For the industry as a whole they are not necessarily so given, and we must therefore find how they are determined.

3. WAGES AND MARGINAL REVENUE PRODUCTIVITY

We have seen that a firm's demand for labour at any wage depends on the marginal revenue productivity of labour. In the whole industry wages themselves depend in part on the marginal revenue productivity of labour. (We shall continue to assume that there is perfect competition in both the factor market and the product market.) As with all prices, the price of labour depends on supply and demand. The problem of the individual entrepreneur in the product market is to equate supply, in the form of marginal cost, with demand, in the form of marginal revenue. In the factor market the individual entrepreneur has to consider supply in the form of marginal cost of the factor, and demand in the form of its marginal revenue productivity.

When we turn from the individual entrepreneur to the whole industry the price of a factor to such an industry, like the price

of the product of an industry, still depends on demand and supply.
We now have supply in the form of labour available at various
wage rates whilst demand depends on the marginal revenue
productivity of that labour—this time to the whole industry.
Since it is the price of labour which we now want to determine,
we have to discover the shape of the demand and supply curves
for labour. As usual it is reasonable to think that the demand curve
for labour will slope downwards and that the supply curve will
slope upwards. It would of course be possible for us to consider
all the conceivable shapes of demand and supply curves for
labour. This would not be very useful. We are mainly interested
in the way in which wages depend on marginal revenue productivity—on the way in which the demand for labour influences
wages; and it will pay us to ignore complicated conditions of
supply for the moment. We shall assume that the total supply of
labour is fixed whatever the wage offered, and that the elasticity
of supply of labour is zero.

This will not always be the case. Nor will it be the normal
case. But it will allow us to simplify our problem. Let us consider what such an assumption means. First, it means that there
is a fixed number of men who will work for entrepreneurs in the
industry quite irrespective of the wage offered. Second, it means
that the labour is 'specific' to the industry. The men can work
in this industry only. They cannot do the jobs required in another
industry, even though wages there may be higher. There is, in
other words, no mobility of labour *into or out of* the industry we
are considering. Third, the vertical supply curve of labour
implies that all the workers are prepared to do a full week's work
whatever the level of wages. We shall, that is to say, ignore for
the moment the possibility that some workers (coal-miners are
supposed to be the chief offenders) will work five days a week if
paid £5 a week, but if they are given £10 a week will work for three
days and spend two days in bed or at the races. We shall also
continue to assume that there is no overtime working. These
assumptions mean that our analysis is simple. But a simple analysis has at least the virtue of showing just which forces are most
important.

We start then in Figure 97 with a vertical supply curve of
labour (MS) showing that there is a fixed number of men (let us
call this OM) willing to work. We now want to see what will be
the shape of the demand curve for this labour. To do this let us
consider two instances; first, where the demand curve is down-

ward-sloping ; and second, where it is horizontal. Which type of
demand curve for labour is more likely to be met with in practice ?

First let us try to discover when the demand curve for labour
will slope downwards. Let us consider the situation shown in
Figure 96.

In Figure 96a we have shown the demand curve of a firm for
labour. This demand curve (the marginal revenue productivity
curve of labour for the firm—MRP) shows the usual humped
shape. The average (net) productivity curve of labour (ANRP)
is also shown. Wages are assumed to be as shown by the line

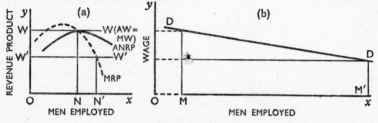

FIGURES 96A AND 96B

WW. The firm is therefore in full equilibrium earning only
normal profits and employing ON men. If we now assume that
wages fall to W'W', then the demand for labour increases from
ON to ON'.

Let us now assume that the industry is composed of ten
identical firms. If this is the case, then, for a given fall in wages,
the demand of the industry for labour will increase by ten times
the amount (NN') by which it increases in the individual firm.
This is shown in Figure 96b. The fall in wages raises the amount
of labour demanded from OM to OM'. It can be seen that the
demand curve of the whole industry for labour slopes downwards.
The elasticity of the demand for labour in response to the given
fall in its price will, in fact, be the same both for the firm and for
the industry in this particular case. It is possible in this way to
deduce the demand curve for labour of the industry from the
marginal revenue productivity curves of the individual firms.

In adding the marginal revenue productivity curves of the
individual firms together sideways, as we have done in Figure 96b,
we have assumed that the price of the industry's product is given
whatever the output of its product. For the individual firm,
shown in Figure 96a, this assumption that the demand for its
product is infinitely elastic is reasonable. For the industry it is

not reasonable. The demand curve for the product of the industry is almost certain to slope downwards. What we have done is to show the marginal revenue productivity curve of the industry as representing marginal physical productivity of the factor × price of product. Really it should be marginal physical productivity per unit of factor × *marginal revenue to the industry*. Nevertheless this simplifying assumption that price, and therefore marginal revenue as well, is constant for the industry whatever the level of output, will ease our task now, and we shall abandon it later on.

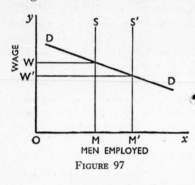

FIGURE 97

If we assume that, when, in Figure 96a, the firm was in the original position with a wage of WW, it was in full equilibrium, we know that the industry too was in full equilibrium. (We are assuming that all firms are homogeneous.) If we also know the supply curve for labour, we can tell what the wage actually would have been. For our assumption, made above, that wages fell from OW to OW' was made simply to show the shape of the demand curve for labour. Having discovered the shape of that demand curve, we must now use it in conjunction with the supply curve of labour to discover what the wage will actually be. This can be seen from Figure 97, where DD shows the demand curve for labour, MS the supply curve, and OW the wage at which supply and demand are in equilibrium.

Let us now assume that whilst the demand for labour remains the same, the supply is increased. Let us imagine that to begin with we are considering a colony with only a fixed labour supply of OM men willing to work in the industry with which we are concerned. Now let us assume that an immigrant ship brings MM' new workers who are willing to work under exactly the same conditions as the existing workers. The supply curve shifts from MS to M'S' but remains a vertical straight line. Elasticity of supply of labour is still zero. The result of this change, seen in Figure 97, is to lower wages to OW' instead of OW. Wages fall because the supply of labour has risen, but demand conditions have not changed. Wages are still equal to marginal revenue productivity of labour, but that marginal revenue productivity itself has fallen now that more men are employed. The implication of this particular analysis is, of course, that the number of firms in the industry remains constant. It is that fact which enables us to assume that there is a downward-sloping demand curve for labour. This further implies that the number of entrepreneurs is fixed. Entrepreneurship is assumed to be a fixed factor of production for the whole industry, whilst labour is assumed to be variable in amount.

The existence of diminishing marginal revenue productivity in an industry thus does not result from the fact, taken in isolation, that the supply of labour has increased. It follows from the fact that we have assumed labour and entrepreneurship to be used in varying proportions. The existence of diminishing returns is a corollary to the fact that entrepreneurs were not increased in number as the supply of labour rose. This is an important fact to remember. It is important because traditional economic theory has often based itself on this assumption and has derived generalisations about wages from it.

There are two clear conclusions which one may draw. First, if it is hoped to maintain wages at the existing level, the immigrant ship should be sunk. Or, to put it another way, if all parents want children to follow them in the same industry, the way to keep up wages of future generations in that industry is to restrict the size of families. Second, if future entrepreneurs are the sons of the present entrepreneurs, workers should encourage entrepreneurs to have large families. The more entrepreneurs there are, the higher wages will be. For the supply curve of labour being given, the more entrepreneurs there are, the farther to the right will lie the demand curve of the industry for labour and the higher wages will be.

Indeed, if one thinks carefully about this second case, it is clear that if the supply of entrepreneurs is infinitely elastic in supply at the current rate of profits in the long run, the long-run demand curve for labour will be a horizontal straight line. This is the horizontal demand curve for labour which we set out to discover. In the first case, that of the downward-sloping demand curve for labour, we assumed by implication that entrepreneurs could earn abnormal profits when wages fall because the number of firms in the industry was limited. Now, however, we are assuming that (in the long run) the supply of homogeneous entrepreneurs is infinitely elastic. All are equally efficient. In this case there will be no (long-run) abnormal profits and the long-run demand for labour will be infinitely elastic. The number of firms will expand in the long run and the demand for labour will increase whenever there is a tendency for wages to fall and abnormal profits to appear.

One may therefore sum up as follows. The demand curve for labour will always slope downwards if the number of firms (and thus of entrepreneurs) in the industry is fixed, as it must be in the short run. But even if the number of firms in the industry is not fixed, as will normally happen in the long run, the demand curve for labour can only be horizontal if entrepreneurship *of the same quality* is in infinitely elastic supply to the industry at the existing level of normal profits. If entrepreneurs are heterogeneous, those outside the industry being less efficient than those within it, the demand curve for labour must slope downwards. Wages will have to fall if less efficient entrepreneurs are to be able to earn normal profits in the industry. Only if 'homogeneous' entrepreneurs are available in large numbers at the existing rate of normal profits can the demand curve for labour be horizontal. We are, of course, assuming throughout that labour is homogeneous.

This situation where the demand curve for labour is a horizontal straight line is, however, even less probable than it appears at first sight. It can only ever exist on our assumption that the price of the product made by the competitive industry is constant, however large or small the industry's output is. But it is unreasonable to think that, even though the industry expands, the price of its product can remain the same. The only hope of maintaining wages if the supply of labour increases is therefore that when the immigrant ships bring new workers they will also bring a shipload of consumers. That is to say, there must be an increase in the demand for the product of the industry in which we are interested, from those working in other industries. We are making the usual assumption of partial equilibrium analysis that the demand for labour in a single industry is independent of the supply. This means that we assume that workers do not buy a significant proportion of the output of their own industry. So, if the supply of labour to an industry increases, then unless consumers increase their demand for its product the price of that product must fall and money wages will therefore drop. Wages will be constant only in terms of the product made, and to measure wages in terms of the product which workers make is not very useful. For if they buy any of the product at all, they will be unlikely to buy it in substantial quantities.

It is clear, then, that a horizontal demand curve for labour is a most unlikely occurrence. We shall therefore assume that the demand curve for labour (as indeed for any other factor) slopes downwards both for the firm and for the industry. This demand curve will, of course, show the elasticity of demand for labour. This elasticity can be measured in the normal way. Broadly speaking, the more rapidly the marginal physical productivity of labour falls off as employment increases, and the more rapidly the price of the product made by labour falls as its output rises, the less elastic the demand for labour will be and *vice versa*.

We have now seen that the wage of labour in a perfectly competitive industry depends on demand and supply. Demand is given by the marginal revenue productivity curve of labour to the industry. Supply is given by a curve showing for each level of wages what the volume of labour offered will be. Wages are determined by the intersection of these two curves.

4. MONOPSONY

We must now see what will happen when competition between the firms buying labour is not perfect. To some extent our analysis will be simpler in this situation. We shall no longer need to study first the single firm, to see how much labour it will employ at a given wage, and then the industry, to see what that wage will be. For in monopsony the demand of the monopsonist is the only demand for the factor of production. The monopsonist's demand for, say, labour will, in conjunction with the supply conditions of that labour, determine wages. We have already discovered that, where there is perfect competition both in the factor market and in the product market, the price of a factor of production is equal both to its marginal revenue product and to the price of its marginal physical product and is determined by demand and supply conditions. Let us now see what forces determine factor prices for a firm which is a monopolist in the product market and a monopsonist in the factor market. We take this particular instance only for the sake of convenience. In the next chapter we shall consider further possible situations in the labour market and the product market.

For this 'monopolist-monopsonist' the demand for labour will still depend on the marginal revenue productivity curve of labour. But the marginal revenue product of any unit of labour cannot be so easily calculated when there is monopoly as it was when there was perfect competition in the product market. With perfect competition marginal revenue product equals marginal physical product multiplied by the (constant) price of the product. If the employment of an additional unit of labour adds ten wheelbarrows to the product of a firm, and the price of a wheelbarrow is £10 whether the individual firm produces 10 or 1000 wheelbarrows, it is clear that the marginal revenue product of labour is £100. The sale of the ten wheelbarrows has added £100 to the earnings of the firm. With monopoly the price of the product is not constant but varies with output. A further complication is therefore introduced.

A marginal worker may still produce ten wheelbarrows. The marginal physical productivity of labour may therefore still be 10 units of output. But the price of wheelbarrows will now fall as output rises. The ten additional wheelbarrows produced by employing a marginal worker who raises a firm's output from, say, 100 to 110 may be sold for £10 each. The value of the marginal physical product is still £100, but the price of wheelbarrows may be lower now that output is 110 and not 100. For example, it may be that when 100 wheelbarrows were being sold, the price of each was £10 10s., but now that output is 110, the price of each has fallen from £10 10s. to £10. So, when this marginal worker is taken on, the firm earns £50 less on the existing output, i.e. 10s. less on each of 100 wheelbarrows. The employment of the marginal unit of labour has therefore added only £50 (net) to the firm's revenue. Ten more wheelbarrows have been sold for a total amount of £100, but £50 less has been earned on the other 100 wheelbarrows previously sold for £1050 and now sold for only £1000. The marginal revenue product of labour is thus only £50, whilst the value of the marginal physical product of labour, i.e. the price at which the marginal physical product is sold, is £100.

In monopoly, therefore, the marginal revenue product of a factor at any level of employment is not marginal physical product × price of product ; it is now marginal physical product × marginal revenue from that physical product. It is still the net addition to the revenue of the firm made by the employment of a marginal unit of the factor. But we now have to allow for the fall in the price of the firm's product which results from the fact that the monopolist's average revenue curve is downward-sloping and not horizontal as the perfect competitor's average revenue curve is.

The result of this is to make the marginal revenue productivity

curve of a factor to a monopolist slope downwards more rapidly
than it would do if he were producing in perfect competition.
Figure 98b shows the demand curve (marginal revenue productivity
curve) for labour of a firm producing in conditions of perfect
competition.   Figure 98a shows the demand curve of a firm with
an identical marginal physical productivity curve but which is a
monopolist and not a competitor.   The difference in the shapes of
the two curves results entirely from the fact that the first firm has

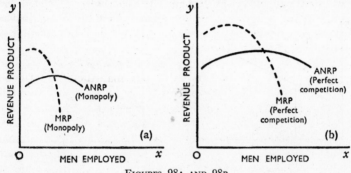

FIGURES 98A AND 98B

a horizontal average revenue curve for its product whereas the
second has a downward-sloping one.

The supply curve of labour to the firm is also different for
our 'monopolist-monopsonist' from what it would be for the
perfect competitor.   Where the firm is buying in conditions of
perfect competition in the labour market, the supply curve can be
shown as a horizontal straight line.   But now that the firm is a
monopsonist, it is the only buyer of labour and it influences the
price of labour by altering its own purchases—by changing the
level of employment.   Wages rise and fall as the firm hires more
or less men, whereas in perfect competition they remain constant
however many men it employs.   This raises a further problem.
When there was perfect competition in the labour market it was
possible for the firm to ignore differences between average factor
cost—the price paid to each unit of factor—and marginal factor
cost—the addition to the total cost of the factor when a further
unit was engaged.   These were all the same thing.   Now there is
a difference between marginal and average factor cost.   Where a
firm is a monopsonist it can lower the average cost of labour—
average wage—by reducing its demand for labour.   Average
wage (total wage bill divided by number of workers employed) is

not equal to marginal wage. This is the addition to the wage bill
when another worker is employed. For example, if employment
rises, the addition to the wage bill—marginal wage—will be
greater than the average wage, in just the same way as marginal
cost is greater than average cost when average cost is rising as
output increases.

The supply conditions facing a monopsonist in the labour
market are shown in Figure 99. The meaning of the curve
showing average wages should be fairly obvious. It shows the

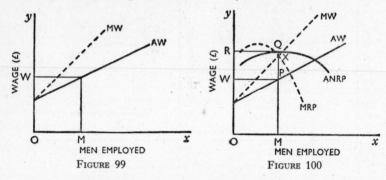

FIGURE 99   FIGURE 100

amount of money paid to each worker when various numbers are
employed. For example, when OM men are employed, they have
to be paid £OW each. The marginal wage curve is more difficult
to explain. *It does not show the wage paid to a marginal worker—
all workers receive the same wage.* It shows the addition to the total
wage bill of the firm when an additional unit of labour is taken
on. Where there is monopsony, an extra worker can be engaged
only if a higher wage is paid to *all* workers in the firm. The wage
of the marginal worker will therefore be smaller than the addition
to the wage bill when he is taken on. Since the average wage curve
rises, the marginal wage curve will be above the average curve.
The wage paid to each marginal unit of labour (and of course to
all other workers) will be less than the addition to the total wage
bill when he is employed.

What, then, is the connection between the two sets of curves
shown in Figures 98 and 99? If they are drawn together as in
Figure 100, we can find the equilibrium position of the firm in
question. We assume that the firm will still wish to maximise
profits even though it is a monopolist in the product market and a
monopsonist in the factor market. The monopsonist will therefore
increase employment until the amount added to revenue (marginal

revenue product) when a marginal unit of labour is taken on is equal to the addition to the wage bill (marginal wage) when he is taken on. This equality occurs at point X.

This equality of marginal revenue product and marginal wage will occur in Figure 100 when OM men are employed at the wage £OW. Abnormal profits earned by the firm will be £WPQR, normal profits having already been deducted in obtaining the average net revenue product from the average gross revenue product. What, then, is the difference between this situation and equilibrium under perfect competition? The marginal revenue product of labour must still equal the marginal cost of labour (marginal wage). But there are two important differences. A change in the output of the product will lower its price because of monopoly in the product market. An increase in the number of workers employed in making the product will therefore lower its price. This makes it impossible to go on expanding employment as long as might have happened without monopoly—the marginal revenue product curve of labour is steeper. Second, the marginal wage curve rises instead of remaining horizontal as in perfect competition.

But there are other differences. When monopsony is absent in the factor market not only does the marginal revenue product of labour equal the marginal wage, but that marginal revenue product also equals the wage itself. Similarly, when monopoly is absent from the product market not only does the marginal wage equal the marginal revenue product of labour, but it also equals the price at which the marginal *physical* product of labour can be sold. On the other hand, if there is monopsony in the factor market the wage itself—the average wage—is less than the marginal wage. Similarly, if there is monopoly in the product market the marginal revenue product of labour is less than the price at which the marginal physical product of labour can be sold. The causes of this are to be found in the downward-sloping average revenue curve of the monopolist and the rising average wage curve of the monopsonist. So where a large firm is both a monopolist and a monopsonist, it is likely to benefit in two ways. It can raise the price of its product, and, at the same time, lower the wage paid to its workers, by restricting output and employment.

It is only reasonable to think that a monopolist will also be a monopsonist. If a producer is making a large proportion of the product of an industry, it seems fair to think that he will also be using a large proportion of the factors used by the industry. A monopolist is therefore likely to have the type of control over both the price of his product and the prices of the factors he uses which will enable him to earn abnormal profits at the expense of consumers and workers alike.

It is this feature of the monopolist's position which has led economists and others to talk of 'monopolistic exploitation'. But unfortunately the idea of exploitation implies some kind of moral judgment—it is an 'emotive' phrase—and we are attempting in

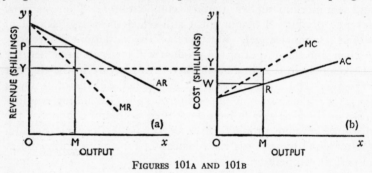

FIGURES 101A AND 101B

this book to avoid making such moral judgments. This makes it difficult to use the word exploitation in this context. We shall, however, retain it, but stress that we are not, in fact, making moral judgments at all.

We have described the equilibrium of the 'monopolist-monopsonist' in terms of revenue product curves and wage curves. But perhaps this does not show the position quite as clearly as one could wish. It may therefore prove useful to show the same equilibrium position in terms of revenue and cost curves. We shall therefore approach the problem in two ways, giving two different types of diagram. In Figure 101 the position of the firm is shown in terms of the usual concepts of money receipts and money costs for various outputs, assuming for the sake of simplicity that the only costs are labour costs.

Figure 101a needs no explanation. It shows the normal average and marginal revenue curves of a firm. It shows how great average and marginal revenue is when output is at various levels. Figure 101b shows average and marginal costs. Since wages are the only cost, it also shows average and marginal wages. But it shows average and marginal wages per unit of output and not per unit of labour as is more usual. In other words, it shows marginal and average (wage) cost per unit of output. At output OM, wage cost per unit of output is MR. Wage cost per unit of output is a less usual concept than is wage per man, but is exactly the same (when labour is the only cost) as average cost.

The dotted line joining the two diagrams shows the output at which marginal revenue per unit of output equals marginal wage cost per unit of output. The firm therefore produces OM units of output, selling them at OP*s.* each. Its wage bill is OW per unit of output. It therefore earns abnormal profits of (PY*s.* + WY*s.*) × OM.

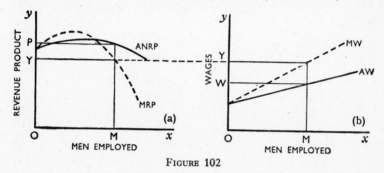

FIGURE 102

Since the firm is a monopolist, these profits need not be competed away, but will be earned so long as the monopoly is maintained.

An alternative way of showing the same equilibrium position of the firm is given in Figure 102. In Figure 102b average and marginal wage per man are shown. Figure 102a shows average and marginal revenue, not per unit of product but per man. It uses the same concepts as we have used throughout our analysis of the theory of factor pricing—marginal and average revenue productivity curves.

Here again the dotted line connecting the two diagrams shows the equilibrium position of the firm. From this we can deduce the numbers of men employed in this equilibrium position. In fact, OM men will be employed at a wage per man of £OW. Average revenue per man is £OP and profits £(PY + WY) × OM. The equilibrium of the firm can therefore be shown both in terms of revenues and costs of products, and in terms of revenues and costs of factors. Figure 101 shows an example of the former type of equilibrium and Figure 102 shows the latter.

We have now provided, in outline, a theory which can be generalised to show how the rewards of all factors of production are determined. Yet, although this theory can be applied equally

S

to all the broad groups of factors—land, labour and capital—there are various distinguishing features of each type of factor which make it important that we should apply the general analysis so far explained to each group of factors in turn. This we shall now do.

SUGGESTED READING

Joan Robinson, *Economics of Imperfect Competition*, London, 1933, especially chapters xvii, xviii, xxi and xxii.

CHAPTER XII

WAGES

1. LABOUR AS A FACTOR OF PRODUCTION

ALTHOUGH our analysis of the pricing of factors of production has so far been carried out very largely in terms of the wages of labour, the theory we have outlined applies equally to *all* factors of production. But each factor has its own peculiarities and problems. In this chapter we shall explicitly apply the conclusions of the theory of factor pricing to labour, explaining at the same time what are the main differences between labour and other factors of production. We can then see how far the theory of the pricing of factors of production needs modifying if it is to take account of these differences.

In Chapter XI we gave general rules by which to explain the pricing of all factors of production. We saw that an entrepreneur will continue to purchase more of any factor until its marginal revenue productivity is equal to its marginal cost—the addition which its purchase makes to the costs of the firm. With perfect competition in both the factor market and the product market, this will mean that in each firm the price of the factor is equal to the value (price) of its marginal physical product. For the whole industry, the price of any factor will be determined by the marginal productivity curve of that factor on the one hand, and by the supply curve of the factor on the other. With monopoly in the product market, the value of the marginal product of a factor will be greater than its marginal revenue productivity. Similarly, with monopsony in the factor market, the marginal cost of the factor will exceed its average cost—its price. So, with both monopoly and monopsony existing at the same time, employment will still be determined at the level where marginal revenue product equals marginal cost, but these will be less than the price of the marginal product and greater than the price of the factor. This formal statement applies equally to any and all factors of production. It is our task now to apply it specifically to labour. Are there any

differences between labour and other factors? If so, can any
valid generalisations be made about them?

The characteristic of labour which distinguishes it from
other factors of production is a sociological one. It is the tradition
in economics to divide the price of factors of production into four
broad groups. One discusses the wages of labour, the rent of
land, interest on capital, and the profits of enterprise (or entrepreneurship). Some economists have suggested that there is no
difference economically between the return to the factor of production labour and the return to other factors of production. It
is said that all are returns to factors of production, and that since
all depend on the marginal productivity of the factor on the one
hand and supply conditions on the other, there is no difference
in principle between them. Indeed, one economist has gone so
far as to say that the classification, land, labour and capital, is no
more useful than would be the classification animal, vegetable and
mineral.

Yet, as has been suggested, and as will be shown later, there
are sociological problems which arise when one studies the wages
of labour which do not arise with the prices of other factors of
production. For this reason it is justifiable to distinguish labour
from the other factors. There are, of course, bound to be some
difficulties in being quite certain whether a specific unit of a
factor is labour or not. The border-line cases will be numerous.
For example, does labour mean only manual labour? Or does
it include clerical, 'white-collar', workers? And how should
managers be classified? We should apparently have to include a
£10,000 a year manager in 'labour'. Yet Mrs. Jones earning
£500 a year from a fish-and-chip shop would be a capitalist
or entrepreneur. It will be impossible to deal completely with
these problems of definition, but in general everyone has a fairly
clear conception of what the factor of production labour would
include.

We shall select a typical case in order to avoid these awkward
problems of definition. We shall consider the problems of those
members of the lower income group whose sole income is obtained
from the work of their hands or brains, and who spend their
lifetime working for an entrepreneur. They are the sort of people
who are not in general very interested in their work as such, but
who carry on fairly cheerfully with a rather dull job under constant
supervision. It seems reasonable to think that this type of factor
of production differs in two main ways from other factors. In

the first place, workers of this kind will usually be found combining together to urge wage claims on entrepreneurs. In the second place, they are, within limits, free to choose whether they will work on a particular day or not, and if they do, for how long. This kind of choice is out of the question for land and capital. Machines and fields, being inanimate, cannot combine together, nor will they refuse to work because they are too tired or too bored. Workers can and do. The main task of this chapter will be to discuss the consequences which result from the ability of labour to influence the conditions of its own employment in these two ways.

2. COLLECTIVE BARGAINING

First, let us see what is the result of workers being able to combine in trade unions to press wage claims. Let us assume that a particular trade union goes to the employers, who agree that every man whom they employ will, in future, be paid £6 a week, neither less nor more. Let us also assume that this agreement is put into force completely, and that once it is in operation the trade union indulges in no strikes, and the employers in no lockouts. Work goes on as usual. What will be the result?

We shall confine our attention in this analysis to situations where a trade union presses for a higher wage but does not make any stipulations about the numbers of workers to be employed. In fact, of course, being a monopolist, a trade union will have to take account of the fact that a rise in the price of labour will probably alter the amount demanded. But in practice the main preoccupation of trade unions is with the level of wages, if only because it would be almost impossible to attempt to control levels of employment. We assume here that when a wage bargain is made, all the members of the union are prepared to offer their services at the agreed wage. The supply curve of labour will therefore be a horizontal straight line at this agreed wage.

Clearly the conditions of demand and supply for labour will be disturbed. For instead of perfect competition between sellers in the labour market, there is now monopoly. If one assumes that the marginal revenue productivity curve for labour slopes downwards, there is a distinct possibility that fewer workers will now be employed. For the supply curve of labour will become horizontal instead of being vertical or upward-sloping, and the equilibrium wage is likely to rise too. Workers are unlikely to combine in trade unions except with the aim of *raising* wages.

But there is more to the problem than this. The results of collect-ive bargaining will differ according to the circumstances in the markets for the factor and the product. There are four main possible combinations of conditions in the factor and product markets. We assume throughout, of course, that there is perfect competition between *buyers* in the product market, but now that there is collective bargaining, we have monopoly instead of perfect competition between *sellers* in the labour market. The four pos-sible situations are these : (*a*) There could be perfect competition between sellers in the product market and between buyers in the labour market. (*b*) There could be a monopoly seller in the product market but perfect competition between buyers in the labour market. (*c*) There could be perfect competition between sellers in the product market but a monopsonist buying in the labour market. (*d*) There could be a monopolist selling in the product market and a monopsonist buying in the labour market. Let us consider the results in each of these four cases sepa-rately.

(*a*) *Perfect Competition in Both Markets*

Where there is perfect competition in both the factor and product markets, then, for the individual firm, the wage will be equal to the value of the marginal physical product of labour, both before and after collective bargaining is introduced. The result of the introduction of collective bargaining will thus depend on whether the new wage is the same, higher than or lower than the existing wage. If wages are merely frozen where they were, there should be no effect at all. The new agreement merely underwrites the existing situation.

Nevertheless it is possible that even where wages are unaltered, the introduction of collective bargaining will have some effect. If collective bargaining is instituted in an industry with a large number of small firms, it is possible that the perfection of com-petition between them may, in fact, not be complete. The hard-hearted business man in the small firm may be able to keep down the wages of his unorganised workers below the general level. In this case the new wage obtained by collective bargaining will improve the position of such underpaid workers by ensuring that they earn their £6 a week. This sort of problem is really one of imperfection of competition, but it may exist in conditions of apparent perfection. The effect of collective bargaining will be to eliminate such accidental imperfections.

What happens when, as will normally happen, collective bargaining is introduced and does not merely underwrite the existing situation but causes a rise in wages? If all firms in the industry are homogeneous, the amount of labour used by each firm will be reduced by the same amount. The wage paid to each worker in each firm will still be the same as to each other worker, but it will now be higher than it was before. Since the marginal revenue productivity of labour in each firm decreases as employment increases, the amount of employment in each firm must be reduced as wages rise if firms are to maximise profits. In the

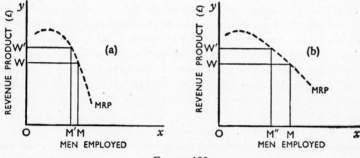

FIGURE 103

industry as a whole there will be less employment offered at the new and higher wage than at the old lower wage. (We are, of course, assuming that everything else, except wages and employment in the industry we are studying, remains the same.) How much less employment will be offered now that wages have risen will depend on the rapidity with which the marginal revenue productivity of labour is falling. The steeper the marginal revenue productivity curve of labour (the lower the elasticity of demand for labour), the smaller the fall in employment will be as wages rise. This can be seen from Figure 103.

Figures 103a and 103b show two different hypothetical firms, A and B. Firm A has a steep marginal revenue productivity curve of labour, and firm B a flat one. In firm A a rise in wages from OW to OW' decreases employment by the small amount M'M. In firm B the same rise in wages reduces employment by the much larger amount M"M. If all firms in an industry are homogeneous and all have marginal revenue product curves like those in Figure 103a, a given increase in wages will lower employment by less than if all curves are like those in Figure 103b. So long as other things remain equal, the effect of the increase in wages resulting from collective bargaining, where there is perfect competition in both markets, will be a certain amount of unemployment. It is therefore possible that the action of philanthropists who raise wages can cause unemployment.

If all firms in the industry are homogeneous and start from a position of long-run equilibrium, the short-run effect will be to reduce profits below normal, whilst firms will reduce employment by moving back along their marginal revenue productivity curves. In the long run, however, because of the losses being made, some firms will be forced to close as a result of the rise in wages. If there really is complete homogeneity, the idea that some firms will go out of business may seem rather difficult to accept. If all are homogeneous, which will go bankrupt? It is inevitable that some must go bankrupt, and so far as we as economists are concerned, we may say, with Phyllis in *Iolanthe*, that we 'don't care which'. Probably it will be sheer accident which firms leave the industry. If the firms in the industry in question are not homogeneous, the solution is easier. The least efficient will leave because of bankruptcy. In either case the result of the advent of collective bargaining will be some unemployment.

We must now consider what will happen in the market for the product. Since employment has fallen now that wages have risen, the supply of the product at each price will be reduced, the equilibrium price will rise slightly, and a smaller amount of the product will be sold. The fact that the price of the product has risen will, of course, cause the marginal revenue product curve of labour to move to the right. Employment will not need to fall so far as it would have done if the price of the product had been constant. But this rise in price cannot increase marginal revenue productivity sufficiently to prevent there being some fall in employment.

The conclusion which one must draw where collective bargaining is introduced into an industry with perfect competition in both the product market and the factor market is that wages will be raised, but that this will not be an unmixed blessing. A certain amount of unemployment seems inevitable, on our assumptions. This is the traditional case of economists against collective bargaining. It is important to remember, however, that this case does depend on the assumption that there is perfect competition in both markets, and also on the fact that we are only concerned with a partial equilibrium analysis. We shall see in Part Two that problems such as these cannot be completely discussed except by a general equilibrium analysis.

(b) *Monopsony in the Factor Market, Perfect Competition in the Product Market*

Where there is perfect competition in the product market and monopsony in the factor market, the situation will be as in Figure 104. Figure 104 shows a firm which is the only purchaser of a particular type of labour, but which sells in a perfectly competitive market.[1] Since the firm is a monopsonist in the labour market, the wage line is not horizontal. The average and marginal wage curves (AW and MW) slope upwards. The monopsonist will maximise profits when he hires OM labour at the wage of £OW. If there is now a collective agreement fixing wages at £OW', the wage line will cease to slope upwards but

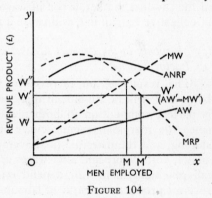

FIGURE 104

will be horizontal, as shown by the line W'W' in Figure 104. This will be because the entrepreneur will have to pay the given wage of £OW' however few or many men he employs. The marginal and average wages will now be equal, as under perfect competition, because of the collective agreement. For the wage has to be £OW' however few or many men are employed.

Let us assume that the collective agreement providing for a wage of £OW' to be paid to all workers is introduced. Earnings per man rise from £OW to £OW', but the volume of employment rises from OM to OM'. There is an increase and not a decrease in employment now that wages are higher. The reason is that the new marginal wage curve (MW'), representing the addition to the wage bill caused by employing one more worker at each level of employment, is the horizontal line W'W'. It is identical with AW'. Thus, at the old level of employment, the marginal wage is now less than the marginal revenue product of labour. If the

---

[1] It is most improbable, though not impossible, that in practice a firm could be the only buyer of labour of a particular kind and yet sell in a competitive market.

enterpreneur is to maximise profits he must increase employment to OM′ when marginal revenue product will equal wage. Employment has risen because collective bargaining has artificially reduced the marginal wage at the old level of employment. Only if the wage fixed by collective agreement was greater than OW″ would employment fall. For only if this were to happen would the new marginal wage exceed the marginal revenue product of labour at the old level of employment (OM). It is quite possible that where there is monopsony in the factor market and perfect competition in the product market, a rise in wages, resulting from the advent of collective bargaining, will cause a rise in employment.

(c) *Monopoly in the Product Market and Perfect Competition in the Factor Market*

The results of an increase in wages caused by collective bargaining will be similar, in this case, to the results where there is perfect competition in both markets. Employment will fall, since the marginal revenue curve of labour will be downward-sloping, and the marginal (and average) wage curve will be horizontal, both before and after wages are increased. The size of the fall in employment will depend on the slope of the marginal revenue productivity curve of labour—on the elasticity of demand for labour.

(d) *Monopoly in the Product Market and Monopsony in the Factor Market*

The effect on employment of a rise in wages in these conditions can be seen from the conclusions of the three previous sub-sections. If the new marginal wage (which is now the same as average wage) is less than the old marginal wage *at the original level of employment*, then employment must increase. Only if the new marginal wage is greater than the old marginal wage at the original level of employment will employment fall off. It is thus perfectly possible that both wages and employment may increase when a collective agreement comes into force.

This, in outline, is how the introduction of collective bargaining will affect wages and employment in various possible situations.

3. THE SUPPLY CURVE OF LABOUR

The second special feature of labour as a factor of production which we must consider, is caused by the fact that workers can decide whether or not they will work on a particular day or on particular terms. In order to carry out this part of our analysis we shall assume that workers can decide how many hours they will work each day. We shall assume that the contract they make with employers is to work for xs. per hour, but that they are free to choose for themselves how many hours they will work. This is not entirely realistic. In reality, the number of hours worked will be fixed by the decisions of workers as a whole in consultation with employers. We also abstract from the problems raised because, in practice, overtime can be worked and higher wages are paid if it is. These simplifications are drastic, but they do not detract from the validity and importance of the general principle which we shall enunciate.

Our analysis of the supply and demand for labour by an industry as a whole has so far been based on the assumption that the supply curve of labour is a vertical straight line. We must now consider in detail whether this assumption is likely to be reasonable either in a single industry or in an economy as a whole. In fact, it is unlikely that normal conditions will be like this. It is more probable that the supply of labour will vary in response to changes in wages. Even if the number of workers is fixed, each can vary the number of hours which he will work. The supply curve of labour, both for the individual and the market, is variable.

If we drop this assumption of a vertical supply curve of labour what shall we put in its place? The normal assumption would be that it rises towards the right. This is a plausible assumption; people will usually work longer hours if they are paid more for doing so. In the case of labour, however, it seems probable that whilst the supply curve will rise, it will not always rise towards the right. Over some ranges it may slope upwards and backwards; it may rise to the left. If wages rise, workers may sometimes work fewer hours. Such a phenomenon may, of course, occur with entrepreneurs. Entrepreneurs may decide to spend more time at home or playing golf when profits rise. It is, however, likely to be most important in the case of labour. If a backward-sloping supply curve for labour is likely to exist, it is essential to understand why and how it occurs. We shall now provide an analysis of this type of behaviour. Let us consider the supply curve of labour of a single labourer.

We must consider the worker's demand for income in exchange for effort. As his wages rise, his income in terms of money will rise also. Since he will be better off, he normally will spend more money on goods of various kinds. It does not follow, however, that he will work a larger number of hours each day now that his income is greater. The worker's standard of living will also include the amount of leisure he is able to enjoy, for leisure is just as much a good as clothes, vegetables and cigars. Our workers will desire freedom to amuse, enjoy or educate himself in his own time. When wages rise he may therefore take the opportunity

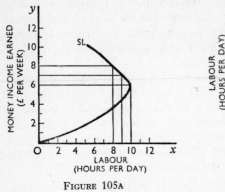

FIGURE 105A

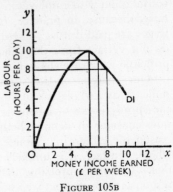

FIGURE 105B

to decide that he will take more time off—that he will spend longer doing nothing.

The worker's ability to make decisions of this kind makes it important to consider the relationship between the demand for leisure and the demand for the more usual kinds of consumer goods. Is it not likely that now that his standard of living is higher he will want both more leisure and more ordinary consumer goods? Is not leisure needed in order that many consumption goods may be enjoyed? Consider the case of visits to the cinema. Higher wages will make it possible to raise one's standard of living by visiting the cinema more often. But this can only be done if one has enough time in the evening to go to see a film. Again, a Bach concert cannot really be appreciated if it has to be heard at a bench as part of 'Music While You Work'. Most of the good things of life must be enjoyed at leisure if they are to be enjoyed at all.

We can explain this kind of behaviour, where an individual worker works fewer hours as wages rise, diagrammatically, as in Figure 105.

In Figure 105a there is shown the worker's total supply curve of labour (effort) in exchange for income earned. As his weekly income rises from zero to £6, the number of hours worked each day rises too. The number of hours worked each day then reaches a maximum where weekly earnings are £6 and 10 hours a day are worked. Once weekly wages exceed £6, however, the hours worked begin to decline. The curve SL in Figure 105a shows how the worker's supply of labour varies as his income changes. In Figure 105b the same information is shown but the axes are reversed. The curve (now called DI) which in Figure 105a showed the supply of labour (effort) in exchange for income, now shows the total demand for income in exchange for effort

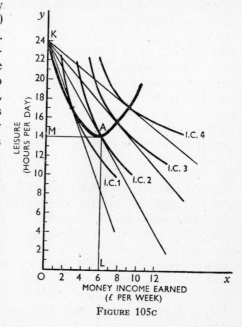

FIGURE 105c

(labour). It will be seen that the demand for income, measured in terms of effort offered in exchange, rises steadily for every increase in income until 10 hours a day are being worked, and then declines. For example, when the income demanded rises from £7 to £8, the number of hours offered each day falls from 9 to 8.

In Figure 105c the way in which a curve giving the same information as that in Figure 105b is derived is shown. This curve shows the demand for income in terms of leisure. As in Figure 105b, income is measured along the x-axis. But instead of measuring daily hours of work up the y-axis, daily hours of leisure are measured. Since there are only the fixed number of 24 hours per day (OK), the number of hours worked can be measured down the y-axis from K. For example, if OM (14) hours per day are taken in leisure, KM (10) hours are being worked. This diagram also shows the indifference curve system between income and leisure. By drawing a series of straight lines radiating from the point K on the *y*-axis, which shows the total hours per day which are available, one can show all the possible 'price ratios' between income and leisure.

The points of tangency between these various price lines and successive indifference curves show the equilibrium position of the worker with respect to income and leisure at the various 'price ratios'. If all such points are joined by a price-consumption curve, one can see the worker's equilibrium position at all possible levels of income. When the price line is very steep—when it coincides with the *y*-axis, income is so expensive in terms of effort, leisure is relatively so 'cheap', that no work is done and the whole day is taken in leisure. As the price line becomes less steep income becomes less expensive in terms of effort (leisure becomes 'dearer') and more and more hours are worked until, with the price line KA, the relative 'prices' of income and leisure are such that OM (14) hours are taken as leisure and KM (10) are worked and £OL (£6) are earned. Any further increase in wages (*i.e.* any further reduction in the price of income in terms of effort) reduces the number of hours worked. If this price-consumption curve is turned upside down so that K coincides with the origin, the total demand curve shown in Figure 105b is obtained, with work measured upwards on the *y*-axis instead of downwards as in Figure 105c. It should be remembered that all that this kind of analysis means is that whilst the elasticity of demand for income in terms of effort is normally greater than one, it may sometimes be less than one. In our example this elasticity becomes less than one once 10 hours a day are being worked. The total demand curve for income therefore slopes upwards once income reaches £6.

It is likely, then, that a rise in wages will often reduce the number of hours worked by labour. This is a point which must never be overlooked. It is not a theoretical curiosity, like 'Giffen's Paradox', but a hard fact of real-world behaviour. Nevertheless, it does not follow that this peculiarity in the behaviour of labour is necessarily unfortunate. There are two important qualifications which should be borne in mind.

First, an increase in income may well raise the efficiency of the worker. If he has previously been badly fed, he may now be able to afford a proper diet. This will very probably increase his productivity per hour. Such an effect is quite likely in backward or undeveloped countries where standards of living are very low. The possibility that this may be the case has long been recognised by economists, who speak of it as the 'economy of high wages'. Second, a reduction in the number of hours worked by an individual may increase his productivity. It has often been found in practice that a reduction in weekly hours worked actually increases total weekly output, because hourly output rises so much more than in proportion to the fall in the number of hours worked. Since this is the case, a reduction in hours may often raise output as well as enabling workers to enjoy the fruits of their leisure.

The general conclusion which can be drawn from this analysis is that for the whole economy, in the short run, since the total number of workers is fixed, the supply curve of labour showing hours of work offered at various wages, will usually slope upwards to the right, though over some ranges it may slope upwards to the left. In the long run, when the number of workers in the economy can alter, the shape of the supply curve can alter, but it is not certain what shape it will take. Economists in the early nineteenth century believed that the supply curve of labour to the economy was horizontal in the long run, and that every increase in wages would, in the long run, call forth a sufficient increase in population to cause wages to return to the original level. This original level was conceived as the minimum amount needed to maintain existence—the subsistence level of wages. It was thought that there was an 'iron law' which ensured that in the long run wages always equalled the cost of subsistence—that the long-run supply curve of labour was horizontal at this level because any rise in wages would evoke a proportionate increase in the size of the population.

This is not the accepted view now. It is agreed that a rise in wages will not always induce a correspondingly large long-run increase in population. In Western countries, at least, people are clearly willing to allow their standard of living to rise and do not always increase their families in such a way as to cancel out the effect of any rise in wages on their standard of living. In countries like India and China this may, of course, still happen. All that one can say is that in Western countries the supply of labour to the whole economy is unlikely to be infinitely elastic to changes in wages in the long run, but that one cannot be sure exactly how responsive to wage changes it will be. This will depend on too many psychological, moral and social factors to permit of satisfactory generalisations. In general, however, it seems that the more advanced a community is, the less likely is a rise in wages to lead to a large long-run increase in its population. Indeed in a rich community there is probably no correlation at all between wages and the size of population. If there is any it is almost certainly negative.

SUGGESTED READING

Alfred Marshall, *Principles of Economics* (8th Edition), London, 1920, Book VI, chapters 3, 4 and 5.

Joan Robinson, *Economics of Imperfect Competition*, London, 1933, chapter xxvi.

Lionel Robbins, 'On The Elasticity of Demand for Income in Terms of Effort', *Economica*, 1930, p. 123.

CHAPTER XIII

RENT

1. ECONOMIC RENT

As the second stage in our discussion of the factors of production and their prices we must now consider the rent of land. In colloquial English the word 'rent' can refer to any periodic payment made regularly for the hire of a good. Examples are, the rentals paid for the hire of bicycles or wireless sets and the rents paid for houses, flats, shops and the like, where these are not bought outright. In economic theory, on the other hand, the term rent is only applied to payments made for factors of production which are in imperfectly elastic supply—with land as the main example.

The type of payment ordinarily known as rent may, of course, include a payment for the hire of land. The rent of a house, for instance, will usually include a contribution to cover ground rent. But it is a payment for other things as well. The landlord has invested his money in the bricks, mortar and wood of which the house is built and he expects a return—interest, as economists call it—on that investment. 'Economic' rent takes account only of payments for the use of land. It excludes interest on a landlord's capital investment. The problems of interest are those to which we shall turn next and we shall therefore ignore them for the moment.

The kind of model which economists most usually use, in explaining what rent is and why it is paid, is one where a tenant farmer rents his farm from a landlord. This is obviously important in practice and it is also the standard case which has been discussed for over a century by economists. Relations between landlord and tenant do, of course, differ from country to country. In this country there is a well-established practice so far as the landlord's responsibility and the tenant's obligations are concerned. The tenant provides all farm machinery, whilst fixed equipment in the form of buildings, and sometimes fences, are provided and maintained by the landlord. Part of the tenant's rent is therefore really interest on the fixed capital provided by the landlord, but the rent usually also includes a fairly substantial payment to the landlord as owner of the land.

This is 'economic' rent. It is sometimes described as a 'surplus' because it does not result from any effort or activity on the part of the landowner. This idea that rent is a reward for the mere ownership of a factor of production and not a payment for effort expended is important in economic theory. Adam Smith commented that 'the landlords like all other men love to reap where they never sowed'.[1] Perhaps the metaphor is a little unfortunate, since reaping is by no means an effortless operation. But even apart from this the statement gives no clue to the reason why rent exists. How is it that landlords are able to reap where they have not sown when other members of the community cannot?

One of the earliest explanations of the nature of rent, and one which is still regarded as coming very near the truth, was provided by David Ricardo in the early years of the nineteenth century. It is not surprising that rent should have been regarded as important in the early 1800's. The scarcity of food, resulting partly from the Napoleonic wars and partly from the pressure of increased population, had raised food prices considerably. Rents had risen greatly and it was widely felt that landlords were profiting from the misfortunes of the rest of society.

It has therefore been suggested that, true to his time, Ricardo developed his theory of rent as an attack on the landed aristocracy as distinct from the tenant farmers. It is sometimes said that Ricardo was a member of the new bourgeoisie and as such was antagonistic to the aristocracy. There may be some justification for this idea, but it is possible to stress it too much. Ricardo was bourgeois by upbringing and inheritance. Yet he is one of the few economists who has made a great deal of money. Going on to the stock exchange he made a fortune in a very few years and, retiring very young, bought an estate in Gloucestershire, becoming a landlord himself as well as a Member of Parliament. It is therefore dangerous to attack Ricardo as being an unrelenting opponent of landowners.

2. RICARDO AND RENT

It will be useful to take the Ricardian ideas on the subject as our starting-point in this discussion of rent. Let us try to see what

[1] Adam Smith, *The Wealth of Nations*, chapter vi.

was the essence of Ricardian theory and where Ricardo's ideas were right and where they were wrong. Ricardo's two main contentions were these. First, rent is a return for the use of the 'original and indestructible powers of the soil'.[1] Second, high rents are not a sign of the bounty of nature. On the contrary, they are an indication of the niggardliness of nature.

It will be easiest to take the second point first. This part of Ricardo's doctrine was probably intended very largely as an attack on a group of French economists known as the 'physiocrats'[2] who laid great stress on the bounty of nature as the cause of the rent of land. In modern terms Ricardo meant that whilst land is clearly useful it is also scarce, that whilst the productivity of land may be a sign of its usefulness and of the bounty of nature, the fact that the total supply of land is more or less fixed is a sign of nature's niggardliness. Ricardo, as we have seen, lived at a time when high rents were causing great anxiety. He saw only too clearly that these high rents were caused by the scarcity of agricultural land and its produce and not by their abundance. It is scarcity and high prices which cause high rents, not bountiful plenty.

What, then, can we say about Ricardo's first point? This assertion that rent is a payment for the 'original and indestructible powers of the soil' is more difficult to judge. Admittedly, the fact that rent is a payment for natural resources and not for consumption goods makes it easier to use such terms. One difficulty, however, is that of deciding which powers of the land are 'original' and which are not. The implication intended by the term 'original powers' is probably that it is both desirable and possible to distinguish, for example, between land with drainage facilities supplied by the landlord, payment for which is really interest, and payment for land with only natural drainage, which is rent. It is well known that the whole landscape of Britain has been changed by man since prehistoric times. The present landscape is certainly not attributable to the original powers of the soil and to nothing else. What land is today depends not only on what nature has given but also on the actions of Ancient Britons, Romans and successive generations of English, Welsh, Scots and Irish. The concept of the 'original' powers of the land is, to say the least, nebulous.

Can it then be said that the powers of the soil are 'inde-

[1] David Ricardo, *Principles of Political Economy* (edited Piero Sraffa), p. 67.
[2] For a study of their doctrines see *A History of Economic Doctrines*, Gide and Rist, chapter i.

structible'? In these days of nuclear physics and atomic energy it is very dangerous to assert that anything is indestructible. But even on a more ordinary plane it is not entirely reasonable to claim that the fertility of the land is unalterable. Changes in climate or farming methods can turn fine arable land into dust bowls and even deserts into grassland. It is not reasonable to regard the powers of the land as indestructible.

It seems more reasonable to attribute the payment of rent not to the original and indestructible powers of the soil but rather to the fact that land is a factor of production which is in almost completely inelastic supply to changes in its price. More land cannot be produced to meet a greater demand for it and such expedients as reclamation from the sea are clearly quantitatively unimportant. What Ricardo was really searching for was surely an explanation of the fact that when the demand for land increased, the supply was incapable of changing in response to that increased demand. The idea that there are 'original and indestructible powers' of the land implies an almost complete inelasticity of supply to changes in price. It is therefore much more satisfactory to explain the rent of land in the more modern terms of a payment to a factor of production with a less than infinite (and in fact extremely low) elasticity of supply. Whilst the Ricardian idea of original and indestructible powers of the soil implies very inelastic supply, very inelastic supply does not necessarily imply original and indestructible powers of the soil, which is all to the good.

3. SCARCITY RENT

In order to explain the theory of rent more fully we shall find it useful to construct a simplified model which will not, in its early stages at least, be a Ricardian model. Let us assume that there is an island of finite size and that this island is made up of homogeneous land. This means, first, that every acre is equal in fertility to every other acre, and second, that no acre is in a superior situation to any other acre or more suited to growing any particular crop. We imply, for example, that there is no inherent difference between the situation of one acre of the island and that of another, as there clearly is between a site, say, in Oxford Street and one in North Yorkshire. These assumptions are not realistic, but they are useful at this early stage in our discussion. These assumptions enable us to rule out the possibility that some parts of the island are better situated than others for serving particular markets. We shall also assume that all the land on this imaginary island is agricultural land and is only able to grow one product. We shall call this product wheat, again for the sake of simplicity. We assume that none of the island will be of any use as country parks, children's playgrounds or aerodromes, and that none of it can produce carrots and potatoes as well as wheat.

So far as the ownership of the land is concerned we shall assume that this ownership is divided between a large number of landowners. We rule out the possibility of a monopoly in the ownership of land. In the past this has sometimes led to confusion in theories of rent. We can assume, for example, that each acre of the island is owned by a different person. Let us assume, for example, that the ancestors of the present landowners came to the island with William the Conqueror. He granted them pieces of land which have all remained in the hands of the same families ever since. This enables us to postulate that no landowner ever wants to farm the land himself and that no-one ever wants to buy or sell land. Finally, we assume that the island is uninhabited, all the landlords being absentee landlords.

Let us now imagine that a farmer arrives and wants to farm on the island. It would be easiest to suppose that he merely needs two factors of production—himself and some land—in order to commence production. It is rather more realistic, however, to think that he will bring a plough. We shall therefore assume that every farmer has one tractor and one plough which can only be used by him. We have, in fact, 'a fixed production coefficient' between farmers and ploughs.

Finally, we must introduce demand into our model. Let us assume that there is a perfectly competitive world market for wheat and that our hypothetical island is small compared with that world market. Then even if the whole island is cultivated, we can assume that any change in the island's output of wheat does not change the world price. This is a realistic assumption. Any group of farmers on a fairly small island would have to take the world price of wheat as being fixed quite independently of their own actions.

When the farmer arrives he will not be likely to want to farm the whole island—we assume it to be fairly large. Nor, since there is perfect competition between landlords, will he need to pay any rent. If any one landlord tries to charge him rent, the farmer will simply move along to the next piece of land. Perfect competition between landlords will ensure that the price of land is zero. Since no rent need be paid, it will clearly be 'rational' for the farmer to go on extending the size of his farm until the last field he takes in produces no addition to his revenue. In other words, he will employ more and more land until its marginal net

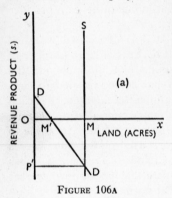

FIGURE 106A

revenue product is equal to its price —which is zero. At this point the farmer will not want to cultivate any more land for he will be maximising profits. It is often said that when the farmer is cultivating just enough land for the last acre he takes into cultivation to be producing no more and no less than it costs to hire it, the *extensive margin of cultivation* has been reached.

This situation can be seen from Figures 106a and 106b. Figure 106a shows the demand and supply curves for land on the whole island. The demand curve DD is given by the (falling) marginal revenue productivity curve of land to the one farmer who is farming on the island. For simplicity we have drawn this curve as a straight line. The supply curve SM is a vertical straight line showing that there is only a fixed amount of land, OM acres, available—the whole island. In this initial situation there is, as can be seen from Figure 106a, no positive price for

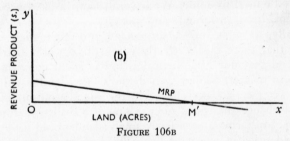

FIGURE 106B

land at which the demand for land equals the supply of land. If all the island were to be cultivated, the landowners would have to pay the single farmer OP's. (=MDs.) per acre. Since presumably no landlord will actually pay people to induce them to farm his land, the one farmer uses OM' acres of land and pays no rent.

Figure 106b shows the equilibrium position for this single farmer. Since he has no rent to pay, he goes on hiring more and

more land until the marginal acre brings him no revenue. He thus
equates the marginal revenue product of land with its marginal
cost. In Figure 106b this happens when the farmer uses OM'
acres but pays no rent for them. The farmer then stops increasing
the size of his farm. It will be seen that when there is only one
farmer the marginal revenue productivity curve of land to the farmer
is the same thing as the demand
curve for land. The two curves
look different in Figures 106a and
106b only because the scale along
the x-axis in Figure 106b is ten
times larger than in Figure 106a.
This is because the individual farm
is so much smaller than the whole
island.

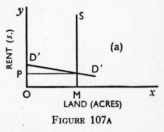

FIGURE 107A

Let us now assume that the success of this pioneer farmer
attracts new entrants to the island's farming industry. We shall
further assume, for simplicity, that all the farmers we are concerned with are equally efficient.

So long as there are not enough farmers to make it worth while
farming the whole island, no rent will be paid. This is because
we are still assuming that there is perfect competition between
landowners. However, if when all the land (OM acres) is taken
there are still farmers who want land and who are willing to pay
a rent for it, a rent will be charged. All the farmers will have

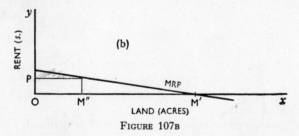

FIGURE 107B

to pay rent—and all will pay the same rent—because all the
land is homogeneous and there is perfect competition between
landowners. The increase in the number of farmers demanding
land will reduce the amount of land used by each individual
farmer. Each farmer will still use only those acres of land
which yield a marginal revenue product at least as great as their
rent. But there are now more farmers and rent is therefore paid.

It is obvious that, given the marginal revenue productivity of land to each single farmer, such a farmer will now only find it worth his while to use a smaller amount of land than he did when land was free. The increase in the number of equally efficient farmers thus reduces the amount of land used by each. For each farmer the revenue product of a marginal acre of land will be the same ; and for each it will also be equal to the rent of an acre of land. All farmers, being equally efficient, will have exactly the same acreage of land.

The situation when the whole island is being farmed is shown in Figures 107a and 107b. These are similar to Figures 106a and 106b. In Figure 107a the curve SM still shows the fixed supply of land OM acres. D'D' is now the demand curve for land by the whole of the island's farming industry and is obtained by adding the marginal revenue productivity curves of all the farmers together sideways. This demand curve slopes downwards only because we assume that the number of farmers on the island is still relatively small. We are continuing to assume a given and constant world price for wheat. The whole island (OM acres) is now used and a rent of OPs. per acre is paid. In Figure 107b we see the position of the individual farmer, as in Figure 106b. The marginal revenue productivity curve of land to each farmer is the same as it was to the single farmer in Figure 106b because all farmers are assumed to be equally efficient. But the rent per acre has risen from zero to OPs. and the individual farmer thus finds it profitable to farm only OM" acres instead of the OM' farmed by the single original farmer. The 'extensive margin of cultivation' has retreated for the individual farmer. We may therefore sum up this part of the discussion as follows. Each farmer will always farm land up to the point where the revenue product of the 'marginal' acre is equal to the cost of a 'marginal' acre. In perfect competition this 'marginal cost' of land will also equal the rent of the land.

We have so far studied the problem of rent mainly from the point of view of the individual farmer who is deciding how many acres to farm. But we can also consider it from the point of view of the farmer who is wondering how many hours to work, or to put it in the terms we are using, how many 'doses' of labour and capital to apply to the land ; each 'dose' being, say, one hour's work by the farmer with his plough. This is not so simple as it sounds. We need to consider the marginal productivity of 'doses' of labour and capital applied to land. Strictly speaking, however, as we have seen, the amount of land used by an individual farmer will change every time rent changes. This means that we ought really to reconsider the marginal productivity curve of labour and capital each time rent changes, for labour and capital would then be applied to a different amount of land. This would be inconvenient. The simplest case to consider is therefore one where the amount of land used is fixed in amount. This will show all the main principles involved in this question but will avoid the difficulties encountered when the amount of land farmed by each farmer can change. We shall also, for the sake of simplicity, talk only of 'doses' of labour— though in fact each unit of labour will have to use a fixed amount of capital.

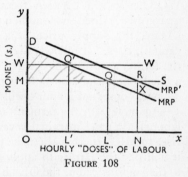

HOURLY "DOSES" OF LABOUR

FIGURE 108

In Figure 108 the marginal revenue productivity curve of 'doses' of labour supplied by a single farmer to a given area of land is the curve MRP. Let us assume that, to begin with, the farmer is in equilibrium in Figure 108 when he applies OL hourly 'doses' of his own labour to the fixed amount of land. The supply of labour curve (MS) shows the amount of money per hour (measured up the y-axis) which the farmer must be paid if he is to be induced to work for any given (marginal) hour (measured along the x-axis). It represents his supply curve of labour in terms of (hourly) income. For the sake of simplicity it is assumed that the farmer asks a constant return of OMs. per dose of labour (and capital), however many or few hours' 'doses' he supplies. He applies his labour to his farm until the 'marginal dose', in this case the OLth, brings no greater reward than he asks. A more intensive effort on his part, say, working for ON hours, would bring a smaller income than he asks, NXs. for the ONth hour instead of OMs. (= NRs.), so he does not work so hard as that. The marginal (OLth) dose yields only just as much as the farmer asks from it. On all the 'intra-marginal' doses, however, the return yielded is greater than the farmer asks. It is from these 'intra-marginal' doses that rent is paid. They yield more to the farmer than he asks, and competition for land between farmers ensures that this 'surplus' goes to the landlord. In Figure 108 the triangle MQD represents the rent paid. The 'marginal dose' of labour, it will be noted, makes no contribution to this rent. It is only just worth applying.

If the farmer now becomes less inclined to work, the supply curve of his labour rises to WW. He still works up to the point where the marginal revenue product of his labour is equal to the reward he demands for applying that marginal 'dose' of labour. But since that reward he asks is now greater than it was, he supplies only OL' 'doses' instead of OL. When this marginal dose of labour (the OL'th) has been applied it is said that the *intensive margin of cultivation* has been reached. Rent is now WQ'D. It will be seen from Figure 108 that the 'intensive margin' is reached sooner when the 'marginal cost' of the farmer's labour, the supply price of a marginal 'dose' of labour (and capital), rises. It follows, therefore, that if the labour used is not the farmer's own but it is hired by him, a rise in wages will cause a fixed amount of land to be worked less intensively. Fewer men —fewer 'doses' of labour—will be used on it.

Again, if with the farmer's original supply curve of 'doses' of labour (MS) the marginal revenue productivity curve of labour rises to MRP' (perhaps because the farmer becomes more efficient), it will pay the farmer to apply ON 'doses' of labour and capital to his land instead of the OL he originally applied. The intensive margin is thus extended, *ceteris paribus*, when the marginal revenue productivity of labour increases. We can see then that each farmer will always push the 'intensive margin of cultivation' to the point where the marginal 'dose' of labour and capital brings a return just equal to the payment necessary to induce it to work—to the point where the marginal revenue product of labour is equal to the marginal cost of labour.

We have now seen that farmers must adjust their operations in two ways if they are to earn maximum profits. First, at each level of rent they must cultivate an area of land of such a size that the 'extensive margin' is just reached. Second, with a given supply curve for doses of their own or other peoples' labour and capital, they must apply so many doses that the 'intensive margin' is just reached. It must always be remembered, of course, that adjustments at both these margins will take place simultaneously to meet changed conditions. We have considered the adjustments separately only because this facilitates the exposition.

The main conclusions we have reached are these. First, since in our model land has zero elasticity of supply no change in rents can bring more land into existence. On our assumption that all

land is homogeneous and that there is perfect competition between
landlords and between tenants, all farmers will pay the same rent—
a rent whose size will be determined by the demand for land and
the supply of land. It follows that a rise in rents will occur in
three main situations. First, rents will rise if the number of
farms increases but the price of their product and their productivity remain constant. Second, rents will rise if the price of
the product rises but the number of farms and the marginal
productivity of land remain constant. Third, rents will rise if the
marginal revenue productivity of land rises but the price of the
product and the number of farms remain constant.

Rent in the situation we have so far studied is known as
scarcity rent. It results from the scarcity of homogeneous land.
The essential feature of pure scarcity rent is this. Whilst a rise
in the prices of other factors of production will often cause an
increase in their supply, at any rate in the long run, a rise in rent
cannot increase the supply of land. Higher earnings can therefore
persist for land even in the long run, whereas with other factors
this is not very likely to happen because supply will increase to
meet the increased demand. It is the fixity of its supply which
distinguishes homogeneous land and its scarcity rent from other
factors of production and their prices. Scarcity rent is essentially
the result of the fact that, both in our model and in the real world,
land is in inflexible supply.

4. DIFFERENTIAL RENT

The problems of scarcity rent can, as we have seen, be discussed in terms of a model in which land is both homogeneous
and scarce. This is not, however, a very realistic model. We
shall now drop the assumption that land is homogeneous. For
land is not all of the same quality. Let us continue to simplify
the analysis by discussing our hypothetical island but let us now
assume that a new stretch of it, not capable of reclamation by
human agencies, is uncovered by the sea.

It is reasonable to assume that this new stretch of land will
not be so fertile as the rest of the island. This means that there
will now be land of two qualities, the new land being less fertile
than the old. We have already assumed that the whole of the
original island is being cultivated and that, since all the land is
homogeneous, each acre pays the same rent. If more new farmers

now arrive on the enlarged island, they will obviously consider
using the new and less fertile land. Since the new land is not so
productive, it will not pay the farmers to hire it at the same rent
as they would have to pay for the better land. If the same rent
were charged for both types of land, it would clearly be sensible
for the farmers to use the better land. Assuming perfect competition between landlords and farmers, rent on the less fertile
land must be lower than on the better land. For example, if the
rent on the better land is £20 per acre, whilst the fertility of the
worse land is such that farmers' earnings are £10 less per acre
than on the better land, the rent on this worse land must be £10
per acre. If rent on the worse land were less than £10, it would
pay farmers to farm it instead of the better land and competition
between farmers wishing to farm on the cheaper land would
raise its price. If rent on the worse land were more than £10 per
acre, it would pay farmers to farm the better land instead. Only
at £10 per acre will there be no inflow or outflow of farmers to
and from the worse land. Competition between farmers, then,
establishes an appropriate difference between the rents of the two
types of land. It follows that if there are yet other grades of land·
these too will earn different rents.

This type of situation represents the kind of situation in which
Ricardo was interested. It is a rather more complicated model
than where all land is equally fertile but it is more realistic than
was the model where rent was mere scarcity rent. For we can now
allow for differing fertilities between different pieces of land.
This type of situation is said to lead to *differential rents*. Rent is
'different' on each grade of land. That grade of land which is
now only just worth cultivating is said to be *on the extensive
margin of cultivation* for the island's farming industry. If the area
under cultivation increases for any reason, rents on all grades of
land rise proportionately and the extensive margin is pushed onto
progressively worse grades of land.

Rent is not due to the existence of land of differing fertility.
As we have seen, rent is caused solely by the fact that land is
scarce and can be paid when land is homogeneous. But differences
between the fertilities of different types of land will cause *differences* in their rents. Rent will be lower on the less fertile land
and higher on the more fertile land. On the other hand, it is
quite possible for very infertile land to pay no rent at all when
land is not all of the same quality. Ricardo considered this kind
of situation and showed that land which, for the whole farming

industry, is on or beyond the 'extensive margin of cultivation' will pay no rent. It will be 'no rent' land.

This idea that different areas of land are of differing fertility is quite realistic. The typical case can be considered if we assume that there is a fertile valley containing several farms and that on either side of the valley there are less fertile hillsides with less and less productive farms as one moves up the hills. Let us continue to assume that only wheat is grown. If the price of wheat rises, progressively less fertile land farther and farther up the hills will be cultivated. The extensive margin of cultivation will move up the hillsides. 'Marginal land', as British farmers have recently come to call it, following economic terminology, will be brought under cultivation. Rents will rise everywhere. But the effect of the increased prices—and hence the increased rents—will be felt on both the extensive and the intensive margins of the wheat industry. More land will be used—the extensive margin will alter. But land will also be used more intensively now that wheat is more expensive—the intensive margin will be extended too. It is very important to remember that whenever circumstances change every farmer will have to adapt his activities at both the extensive and the intensive margins so as to bring himself back into equilibrium. And because individual farmers will always behave in this way it follows that the farming industry as a whole will also maintain equilibrium at both the extensive and the intensive margins.

One can also see from this kind of model that some land can earn no rent. As the extensive margin of cultivation advances there will always be some land ' on the margin of cultivation' which is so infertile that it pays no rent. It will only be worth cultivating at all if it can be used free of charge. If rent had to be paid, the farmer would refuse to cultivate it. He would find it more profitable to work on the better land instead. For although there would be a rent to pay on this better land, the land would be sufficiently more fertile to allow the farmer to pay the rent and yet earn larger profits than on the worse land.

We have seen throughout our analysis of rent that there are three main circumstances which can lead to a rise in rents. These are : an increase in the number of farmers ; an increase in the productivity of each farmer ; and a rise in the price of the product which the farmers are growing. In fact, it is usually the last of these three explanations—a rise in price because demand for the product has increased—which is the cause of rising rents in the real world. If the price of the product rises, it rises equally for all farmers however much or little they produce, for we are assuming that competition is perfect. So, the higher prices are, the less fertile is the 'marginal' land which it is just possible to cultivate and yet earn normal profits. Similarly, the higher crop prices are, the higher are rents on the better grades of land. It is usually changes in the prices of agricultural products, and consequent changes in the demand for land, which cause changes in rent. And since land is in fixed supply, such rises in the price of the product of land will cause increases in rent. High prices are the cause of high rents—not *vice versa*.

It is always possible to show whether or not the earnings of a given piece of land are rent by taxing those earnings. Since the supply of land is completely inelastic, any rise or fall in the receipts of landlords cannot affect the supply of land. Landlords cannot produce more land however high rents are. So long as there is perfect competition between landlords, they will always find it worth while to leave their land in cultivation, to pay the tax and keep what is left, however little it may be. The land exists in any case, and landlords will feel that it is sensible to take what rents they can get—even if these are taxed. There will be no reduction in the supply of land if its rents are taxed. There is, however, little likelihood that the supply of *other* factors of production would remain unaltered in this way if their earnings were to be taxed.

This analysis of rent has been very abstract but it has enabled us to distinguish two different types of rent. In the first place we have seen that rent can be earned where all land is homogeneous—provided that it is also scarce. In this case, because there was perfect competition between landlords, the homogeneous land on our hypothetical island was in *perfectly elastic* supply until all was used, and therefore until it was all used no rent could be charged. Once all the land was used, however, land was in *perfectly inelastic* supply to changes in the demand for it and a scarcity rent began to be paid. This accrued equally to each and every acre of land. The rent was a pure scarcity rent and no differential elements existed at all. It will be remembered, of course, that we were assuming that the land could only grow wheat. In technical language, it was 'completely specific' to wheat-growing. We shall have to see soon just what difference this simplifying assumption makes.

In our second model, when there was a supply of land large

enough for some of it to pay no rent at all, there was no scarcity
rent as such. But this land was not homogeneous. Some was
more fertile than the rest, and it was possible in such a situation
for a differential rent to be earned by this better land. Land may
or may not now be specific to wheat-growing, though for the
moment it will be easier to assume that it is. The land cannot,
however, be in completely elastic supply since it is not all of the
same quality. Some acres are only imperfect substitutes for others.
Better areas of land will therefore earn a larger rent than worse
ones because of the differences in fertility between them. The
land is in *imperfect elastic* supply to changes in its price and in
such circumstances it is always possible for rent to be earned.
Of course, as Marshall has said, 'in a sense all rents are scarcity
rents, and all rents are differential rents'.[1] Differential rents arise
only because land of each particular quality is scarce. Nevertheless the distinction between these two kinds of rent is worth
making.

Another qualification needs to be made to the theory of rent
outlined above. We have so far relaxed our initial assumptions
only to the extent of admitting the possibility that land may not be
homogeneous. We must now make a similar change in our
assumptions to allow for the fact that land is not all in the same
place and that some acres of land are therefore less accessible than
others. Differential rents may occur because of differences in
situation.

To some extent differences in the situation of land come to
the same thing as differences in its fertility. Land may be described
as bad for corn-growing either because it is situated on the chalk
of the South Downs or because it is half-way between Brighton
and Eastbourne. Both come to the same thing in the end, but
the first explanation is in terms of soil fertility and the second
is in terms of situation. Sometimes, therefore, differences in
fertility and differences of situation amount to the same thing.
But even where land is homogeneous from the point of view of
inherent fertility there may well be differences in rent because of
differences in situation. As we have seen, the rent of land is
determined in the last resort by what consumers will pay for the
product of the land. The receipts from a particular crop will
therefore depend in part on how much it costs to transport it to
market. The existence of transport charges means that land near
a market can pay higher rents than land farther away. Those

[1] *Principles of Economics*, p. 422.

farming the nearer land have to pay less to send their produce to market, and competition between farmers will thus ensure that rent on this land is higher than on less accessible land.

The same type of situation arises in the case of perishable foods. It will be more profitable to grow green vegetables, milk and strawberries for a town market near that particular town than to grow them six hundred miles away. A smaller amount of the goods will go bad in transit. In competitive conditions, then, two market gardens of equal fertility and run with equal efficiency will pay different rents if one is much nearer to, say, London than the other, rents differing by the difference in transport costs. It is important, therefore, to allow for differences in situation in constructing any really satisfactory theory of rent. Differential rents are just as likely to exist in the real world because of differences in situation as because of differences in the innate fertility of the land. Since we have drawn our illustrations of the importance of situation as a cause of differences in rents from agriculture, it is probably desirable to say explicitly that rents in industry will differ for similar reasons. A factory near a large market will pay a higher ground rent than an identical factory far away. Also, very great differences exist between the rents paid by shops in, for example, the centre of London and in a village in central Wales. Rents are much higher where trade is more easily attracted. The advantages of a site in a good shopping or trading centre have to be paid for in the form of high rents.

5. TRANSFER EARNINGS

One final and most important qualification to our theory of rent remains to be made. It should be obvious to the reader that by confining our attention to the payment made for land which is completely 'specific' to growing one crop we have been able to avoid a very important problem. We have been able to imply that the whole of a rent earned by land is a payment for a 'free gift of nature'. Being a free gift, land is not reproducible. It does not need to be paid if it is to be kept in existence. There is therefore no problem of the kind which would exist if some of the earnings of land were devoted to keeping it alive. For if that happened, some of the earnings of land would be a 'wage' to keep it alive. Only the remainder would be a rent due to its scarcity. But an analogous problem does arise if we consider the rent of land from the point of view of a particular industry. It is this problem which we have avoided by assuming that the land could do nothing but produce wheat. Since the land was assumed to be valueless in any other use, it was possible for us to assume that the wheat farmer did not need to make any payment to keep the land in the wheat industry. It would remain in existence whatever happened and its earnings could therefore be described as rent. This is not realistic. Most land can produce various crops and to keep land in any one crop-growing 'industry' it must be paid enough to prevent it from leaving that particular 'industry'. For example, let us assume that a marginal acre of wheat land, whilst able to remain in the wheat-farming industry so long as rent was not more than £6 an acre, could, if need be, profitably turn to the production of turnips if only rent fell to £4 an acre. In this situation, the wheat farmer must pay at least £4 an acre in rent to the landlord or he will hand the land over to the turnip industry.

This £4 per acre is known as the land's *transfer earnings*. Unless the acre earns at least £4 in the wheat industry it will transfer to the next most lucrative (in this case the turnip) industry. We may therefore define the rent from the point of view of any one industry more accurately as *a payment in excess of its transfer earnings*. In our example, from the point of view of the wheat industry paying £6 an acre for land, the 'true' rent is £2 and transfer earnings £4. If now some revolution in the supply or demand conditions for turnips, the most profitable alternative crop, should make it possible for turnip farmers to pay £10 an acre for land whilst wheat farmers can still offer only £6, land will move into the turnip industry. From the point of view of the turnip industry the transfer earnings of any acre of land will now be the £6 required to prevent it from returning to the wheat industry. Its rent will be £4—the difference between its transfer earnings of £6 and the £10 it actually earns.

On the basis of the concept of transfer earnings it is not difficult to show that it is quite possible for land, which is in *perfectly inelastic* supply to the economy as a whole and which therefore, from the point of view of that economy, earns nothing but rent, to be in *perfectly elastic* supply from the point of view of a particular industry and therefore to earn no rent at all so far as that industry is concerned. For example, let us revert to our original imaginary island of homogeneous land. Let us imagine that it is all used to grow wheat and that the rent per acre is £6. Now if a small group of farmers decides to grow, say, turnips, it will be able to obtain as much land as it wants for slightly more than

U

£6 an acre, so long as it does not want to use the whole island. From the point of view of the 'turnip industry' the whole payment of a little over £6 will be transfer earnings needed to entice the land away from wheat-growing, and the land will earn no rent so far as the 'turnip industry' is concerned.

Now, as we have seen, land can earn more than its transfer earnings and any such excess over transfer earnings is rent from the point of view of the industry using the land. It must always be remembered, however, that this analysis of transfer earnings has only been undertaken from the point of view of a single industry. Such an individual industry does have to pay money to keep land from transferring to the next most lucrative use. For the economy as a whole, however, land has no alternative use at all. The transfer earnings of land from the point of view of the economy as a whole will therefore be zero, and all the earnings of land will be rent.

The same kind of problem can be studied from the point of view of the individual farmer. To him land has a cost in just the same way as any other factor does. Unless he pays the rent per acre which is determined by competition between landlords and between farmers, the land will go to someone else. *For the individual farmer the whole rent will be a cost—the cost of keeping the land from transferring to someone else.* This concept of transfer earnings helps to bring the simple Ricardian theory—where transfer earnings are zero because it is the whole economy which is being studied—into a closer relation with reality.

6. RENT OF ABILITY

We have seen that land earns rent because it is a factor of production which is in inelastic supply to changes in its price. There are, however, other factors of production which cannot be reproduced at will—or at all—and which are therefore also in imperfectly elastic supply so far as changes in their prices are concerned. All such factors can earn rent. Rent can therefore be defined, more accurately than we have done so far, as the difference between the reward to *any* factor of production in imperfectly elastic supply with respect to changes in its price and its transfer earnings. Natural ability, which cannot be reproduced even if earnings rise, is quite frequently found in some units of the factor of production labour. The genius clearly possesses scarce and non-reproducible ability, and whilst such ability is clearly not 'indestructible' (though it may be original), it is undoubtedly born and not made. The supply of genius over periods of time may be variable, but it does not vary in response to changes in its price. Human ability just happens.

Natural ability of this kind cannot be produced even by the best education. From the point of view of the whole economy it is therefore in completely inelastic supply to price changes. Such ability may be either general or specific. If the skill is completely specific to one occupation, the person concerned will earn a very large income in that occupation. Let us assume, for example, that we are concerned with a brilliant violinist. His talent is natural and he is able to earn £80 a week by his playing but nothing at all by doing anything else. The money he earns represents a true economic rent. It is a payment for completely 'specific' ability.

It is, however, much more likely that the violinist's talent will not be entirely specific but that he may be able to earn a much smaller income in another occupation. As a soloist he earns £80 a week. If he had to choose some other job he could always earn £20 a week by playing in a dance band. Thus, so long as he is paid at least £20 a week he will remain a soloist, but since we assume he is 'rational', he will turn to playing jazz if he is offered less than £20. The same principle can be seen if we apply the acid test of a tax to our example. If the violinist is taxed £60 a week he will continue to play his Beethoven and Mendelssohn. Only if the tax on solo violinists exceeds £60 a week will he (being 'rational') turn to jazz. The £60—the difference between his total earnings and his transfer earnings—is the violinist's economic rent from the point of view of the 'solo violin industry'. It represents *rent of ability*.

7. QUASI-RENT

There are some factors of production whose supply is elastic in the long run but inelastic in the short run. These will, in Marshall's words, be 'machines and other appliances made by man.'[1] They are not in fixed supply like land, so that the earnings from their use cannot be called rent in the economic sense. Nevertheless, in the short run their supply cannot be increased or decreased, since they are relatively durable in use and take time to make. The reward from them is therefore not

[1] *Principles*, p. 74.

quickly adjusted to changes in market conditions. It is not closely akin to the rate of interest on free or floating capital, but is rather a sort of rent. Marshall attached great importance to the analysis of these earnings from machines, and coined a special term for them, namely, quasi-rent. There is no explicit, formal definition of quasi-rent in Marshall, and the term has been used both by him and by other writers in a variety of related but not identical senses. In Marshall, the main 'model' appears to be as follows.

An entrepreneur hires a machine, on an annual contract, and pays a given weekly sum for its use. This payment is a fixed and not a variable cost for the entrepreneur. But, by using the machine in conjunction with one or more variable factors, he earns from it a profit which varies with changes in demand conditions and in other cost conditions, for example, wage rates. If the entrepreneur has only one fixed factor (the machine) and one variable factor (labour), his total receipts from sales of product minus his total wage bill is quasi-rent earned by the machine. Now this quasi-rent may be less than or equal to or greater than the weekly rental of the machine. In Figure 109 the firm initially faces the average revenue (demand) curve PD. Total weekly wages are OMST; weekly rental of the machine is LQST: quasi-rent is PRST. In this case the entrepreneur is doing well. He is earning abnormally high profits or 'abnormally high quasi-rent' in the short run. It is only in the long run that the supplies of the machine can be increased, and such abnormally high quasi-rent competed away. If the demand curve fell, in the short run, from PD to P′D′, the machine would still be earning a positive quasi-rent of P′R′S′T′, but this would be smaller than the weekly rental of L′Q′S′T′ (=LQST). The quasi-rent would now be 'abnormally low', and in the long run the number of machines in existence would fall so that quasi-rent returned to the 'normal' level. It should be noted that if demand fell still further, quasi-rent might become zero, with the demand

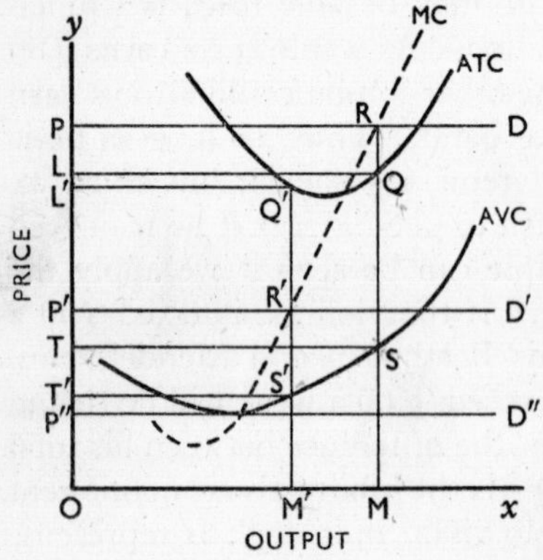

FIGURE 109

curve $P''D''$. However, with a demand curve below $P''D''$, it would pay the firm to close down altogether rather than produce in a situation where total receipts were less than the total wage bill for any positive output. We have already seen that a firm will then minimise its loss by closing down temporarily. It may be noted that, on this assumption, quasi-rent can never be negative.

Let us attempt a formal definition of quasi-rent. The quasi-rent of a machine is its total short-run receipts less the total costs of hiring the variable factors used with it and of keeping the machine in running order in the short run. In long-run equilibrium quasi-rent will become equal to the (constant) normal earnings of the machine. Quasi-rent, in other words, will be at its 'normal' long-run level, where it is just equal to the cost of keeping the machine in continued existence.

It follows that whilst in the short run any receipts of a machine in excess of the prime costs of running it can be regarded as akin to rent, such returns are in the long run quite essential to the continued existence of the machine. In the long run, any quasi-rent 'is expected to, and generally does, yield a normal rate of interest . . . on the free capital, represented by a sum of money that was invested in producing it'.[1] As Marshall says, 'it is . . . just as essential in the long run that the price obtained should cover general or supplementary costs as that it should cover prime costs. An industry will be driven out of existence in the long run as certainly by failing to earn even a moderate interest on the capital invested in steam engines, as by failing to replace the price of the coal or the raw material used up from day to day.'[2] Consequently one may say that 'the confident expectation of coming quasi-rents is a necessary condition for the investment of capital in machinery and for the incurring of supplementary costs generally.'[3]

The principles lying behind rent and quasi-rent are well illustrated by what is known as Marshall's 'parable' of the meteor stones.[4] We shall use Marshall's analysis as the basis for our own. Let us assume in the first instance [5] that a single shower of homogeneous meteoric stones falls in a particular area. All the stones fall within a very small radius and they are all immediately found. It is then discovered that since the stones

[1] Marshall, *op. cit.* p. 424 (footnote).   [2] *Ibid.* p. 420.
[3] *Ibid.* p. 424 (footnote).   [4] *Principles*, pp. 415-21.
[5] Cf. Marshall, *ibid.* p. 415.

are harder and more durable than diamonds they are very useful
in industrial production. The owners of the stones are therefore
able to charge a 'scarcity rent' for them. They own a 'free
gift of nature' in perfectly inelastic supply to changes in its
price.

This hypothetical situation is depicted in Figure 110a. The
fixed (long and short run) supply of stones, OM, is demanded by
industrialists who are willing to pay for varying amounts of them
the amounts of money shown by the demand curve DD. This is
the marginal (net) revenue productivity curve of stones to industrialists. It slopes downwards for the usual reasons. The

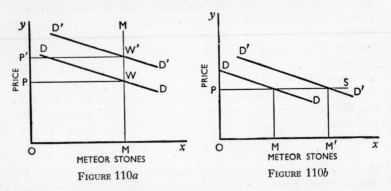

FIGURE 110a   FIGURE 110b

price of each stone, in perfect competition, is therefore OP and
all the stones are used. The owners earn an amount of rent
OMWP. If now the demand for these stones increases, perhaps
because of an increase in the price of industrial output, the demand
curve may rise to D'D'. The price of the stones would then increase to OP' in both the short and the long runs and an additional
amount of rent PWW'P' would be earned. Since the supply of
stones is completely fixed there can be no change in the supply
curve MM. All the earnings of the stones are rent—being paid
both in the long run and the short run. This limiting case is
therefore akin to the case of scarcity rent, with homogeneous land.
Since we assume that the stones are homogeneous it is a 'pure
scarcity rent'. All the stones earn rent and all earn the same rent.

At the other end of the scale, however, is the case [1] where the
meteor stones fall in such a way that they are available in unlimited quantities, provided that the buyer pays the cost of finding

[1] Cf. Marshall, *Principles*, p. 418.

the stones. If we assume that the stones are all equally easy to find, the production cost of stones will be constant and the supply curve PS will be horizontal, as in Figure 110*b*. In the original demand conditions in Figure 110*b*, shown by the demand curve DD, the price of stones is OP and the amount of stones OM is demanded. If, however, the demand curve now rises to D'D', the supply of stones, being perfectly elastic, even in the short run, adjusts itself completely to the changed demand conditions and the quantity of stones OM' is supplied. The price of stones remains OP, which is, as stated already, just enough to pay for their production. The owners of the stones earn no rent as a result of the increased demand. This is the other limiting case where, because supply is

perfectly elastic both in the short and long runs, rent is entirely absent in both the long and the short runs.

Let us now consider one of the intermediate cases where supply takes some time to react to a changed demand and where quasi-rent is therefore earned.

In Figure 111, for example, the original situation is one where a quantity of OM stones

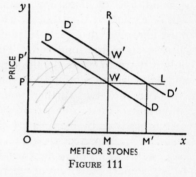

FIGURE 111

is available at a price of OP, but where no more stones at all are available in the short run whatever price is offered. In the long run, however, further stones can be provided at the same cost as the original ones. The short-period supply curve PWR therefore rises vertically once more than OM stones are demanded. Short-run supply is infinitely inelastic. If, therefore, the demand curve DD now rises to D'D', the price of stones will rise to OP' but still only OM stones are available, in the short period. Assuming that there are no short-run costs of maintaining the stones in working order, all the short-run earnings of the stones (OMW'P') represent quasi-rent. This quasi-rent is earned only because the homogeneous stones are in imperfectly elastic supply in the short run. In the long run, however, the supply curve PWL is horizontal and the price of stones falls to OP again, OM' stones now being supplied, and no rent at all is earned in excess of costs of production. The short-period return is therefore a 'quasi-rent' and only in long-run equilibrium can it be regarded as part of costs of production. Quasi-rent will be earned whenever any factor of production is in fixed short-run supply, and earns something more than prime costs. (In Figure 111 these are zero.) These hypothetical illustrations referring to meteor stones therefore show that a situation where factors of production earn 'pure' rent is only one limiting case. The other limiting case is the situation where no rent at all is earned because factors are in perfectly elastic short-run supply. Between these limits one can find various different situations where, because in the short run factors are in imperfectly elastic supply, they earn quasi-rent. In the long run prices will fall again. But they may not fall to the original level if the supply curve for stones slopes upwards—if the stones are being produced in conditions of increasing costs. In this case differential rents will be earned by the stones. Those stones which were produced most cheaply will earn a surplus payment over and above their cost—even in the long run. Those stones whose production is only just worth while (in the long run) will be 'marginal stones' and will earn no rent at all in the long run.

There are two further points about quasi-rents which are important. First, quasi-rent can be earned by human beings just as easily as by inanimate capital goods. Possessors of ability which is in imperfectly elastic supply in the short run will earn quasi-rent. This quasi-rent will be of two kinds. First, there will be an ordinary scarcity rent where all units of the factor are homogeneous. Let us assume, for example, that a new method of teaching entrepreneurs is discovered by one university which is able to prevent any other university from finding out what the method is. The graduates of this fortunate university will be able to go into business and, having been taught very efficiently, they will make large profits. We will assume, to begin with, that all these new entrepreneurs are equally capable so that the new factor of production is homogeneous. All the graduates of the 'innovating university' will therefore all earn exactly the same amount of money and this will be a larger amount than can be earned by business men taught elsewhere. In the short run these extremely large earnings will persist because there are very few of these 'super-entrepreneurs'. They earn a quasi-rent. In the long run, however, the innovating university will be unlikely to maintain its monopoly of the new teaching methods. Its secrets will leak out and other universities will make use of them. Quite apart from this, the university will itself be turning out very large numbers of these expert business men and they will ultimately cease to be in such limited supply. The quasi-rents will then disappear.

The second important point to remember is that transfer earnings will enter into the picture with quasi-rent just as they do with rent. Maintenance costs will arise too. From the point of view of the economy as a whole, rent is *any* earning over and above what is required to keep a factor of production in existence. Capital goods, like land, will remain in existence in the short run whether paid or not. But they may go rusty, even in the short run, and it will pay to spend just enough money on them to keep them in running order. Some short-run earnings of machines will represent maintenance costs and not quasi-rents, from the point of view both of the individual industries and of the economy. Human beings also must be paid something if they are to be kept alive. Even from the point of view of the whole economy, labour has 'transfer earnings'. It must be paid something or it will 'transfer' to the next world.

From the point of view of individual industries, of course, all factors of production are likely to have transfer earnings and these should be carefully separated from quasi-rents. For example, let us suppose that the new method of business training which we discussed above is more suited to the automobile industry than to others. A man trained in the new way might earn £20,000 a year making cars. But he might be able to earn £10,000 a year in several other industries. In this case his transfer earnings from the point of view of the motor industry will be the £10,000 needed to keep him in the motor industry. His quasi-rent will be £10,000.

We have now seen that the theory of rent can be generalised so that it will apply to all types of factors of production. It is usually assumed, however, that rent is in some way peculiarly connected with land. Is this true? The usual justification is that land is the only 'original' factor of production. This is not true. Inherent human ability, as we have seen, is often 'original' in the sense that more cannot be created if its 'price' rises. Again, it is reasonable to think that the connection between wages and the birth-rate is now less close than many people, especially during the nineteenth century, imagined. It is difficult to maintain that land is the only factor of production which is a 'free gift' of nature and which cannot be 'produced' in larger quantities if its price changes. Nevertheless, it is likely that land is the only factor whose total supply is *completely* inelastic. It does seem that there is some justification for regarding the rent of land as rather different from the rents of other factors—in describing the rent of land as 'the leading species of a large genus'.[1]

SUGGESTED READING

David Ricardo, *Principles of Political Economy* (edited by Piero Sraffa), Cambridge, 1951, chapter ii.

Alfred Marshall, *Principles of Economics* (8th Edition), London, 1920, Book V, chapters 9, 10 and 11 ; Book VI, chapters 9 and 10.

Joan Robinson, *Economics of Imperfect Competition*, London, 1933, chapter viii.

[1] Marshall, *Principles*, p. 421.

CHAPTER XIV

INTEREST

1. CAPITAL

In our study of the pricing of the various factors of production we have so far discussed the wages of labour and the rent of land. This chapter deals with interest on capital. It is important at the outset that we should be quite clear what is meant by capital. The fundamental distinguishing feature of capital is that it is made by man. Labour and land are gifts of nature and their amount cannot, in general, be increased by human action. The term capital is used to describe all those instruments of production which are deliberately made by man to be used to carry on production in the future. The chief types of capital asset are machines, factories, railways, vehicles and the like. Capital is therefore unique among the factors of production in that man exercises complete control over its creation.

In the past, economists have argued at considerable length whether such things as houses are capital goods or not. It will be seen from the previous paragraph that we have excluded such items from our definition of capital. It seems better to call them durable consumer goods. For whilst capital goods and durable consumer goods have several properties in common—especially the length of time over which they provide satisfactions—they do serve rather different purposes. It will be desirable to confine our attention in this chapter to those capital goods which are bought and sold simply as factors of production.

We shall discover that the problems of capital and interest are rather more difficult to solve than those in other parts of the theory of factor pricing. This is especially a result of the fact that capital is produced by human agencies and that a deliberate decision to make each capital asset has to be taken. In the case of land and labour no such deliberate decisions on the part of their owners are usually possible. The early economists Adam Smith and David Ricardo could offer no real solution to the problem of how the return on capital was determined, and the first broad outline of the modern theory of capital was given by Nassau Senior some twenty years after Ricardo had made his contribution.

The essence of the theory put forward by Senior was that interest—the price of capital—depends on the two forces of demand and supply. In Senior's view the supply of capital goods depended on the willingness of consumers to abstain from consumption in order that resources might be freed to produce capital goods. The demand for capital, Senior thought, depended on its productivity. As in the case of other factors of production, it was the output of consumer goods which entrepreneurs expected capital assets to produce which determined the demand for such assets.

Senior's theory of capital was not accepted by everyone. In particular, Karl Marx objected to the idea that the rich underwent anything meriting the title of abstinence. The notion that the capitalist practised virtuous thrift or suffered from the rigours of abstinence struck Marx as ridiculous. It was mainly to avoid such criticisms that Marshall [1] substituted the colourless term 'waiting' for the more doubtful 'abstinence'. This term 'waiting' also has the advantage of giving a reminder that the passage of time is of crucial importance where capital is concerned. It makes one remember that production with capital means the use of lengthy processes. Spending time making machinery which can ultimately be used to make consumer goods instead of producing the consumer goods directly, is rather like choosing to have a birthday present next year instead of this year. The choice of a present next year will only be worth while if it is a better present than there would have been this year. For it is a fundamental feature of human nature (to change the metaphor) to prefer a bird in the hand to the same bird in a bush. A birthday present this year is normally regarded as worth more than a promise of exactly the same present next year.

The essence of the services rendered by machines, then, is that they represent productive and efficient but 'roundabout' processes. We shall have to say a great deal in the next few pages about such roundabout processes. We may note at the outset, however, that the time-lag between the moment when work is started on a new machine and the moment when it is actually completed is usually considerable. Production is carried on in a 'roundabout' way because energy and time are expended on

[1] See his *Principles of Economics*, p. 233.

making a machine which will produce the final consumer goods, instead of being expended directly on producing the consumer good itself. It is the 'roundaboutness' of production which uses capital which causes most of the difficulties in constructing a simple and straightforward capital theory.

In our analysis so far we have largely succeeded in evading the problem of time. We have, of course, made great use of the distinction between long and short time-periods—a distinction about the response of supply over time to a change in demand which took place at a particular moment of time. But now we find that capital goods represent a whole class of factors of production which is intimately and peculiarly connected with time. This is a second reason, in addition to the fact that capital is man-made, which distinguishes capital from other factors of production. It also accounts for the difficulty of capital theory. Because capital theory is not an easy subject it is hard to construct a useful and yet simple analysis. Economists have spent a great deal of energy in constructing precise models.[1] These have turned out to be very complicated. Yet, even so, the results have not been altogether happy. We shall therefore content ourselves with the construction of simple, and not at all rigorous, models.

2. ROBINSON CRUSOE INVESTMENT

The simplest model one can construct is of a man shipwrecked on a desert island. We shall assume that the island is completely uninhabited and that it grows no food. The only possible food is fish. These can be caught either from the sea or from rivers. We shall also assume that the castaway has not been able to salvage any capital equipment—fishing-rods, lines or nets—from the wreck. If he wants to live he must catch fish. But unless he makes himself a net he will have to catch the fish by hand. We therefore have only one consumption good—fish. Our Robinson Crusoe has to decide how he will catch enough fish to remain alive. At first he will doubtless catch fish by hand until the idea strikes him that it ought to be possible to make some sort of net from twigs and creepers. What will it cost him to make the net— his primitive piece of capital? Assuming that it takes Crusoe a day to produce the net, the cost will be the fish which have to be forgone because on that one day he has no time to go fishing.

[1] Readers who are anxious to see one such model for themselves should consult F. A. Hayek, *Pure Theory of Capital*.

The castaway will have to go without food for a day in order to make the net.

The decision which Crusoe has to make is whether the cost of the net—one day without food—will be worth while. This will depend on the returns which he expects to obtain from the net if he makes it. If Crusoe is able to catch 5 fish a day by hand and still only expects to catch 5 when the net is made, it will clearly not be worth making it. If, however, there are prospects of catching 10 fish each day once the net is made, its construction may be worth while. Crusoe will decide whether to make the net on the basis of what economists call his 'rate of time preference'. This will show how highly he rates the desirability of having fish today instead of tomorrow—how strongly he prefers present to future satisfactions. If Crusoe's rate of time preference is such that he regards 5 fish today and 5 fish each day in the future as worth more than no fish today but 10 fish every day in future, then he will not make the net. If, however, the choice was not between 5 fish every day and 10 fish every day after (and including) tomorrow, but between 5 fish every day and 20 fish every day after tomorrow, our shipwrecked mariner might well decide to go hungry for one day and make the net. He reaches his decision by comparing the returns from investment in the capital good with its cost—the day without food. Taking the undesirability of a day without food as given, the more productive the net is expected to be the more likely it is to be made.

But the productivity of the net will not only depend on how many fish can be caught with it each day, but also on how many days the net can be used. Let us consider two possible situations in which the net may not be worth making. In the first place, if the mariner is certain he will be rescued within a week he may feel that the extra 85 fish which the '20-fish' net would catch during those seven days will not repay him for a day's hunger. On the other hand, if he expects to be stranded for a year the extra fish he will catch will run into thousands. Again, if Crusoe knows the net will fall to pieces after a week, he will feel less inclined to make it than he will if he thinks it will last for a year. What the investor, making the net, has to compare are not two figures for fish caught, one for today and the other for tomorrow. He has to compare two supplies of fish, of different size and which he can choose between, that stretch out into the future, probably for different lengths of time.

Perhaps the most important fact to notice about Crusoe's

(and any other) investment decision is that whilst the cost of the capital good is likely to be easily discovered, since it is in the present, the returns expected from it—its *prospective yield*—are a matter for conjecture rather than accurate estimate. This is because the prospective yield of any asset depends on expectations of what the future holds in store. A Crusoe making a net or a business man buying a factory will both be basing their actions on their own estimates of the future earning powers of these capital assets. Both may prove to be wrong. Crusoe may expect to catch 20 fish a day but may actually only catch 10. A business man may build a railway system expecting to earn a fortune but may be sent bankrupt by the development of competitive road and air transport systems whose growth he had not been able to foresee. Investment in capital assets therefore depends to a very large extent on business men's expectations of the future. If these are wrong a capital asset may turn out to be incapable of fulfilling the hopes of those who have made it. This close connection between investment and expectations must never be overlooked.

Finally, even on his island Crusoe would be able to choose between different kinds of nets. Assuming that both lasted for the same length of time, he might be able to make a rather useless one in a day but a very productive one in a week. Which would be better? Again he would have to balance the cost of going hungry against the expected returns from the two nets. On our assumption of 'rationality' he would choose that type of net which promised to give the greatest satisfaction compared with its cost.

This extremely simplified model of a Robinson Crusoe economy is none the less useful. For the problems which Crusoe faces are precisely the same as those faced by the modern economy. In both cases demand and supply have both to be taken into account. Let us therefore sum up the problems of the Crusoe economy under the heads of demand and supply. The supply of capital assets depends on their costs. In the Crusoe economy this is measured in terms of the mariner's rate of time preference between fish today and fish tomorrow. On the demand side one must first of all assume that the capital asset is more productive than the unaided mariner. It is reasonable to think that such an asset would be more productive than Crusoe fishing with his hands. It is not, however, inevitably certain that a larger and more complicated net will be correspondingly more productive. It may fail to work at all. Granted that the net does work, however, the main element determining the demand for the net will be its expected productivity. This will have to be balanced against its cost. As we have seen, human beings normally prefer a thing today rather than the same thing tomorrow or next year. The individual's rate of time preference is normally in favour of the present. It is for this reason that a capital asset must promise a return over and above its cost if it is to be considered worth making. The investor must be offered a positive reward in order to persuade him to postpone his consumption. This price is interest. Unless interest is expected, neither a Crusoe nor a business man will make or buy a capital asset.

Perhaps the nature of interest in a 'Crusoe Economy' can be seen most clearly from a more rigorous hypothetical model. Let us assume that Crusoe knows that he will only be shipwrecked for six days, during which time he can catch 30 fish by using his hands only. He can, however, choose to spend one day making a net and five days using it to catch fish. If the net is to be made, it must catch at least 30 fish, or Crusoe will be worse off. But, in order to make the net, Crusoe will have to go without food for one day, and since we may reasonably assume that Crusoe prefers present to future satisfactions, he will need to be offered more than 30 fish to make the postponement of satisfactions worth while. If he catches 33 fish with the net, the interest on it will be 3 fish. If these fish are just sufficient to induce Crusoe to make the net, his rate of time preference is such that one day's hunger must be repaid by 3 extra fish—representing interest—within the next five days. Crusoe calculates whether the net is worth while by comparing the interest earned from it with his rate of time preference. If these two are just equal, the net is just worth making.

Alternatively, we may say that Crusoe 'discounts' the future receipts from the net. Since the fish which Crusoe can catch with the net will only materialise in the future, he will prize them less highly than fish caught in the present. He will therefore have to decide how many fish caught with the net (after a day's lapse) equal the 30 fish caught by hand, some of which can be caught on the present day. If Crusoe decides that 33 fish caught with the net are just worth 30 caught by hand, he is 'discounting' the future yield of the net; and he finds that the rate at which he discounts the future is such that 33 'future fish' just equal 30 'present fish'. One can therefore compare the future yield of an asset with the cost of that asset, either by discovering what 'interest' it will yield, or alternatively by deciding how heavily its returns—being future returns—must be 'discounted' in order to give them a present 'lump-sum' value, which can then be compared with the (present) cost of the asset. One of the crucial problems of capital theory is how to 'capitalise' the returns from an asset so that this capitalised value can be compared with its cost, which is itself a given capital sum.

3. SOCIALISED INVESTMENT

We have seen how the process of creating capital assets will be carried on in a one-man economy. This is the simplest possible case to study. It has the virtue of showing very clearly that a decision to invest means that there must also be a decision to refrain from consumption. The necessity for such a choice between consumption and investment is made perfectly clear because the consumer and the investor are one and the same person. Perhaps the greatest difficulty in analysing the real-world economy is that the people who refrain from consumption and the people who invest are rarely the same. This causes complications. It is therefore important to stress the direct connection between consumption on the one hand and investment on the other.

Fortunately, there is one instance of a modern economy where the connection between investment and consumption can be seen very easily. This is the planned economy. By a planned economy, in this context, is meant an economy such as that of the U.S.S.R., where all economic activities are controlled by the State. In such a case, the State is the only body able to decide that it will increase investment in capital assets. It will be only too well aware that to do so it will have to reduce the consumption of some members of the community.

The main aim of the series of five-year plans which the Soviet Union has carried out has been to industrialise the country as rapidly as possible. The alternative courses between which the Soviet Government had to choose are clear. On the one hand, it could have made use of existing capital equipment and attempted to raise the productive efficiency of the country by making people work more efficiently to produce consumer goods with the existing machines. On the other hand, it could use the greatest possible proportion of the existing resources to produce more and better investment goods—at the same time reducing the proportion producing consumer goods.

X

In fact the Soviet Union chose the second course. This has meant that the flow of consumer goods has been reduced below the level which could have been attained in the short run, in order to build up stocks of capital goods. There has been a deliberate act of self-denial and abstinence in the present so that the future standard of living might be raised. The cost of investment in the planned economy is thus likely to be a reduced standard of living in the present just as on the desert island it is a day without food. In neither case is it possible both to have a large increase in one's stock of capital assets and to build up one's standard of living at the same moment. One has to 'wait'.

The rulers of a collective economy will often disapprove of the idea that there is such a thing as interest, on political grounds. They will, however, have to base their choice between current and future satisfaction on what is in fact interest. The planners will have to decide how great a surplus over its cost any piece of investment will yield, and decide whether its construction will be worth the sacrifice it entails. This surplus over cost will be interest. It will show how great the rise in the standard of living at a later date is expected to be. Alternatively, one may say that the planners have to 'discount' the future yields of assets and compare these 'discounted values' with their present costs. The choice between present and future satisfactions has to be made in every collective economy. In the case of those, like the Soviet Union and China, where the original standard of living is low, it will be a painful choice.

4. MARGINAL PRODUCTIVITY AND INVESTMENT

We have now reached a position where we can discuss capital and interest as they are in the modern market economy. We must discover how investment will be carried out in the modern economy, how the return from a capital asset can be calculated, and how that return can be compared with the cost of the asset. We shall find that in a market economy the most important difficulty in discussing the purchase of capital assets is that decisions to invest and decisions to refrain from consumption are not now made by the same persons. In both the Crusoe economy and the planned economy a decision to invest means a simultaneous and synchronised decision to refrain from consumption, for both decisions are made by the same person or body of persons. In a market economy, however, decisions to invest and decisions to refrain from consumption are not normally made by the same person.

This important difference between the one-man and the market economy makes for difficulties when one considers certain problems—especially the sort of problems we shall study in Part Two. For the moment, however, we can avoid these pitfalls by making two simplifying assumptions. Throughout the rest of this chapter we shall assume, first, that all money which is saved at a given rate of interest is immediately used to buy capital assets. This rules out the possibility that people may save their money and put it aside in the form of cash. Second, we shall assume, as we are entitled to do in particular equilibrium analysis, that the demand for capital assets is entirely unconnected with the supply of savings with which they have to be purchased. We shall assume, for instance, that if savings increase, and people spend less money on consumer goods, this does not cause any falling off in the demand for capital goods. Since capital goods are bought in order to produce such consumer goods, this is not a very realistic assumption, but we shall find it a useful assumption to make as a first approximation. With these two simplifying assumptions we may now consider investment in the modern market economy.

We have already seen that in the short run there can, by definition, be no change in the volume of capital goods in an economy. Similarly, the earnings of machines are really quasi-rents, and we have already discussed such earnings. Only in the long run, when investment *can* be undertaken, is a change in the stock of capital goods possible. In order to study these long-run problems, we must again study supply and demand. Capital assets are both scarce and useful, and for that reason they earn a reward.

Let us first consider demand. Why are capital assets demanded? Capital assets are demanded because they can be used to produce consumer goods—because they have a revenue product like all other factors. For any given type of capital asset—say a lathe—it will thus be possible to draw a marginal revenue productivity curve. It will be possible for an entrepreneur to calculate how much he thinks the employment of an additional lathe will add to the total revenue of his firm at each level of employment. But the marginal revenue productivity of capital is not a simple concept. In particular, the problem of time enters in at two stages. First, capital goods, as we have seen, are not used up when they are hired in the way that consumer goods are used up. Capital goods have a working life of many years. Therefore, if a firm borrows money in order to buy a machine, it must feel certain that it can repay the money with interest over a period of years. The business man has to consider the productivity of the machine not now, but in the future. What matters is the productivity of the machine over time—its expected future productivity or 'prospective yield'. Second, the machine itself takes time to build. It is some time before anything at all is produced, but money has to be continuously spent on preparing the machine to carry out its job efficiently. And interest will have to be paid on this money.

The easiest way in which to study the act of investment will be to construct a series of models, beginning with a very simple one, and introducing successive complications. As our first model, let us assume that a business man is considering whether to buy a given machine. This machine costs £100. It has a working life of one year, all of which is spent in producing a single product which is finally completed on the last day of the year. The entrepreneur thinks that when all other factors used with the machine have been paid, the *net* product of the machine will be worth £103. Having produced this product worth £103 at the end of the year the machine drops to pieces. The entrepreneur therefore finds that the machine has a product of £103 to be compared with its cost.

Now, we shall have to see later what it is which determines the rate of interest in the economy as a whole. But from the point of view of the single entrepreneur one may take that rate of interest as given. Assuming that there is perfect competition in the capital market, one entrepreneur can borrow money at just the same rate as another. Let us assume that everyone has to pay interest at 3 per cent to borrow money for a year. In order to pay for the machine, the entrepreneur will need to borrow £100. At the end of the year he will need to find £100 to repay the loan— for the machine has now ceased to exist and must have repaid its cost if it is to be worth buying—as well as £3 interest. Since we have assumed that the machine is expected to produce just £103, the entrepreneur will find it just worth his while to buy it. It will be a 'marginal' machine. If the machine is expected to produce more than £103, he will buy it cheerfully; if less, he will decide not to buy it. An entrepreneur buying a machine therefore has to expect the machine in question to earn at least enough to repay the money borrowed to buy it, and to pay interest on this loan. The revenue product of a machine must at least equal its cost, plus interest at the market rate, if the machine is to be bought.

We may say, alternatively, that the entrepreneur is discounting the future yield of the machine. Instead of saying that the machine can, for one year, earn interest at 3 per cent over and above its cost of £100, we can say that the machine's future return of £103 can be discounted at (slightly less than) 3 per cent and yet prove equal to its cost. The entrepreneur will be prepared to buy the asset if the value of its expected earnings, when discounted, is at least equal to its cost. In our hypothetical model, the entrepreneur will just be prepared to buy the machine so long as the 'market' rate of discount is a fraction under 3 per cent.[1] For in this case the present value (£100) of the machine's future yield of £103 will be equal to the cost of the machine.

As our second model, let us assume that a farmer is buying a sheep which will live for ten years, and which is expected to produce £3 worth of wool each year for ten years and £100 worth of meat also at the end of the tenth year. The sheep costs £100. Now, if the market rate of interest is 3 per cent per annum, the sheep will be able to meet, each year, the interest charge of £3 on the loan required to buy it and will also be able to pay off the whole loan (by the sale of £100 worth of meat) at the end of the tenth year. The 'asset' will earn interest of £3 each year on a cost of £100. Similarly, if one discounts the value of the sheep, the discounted value of its earnings will just have a present value of £100 if discounted at something less than 3 per cent per annum. The farmer will buy the sheep, assuming he is 'rational', if the market rate of interest is 3 per cent or less, and the market rate of discount is, at most, rather under 3 per cent. This second model is perhaps not a very usual one, but it is useful because it avoids the problems of compound rates of interest and discount.

The third model we shall consider is where an entrepreneur is deciding whether to buy a machine which will last for ten years. We assume that this machine produces nothing until the end of the tenth year, when it produces a product worth £134.

[1] It should be obvious that if a rate of interest of 3 per cent makes £100 into £103, a rate of discount of slightly *less* than 3 per cent will reduce £103 to £100.

The machine then falls to pieces. The entrepreneur who is wondering whether it will pay him to install the machine will have to borrow money to do so, and having borrowed the money, will have to pay interest on it. If he borrows at compound interest of 3 per cent per annum, the total amount owing at the end of ten years, including the £100 loan, will be £134. Thus, if the rate of interest is less than 3 per cent, the entrepreneur will find the machine worth buying. For the total amount owing at the end of the year will then be less than the £134 which the machine yields. Similarly, if the rate of interest is more than 3 per cent he will not find it worth his while to buy the machine. Alternatively, one can say that the machine will certainly not be bought so long as its future earnings have to be discounted at more than 3 per cent per annum. If the rate of discount is (rather less than) 3 per cent, the present value, £100, of the machine's yield (£134) is just equal to its price of £100. In this model we have been able to allow explicitly for the existence of compound rates of interest, but have simplified the problem by assuming that no repayments of capital are made for ten years.

In our final model, let us try to achieve greater realism. Let us assume that an entrepreneur is considering installing a machine which will take nearly a year to build and that it will then work for four years before falling to pieces. Let us assume that in the first year the machine works for long enough to earn just £4. In the next four years it earns £27 10s. each year. Let us also assume that the machine costs £100 and that the rate of interest at which the entrepreneur can borrow is 4 per cent. If the entrepreneur borrows the £100 to buy the machine, he will have to wait nearly a year before he earns anything from the machine. By the end of that year he will owe £4 interest on the £100, but this will just be cancelled out by the £4 worth of goods produced by the machine. The entrepreneur will thus begin the second year owing just £100. At the end of this year he will again owe £4 interest, making a total of £104. Of this he can pay £27 10s., leaving £76 10s. owing.

At the end of the second year, interest on the £76 10s. will amount to approximately £3—a total now of £79 10s. If £27 10s. is now paid off, £52 will be outstanding. At the end of the third year, interest will be about £2, making a total owing of £54. If £27 10s. is paid off, £26 10s. will be owing. This will mean interest of £1 in the fourth year, leaving a total of £27 10s. owing, all of which can be paid off at the end of that year. Thus if the

rate of interest is 4 per cent, the producer will just be able to pay
for the machine by the end of the fourth year—after which it
ceases to exist. If the rate of interest is more than 4 per cent,
the entrepreneur will lose on the transaction so he will not buy the
machine. If the interest is less than 4 per cent, he will buy the
machine. Alternatively, it may be said that if the rate of discount
is (roughly) 4 per cent, the future earnings of the machine, when
discounted, would just equal the costs, and the manufacturers
would be on the margin of doubt whether to buy it. Similarly,
a rate of discount of rather less than 4 per cent would make the
present (discounted) value of the prospective yield of the machine
greater than its cost. It would be worth buying. A rate of
discount of 4 per cent or more would make the discounted
prospective yield of the machine less than the cost. It would not
be worth buying.

It is possible to sum up this discussion as follows. An entrepreneur wishing to buy a particular asset will have to consider,
first, the prospective yield of the asset, calculated by adding
together all the earnings from it over its whole working life, second,
the cost of the asset, and third, the rate of interest or discount.
The entrepreneur can then either compare the *net* prospective
yield [1] of the asset (minus the cost of the asset) with the interest
which will have to be paid on the money borrowed to buy it ; or
alternatively, he can compare the cost of the asset with the discounted value (the present value) of its prospective yield. In
either case, he will reach the same decision about whether to buy
the asset or not. If the *net* prospective yield of the asset (minus
its cost) exceeds the interest which will have to be paid to borrow
the money needed to buy it, or if the discounted *net* prospective
yield exceeds the cost of the asset, it will be bought. On the
other hand, if the interest (and capital) payments to repay the
loan are greater than the net prospective yield of the asset, or
the cost of the asset is greater than its (discounted) net prospective yield, the asset will not be bought; for this will mean that
the cost of the asset (over its life) will be greater than the returns
from it.

Now, since for any single kind of asset an entrepreneur can
calculate the prospective returns which any given unit of it is
expected to produce, the yields of various amounts of an asset
of a given type, either to the entrepreneur or the industry, can be
similarly calculated. Let us, for example, consider the prospective

---

[1] *I.e.* excluding the expected cost of co-operating factors.

yields of differing amounts of a particular kind of asset to a given entrepreneur. We assume that the capital good in question is productive. It is therefore possible to draw a marginal productivity curve for the asset we are considering, showing how much will be added to the receipts of the firm when, with any stock of the asset, another unit of the asset is added. But it should be clear that this marginal revenue productivity of a particular asset is exactly the same thing as the prospective yield from employing another marginal asset of this kind with any given stock of assets. The marginal revenue productivity and 'marginal' prospective yield of any given asset amount to the same thing.

There are two important points to bear in mind when one speaks of the prospective yield of an asset. First, whilst this prospective yield is determined by the returns to the asset over a period of time, the returns *per unit of time* will not necessarily be equal. There is a danger that they may be looked upon as equal. Yet in a dynamic world this is most unlikely to be the case. Second, it must always be remembered that prospective yields are *anticipated* yields, not realised yields. Business men can make wrong guesses about such yields, and if they do, capital assets will not yield what was expected from them.

We have seen that since assets do not all have the same length of life, the returns expected from those with a long life need to be more heavily discounted than from those with a short life, even if both are expected to yield exactly the same total amount of money during their lives. For larger interest payments will be needed to acquire the latter because the money borrowed to pay for them will be needed for a longer period of time. The only way of calculating and comparing the productivities of different kinds of assets with different lengths of life is thus to compare not their marginal productivities (prospective yields) but their *discounted* marginal productivities (*discounted* prospective yields). Once one knows the current rate of discount, one can bring the yields of assets of different kinds, with different prospective yields and different lengths of life, to a comparable basis by discounting these yields. This process gives, for each unit of each asset, a capital sum representing the present value of its prospective yield. The marginal revenue productivity curves—the demand curves for capital assets—will therefore show the *discounted* marginal productivities of the assets. They will show the present value of the additional receipts which an entrepreneur expects to earn in the future if he employs another unit of any given asset, these receipts being discounted at the current rate of discount.

This curve of discounted marginal revenue productivity of an asset will show the demand for the asset. It will show the discounted (present) value of the returns an entrepreneur will expect to receive from employing additional units of a particular kind of asset. This demand curve will slope downwards from left to right in the normal way. The more machines of a given kind an entrepreneur has, the less money he will expect to earn by hiring one more machine of the same kind. The supply curve for the same assets will be given by their price, and for each asset this curve will be a horizontal straight line to the individual entrepreneur, assuming that competition in the market for the asset is perfect. The entrepreneur will therefore increase his purchases of the asset until the last unit he buys has a discounted marginal productivity just equal to its cost.

Now, if we take the prices of capital assets as given, it follows that a fall in the rate of interest (and discount) makes entrepreneurs willing to buy more capital goods. For with a lower rate of interest (and discount) the cost of borrowing money to buy assets will fall, and the returns expected from them will thus have to be discounted less heavily. Entrepreneurs will find that units of the asset which they did not think worth buying at higher rates of interest (discount) can now be bought. Their discounted prospective yields now exceed their supply price because these yields do not have to be discounted so heavily. In other words, the demand curve for capital assets of each kind has shifted bodily to the right.

Alternatively, it is possible to express the demand for capital goods by showing (on a curve) how many units of each will be bought (given their price) at varying rates of interest. This demand curve will also slope downwards to the right. The demand both for individual capital goods and for capital goods in general will increase as the rate of interest falls (provided the price of capital goods is constant). This will be true for individual firms, for individual industries, and for the community as a whole. The lower the rate of interest, the more capital goods will be demanded. We can thus construct a downward-sloping demand curve for both capital goods or for loanable funds—for money to be used to buy capital assets—which will slope downwards from left to right. The latter curve will show that more loanable funds will be demanded by all entrepreneurs in the country taken together the lower the rate of interest is. Since more assets are demanded as the rate of interest falls, more money is required to purchase them. The curve shows us the demand for 'money capital' at various rates of interest.

We must now see what will determine the supply conditions for money capital. How will the amount of money which people will lend out to business men wanting to build machines and factories vary as the rate of interest changes? It will be remembered that we are assuming that all money which people save is lent to entrepreneurs to enable them to build capital assets. But if people are to be persuaded to save money and to lend it to entrepreneurs, they must be offered interest. We have already seen that if people are to be persuaded to save and to put their money into capital assets, they will ask for some future return over and above the initial loan, because they must abstain from present consumption. But if a man has £100 and is asked to part with it for a year, he is not only forgoing consumption, he is also running the risk of losing his money. The risk may be small or large, and the larger it is the less anxious he will be to lend his money. For if he could put his money in a stocking or up the chimney, he would at least be sure that it would be safe (barring robbery). If he invests it, he cannot be so certain. Interest on capital has therefore to be paid, partly in order to persuade people to postpone consumption and invest in capital assets, and partly to persuade them not to hoard their savings, so as to avoid any risk of loss, but to allow them to be risked in business.

The supply curve of loanable funds to all industry will therefore slope upwards to the right. On the one hand, the more money capital people lend out, the more consumption they have to postpone, the greater will be the reward (per cent) they will ask to make such a postponement worth while. In other words, as more money is borrowed it has to come from people whose 'rates of time preference' are progressively more strongly weighted in favour of present satisfactions. On the other hand, as more money is borrowed it will have to be borrowed from people who are progressively more worried about the risks being run. More money can be borrowed if, but only if, a higher return is offered. Thus if more money is to be lent out, rates of interest normally have to rise to induce 'marginal lenders' to forgo present satisfactions and to allow their resources to be tied up in machines and factories instead of being kept in the form of more 'liquid' capital assets.

The actual level of the rate of interest will therefore be determined by the intersection of a downward-sloping demand curve for loanable funds to be used to buy capital goods and an upward-sloping supply curve for such loanable funds.

SUGGESTED READING

Irving Fisher, *The Theory of Interest*, New York, 1930, especially chapters i–ix.

CHAPTER XV

PROFITS

1. THE ENTREPRENEUR

IN this chapter we shall discuss the profits of the entrepreneur and so complete our study of the pricing of the several factors of production. The word entrepreneur is one which we have used before. It is not a pleasant word, but, compared with the alternative words 'undertaker' and 'enterpriser', it seems the most desirable. The entrepreneur has so far been regarded as a human calculating machine. We have assumed that he is the one person in the firm who hires factors of production and that his decisions are always based on an attempt to maximise profits. His chief aim is to avoid losing money. It is clear, therefore, that the entrepreneur is a special type of factor of production. He is the only factor of production whose duty it is to combine and organise other factors of production. Nevertheless even the entrepreneur is really a human being. He is not a true calculating machine. No calculating machine would be described as *attempting* to maximise profits. It *would* maximise them. In addition, the entrepreneur (and for that matter the calculating machine) may do his best to maximise profits but the information at his disposal will rarely be adequate to allow him to know whether or not he has succeeded.

We have spoken so far in this book as though the entrepreneur bases his actions on objective and completely certain figures of cost and revenue. But the data on which the real-world entrepreneur has to make his decisions are not objective. He has to decide, in advance, what revenues and costs will be, and his ideas about them are therefore subjective estimates embodying his own hunches and guesses. And like all guesses they may well turn out to be wrong. The best that the entrepreneur can do is to equate his estimate of marginal cost with his estimate of marginal revenue. He can never be quite certain in advance what either marginal cost or marginal revenue will be. This realisation of the true nature of the kind of data on which enterpreneurs' decisions are based brings us face to face with a new element of our theory. We must study the expectations of the entrepreneur. Despite our attempts so far to avoid the problem of uncertainty we have not altogether succeeded. In the discussion of interest we found it necessary to acknowledge the uncertain nature of business men's estimates of the prospective yields of the capital assets they are wondering whether to buy or to make. And in this discussion of enterprise we shall be forced to devote the major portion of our analysis to studying the way in which uncertainty about revenues and costs influences business men who are deciding how to fix their prices and their output.

It is important to realise that uncertainty enters economics once conditions can change. So long as one is concerned only with a static or changeless world, uncertainty can be ignored. But when, as in capital theory, allowance for future changes has to be specifically made, uncertainty appears. With profits uncertainty, as we shall see, is the essence of the matter. The entrepreneur can never be certain what he will earn from producing goods until *after* he has decided to produce them. He is never certain whether he will make a profit or suffer a loss.

There is one final feature which distinguishes the entrepreneur from other factors of production. The fundamental difference between them lies in the fact that whilst land, labour and capital are all, at least in principle, hireable, enterprise is not. For this reason the entrepreneur is not on all fours with other factors of production. We shall not place any great stress on this feature of entrepreneurship. But it is quite important and should be borne in mind.

2. RISK AND UNCERTAINTY

Once one looks upon the entrepreneur as more than a mere calculating machine it is possible to claim that he does fulfil a useful social function in the productive process, that he *is* productive. The entrepreneur can be considered as possessing a marginal revenue productivity in just the same way as any other factor of production. What, then, is the function of the entrepreneur in the economic system ? Why is he productive ? An answer to this important question has been given by Professor F. H. Knight.[1] We shall base the following analysis of profits on his explanation.

[1] See F. H. Knight, *Risk, Uncertainty and Profit*, especially chapters v-xi.

Some idea of the difficulty in finding an answer to this question, 'Why do entrepreneurs earn profits?' can be seen from the fact that the economists of the nineteenth century failed to answer it. The main reason for the failure of these economists to provide a satisfactory theory of profit seems to have been that they did not distinguish profits from interest. Because the typical entrepreneur of the nineteenth century was also the owner of the capital of his firm, economists confused the returns which he received *qua* entrepreneur with the money he earned *qua* capitalist. They did not realise that the receipt of interest as a reward for waiting and the receipt of profit as a reward for taking the risks of business are not the same thing.

The modern theory of profit regards the entrepreneur's contribution to the process of production as that of bearing 'non-insurable risks and uncertainties'. The distinction between insurable and non-insurable risks is an important one. Every entrepreneur faces many risks besides the most important risk— that he may lose money as a result of misjudging market conditions. There is always the risk that fire, theft, death and the like may cause business losses. But these latter risks can be insured against. Indeed, the modern economy provides a whole industry to deal with insurance against the risks of this kind. The business man need not worry about what will happen to his dependants if he dies, for he can insure his life. Nor need he lose sleep over the danger of losing plant or stock through fire. Fire also can be insured against.

It is clear, then, that the entrepreneur only has to meet those risks which cannot be insured against. We must therefore decide what kind of risks these will be and discover why they cannot be insured against. What is the main difference between insurable and non-insurable risks? The difference lies in the fact that the probability that some events will occur can be calculated mathematically whilst the probability that others will occur cannot. For example, statisticians are able to calculate the probability of fires occurring quite accurately. An insurance company therefore knows that, say, 1 per cent of factories in the country will have a fire each year. It is impossible to say which particular factory will catch fire; but it is possible to say with considerable accuracy what percentage of factories in general is likely to suffer from fire in any one year. It is therefore possible for business men to insure against this type of risk. The insurance company knows how high a premium it must charge in order to be able to meet fire insurance claims. The business man knows what that premium is and he knows also what the risk of fire is. Since no-one wants deliberately to take risks which can be avoided, the entrepreneur is only too pleased to pay the premium and avoid the risk. The reason why this can be done, as has been stated, is that an accurate quantitative estimate of the danger of fire can be made. The fire insurance premium is a cost of production just as much as payments for labour or raw materials are.

We must now move away from these definite and calculable risks to the sort of risk which is more vague and uncertain. What are these risks, taken by entrepreneurs, which are incalculable and which no insurance company will dare to insure against? The kind of decisions made by entrepreneurs are decisions about, for example, whether it will pay to increase or decrease the output of a given article. The entrepreneur has to guess what his cost conditions will be, which is usually quite simple. He also has to guess what demand conditions will be, and this is often extremely difficult. He may earn a profit or he may make a loss. But no-one can say which with any real degree of certainty. Nor can anyone say with certainty how large that profit or loss will be. It is therefore no accident that it is impossible for entrepreneurs to insure against commercial losses. It is possible for an insurance company to estimate accurately that, say, 1 per cent of all firms will have a fire each year. It is quite impossible to say whether 5 per cent, 25 per cent or 50 per cent of firms in an industry will make losses or how much will be lost. It is quite possible that all might make profits or that all might suffer losses. No statistician can work out the numerical probability that a given group of firms will make profits or losses in any year. It is therefore impossible for any organisation to insure firms against loss. It would not know what premium to charge and in a slump would probably go bankrupt itself.

We can now explain why entrepreneurs earn profits. It is because they have to trust their own judgment about the likelihood of success or failure if they expand or contract their output, raise or lower their prices. If a business man refuses to insure against fire but relies on his ability to design efficient fire-fighting devices, he is fulfilling the function of a true entrepreneur. Since fire insurance is not expensive, there is no need for him to do this—so he will not normally do so. The real function of the entrepreneur is to take those risks where the unknowns to be dealt with are more intangible than the danger of fire. The sort of question which the entrepreneur has to answer is, 'Will consumers like my new frying-pan?' The responsibility for making this kind of decision cannot be shifted, and it is because this kind of decision is typical of entrepreneurial decisions in general that being an entrepreneur is much more risky than being a wage earner.

We have now succeeded in isolating a specific function which may be ascribed to the entrepreneur. He has to take the risks of making price-output decisions. Having attempted to draw this sharp distinction between the function of the entrepreneur and the functions of the other factors of production, we must now consider the similarities between the entrepreneur and the other factors of production. There is no such thing as a disembodied entrepreneur. Entrepreneurs usually own some other factors of production. Let us take the case of the owner of a shop. He is clearly an entrepreneur for he decides what to sell and at what prices. But he also owns some, at least, of the capital of the shop— if only the stock. He is also likely to serve behind the counter. He owns labour as well. Such an entrepreneur therefore represents capital and labour as well as enterprise. His reward will be made up of wages and interest as well as profits. Again, in theory at any rate, it is possible for an entrepreneur to be his own labourer and yet to own none of the capital of his business at all. It is quite conceivable that he might borrow the whole of the capital of his business at a fixed rate of interest. On the other hand, an entrepreneur may own either a part of the capital of his business, or even the whole of it, and yet not himself provide any labour at all. It is therefore not always easy to sort out the rewards of labour and capital from the rewards of enterprise.

Nevertheless the problem is not insoluble. It is always possible to make some sort of estimate of the shares of the various factors of production which he owns in the earnings of a business man. So far as his capital is concerned it is not difficult to decide what the return on that capital would have been if it had been invested elsewhere. The market price for loans—the rate of interest—shows the general level of returns on investments. So, if an entrepreneur who also owns the capital of his firm—but who gives no labour to it—discovers that his earnings exceed the current rate of interest on his capital, one may assume that he is earning profits of enterprise in addition to interest on his capital. It is a sign that he is performing a useful function for the business in addition to providing capital. Taking industry as a whole, it seems likely that profits do exist, and that business men who put their capital in their firms get returns which are somewhat in excess of the market rate of interest. In the short run, of course, there will be a rent element in entrepreneurial earnings and profits may be abnormally high or low. In the long run, however, provided competition is perfect, any excess of the earnings of entrepreneurs over the rate of interest will represent the reward of enterprise alone. We see, therefore, that whilst the rewards of the business man *qua* capitalist are not always immediately distinguishable from his rewards *qua* entrepreneur, this does not mean that the distinction between these two rewards is not valid. It is.

The same sort of procedure of separating true profits from the other earnings of entrepreneurs can be used where the entrepreneur provides labour to the firm. Where the shopkeeper serves behind the counter as well as making entrepreneurial decisions it is not likely that he will pay himself two separate amounts of money: one for his labour and another for his entrepreneurial skill. Yet his earnings will be made up of an amount of money, as large as he could have got elsewhere as a general manager in a shop, and representing the wage for his labour, and of an additional sum of money earned by his entrepreneurial skill.

The most realistic model to use therefore seems to be one where the entrepreneur invests some capital in his business and also provides his own labour. Here, however, there is often difficulty in deciding on the border-line between enterprise and labour. It is not always easy to separate the functions of the entrepreneur from those of the manager who is really only a special type of labour. The duty of a manager is to co-ordinate hired factors as effectively as possible. Clearly, most business men do in fact do this, but this is not the true function of an entrepreneur. The true entrepreneur, the output and price fixer, is the man who risks losses and earns profits. It is not necessary that he should co-ordinate and manage factors of production at all. He can easily hire a manager to do this and pay him a wage for his work.

The idea of the entrepreneur as a co-ordinator is sometimes stressed by economists. But co-ordination is not an essential part of the entrepreneur's duty. He can choose whether or not to act as a manager in this sense, but he cannot ever evade the dangers of losses if he makes wrong price-output decisions. This type of confusion is best avoided by being quite clear what one means by

Y

co-ordination. If co-ordination is stretched to include decisions about the scale of activity, the best product to make, and what to charge for it, it is being made to include the entrepreneurial function. This is the reason why economists sometimes speak of the entrepreneur as a co-ordinator.

In practice, of course, the distinction between the entrepreneurial and the managerial function is very difficult to make. The typical entrepreneur does not sit on the Riviera whilst the dividends roll in. Such persons cannot justly be described as entrepreneurs at all—though they may occasionally reap the reward of other people's entrepreneurial decisions. Most entrepreneurs find it easier to make entrepreneurial (price-output) decisions if they are inside their factory for much of their time. If this is the case, they are likely to make large and small *managerial* decisions as well—as a matter of course. Some time spent as a co-ordinator is really just as necessary for the real-world entrepreneur as is the ownership of some or all of the capital of his firm. It is for this reason that the earnings of entrepreneurs will usually include what are often regarded as 'the wages of management'. These are payments earned for performing the tasks of general management and organisation. As we have said before, the entrepreneur is not a disembodied spirit.

3. OWNERSHIP AND CONTROL

It will probably be objected that this analysis of the entrepreneur is unrealistic in these days. There is much justification for such an objection. The modern economy with its growing scale of industry and, above all, with its own creation, the limited liability company, has replaced the one-man entrepreneur of the nineteenth century. The twentieth-century joint-stock company functions through the shareholders' meeting, the board of directors and the managing director. Who, then, performs the function of the entrepreneur in this type of organisation ? The shareholders are clearly the people who actually make profits or losses when entrepreneurial decisions turn out to be right or wrong. But the shareholders do not make these decisions about what price and output should be themselves. The most that the shareholders' meeting can do is to start a row afterwards if losses have been made. Even so, it is usually necessary for the shareholders to be 'quasi-entrepreneurs' themselves if they are fully to understand and appraise the decisions which have been made.

It is also difficult to decide how far the board of directors is really responsible for making price-output decisions. The board will usually give final instructions about what price and output are to be ; but it will usually do so on the basis of reports provided by accountants and other senior employees of the firm. It is possible that many boards of directors act largely as a 'rubber stamp' to decisions already taken by senior executives of their firm. Again, it must never be forgotten that such things as guinea-pig directors and sleeping partners do exist. This means that whilst in theory the board of directors has sole power to make entrepreneurial decisions, it will often be guided by others in deciding what decisions to make. In fact, it seems likely that the real decisions on price and output policy in many modern firms are made by the general manager or managing director and a few of his chief advisers. Such men may or may not own shares in the firm. Whether they do or not, it is likely that only a very small part of their (usually large) incomes are derived from their share-holdings. Most of their incomes will come from a fixed salary. If this is true it means that the man who really makes entre-preneurial decisions in the modern business often does not receive a payment which is large when he guesses rightly and small when he guesses wrongly. It does, of course, often happen that a manager who has made several wrong decisions is sacked or demoted and thereby suffers a reduction in income, whilst a man who has made several right decisions is given an increase in salary. But there is no automatic connection between a manager's price-output decisions and his income. It looks as though the 'managerial revolution' foreshadowed by James Burnham may already be upon us.

It is undoubtedly true that though many 'small men' remain in business, the largest and most important companies today are not run by *an* entrepreneur. It is therefore difficult to decide whether the entrepreneurial function in these firms is fulfilled by the managers, who make (or at any rate suggest) the price-output policies, or by the shareholders, who lose money if these are unwise policies. Modern industry cannot point easily and unequivocally to *the* entrepreneur. How, then, can there be a managerial function ? One could give a paradoxical answer. Perhaps it is that the theory is right but the facts are wrong. This explanation may seem unscientific. It may be held that the duty of a theory is to explain real concrete facts. If the facts differ it is the theory which is at fault. But is this necessarily so ?

The analysis of the entrepreneurial function is perfectly reasonable and internally consistent. Its only real fault is that it is about a hundred years out of date so far as large businesses are concerned, though there are still thousands of small one-man firms. It is the development of joint-stock companies which spoils the picture. The theory of the individual entrepreneur no longer applies to the whole, or even the most important parts of the economy. Yet it applies still to other facts and to other times.

A theory of the past may be worth looking at. Especially if, as seems likely, present-day conditions in other countries fit it more closely. If one really believes in the 'rugged individualism' of the United States, one could agree that the theory fits in with conditions in present-day America and nineteenth-century Britain. The inability of the theory to explain what happens in modern Britain can be attributed to the decline of capitalism. The tendency is towards the large bureaucratic combine. The business man is becoming more like a civil servant than a business man. Entrepreneurship as a function of individual enterprise and individual enterprise itself appear to be dying out. Yet the theory did apply once. The most interesting feature of the whole problem is that the theory was not developed in full until the conditions to which it applied had begun to pass away.

4. MARGINAL PRODUCTIVITY AND PROFITS

Our theory of the pricing of factors of production has relied throughout on the contention that each factor earns a reward depending on its marginal revenue productivity—that the demand curve for any factor is the same thing as its marginal revenue productivity curve. This holds equally for enterprise. The number of entrepreneurs in an industry will depend on how much they can earn there—on their revenue productivity. What, then, will the marginal revenue productivity curve of entrepreneurship look like? This question can best be answered by studying the marginal revenue productivity of entrepreneurs in a particular industry. This is important. With land, labour and capital it is possible to calculate the marginal revenue productivity of the factor to an individual firm. With entrepreneurship this is not possible. One cannot, so far as a single firm is concerned, compare the revenue product of half an entrepreneur with that of a whole one or the revenue product for three entrepreneurs with that for four or five. Nor can one really measure the contribution of the entrepreneur by the length of time he takes to make his decisions or in any other physical units. There are no rules for measuring entrepreneurial activity. It is therefore unrealistic to try to estimate the marginal revenue productivity of entrepreneurship for a single firm.

But whilst it is useless to try to calculate the marginal revenue productivity of entrepreneurship to a single firm, it is not difficult to do so for the industry. In a whole industry the numbers of entrepreneurs can be altered and the results of such alterations can be studied. Let us assume that in the industry with which we are concerned all entrepreneurs are homogeneous. This means that one can measure entrepreneurship in homogeneous physical units along the x-axis, as is done in Figure 112.

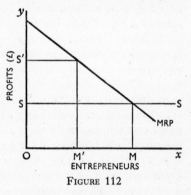

FIGURE 112

In Figure 112 the marginal revenue productivity curve of entrepreneurship to a particular industry is shown by the curve MRP which is drawn for convenience as a straight line. It is reasonable to think that such a marginal revenue productivity curve will fall throughout its length. The more entrepreneurs there are in an industry the smaller will be the profits each is likely to be able to make. The marginal revenue productivity of entrepreneurship, like that of all other factors, is lower the more entrepreneurs there are. The supply curve of entrepreneurship is shown by the curve SS. Since we are assuming that all entrepreneurs are equally efficient, all must earn the same amount of profit (in this case £OS) if they are to remain in the industry. This profit of £OS represents their transfer earnings. All the entrepreneurs, being identical, can earn £OS in some other industry and will leave our particular industry and go to this other industry unless they can earn £OS in our particular industry. The supply curve of entrepreneurship is therefore a horizontal straight line.

It can be seen from Figure 112 that equilibrium will occur when there are OM entrepreneurs in the industry and all are earning just their transfer earnings of £OS—when all are earning 'normal' profits. This will in fact be the long-run equilibrium position in perfect competition. In the long run, entrepreneurs (and firms) will enter or leave the industry until all are earning normal profits. In the short run, however, the industry might only have OM' entrepreneurs and each would then earn £OS'. All would be earning abnormal profits of £SS'. Such abnormal profits would be competed away, in perfect competition, in the long run. If, however, there were imperfect competition in the industry, entrepreneurs could still earn abnormal profits even in the long run, because there would not be completely free entry into the industry and newcomers would not be able to compete all existing profits away.

It is, of course, possible for entrepreneurs to earn rent of ability in addition to profits. A Lord Nuffield or a Henry Ford would earn more than a third-rate entrepreneur. There are two ways of analysing the problems of rent of ability earned by entrepreneurs. First, one could assume, as we did in Chapter VI, that all entrepreneurs are equally efficient from the point of view of all other industries except the one in which one is interested, but that their abilities differ so far as this particular industry is concerned. In such a situation the transfer earnings of all entrepreneurs would be the same, but since some entrepreneurs would have greater ability (which was specific to this industry), they would earn a rent of ability over and above their transfer earnings. It would be the marginal entrepreneurs alone who would earn no rent—their profits being just equal both to their transfer earnings and to their marginal revenue productivity.

Second, one could assume that entrepreneurs are not of equal efficiency either in the particular industry one was studying, or in any other industry. This is a more realistic assumption. The simplest way of making it will be to assume that entrepreneurs who are best in one industry are best in all others, that those who are worst in a given industry are worst in all others, and so on. In other words, we can assume that entrepreneurial skill is never completely specific but is always completely general. Entrepreneurial rent will now be unlikely to exist, so far as the individual industry is concerned. For although some entrepreneurs earn more than others in any given industry, they could do the same in other industries too. Differences in entrepreneurs' earnings thus represent differences in transfer earnings, and not differences in rents of ability. The entrepreneurs who earn most money in an industry will have the highest transfer earnings and *vice versa*.

This assumption that entrepreneurs have general rather than

specific ability seems the most sensible one to make. Entre-preneurs who are best in one industry probably are best in others too. Henry Ford would probably have made a fortune in any industry. This may well mean that the entrepreneurs who have the highest earnings in one industry probably have the highest elsewhere. They may often be the first to leave a declining industry rather than the last. Entrepreneurial skill is not likely to be 'specific', because running one firm is very much like running another.

There is one final point which is of interest. We have seen that profits are earned as a reward for taking risks, so that where there are no risks there can be no profits in the long run, provided only that competition is perfect. It follows that in an economy where nothing changes there can be no profits. There is no uncertainty about the future, so there are no risks and no profits. Alternatively, if there were changes but all of these changes were correctly foreseen there could again be no profits. For in the long run at any rate, everyone would be able to adapt himself completely to these foreseen changes and no-one would earn profits. Thus in a static or omniscient society no industry would yield long-run profits so long as there was perfect competition. In the long run the marginal revenue product of entrepreneurship would be zero.

This is an interesting idea because it suggests that in a static world long-run profits could only exist because imperfections in competition prevented abnormal profits being competed away. In other words, there could be 'monopoly profits', but 'pure profits'—the reward for risk-taking—would not occur. There might also, in such a world, seem to be some profits being earned by entrepreneurs who ran the management of their own firms. But in fact these would turn out, on examination, to be 'wages of management'. Similarly, entrepreneurs might earn interest on money invested in their firms and it is important that any such rewards should not be confused with 'pure' profits. So long as any such confusion is avoided, however, long-run profits will be found to be earned only because we live in a dynamic, a changing, world where, with our existing state of knowledge, uncertainty about the future is always present.

SUGGESTED READING

F. H. Knight, *Risk, Uncertainty and Profit*, London, 1933, chapters v-xi.

CHAPTER XVI

INTER-RELATIONS BETWEEN FACTORS OF PRODUCTION

1. RELATIONS BETWEEN MARGINAL PRODUCTIVITIES

WE have now completed our analysis of the demand for a single variable factor of production, and have studied the individual peculiarities of each of the four broad groups of factors. We must now study the inter-relations between two or more variable factors. In particular we must see how marginal productivity can be calculated where there are two or more variable factors, and what the relationship between the marginal products of such factors is.

We shall assume throughout this chapter that it is possible to vary the amounts of all factors freely. Thus when the amount of one factor is altered the amounts of the other factors can be altered less than in proportion or not at all. We have already mentioned [1] that there may be *fixed production coefficients* between factors of production, when the factors in question must always be used in a given proportion if they are to be used at all. This is the same kind of situation as where the elasticity of substitution between ordinary commodities is zero. But if factors do have to be used in fixed proportions in this way, there is no means of discovering what the marginal product of either factor is, since without a fixed amount of the one factor the other is of no use at all. We therefore assume now that all factors can be used in varying proportions. This condition is necessary if the marginal productivity of a factor is to mean anything. In this situation, the marginal product of any factor can be defined as the addition to the total product when a small additional amount of that factor is used, the amounts of *all other factors* remaining constant. We shall therefore assume throughout this chapter that each and every factor can be varied separately both in a small and in a large degree, and its marginal productivity thereby discovered.

To study marginal productivity in this kind of situation we

[1] See p. 277.

shall consider the case of an entrepreneur using two hired factors. For one can deal with all the important problems which arise when there are several factors of production so long as there are at least three of them: an entrepreneur, and two hired factors which we shall call A and B. If the entrepreneur's firm is to be in equilibrium maximising profits, he must be equating the marginal revenue product of each factor with the marginal cost of that same factor, in the way shown in the previous few chapters. The entrepreneur will always be able to do this so long as our assumption that factors can be used in varying proportions holds good; for he can then always vary freely the amount which he uses of each factor. It follows that when the firm is in equilibrium, the ratio between the marginal physical productivities of the various factors will be equal to the ratio between their prices. Since the price of the firm's product is given, it follows that if the ratio between the marginal physical products of any factors is not equal to the ratio between the prices of these factors, the firm can always increase its profits by expanding or contracting the amount of one factor until the two sets of ratios are equal.

It should also be remembered that if there is perfect competition, the marginal revenue product of any factor will be equal to the value (or price) of its marginal product. So whenever there is perfect competition—and we shall assume throughout this section that there is—one can express the marginal product of a factor either as the addition to the revenue product resulting from the addition of one more unit of the factor, or as the addition to the physical output of the firm (resulting from the addition of the same unit of the factor) multiplied by the price of the product.

Let us sum up the argument so far. In this chapter we shall assume that the amount of the product of any firm depends on the amount of the factors A and B which it is using, and that the amounts of each of these factors can be varied separately. We can therefore also assume that the marginal product of (an extra unit of) factor A, with factor B held constant, and the marginal product of factor B, with factor A held constant, can be calculated by the entrepreneur independently of each other. We assume that this is so because only if this condition holds can the entrepreneur determine the optimum purchases of each factor, where its price equals its marginal revenue product.

On the basis of these assumptions we may proceed to analyse the relationship between the productivities of two hired factors, A and B. First of all, we can say that the marginal product resulting from a unit increase in the amount of factor A used (with factor B held constant) plus the marginal product resulting from a unit increase of factor B (with factor A held constant) is approximately equal to the addition to the product resulting when both factors are simultaneously increased by these same amounts. We shall call the addition to the product when both factors are increased simultaneously in this way the *combined marginal product*. So we can say, more shortly, that the sum of the marginal products of the hired factors will be equal to their combined marginal product.

This proposition holds strictly only where the changes in the amounts of the factors are very small. For if the changes are small, then neither the proportions between the factors, nor the scale of the firm's operations, is significantly changed either when the amounts of the factors are altered separately or when these amounts are changed simultaneously. Let us assume that an entrepreneur is employing the two factors A and B. First he hires a (small) extra unit of factor A, with factor B held constant. Then he hires a (small) extra unit of factor B, with factor A held constant at the original level. If he finds that both these changes will pay him, he can then confidently expect that if he increases both factors simultaneously by these same amounts, he will not lose money.

If, on the other hand, the changes in the amounts of factors are very large, to change the amount of factor A, with factor B held constant, will mean that the proportion of factor A to factor B increases greatly. Similarly, if factor B is changed in amount, with factor A held constant, the proportion of B to A will increase greatly. The result will be that if an entrepreneur increases the employment of factor A by, say, 25 per cent (with factor B held constant), he may find that this raises total output by 200 units. If he then alters the amount of factor B by 25 per cent (with factor A held constant at the original level), he may find that this also yields an increase in total output of 200 units. But if he increases the amounts of both factors simultaneously by 25 per cent, total product may rise by more or less than 400 units.

It will probably be useful to see in greater detail why this is, and, in particular, why the change in the proportion between the factors when each factor is varied separately is so important. Let us consider first a situation where the production function is homogeneous of the first degree. This means that along each scale line the proportions between factors and the returns to outlay will be constant. Where the proportions between the factors are altered, returns to outlay will diminish. There will therefore be a greater increase in output if both factors are increased in the same proportion than if each is changed separately. For if both factors are increased in the same proportion, returns to outlay (along a scale line) will be constant, but if each factor is increased separately, returns to outlay will diminish.

A similar relationship will exist where returns to outlay are increasing along each scale line, so long as these scale lines slope upwards to the right. A (large) increase in the amount of factor A alone will give a smaller increase in output than would be given by the same increase in outlay along the scale line appropriate to the relative factor prices. Similarly if B alone is increased. If, however, both factors are increased at the same time in the proportions given by the slope of the scale line, there will be the same proportionate increase in total outlay. There will now be a (large) composite increase in the amounts of both A and B—along the scale line—and the combined marginal product will exceed the sum of the individual marginal products since returns to outlay are increasing. With diminishing returns it is not possible to generalise in this way. But unless returns to scale are diminishing very rapidly the conclusion will not need to be reversed. With large changes in the amounts of factors, then, the first proposition about marginal products with more than one factor does not hold.

This first proposition is that the sum of the individual marginal products of any number of variable factors will equal their combined marginal product. This will hold approximately for small changes in the amounts of factors and holds strictly for infinitesimally small changes in their amounts.

2. THE 'ADDING-UP PROBLEM'

Our second proposition about the relationship between factors of production is this. When returns to scale in any firm are constant, as happens at the minimum point of the firm's cost curve, and when each unit of each factor used by the firm is paid a reward equal to its marginal product, the rewards of all factors when added together will just equal the total product of the firm. In other words, the marginal product of factor A multiplied by the amount of factor A employed, plus the marginal product of factor B, multiplied by the amount of factor B used, equals the total product of the firm. In competitive equilibrium, factors of production will in fact be paid a reward equal to their marginal products and they will, therefore, just exhaust the total product of the firm. The problem of demonstrating that this proposition will hold, and why, has been called the 'adding-up problem'. We must now see how the validity of this proposition can be proved—how the 'adding-up problem' can be solved. Let us first take the simplest case where there is only one factor of production and the production function is homogeneous of the first degree. There will, therefore, be constant returns to the factor at all levels of employment. Since there is only one factor, constant returns at all levels of employment means that marginal product is always equal to average product whatever the output. Now, at any given output total product equals average product multiplied by the number of units of the factor which are being used. But since, here, marginal product equals average product, we can also say that marginal product, multiplied by the number of units of the factor, equals the total product. In this case, then, the solution of the adding-up problem is trivial.

This example is clearly far too simple. In practice one does not find a single factor of production working on its own with no entrepreneur to hire it. A more reasonable model is therefore one where there is an entrepreneur and one hired factor, say, labour. Since, as we have seen, a single firm can only have one entrepreneur, we cannot consider what will be the marginal product of entrepreneurship as more entrepreneurs are added. For the number of entrepreneurs in each firm cannot alter. The entrepreneur has no marginal product to the individual firm. Let us assume, as is usual, that the cost curve of the (perfectly competitive) firm is U-shaped, with increasing returns at small outputs and decreasing returns later on. The productivity curve of the variable factor will thus be shaped like an inverted U. If the firm is in competitive equilibrium, average cost will be at a minimum, and average product will be at a maximum. The total product of the firm in this situation will equal average product multiplied by the number of units of the variable factor which are being used. But since the firm is in competitive equilibrium, the average product of the factor will be equal to its marginal product. It follows that if each unit of the factor is paid a reward equal to its marginal product, the total product of the firm will just be exhausted. This happens at, but only at, the equilibrium position. For only in that position is the firm producing at the minimum point of its average cost curve and the maximum point of its average productivity curve with average product equal to marginal product. At this output, since average product is at a maximum, returns to scale are momentarily constant. They have just ceased to rise and have not yet begun to fall. In competitive equilibrium with only one factor of production the 'adding-up problem' is solved. Equilibrium occurs where returns to scale are momentarily constant, and the firm's total product is just exhausted when each unit of the hired factor is paid a reward equal to the marginal product of the factor.

Let us now consider a model where all the essential complications are present—where two hired factors are being employed by an entrepreneur. We saw in the previous section that in this situation the marginal product of a small unit of factor A plus the marginal product of a small unit of factor B equals their combined marginal product. Let us assume in the first place that there are constant returns in the full sense, so that if each hired factor is increased in the same proportion, the product increases in that same proportion and, given factor prices, outlay on the factors also increases by the same proportion. If returns to scale are constant in this sense, then combined marginal product will also bear this same proportion to the total product. Now the combined marginal product is equal to the (small) increment of factor A multiplied by its marginal productivity, plus the (small) addition to B multiplied by its marginal productivity as we saw in the proposition outlined above. It follows that the firm's total product equals the total amount of factor A multiplied by the marginal productivity of factor A, plus the total amount of factor B multiplied by the marginal productivity of factor B. The amounts in this instance will, however, be greater (say by 100 times) than in the previous sentence.

If there are constant returns to scale everywhere on the equal product map, the total amount of factor A, the total amount of factor B and the total product can each be looked upon as the sum of the corresponding marginal quantities. If production were started at a very low level and then gradually increased to a given total, the above solution of the adding-up problem would hold at all stages. This model has the advantage that it represents a very simple production function and is not incompatible with diminishing marginal physical productivity. We saw in Chapter X[1] that with such a production function returns

[1] P. 226.

are constant along any scale line, but that returns will *always* diminish along any horizontal or vertical line. The one disadvantage of this model is that in perfect competition, which we are assuming throughout this section, the equilibrium output of the firm is indeterminate. If it pays to produce anything at all, it will always pay to produce more and more without limit.

Fortunately, as we have already seen, the solution of the adding-up problem does not depend on the unreal assumption of constant returns to scale *throughout* the equal product map. It can apply also to more realistic cases where returns to scale first increase and then diminish. It applies here at the lowest point on the firm's long-run average cost curve, for at this point returns to scale are momentarily constant. This is fortunately an important case because any firm which is in full competitive equilibrium will be producing at this minimum point on its long-run average cost curve.

Let us assume that in this equilibrium position there is a small addition to each factor. Since it is the full equilibrium position, the marginal revenue of the firm just equals the combined marginal cost of the two factors A and B, with nothing left over for the entrepreneur. So at this equilibrium point the whole of the combined marginal product of the two factors (which is the same thing as marginal revenue) goes to the two factors. It is divided between them in proportion to their marginal products. If it were not so divided, it would pay the firm to go on hiring more of one or other of the factors and the firm would not be in equilibrium. But, at this equilibrium point, returns to scale are momentarily constant. It follows, for infinitesimal changes, that if the increased amount of factor A and the increased amount of factor B are in the same proportion as total A and total B, then total product, total amount of factor A and total amount of factor B bear the same proportion to each other as combined marginal product, increased amount of factor A and increased amount of factor B. Therefore since, by our first proposition, the combined marginal product equals the marginal productivity of A multiplied by the increase of A, plus the marginal productivity of B multiplied by increase of B, then total product equals the total amount of A multiplied by the marginal productivity of A, plus the total amount of B multiplied by the marginal productivity of B. The whole of the product is thus paid out when each factor is paid according to its marginal productivity.

Finally, we must say more about the assumption made

throughout that the entrepreneur has no marginal productivity
to the firm since he cannot be varied in amount. For the industry,
as distinct from the firm, zero marginal productivity of entrepreneurs does mean something. It means that if the number
of entrepreneurs in the industry increases, say from 100 to 101,
and the other factors are redistributed between these 101 firms,
there will be no addition to the total product of the industry.
The marginal productivity of entrepreneurship to the industry
will be zero. This, as we saw in the previous chapter, is what
will happen in static competitive equilibrium. So, since the
adding-up problem is solved in the competitive equilibrium
position, we are justified in assuming that entrepreneurs receive
no profits.

It may also be noted that whilst, when each factor is paid its
marginal product, the total product is just exhausted if returns
to scale are constant, more than the total product would be paid
out if returns to scale were increasing and less if returns to scale
were diminishing. In a sense it would be better to talk of the
'dividing-up problem', for in practice the total product is always
all shared out. But where a perfectly competitive equilibrium
does not occur the entrepreneur takes a residual share.

3. A MATHEMATICAL NOTE ON THE 'ADDING-UP PROBLEM'

The three solutions for the 'adding-up problem' which we
have given in words in the previous section can be put in mathematical form. In order to do this we must start from the production
function relating to the particular solution which we are studying.
We have already seen that a production function can be written
in the general form $P = f(A, B)$, where A and B are two factors of
production and P is the product. Such a production function
shows that the product is a function of, or depends on, the
amounts of factors A and B which are being used.

In the first case which we studied in the previous section,
returns to scale were constant and there was only one factor of
production. In this situation the production function can be
written in the particular form $P = kA$, showing that the product
(P) equals a constant (k) times the amount of factor (A). In
other words, as the amount of factor A is increased, the product
always increases in a given and constant proportion. To show
that the adding-up problem is solved in this case we need to show
that the marginal product of A multiplied by the amount of A

which is being used, is equal to the total product P. The only
unknown is therefore the marginal productivity of factor A.
Now the marginal productivity of factor A, since it shows the
addition to the total product resulting from a given (small)
increase in factor A, can be looked upon as the rate of change of
total product compared with the rate of change of the employment
of factor A. This is given by what is known as the *differential
coefficient of P with respect to A*. If we can calculate this differential
coefficient, we can show whether the product is exhausted or not
when each unit of factor A is paid a reward equal to the marginal
productivity of factor A. Now since

$$P = kA, \qquad \cdot \qquad \cdot \qquad \cdot \qquad \cdot \qquad (1)$$

it follows that
$$P + \delta P = kA + k(\delta A), \qquad \cdot \qquad \cdot \qquad \cdot \qquad (2)$$

where δP is the (small) change in production resulting from the
small increase (δA) in the amount of A employed. Subtracting (1)
from (2) we have

$$\delta P = k(\delta A),$$

$$\therefore \frac{\delta P}{\delta A} = k.$$

As δA approaches nought as a limit, $\frac{\delta P}{\delta A}$ approaches to the rate
$\frac{dP}{dA}$. This latter expression is the differential coefficient of P with
respect to A, and shows the marginal productivity of factor A at
any given level of employment. In this particular instance the
marginal product of factor A is k at every level of output. We
know, however, that the total product (P) equals kA. Therefore,
if each unit of factor A is paid its marginal product, k, the total
product (P) is just exhausted.

In the second case discussed in Section 2, there was still only
one hired factor, but its returns to scale varied, since it was being
combined with an entrepreneur (who had no marginal product).
The production function for this situation can be written as
$P = f(A)$. The total product depends on the amount of factor A
used, but it does not now vary in exact proportion with the
amount of A. We need to show that in this situation the total
product will just be exhausted when, in competitive equilibrium,
each unit of the factor is paid a reward equal to the marginal
product of the factor. Now, since we are only concerned with the

competitive equilibrium position,[1] we know that average product equals marginal product, that is to say, $\dfrac{P}{A} = \dfrac{dP}{dA}$. If we now multiply both sides of the equation by A, then $P = A \cdot \dfrac{dP}{dA}$, which is what we set out to prove.

Let us now turn to the more interesting and important case where there are two hired factors so that the production function now is $P = f(A, B)$. Here A and B are both independent variables—the amounts of factors A and B can be varied separately in large or small degree. We therefore have now to calculate what is known as the *partial differential coefficient* or *partial derivative* of P with respect to A or B, according to which factor we are momentarily interested in. The partial differential coefficient of P with respect to A is similar to the differential coefficient used in cases one and two above, except that we now regard B as being held constant whilst A is varied. The partial differential coefficient of P with respect to A thus shows the rate of change of P compared with the rate of change of A, when the amount of A is altered but that of B remains unchanged. Since

$$P = f(A, B), \qquad . \qquad . \qquad . \qquad (1)$$

it follows that $\qquad P + \delta P = f(A + \delta A, B + \delta B). \qquad . \qquad . \qquad (2)$

Subtracting (1) from (2) we have

$$\delta P = f(A + \delta A, B + \delta B) - f(A, B). \qquad . \qquad . \qquad (3)$$

By subtracting $f(A, B + \delta B)$ from each term on the right-hand side of the equation (so that the total is not affected) we can rewrite the equation as

$$\delta P = [f(A + \delta A, B + \delta B) - f(A, B + \delta B)] + [f(A, B + \delta B) - f(A, B)]. \quad (4)$$

In equation (4) the first pair of terms (in the first square bracket) differ only in the amount of the first factor, factor A. This difference is approximately equal to the change in the amount of the factor A (δA) multiplied by its rate of marginal productivity $\dfrac{\partial P}{\partial A}$.[2] Similarly, the difference between the second

---

[1] As we have seen, at any point except that of competitive equilibrium, returns to scale will not be constant, and if each unit of each factor is paid an amount equal to the marginal product of the factor, the total payments to factors will not equal the total product.

[2] This is written $\dfrac{\partial P}{\partial A}$ and not $\dfrac{dP}{dA}$ because we are now concerned with partial derivatives and not ordinary derivatives.

pair of terms (in the second square bracket) is approximately equal to the change in the amount of the factor B used (δB), multiplied by its rate of marginal productivity $\frac{\partial P}{\partial B}$. We can therefore rewrite equation (4) as

$$\delta P = \delta A \cdot \frac{\partial P}{\partial A} + \delta B \cdot \frac{\partial P}{\partial B} \text{ (approximately).}$$

The reason why this relationship is only approximate springs from two different sources. First, there is the usual fact that $\frac{\partial P}{\partial A}$ gives the rate of marginal productivity only for infinitesimal changes in factor A $\left(\text{and similarly with } \frac{\partial P}{\partial B} \text{ for factor B}\right)$, whilst we are considering small but finite changes in A (and B). Second, as we have seen, the first pair of terms in equation (4) differ only in the amount of factor A, which is being used with a constant amount of factor B. But this amount of B is B + δB, and not the original amount of B to which the partial differential really refers.

An exact relationship can, however, be obtained by using the notion of *the differential*, written as dP, dA or dB according to whether we are considering P, A or B. The differential dA means a finite increment in factor A. The differential dP shows what the finite increment of product δP would have been if, over the whole range of the finite increment of the factor δA, the rate of marginal productivity $\frac{\partial P}{\partial A}$ were the same as at the original employment of factor A. We can thus write a further equation, using these differentials, where $dP = dA \cdot \frac{\partial P}{\partial A} + dB \cdot \frac{\partial P}{\partial B}$. This is known as the equation of the complete or total differential. It is, in fact, another way of saying that the relationship $\delta P = \delta A \cdot \frac{\partial P}{\partial A} + \delta B \cdot \frac{\partial P}{\partial B}$ holds approximately, being a better approximation the smaller the finite changes δA and δB.

With the aid of the equation of the complete differential we can now proceed to solve the adding-up problem for a production function of two independent variables. Let us consider a homogeneous production function of the first degree where, as we know, returns to scale will be constant and the proportion between the factors along any scale line will always be the same. If the production function is P = f(A, B), we can say that, since it is a homogeneous function of the first degree, $f(\lambda A, \lambda B) = \lambda f(A, B)$ for any value of λ. That is to say, if we increase the amount of each of the factors A and B in a given proportion, we multiply the output in that same proportion. Let us now give λ the particular value $\lambda = 1 + \dfrac{dA}{A} = 1 + \dfrac{dB}{B}$, so that the amounts of the factors become $A + dA$ and $B + dB$. Then,

$$P + dP = f(\lambda A, \lambda B) = P\left(1 + \frac{dA}{A}\right) = P\left(1 + \frac{dB}{B}\right). \qquad . \quad (1)$$

Thus, dividing through by P, $\dfrac{dP}{P} = \dfrac{dA}{A} = \dfrac{dB}{B}$. Substituting for dA and dB in terms of dP in the equation $dP = dA\dfrac{\partial P}{\partial A} + dB\dfrac{\partial P}{\partial B}$ (the equation of the total differential), we have

$$P = A \cdot \frac{\partial P}{\partial A} + B \cdot \frac{\partial P}{\partial B}. \qquad \text{Q.E.D.}$$

As we have seen, the fact that we are considering the differential dP and not the actual increment of product δP in equation (1) means that the proof is not entirely rigorous.[1] For $f(\lambda A, \lambda B)$ refers to the actual output corresponding to λA, λB, whilst dP shows what the output would be if $\dfrac{\partial P}{\partial A}$ and $\dfrac{\partial P}{\partial B}$ were the same at the increased employments $A + \delta A$ and $B + \delta B$ as at the original employments A and B. This result, showing that when the production function is homogeneous of the first degree and each factor is paid a reward equal to its marginal product, the whole product is just exhausted, exemplifies what is known as Euler's Theorem on homogeneous functions of whatever degree. This is often quoted as

$$A \cdot \frac{\partial P}{\partial A} + B \cdot \frac{\partial P}{\partial B} = nP.$$

This formula gives the result for a homogeneous function of the nth degree. By a homogeneous function of the nth degree we mean a function such that $f(\lambda A, \lambda B)$ is equal to $\lambda^n f(A, B)$. In our particular case, of course, $n = 1$.

The above proof relates to homogeneous production functions of the first degree in the general form $P = f(A, B)$. It may be useful if we consider a particular function of this form in some

---

[1] Students requiring a rigorous proof should consult R. G. D. Allen, *Mathematical Analysis for Economists*, pp. 317-18.

detail. Let us consider the function $P = \sqrt{AB}$. It is not difficult to show algebraically that with this function the adding-up problem is solved.   Since

$$P = \sqrt{AB},$$

then $\qquad \dfrac{\partial P}{\partial A} = \tfrac{1}{2}\sqrt{\dfrac{B}{A}}$ [1] $\quad$ and $\quad \dfrac{\partial P}{\partial B} = \tfrac{1}{2}\sqrt{\dfrac{A}{B}},$

therefore $A \cdot \dfrac{\partial P}{\partial A} + B \cdot \dfrac{\partial P}{\partial B} = \tfrac{1}{2}A \cdot \sqrt{\dfrac{B}{A}} + \tfrac{1}{2}B \cdot \sqrt{\dfrac{A}{B}}$

$$= \tfrac{1}{2}\sqrt{A} \times \sqrt{A} \times \sqrt{\dfrac{B}{A}} + \tfrac{1}{2}\sqrt{B} \times \sqrt{B} \times \sqrt{\dfrac{A}{B}}$$

$$= \tfrac{1}{2}\sqrt{AB} + \tfrac{1}{2}\sqrt{AB} = \sqrt{AB} = P.$$

Therefore, if each factor is paid its marginal product, the total product is just exhausted.

The proofs so far given for the case of two hired factors relate only to firms with constant costs at all scales of output. Since, in perfect competition, such firms can never be in equilibrium, it will be useful to give a further solution for the adding-up problem in the more realistic case where a firm using two hired factors is in competitive equilibrium. The general form of the production function for this kind of firm, with decreasing costs to begin with as the scale of operations increases, and increasing costs after the optimum output has been passed, can be written as $P = f(A, B)$. The total cost of production will be $Ap_A + Bp_B$, where p_A and p_B are the prices of factors A and B respectively. Let us write average cost per unit at an output of P units as π_P.   Then

$$\pi_P = \frac{1}{P}(Ap_A + Bp_B). \qquad . \qquad . \qquad . \quad (1)$$

Since we are considering a competitive equilibrium position, $\pi_P = p_P$ or, in other words, average cost of production = price of product.

In order to get the conditions for π_P to be a minimum (as in competitive equilibrium) we must differentiate π_P partially with

[1] This is equivalent to differentiating $kx^{\frac{1}{2}}$ where, in our particular case, $k = \sqrt{B}$ and $x = A$. With this type of function the differential coefficient can be obtained by reducing the power by one and multiplying by the original power. Thus the differential coefficient of $kx^{\frac{1}{2}}$ is $\tfrac{1}{2}kx^{-\frac{1}{2}} = \tfrac{1}{2}\dfrac{k}{\sqrt{x}}.$

respect to A, that is holding B constant. The partial differential coefficient of π_P with respect to A is $\dfrac{\partial \pi_P}{\partial A}$, which can be written as

$$\dfrac{\partial \dfrac{1}{P}(Ap_A + Bp_B)}{\partial A}.$$ We therefore wish to differentiate the product $\dfrac{1}{P}(Ap_A + Bp_B)$. This we can do by using the well-known rule for differentiating a product. If we consider the product uv, where u and v are both functions of A, then

$$\frac{\partial(uv)}{\partial A} = u\frac{\partial v}{\partial A} + v\frac{\partial u}{\partial A}.$$

In our particular case $u = \dfrac{1}{P}$ and $v = Ap_A + Bp_B$, so

$$\frac{\partial(uv)}{\partial A} = u\frac{\partial v}{\partial A} + v\frac{\partial u}{\partial A}$$

can be written

$$\frac{\partial \pi_P}{\partial A} = \frac{1}{P} \cdot \frac{\partial(Ap_A + Bp_B)}{\partial A} + (Ap_A + Bp_B)\frac{\partial \dfrac{1}{P}}{\partial A}.$$

This can be rewritten as

$$= \frac{1}{P}\frac{\partial(Ap_A + Bp_B)}{\partial A} + (Ap_A + Bp_B)\frac{d\dfrac{1}{P}}{dP} \times \frac{\partial P}{\partial A},$$

since $\dfrac{\partial \dfrac{1}{P}}{\partial A} = \dfrac{d\dfrac{1}{P}}{dP} \times \dfrac{\partial P}{\partial A}$. For $\dfrac{\partial \dfrac{1}{P}}{\partial A}$ means the rate of change of $\dfrac{1}{P}$ compared with the rate of change of A. This can be split up into the rate of change of $\dfrac{1}{P}$ compared with the rate of change of P and the rate of change of P itself compared with the rate of change of A.

Now $\dfrac{\partial(Ap_A + Bp_B)}{\partial A}$ is equal to p_A, since in the partial differentiation p_A, B and p_B are treated as constant. Also $\dfrac{d\dfrac{1}{P}}{dP} = -\dfrac{1}{P^2}$, by the usual rule for differentiation.[1]

---

[1] See footnote, p. 340.

Therefore
$$\frac{\partial \pi_P}{\partial A} = \frac{1}{P}p_A - \frac{1}{P^2}\frac{\partial P}{\partial A}(Ap_A + Bp_B)$$

$$= \frac{1}{P}p_A - \frac{1}{P^2}\frac{\partial P}{\partial A}(P\pi_P).$$

Therefore
$$\frac{\partial \pi_P}{\partial A} = \frac{1}{P}\left(p_A - \frac{\partial P}{\partial A}\pi_P\right).$$

For this equation to relate to a competitive equilibrium where π_P (average cost) must be at a minimum, we must have $\frac{\partial \pi_P}{\partial A} = 0$, or alternatively $\frac{1}{P}\left(p_A - \frac{\partial P}{\partial A}\pi_P\right) = 0$. Now since P (output) must be a finite quantity, $\frac{1}{P}$ cannot be 0. So, if the whole term is to equal 0, $\left(p_A - \frac{\partial P}{\partial A}\pi_P\right)$ must equal 0, therefore

$$p_A = \frac{\partial P}{\partial A}\pi_P = \frac{\partial P}{\partial A}p_P.$$

Similarly,
$$p_B = \frac{\partial P}{\partial B}\pi_P.$$

Substituting for p_A and p_B in equation (1), we have

$$\pi_P = \frac{1}{P}\left(A\frac{\partial P}{\partial A}\pi_P + B\frac{\partial P}{\partial B}\pi_P\right).$$

Multiplying both sides by $\frac{P}{\pi_P}$, we have $P = A\frac{\partial P}{\partial A} + B\frac{\partial P}{\partial B}$.   Q.E.D.

Thus in competitive equilibrium where there are two hired factors the adding-up problem is solved.

4. THE DEMAND FOR FACTORS OF PRODUCTION

The final problem which we must discuss is the nature of the demand for several variable factors of production. We have seen in the last few chapters that the demand curve for a single hired factor is its marginal revenue productivity curve. But not all factors will have the same shaped marginal productivity curve, so that the size of the increase in the demand for a factor when its price falls (and hence the elasticity of demand for the factor) will vary according to the circumstances. In particular, the demand for any factor will be less elastic the lower the elasticity of demand for the product, and the more quickly the factor's marginal physical productivity falls off when its employment rises and *vice versa*.

We have also seen that when there are several variable factors of production, the demand for any one of them will still depend on its marginal revenue productivity. We have already shown, in our discussion of the 'adding-up problem', how marginal revenue productivity can be measured when there are more than two factors. If we vary slightly the amount of one factor A whilst holding the amount(s) of the other(s) constant, we can calculate the marginal (net) physical (and hence marginal (net) revenue) product of factor A in any given situation. Similarly, with any other factor if we vary its employment by a small amount, holding the amount of the other factors constant, and find the resultant addition to the revenue of the firm, we shall have discovered its marginal (net) revenue productivity. It will always pay an entrepreneur to go on hiring more and more of any factor until its marginal net revenue product equals its marginal cost. Thus, in equilibrium, the marginal net revenue products of all factors will equal their marginal costs.

Let us now consider what will be the main effect on the demand for any given variable factor when its price changes, assuming for the sake of simplicity that the prices of all other factors remain constant. It is important at the outset to stress again the fact that the demand for every factor of production is a *derived* demand. Factors of production are only useful because they can help to produce consumer goods and the demand for factors is 'derived' from the direct demand for those consumer goods. This is an important difference between the demand for factors of production and demand for consumer goods. There are, however, some similarities between the two cases. In particular, some factors of production will be competitive and others complementary.

Where there are only two factors of production, shown for example on an equal product map, these factors must be substitutes for each other in the sense that, if the product is to remain constant, less of one factor must be used when more of the other is employed. If, in these circumstances, the price of one factor falls, more of it will be bought. The size of this increase in purchases will depend partly on the scale effect and partly on the extent to which substitution between the factors is possible—just as the extent to which a fall in the price of a consumer good leads to an increased demand for it depends partly on the income effect and partly on the extent to which it can be substituted for the good. If the factors have to be used in a given proportion, such substitution will be impossible. Elasticity of substitution between the factors will be zero. If the factors are perfect substitutes, elasticity of substitution will be infinite. And, between these limits, substitution between the factors will be possible in differing degrees.

Where there are three (or more) factors of production, the relationships between them will be more complex than where there are two. The problems we must now consider are like those considered in Chapter IV where we studied the relationships between three consumer goods. First, some factors will be very closely competitive; for example, hand looms and power looms, or paint brushes and paint sprays. A fall in the price of one out of each of these pairs of factors will thus have a considerable effect on the demand for the factor itself—and on the demand for the substitute.

Let us consider the likely effects of such a fall in price, by studying a problem which was of considerable importance to nineteenth-century economists—the introduction of power looms in the place of hand looms in an industry making woollen goods. Let us assume that the demand and supply, both for the product of the industry and for the factors it uses, are originally in equilibrium, and the equilibrium is now disturbed, because the price of power looms has fallen as the result of a technical change in their supply conditions. Since power looms are now cheaper, it will pay entrepreneurs to employ them in place of hand looms. The number of hand looms will fall and more power looms will be used instead. The extent to which the demand for hand looms will fall will depend on the extent to which it is possible to substitute power looms for them. In fact, such substitution is likely to take place on a large scale. The two kinds of loom are bound to be very close substitutes in the kind of conditions that existed in the early nineteenth century. A small fall in the price of power looms will cause a large fall in the demand for hand looms.

We can ascribe this result partly to a substitution effect and partly to a scale effect. Since power looms are now relatively cheaper, it would have paid to use fewer hand looms *even if* the output of the industry had remained unaltered ; power and hand looms are thus 'competitive' factors of production. They are competitive in the sense that (the level of output remaining the same) if the price of power looms falls, more power looms and fewer hand looms will be used. But in fact, if the price of power looms has fallen, it is likely that costs of production in the woollen industry as a whole will have fallen and that this will increase the output of woollen goods. More will now be bought because they are cheaper. Because of this 'scale effect' more factors of all kinds will be used. And it is just possible that more hand looms may be used as a result. For whilst, if output had not increased, fewer hand looms would have been used, the fact that output has risen *may* mean that more hand looms are used, as well as more power looms. This would be analogous to the possibility of an increase in the demand for any consumer good when the prices of competitive goods fall—if the income effect is strong enough. Nevertheless, it seems unlikely that, in this case of hand and power looms, any practicable increase in the scale of operations will be sufficiently large to offset the strong substitution effect working to reduce the demand for hand looms now that they are dearer relatively to power looms.

But this is not the whole story. We have so far considered only the relationship between the demand for power looms and the demand for hand looms. What of the effects on the employment of weavers, assuming they can work either kind of loom ? Since fewer hand looms are being used, it is likely that the demand for weavers will fall off. For one weaver per loom must be used as a minimum, whilst power looms may only need one man to work several looms. Only if there is a considerable increase in the output of woollen goods will the demand for weavers increase. The fact that power looms and hand looms (and hand-loom weavers) are close substitutes means that a fall in the price of power looms reduces the demand for hand looms and for weavers. There is a substitution effect reducing the employment of the factor whose price is relatively higher. How strong this effect is will depend on the extent to which it is possible to substitute power looms for hand looms. On the other hand, if output increases considerably now that power looms are being used (perhaps because prices of woollen goods have now fallen) and elasticity of demand for them is very high, the demand for weavers may rise. This is the scale effect. Nevertheless, it is clear that the scale effect must be extremely strong if it is to outweigh the substitution effect. For since fewer men are needed to work each power loom, and since the power looms will be at least as productive as the hand looms, the number of weavers employed is likely to fall, even if output does increase somewhat because of a scale effect. We are assuming here that hand-loom weavers are capable of operating power looms. If this is not the case, there is bound to be unemployment of hand-loom weavers.

Because there are so many influences to be considered, it is not easy to be dogmatic about the effect of a fall in the price of power looms either on the employment of weavers or on the demand for hand looms. Both are likely to fall. But both may increase if the scale effect is sufficiently strong. An early analysis of this kind of problem can be found in Ricardo's *Principles of Economics*, in the chapter 'On Machinery'.[1]

5. JOINT DEMAND FOR FACTORS OF PRODUCTION

Some factors of production are not competitive in the way that hand looms and power looms are. Instead of at least one factor out of a set of factors being used in smaller quantities if the price of one other has fallen, more of every factor is used. Such factors are, for example, sugar, flour and butter used together in cake-making, and malt and hops used in brewing beer. It is therefore said that such factors of production are in *joint demand*. We have already used the term, joint demand, in Chapter IV to describe related demands for consumer goods. But joint demand was a term originally invented by Marshall to apply to factors of production. He says, 'there is a *joint demand* for the services which any . . . things render in helping to produce a thing which satisfies wants directly and for which there is therefore a direct demand'.[2]

In discussing joint demand Marshall [3] studied the effects of a strike by plasterers on their wages and on the prices of other factors of production, say carpenters and bricklayers, when all are being used together to build houses. Let us use a similar model. Let us consider the effects of a strike for higher wages by plasterers who are building houses in conjunction with bricklayers and carpenters. We shall assume as Marshall did that the demand curve for houses remains unaffected throughout, and that the supply curves for bricklayers and carpenters do not alter. Bricklayers and carpenters, that is to say, continue to offer their labour in the same amounts as before at the same wage levels.

---

[1] Ricardo, *op. cit.* chapter 31 (Sraffa Edition).
[2] Marshall, *Principles of Economics* (8th Edition), p. 381.
[3] *Op. cit.* pp. 382-7.

The refusal of plasterers to continue to work will clearly reduce the number of new houses being built and will have some effect on their price, which will tend to rise slightly. We can assume, however, that the prices of other factors of production used in building will not rise now that fewer houses are being built, and they may well fall. The extent to which the plasterers' claim for higher wages can succeed will depend ultimately on the extent to which the price of houses rises, and the extent to which the wages of bricklayers and carpenters fall because the demand for them has declined. The price of houses having risen, and the wages of other factors having (at most) remained constant, house-builders will be able to pay higher wages to plasterers and yet earn normal profits.

Marshall lists the following conditions as being conducive to a large increase in the wage offered to a factor of production if the amount supplied is reduced by a strike or some other disturbance.

The first condition is that there should be no competitive substitutes for the factor in question available at a similar price. Second, it is necessary that the demand for the product which the factor is making should be very inelastic so that a small reduction in its output causes a large rise in its price. Third, it is necessary that the cost of the factor should represent only a small proportion of the cost of the product. For example, if the wages of plasterers represent only 1 per cent of the cost of houses, an increase of 100 per cent in wages will only raise the cost of producing houses by 1 per cent. Fourth, it is necessary that the supply of other factors should be very inelastic so that a small fall in house-building, and hence in the employment of such factors, causes a large drop in their wages.

Marshall points out that if there are good substitutes for plasterers, the rise in their wages may not be at all great. The demand for plasterers will be elastic and to obtain a large wage increase they may have to be prepared to see a large fall in their employment. The above analysis thus relates to a situation where all factors are in joint demand, and where a fall in the quantity of the one factor (plasterers) causes a fall also in the number of co-operating factors (bricklayers and carpenters) demanded. Similarly, an increase in the number of plasterers hired (if their wages fell) would cause an increase in the demand for bricklayers and carpenters.

It is important, however, to consider the reasons for which factors of production are in joint demand in greater detail. We

saw in Chapter IV that consumer goods may be jointly demanded
either because they are complementary or because, though they
are competitive, there is a strong income effect when the price of
one of the goods falls. A similar distinction can be made here.
In the example given above it seems likely that plasterers and
bricklayers are jointly demanded because they are not very
competitive—they are not very good substitutes for each other in
house-building. The scale effect resulting from a reduction in
house-building thus easily overcomes the substitution effect which
will tend (in our example) to work in the direction of increasing
the demand for both bricklayers and carpenters now that plasterers
are more expensive to hire. The factors are jointly demanded
only because the scale effect is considerable and they are only
moderately and not *highly* competitive, as for example power and
hand looms are likely to be.

It is quite likely, however, that some factors of production
will bear a complementary relationship to each other. If one first
of all eliminates the scale effect (by keeping output constant) it is
possible to discover whether factors are complementary. For
example, continuing to discuss house-building, consider the three
factors—bricks, wood and bricklayers. Let us suppose that the
price of bricks falls, that the prices of all other factors remain
constant and that there is no change in the number of houses
produced. It is likely in this case that less wood, but more
bricks and more bricklayers, will be used. Bricks and bricklayers
are thus complementary factors. Although the volume of houses
produced remains unaltered, bricks and bricklayers are used in
greater amounts and less wood goes into each house. As with
consumer goods, it is of course impossible for *all* the factors
making a particular product to be complementary. Given any
number (n) of factors, it is impossible for more than n – 1 of these
to be complementary. One factor, at least, must be competitive
with the rest.

It is thus possible to discover whether factors of production
are or are not complementary by eliminating any scale effect, just
as we eliminated the income effect when considering complementarity between consumer goods. It is important to distinguish
in this way between scale effects and substitution effects in any
discussion of the demand for several factors of production, for only
by drawing such a distinction can one tell whether factors are
competitive or complementary. Moreover, the forces which
determine the nature of the scale effect are essentially different

from those underlying the substitution effect, so they should be carefully distinguished.

SUGGESTED READING

R. G. D. Allen, *Mathematical Analysis for Economists*, London, 1937, chapter xii.

J. R. Hicks, *Theory of Wages*, London, 1932, appendix.

Joan Robinson, 'Euler's Theorem and the Problem of Distribution', *Economic Journal*, 1934, p. 398.

Alfred Marshall, *Principles of Economics* (8th Edition), London, 1920, Book V, chapter 6.

J. R. Hicks, *Value and Capital*, Oxford, 1946, chapter vii.

Joan Robinson, *Economics of Imperfect Competition*, London, 1933, chapter xxii.

David Ricardo, *Principles of Economics* (edited by Piero Sraffa), Cambridge, 1951, chapter xxxi.

PART TWO

EMPLOYMENT THEORY

CHAPTER XVII

GENERAL EQUILIBRIUM AND EMPLOYMENT

1. SAY'S LAW

PART ONE has been concerned with the analysis of the prices of individual goods and has shown how they are determined. As we have seen, it is possible to analyse such price problems in terms of 'partial' (or 'particular') equilibrium theory. So far we have not attempted to show how the general level of activity in a country will be determined, or whether it will be high or low. It is, however, impossible to provide an adequate explanation of the forces determining the general level of employment in a country on the basis of partial equilibrium analysis. Partial equilibrium analysis can show that unemployment may occur in particular industries ; but it is almost impossible to show whether employment in *all* industries will be high or low, except by using a general equilibrium analysis.

Until the 1920's and 1930's economists seem to have usually assumed that general unemployment was unlikely. The 'classical economists' [1] tended to ignore the problem of what determines the general level of employment. Nevertheless, on the (few) occasions when such economists did discuss the possibility of unemployment, they seem to have taken the optimistic view that general over-production—and hence general unemployment—were impossible. In 1936, however, J. M. (the late Lord) Keynes wrote his *General Theory of Employment, Interest and Money*,[2] refuting the 'classical' optimism and showing that, far from being a logical impossibility, general unemployment is logically quite

---

[1] Keynes says that '"The classical economists" was a name invented by Marx to cover Ricardo and James Mill and their *predecessors*, that is to say for the founders of the theory which culminated in the Ricardian economics. I have become accustomed, perhaps perpetrating a solecism, to include in " the classical school" the *followers* of Ricardo, those, that is to say, who adopted and perfected the theory of the Ricardian economics.' These economists include (for example) J. S. Mill, Marshall and Edgeworth. *General Theory of Employment, Interest and Money*, footnote to page 3.

[2] For brevity, this book is referred to hereafter as the *General Theory*.

possible. To Keynes full employment is only a limiting case. Just as perfect competition is a limiting case to differing degrees of monopoly or imperfect competition, so full employment is merely the limiting case to various possible situations of under-employment equilibrium, each with a different amount of unemployment. In Part Two of this book we shall summarise Keynesian employment theory. Before doing so, however, it will be useful to see in greater detail the kind of conclusions about unemployment which some earlier economists drew from theories of relative prices similar to the theory outlined in Part One. This will also allow us to see the shortcomings of particular equilibrium analysis if one attempts to use it to deal with the problems of unemployment.

One of the most important conclusions provided by the 'classical economists' is known as 'Say's Law of Markets'. It was this so-called 'law' which gave a concrete formulation to the idea that general over-production, and hence general unemployment, were impossible. J. B. Say (1767–1832) was a French economist whose *Traité d'économie politique* passed through several editions and was the first really popular treatise on political economy published in France. In the chapter in his *Traité* on 'Des Débouchés' Say gives his reasons for disbelieving those business men and merchants who think that general over-production and unemployment are common occurrences. He rejects this view by arguing that 'supply always creates its own demand' as the currently accepted version of his 'law' holds. Unfortunately, it is difficult to find a really apt quotation from Say himself, although the phrase 'supply creates its own demand' certainly sums up very accurately the drift of his argument in this chapter. Probably the nearest one can come to an explicit statement by Say is 'it is production which creates markets for goods'.[1] It does not require very free translation to render this as 'it is supply which creates demand'. Say is prepared to agree that the supply of the products of particular industries may temporarily outrun the demand for the product of those particular industries if entrepreneurs misjudge the demand for their goods. But *general* over-production is impossible, according to Say.

Say's Law was explicitly accepted as the true explanation of the working of the economic system by many English economists during the early part of the nineteenth century, and has underlain

---

[1] 'C'est la production qui ouvre des débouchés aux produits.' *Traité d'économie politique*, p. 144 (2nd Edition).

implicitly most economic writings prior to the 'Keynesian Revolution' of the 1930's. James Mill has a chapter in his *Elements of Political Economy*, showing that 'consumption is co-extensive with production', and claims that 'Production is the cause, and the sole cause, of demand. It never furnishes supply without furnishing demand, both at the same time and both to an equal extent.'[1] Mill claims that 'whatever the amount of the annual produce it can never exceed the amount of the annual demand'.[2] David Ricardo, in a letter to T. R. Malthus,[3] another eminent economist of the early nineteenth century, speaks approvingly of Mill's claim that 'in reference to a nation, supply can never exceed demand'.

Perhaps the most explicit statement of Say's Law given by any English economist appears in John Stuart Mill's *Principles of Political Economy* published in 1848. J. S. Mill, the son of James Mill, takes great pains to refute the idea that the demand for commodities in general might fall short of supply and thus cause over-production and unemployment. He says, ' is it . . . possible that there should be a deficiency of demand for all commodities, for want of the means of payment ? Those who think so cannot have considered what it is which constitutes the means of payment for commodities. It is simply commodities. Each person's means of paying for the productions of other people consists of those which he himself possesses. All sellers are inevitably and *ex vi termini*[4] buyers. Could we suddenly double the productive powers of the country we should double the supply of commodities in every market, but we should by the same stroke double the purchasing power. Every one would bring a double demand as well as supply : everybody would be able to buy twice as much because everybody would have twice as much to offer in exchange. . . . It is a sheer absurdity that all things should fall in value and that all producers should, in consequence, be insufficiently remunerated.'[5]

It is difficult to find explicit statements of this kind in later writings, but there is no reason to doubt that the idea that demand in general might fall short of supply in general and cause general

---

[1] *Op. cit.* 3rd Edition, p. 237. The chapter from which this quotation is taken, chapter iv of Section 3, is devoted to a discussion of the impossibility of general over-production, and is worth reading in the original text.

[2] *Op. cit.* p. 233.

[3] Letter of 16th Sept. 1814.

[4] By the meaning of the word. (Our footnote.)

[5] *Op. cit.* Book III, Section 2, chapter xiv.

over-production was regarded as heretical. Not, of course, that heresy had been absent even in the earliest days of Say's Law. T. R. Malthus, in particular, tried to convince Ricardo, who, as we have seen, took the same kind of view as Say, that demand might be deficient and cause unemployment, but without success. As Keynes says, 'Malthus, indeed, had vehemently opposed Ricardo's doctrine that it was impossible for effective demand to be deficient; but vainly. For since Malthus was unable to explain clearly (apart from an appeal to the facts of common observation) how and why effective demand could be deficient or excessive, he failed to furnish an alternative construction; and Ricardo conquered England as completely as the Holy Inquisition conquered Spain. Not only was his theory accepted by the city, by statesmen and by the academic world. But controversy ceased; the other point of view completely disappeared; it ceased to be discussed. The great puzzle of Effective Demand with which Malthus had wrestled vanished from economic literature.'[1]

2. WAGES AND UNEMPLOYMENT

It will be seen from the quotation from J. S. Mill given above that, for economists like him, the demand for good X is exactly the same thing as the supply of other goods Y, Z, etc., in the economy. Similarly, the demand for good Y is the supply of other goods X, Z, etc., in the economy. Therefore the demand for all goods together is identical with the supply of all goods together, and general over-production is ruled out by definition. J. S. Mill would admit that it is possible that there may be a temporary excess of the supply of X over the demand for X, or of the supply of Y over the demand for Y. But excess of the supply of X, Y and Z together over the demand for X, Y and Z together is a contradiction in terms. Even the partial over-production of any one good alone, say good X, was conceived by 'classical economists' as being possible only because the ruling price of X was too high. It was only at a price above the equilibrium price of X that the supply of X could exceed the demand for X. Once the price of X had fallen relatively to the prices of Y, Z, etc., this excess supply would disappear. The conclusion which one would obviously draw from this kind of analysis was that if the price of a particular commodity were high, compared with other prices, thus causing over-supply, the solution would

[1] *General Theory*, p. 32.

be to reduce costs in the industry making the product in question. In these circumstances the 'classical economists' would advocate a reduction in the wages of workers in the industry suffering from over-production. This would reduce the cost of the product to an extent depending on the importance of wages in the total costs of the industry. Now, since in partial equilibrium analysis one can assume that the individual industry is a relatively small part of the whole economy, one can also assume that the demand curve for the product of a single 'over-producing' industry remains the same after the wages of its workers have been cut. The amount of the product demanded would increase and would catch up with the supply. Over-production would therefore disappear, provided only that wages (or other costs) were reduced sufficiently.

This kind of conclusion is perfectly valid when one is merely attempting to apply partial equilibrium analysis to the over-production problems of a particular industry. But 'classical economists' who used this kind of analysis often extended their conclusions to the economy as a whole. They suggested that *general* unemployment and over-production could be met in the same way by a *general* cut in wages. But if there is general over-production it is unreasonable to try to solve the problems created by applying partial equilibrium analysis. The suggestion that wages should be reduced may well now be methodologically unsound. When there is general unemployment a general cut in wages in *all* industries cannot be assumed to leave demand unaltered, for part of that demand results from spending out of such wages. It is thus likely that a *general* cut in wages will merely cause a reduction in demand and will not in itself remove unemployment. The real solution to this kind of problem can only be analysed fully with the kind of theory we are about to discuss and we shall therefore postpone a complete explanation until the end of Part Two. It is, however, clear that partial equilibrium analysis is unable to analyse the problem thoroughly, and that some kind of general equilibrium analysis is needed.

This criticism of particular equilibrium theory applies to its analysis of other problems of this kind. General equilibrium analysis shows that every part of the economy is connected with every other part of the economy and the repercussions of a change in one part on conditions in another cannot be ignored. In particular, since all the parts of the economy are linked together it is unreasonable, in general equilibrium theory, to regard the demand for consumption goods and the demand for investment goods as being independent of each other, as we did in Chapter XIV. We there assumed that if saving increased, that is to say if the demand for consumption goods decreased, the demand for capital goods would rise because entrepreneurs had more money to spend on such investment goods. In partial equilibrium analysis this is a perfectly valid assumption; but in general equilibrium analysis it is no longer possible to use it.

To see why this is, let us assume that money wages throughout an economy are constant. Now it should be clear that since all workers must work in either the consumption goods industries or the investment goods industries, the volume of employment in the community depends on money expenditure on consumption plus money expenditure on investment. Only if money is paid to the employers in these industries, in return for goods, will labour be demanded. It follows that if consumption expenditure remains constant whilst investment expenditure increases, employment will rise. More money will be paid to entrepreneurs who are making capital goods and they will hire more labour. Similarly, if investment expenditure is constant but consumption expenditure is increased, employment will again rise. But, in fact, the demands for consumption and investment are interdependent. The relation between them is similar to that of complementarity between consumer goods. When consumption expenditure increases, investment expenditure will increase too. Since consumers are buying more consumption goods, entrepreneurs will feel willing to purchase machines and factories to produce such goods. Similarly, if investment expenditure rises, consumption expenditure rises too. For when there is more investment expenditure, more money will be paid to workers in investment industries, and they will spend this money on the products of the consumption goods industries. This complementary relationship between consumption demand and investment demand is important in employment theory, but it cannot be analysed except by general equilibrium theory. This is a further reason why we must now turn from particular to general equilibrium analysis.

3. THE 'MONEY ILLUSION'

We saw in the previous section that when there is general unemployment, theoretical analysis shows that *general* wage cuts may fail to remove that unemployment. And there is an important practical objection to cuts in wages in any economy where money is used. For in such an economy there is often what is known as a *money illusion*. That is to say, money is often regarded as having a fixed purchasing power in terms of commodities. The term money illusion is due to Professor Irving Fisher, who explained [1] that there is a money illusion, 'a failure to perceive that the dollar or any other unit of money expands and shrinks in value'. We simply take it for granted that 'a dollar is a dollar', that 'a franc is a franc', that all money is stable.

It follows from the existence of the money illusion that even if general unemployment *were* caused by wages everywhere being too high, the solution would probably be to cut workers' *real* wages, but not to cut their money wages. As Keynes says, 'whilst workers will usually resist a reduction of money wages, it is not their practice to withdraw their labour whenever there is a rise in the price of wage-goods'.[2] It is, of course, obvious that a very steep rise in the cost of living will cause considerable discontent amongst workers. But disturbances caused by falling purchasing power of money are likely to be very much less serious than those which would result from an attempt to cut money wages. One reason for the existence of the 'money illusion' may be that whilst workers do realise that a rise in prices reduces their real wages, they know that it does so as well to workers in all other industries. And it is possible that workers are more concerned with maintaining their position relatively to workers in other industries than with maintaining their absolute money wage. They are perhaps very concerned to keep their own money wages as high as possible compared with everyone else's, but they are not quite so worried if a rise in prices causes a proportionate fall in real wages in all industries at once. An additional reason for avoiding cuts in money wages is that whilst workers feel that a cut in money wages can be resisted by strikes, since it will be imposed by employers, they know that a fall in real wages is the result of more general economic forces which cannot normally be altered as a result of strike action. For all these reasons it is likely that *even if* more employment can be created only by a reduction in real wages, it is preferable for this to happen because of a rise in prices rather than because of cuts in money wages.

These considerations suggest that the existence of money can be an important factor in influencing the level of employment in

---

[1] *The Money Illusion*, p. 4. This book is based on a series of lectures given in the summer of 1927 at the Geneva School of International Studies.

[2] *Op. cit.* p. 9.

an economy. In fact the 'money' which we made use of in Part One was merely a 'measuring rod' introduced in order to enable us to discuss and compare the prices of different goods and factors of production. Money in the real world is a much more active force than the passive standard of value of Part One. In particular we assumed in Part One that it was impossible for people to save their income and hold it in the form of money. For example, in Chapter XIV we assumed that if people did not spend their money on consumption goods they spent it on investment goods. In the real world, however, it is possible for people to save a part of their incomes and hold it in the form of money, spending it neither on consumption goods nor on investment goods. This situation can occur because money performs the function of acting as a means of storing purchasing power in addition to its function of acting as a standard, or measure, of value. Money serves more than one purpose, and if we are to fully understand its importance we shall have to discuss the nature and functions of money in greater detail.

We have found in this chapter, then, that on the one hand the problems of unemployment are only capable of really satisfactory analysis in terms of general equilibrium theory, and that on the other hand the behaviour of money is one of the more important of the many factors determining the level of employment in the modern economy.

SUGGESTED READING

J. M. Keynes, *General Theory*, London, 1936, chapter ii.
Dudley Dillard, *The Economics of J. M. Keynes*, London, 1950, chapter ii.
Irving Fisher, *The Money Illusion*, London, 1928.

CHAPTER XVIII

MONEY

1. THE NATURE OF MONEY

THE previous chapter has shown us that the economy which we studied in Part One was an economy in which the complications caused by the fact that money is used were absent. It also showed that we can no longer afford to avoid discussing the economic significance of money, because the problems of unemployment are, to a large extent, problems peculiar to a monetary economy. In this chapter, therefore, we shall consider the nature and importance of money.

Throughout the history of the world, countries have found it necessary to begin to use money at an early stage of their development because of the extreme inconvenience of exchange by direct barter. The most troublesome feature of trade carried on by direct barter is that it means that there must always be a coincidence of wants between buyers and sellers. In practice, a man wanting to exchange goats for cabbages may spend several weeks before he finds anyone who has cabbages for sale and happens to want goats. This inconvenience can be avoided by the use of money. For the seller can sell his goats for money and keep this money until he finds cabbages for sale. So, from very early times, civilised societies have found that the most satisfactory method of carrying on trade is through the medium of one particular good, which then becomes money. All members of the society are henceforth prepared to receive payments in the form of this good, which is demanded even though it may not be edible and probably cannot be consumed in any other way. For everyone knows that everyone else will accept the 'money good' in payment for all other goods or services.

It is clearly natural to ask several questions at this stage. First, what exactly decides whether or not a good is money? Second, what are the functions of money? Third, how does money differ from other goods? To answer these questions, we must consider the demand for money and the supply of money. We shall therefore begin by discussing the nature and uses of money—by discovering what it is and why it is demanded. Later, we shall consider the supply of money and the factors which influence that supply.

Money, like all other goods, is demanded because it is useful. Money and other goods thus have one feature in common. But the reasons why money is useful are rather different from those which account for the usefulness of other goods. As we have already seen, such other goods can be divided into two categories. On the one hand there are consumer goods. These are goods which we can eat, wear, burn, or otherwise consume. On the other hand there are producer (or capital) goods, which aid the production of consumer goods. Machines and factories are not directly useful, but because they are useful indirectly they are essential for efficient production in modern societies.

How, then, does money compare with these ordinary consumer and producer goods? Money is not usually a consumer good. It cannot normally be eaten, drunk or consumed in any way. There do, admittedly, appear to be exceptions to this. For example, in Germany in the months just after the defeat of 1945 cigarettes took on the function of money. This seems to disprove our argument that money differs from consumer goods, but the state of affairs in Germany in 1945 was exceptional. Yet, even if such exceptions do exist, it is important to realise that the good which becomes money in such situations immediately takes on a distinct and separate function. The German in 1945 who owned cigarettes did not dream of smoking them if he could possibly avoid it. Having become money, cigarettes were quite different things, and their original function, that of acting as consumer goods, was sharply divided from their new one—that of acting as money. Money is never quite like an ordinary consumption good. Neither is money quite like a capital good. The essential feature of capital goods is that they manufacture their products by transforming them physically. The grains of wheat are made into flour, or the bars of steel into steel strip by a physical process. Money, on the other hand, is unable to perform such feats of physical transformation. Money performs an essentially different operation from that performed by capital goods.

It is clear, then, that money differs from both consumer and producer goods. Because of this, some economists have denied that money is useful at all. This view, of course, is wrong. Money *is* useful, but its usefulness is of an unusual kind. Money is *the* exchange good. It is useful only in an economy where exchange takes place, whilst the other goods are useful, at any rate in principle, in a one-man economy where there can be no exchange. A Robinson Crusoe finds food useful for the same reason as we do. He finds capital goods useful in the same way. But money is of no use to him at all. Only when Man Friday arrives does money become useful to a Crusoe. Money is useful in an exchange economy—and only in an exchange economy.

The *sine qua non* of any kind of money is that it must be *generally acceptable* to each and every member of the society which uses it. Money is useful to A because he knows that he can pay his debts to B with it. Similarly, money is useful to B because with it he can pay wages to C, and so on. But acceptability of this kind is not a physical attribute possessed by some goods and not by others. Acceptability of this kind is essentially a social phenomenon and all sorts of goods have, at various times and places, become money simply by acquiring this social quality. They then became acceptable to all and sundry, in payment of debt.

It is not necessary to be an anthropologist to see that it is society and not any physical characteristic which decides which goods shall and which shall not be money. There is no common physical characteristic of coins, bank notes and bank balances. Indeed, the bank balance, which is so vital a kind of money in modern society, has scarcely any physical constitution at all. Bank balances amount to no more than marks in ledgers. Yet all these types of money are accepted by everyone in payment of debt. For that reason, and for that reason alone, it is worth keeping stocks of them. The history of money—the study of all those goods which have been money at various times—is fascinating. But ours is a study of economic theory and we must ignore history. What is essential for our present purpose is to understand the nature and importance of the various kinds of money in present-day societies.

The main type of money in Great Britain at the moment is not coins or notes, but bank credit—the balances which people hold with the 'commercial', or 'joint-stock' banks.[1] Admittedly there is a large number of notes and coins in existence, but there is much more bank credit. Changes in the amount of money can nowadays usually be regarded as changes in the volume of bank deposits. It is true that many people deal in notes and coins, but they are mainly in the lower income groups. It is not

---

[1] The 'joint-stock' banks are independent institutions which are distinct from the 'central' bank, the Bank of England.

part of our present purpose to explain why these people are in the lower income groups ; but, acknowledging the fact that they are, we may note that they will play a far less significant part in the market than those richer people who deal almost exclusively in cheques. For the purposes of a theoretical analysis of this kind it is useful to ignore all those types of money which are analytically unimportant. We shall therefore concentrate our attention on bank deposits.

Another useful simplification which it will be convenient to make will be to rule out one or two complications which are historically and legally important but economically insignificant. First, we shall find it convenient to ignore the concept of legal tender. In Britain the only forms of legal tender are Bank of England notes to any amount, and coins of the realm to restricted amounts. Technically the State only recognises payments which are made in legal tender. The State can, and sometimes does, refuse to accept cheques in payment of fines. Bank deposits are thus not perfect substitutes for legal tender for all purposes. For most ordinary purposes, however, there is no distinction, though when goods are bought by cheque they often cannot be delivered until the cheque has been cleared.

It must always be remembered, however, that even legal tender may not function as money. Even though the State may give its sanction, or 'fiat', to a particular kind of legal tender, it will not function as money unless it is generally accepted. During the German inflation of the early 1920's marks were legal tender, but they were losing value so rapidly that they ceased to be generally acceptable, and therefore ceased to be money. To sum up, then, from the point of view of the economist, the notion of legal tender is not now very important.

Second, we shall ignore the precious metals which have for so long played a vitally important part in monetary systems. It seems inevitable that human ideas should lag somewhat behind events. This is especially true of ideas about money. Many people still think of money as in some way 'backed' by gold. This is not now the case in most countries. It is, of course, not very long since even the relatively small change of many economies was in the form of actual gold coins. Now they scarcely exist. Only in international trade is gold now of supreme importance. In international trade gold comes back into its own. We, however, are concerned with a closed economy and shall ignore gold. It should be remembered, however, that gold is nowadays not often used even as a basis for the credit structure. Few countries now hold a fixed proportion of gold as 'backing' for their bank notes. We in Britain disposed of much of our gold in the days before Lease-Lend when we had to finance the 1939–45 war on our own slender resources. Yet the fact that gold has ceased to 'back' the currency has not weakened confidence in the pound. The conventional foundation of the credit system has been taken away, but the structure itself remains as firm and strong as ever. People have ceased to worry whether notes are backed by gold or not. Money has only to be 'generally acceptable' to be money.

This idea that the sole prerequisite of any form of money is that it should be 'generally acceptable' troubles some people. They feel that it is far too slender a basis to bear the heavy burden of anything so important as money. The idea that you trust money because I do, and that I trust it because you do, sounds improbable to such folk. There may be some justification for such scepticism—but there is obviously not much. For there are many conventions of this type in our modern society. A university professor, for example, turns up promptly at 10 A.M. each Wednesday to lecture on economics. He does so because he has confidence that his class will come to hear him. Similarly, the class arrives each week because they have confidence in the fact that there will be a lecture. The convention stands because each side has confidence in it, and it even enables students to learn sufficient economics to pass examinations. So it is with money. As long as the convention holds and money is generally acceptable to everyone it retains its value.

2. THE FUNCTIONS OF MONEY

Having seen what are the essential characteristics of money, we must try to see what functions it has to perform. There are four functions of money. First, it must serve as a unit of account. The individual member of the economy has to have some common denominator which can perform the task of measuring the relative prices of such different commodities as wallflowers and washbasins, steam-rollers and sardines. This important task is performed by money. We have already seen that the main disadvantage of a barter economy is that wants must always coincide. Another is that rates of exchange between commodities cannot easily be worked out. It is extremely difficult to do this, except in terms of some standard measure, for precisely the same reasons as it would be very difficult to compare the lengths of the *Queen Mary* and the *Mauretania* if there were no unit of linear measurement. One would be forced to resort to some standard of measurement, whether paces, pieces of string or planks of wood. And if one has to use such standards each time one measures anything, it is only sensible that one particular standard should be accepted as *the* standard. Money is *the* standard for measuring value, as the foot, yard or metre is *the* standard for measuring length. This function of money as a standard measure of value is known as its function of acting as a 'numeraire'. It is for this purpose alone that we have used money so far in our analysis.

It is clear, on reflection, that if a particular commodity is to be used as a unit of account, it will be very convenient for it to act also as the commodity through which exchange is carried on. This leads us to the second function of money. It acts as a medium of exchange. This is the most obvious function of money and it is in the performance of this particular function that the notion of general acceptability is most clearly brought out. A good will not act as a convenient circulating medium unless it is accepted by everyone. But it is important that just because this is the most obvious function of money it should not be thought of as the only function of money. The other functions are little less important.

Third, money functions as a store of value. The good chosen as money is always something which can be kept for long periods without deterioration or wastage. It is a form in which wealth can be kept intact from one year to the next. Money is a bridge from present to future. It is therefore essential that money should always be a commodity which can be easily and safely stored. This explains the popularity of gold in the past. For it does not suffer from physical deterioration. It also explains the popularity of bank deposits now, for they are perfectly safe unless the bank's ledgers are burned or stolen, both unlikely contingencies. Fourth, and last, money acts as a standard of deferred payments. Loans are usually made in money and not in tobacco or chocolates. Since this is the case, it would be a little odd if repayments were made otherwise than in money. It is also always convenient for debts to be measured in terms of what is usually a stable store of value—money.

One of the conveniences of using money, then, is that it usually represents a stable medium in which debts can be contracted and repaid. The importance of this stability can be seen when one considers the consequences of an inflation which is serious enough to cause monetary breakdown. It is losing its value so rapidly. The first consequence is invariably that money ceases to fulfil its function as a standard of deferred payments. Instead of being contracted in terms of the currency of the country in question, debts are contracted in terms of the currencies of other countries whose monetary systems are more stable; in terms of precious metals, or in terms of commodities, perhaps wheat. Money ceases to function as a standard of deferred payments even if for the time being it fulfils its other functions. Logically, then, these functions can be separated. If necessary, each function could be performed by a different good. But in practice they are connected, and in any normal economy the functions are performed by the same good. In our analysis we shall assume that this is always the case.

In practice, once money has ceased to function as a standard of deferred payments, it also ceases to act as a store of value. If it is not worth while agreeing to pay debts in money because money is losing value too rapidly, it will not be worth storing money. For the value of the store may be decimated overnight. Once money ceases to fulfil this third function, its ability to perform the first two functions will be called into question as well. Calculations of prices involving vast numbers are difficult, and both accountants and ordinary citizens will long to return to the simple arithmetic when a loaf of bread cost 2 marks and not 29,234,768,221. Quite apart from this, when inflation has reached such a stage, no producer or consumer will know from one day to the next how high prices ought to be, and the sheer labour of recalculating all prices daily, or even more often, will be unbearable. The last function which money is likely to fail to fulfil is that of acting as a medium of exchange. So long as one can spend one's money fast enough to prevent prices rising too far before one's dealings are complete, money will still be exchanged for goods. But when inflation is really serious—when there is 'hyper' inflation—the position is likely to arise where no-one wants to keep money—even for a few minutes. Once this happens, a completely new money will have to be used.

3. DEMAND FOR MONEY

The explanation of the four functions of money given above is the traditional one and it is certainly one which has retained its usefulness. But for our purposes in discussing employment theory, we shall find it useful to discuss money also in other, more modern, terms. Instead of considering the functions of money in more detail, it will be useful to classify the reasons for which money is demanded, that is to say, the reasons why people want a stock of money to hold.

The demand for money, or 'liquidity preference' as Keynes called it, depends on three motives. These are : (i) the transactions motive, (ii) the precautionary motive, (iii) the speculative motive. Let us consider these motives upon which the demand for money depends in detail.

(i) THE TRANSACTIONS MOTIVE

People receive their income weekly, monthly, or sometimes quarterly or even yearly. But they spend this money at much shorter intervals. Although some payments, among them those for rent, gas or electricity, are made weekly, monthly or quarterly, many payments are made daily, for food, travel or amusement. Because income is received at discrete intervals of time but is paid out more or less continuously, it is inevitable that people should need a certain small stock of money all the time, to enable them to carry out their transactions. The sort of inconvenience which people would suffer if they held no money to satisfy the transactions motive are typified by the feelings of the man who finds himself on the top of a bus without as much as a farthing, or learns that one of his cheques has been returned marked R/D. Everyone holds some money, however little, to satisfy the transactions motive.

The transactions motive can be looked at from the point of view of two sets of individuals, (a) consumers and (b) entrepreneurs.

(a) *The Income Motive.*—From the consumer's point of view the amount of money which he will hold to satisfy the transactions motive will depend both on the size of his income and on the intervals of time between the receipt of the various instalments. His demand for money can thus be classified as depending on the *income motive*. It is fairly clear why the amount of money held will depend on the length of time between the receipt of instalments of income. Let us consider two men, both earning £8 per week, one being paid weekly and the other every two months. Assuming that they both spend £8 each week, the first man will hold, on average, £4. At the beginning of the week he will have £8, and at the end of the week he will have nothing. On the average he will have £4. The second man will receive £64 every two months. Assuming that he spends £8 each week throughout the two months, he will have an average of £32 in his bank account, or in notes. The demand by consumers as a whole for money under the transactions motive thus depends on the (average) length of the interval between successive pay-days.

It may not be quite so clear why the amount of money held under the income motive will vary with the *size* of a person's income. Assuming that there are two men, one earning £40 a month and the other £80, and that they both spend $\frac{1}{30}$th of their income each day during the month ; the one with the larger income will hold £40 on average to the other's £20. It is, of course, not really likely that each will, in fact, spend the whole of his income so evenly through the month. It does, however, seem reasonable to think that a rich man will hold more money to satisfy his income motive than a poor man will. The income motive is likely to mean that there is a greater demand for money, both by individuals and by society as a whole, as income increases. Thus, the community's demand for money will be in rough proportion to the size of the national income.

(*b*) *The Business Motive.*—Entrepreneurs will also wish to hold a certain amount of money in the bank accounts of their firms. They will need money in the bank all the time in order to pay for raw materials and transport, to pay wages and salaries and to meet all the other current expenses incurred by any business. Money held by producers in this way is said to be held to satisfy the business motive. It is clear that the amount of money held under this business motive will depend to a very large extent on the turnover of the firm in question. The larger the turnover the larger, in general, will be the amount of money needed to cover current expenses.

It follows that the amount of money held under the transactions motive will depend (*a*) on the size of personal incomes and (*b*) on the turnover of businesses. As incomes rise and as businesses become more prosperous, the amount of money demanded for the transactions motive will rise. This money held under the transactions motive, will, broadly speaking, be fulfilling the function of providing a medium of exchange.

(ii) THE PRECAUTIONARY MOTIVE

The money which people hold under the precautionary motive will be devoted, broadly speaking, to fulfilling the function of a

2 B

store of value. It is possible to liken the amount of money held under the transactions motive to water in a bath. It is as though water is being fed into the bath through one hose-pipe and is being taken out of it through another. The aim of the individual concerned is to see that there is enough water in the bath all the time for something to be running out, even when nothing is running in. Carrying on the simile, money held under the precautionary motive is rather like water kept in reserve in a separate tank. Money held under this motive is kept to provide for a rainy day. People hold a certain amount of money to provide for the danger of unemployment, sickness, accidents and other more uncertain perils. The amount of money held in this way will depend on the individual and on the conditions in which he lives. If he is nervous, he will hold much money; if he is sanguine, he will hold little. If times are prosperous, he will be optimistic; if there is depression, he will not. The amount of money held is not likely to represent a constant proportion of a man's income, though in general a rich man is likely to hold more money than a poor one to satisfy this precautionary motive. But this is not necessarily so. The amount held will depend on the individual.

(iii) THE SPECULATIVE MOTIVE

The third motive for holding money is the speculative motive. The notion of the speculative motive for holding money was not an evolution from the traditional functions of money, but is a new, typically Keynesian, idea. Money held under the speculative motive constitutes a store of value just as money held under the precautionary motive does. But it is a store of money intended to fulfil a different purpose. The store of value implied by the precautionary motive is one which helps the holder in times of difficulty. He is able, let us say, to avoid selling his house if bad times come.

Money held under the speculative motive, on the other hand, constitutes a store of value—a liquid asset—which the holder intends to use for gambling, to make a speculative gain. The money is held in a bank account to be invested in securities at an opportune moment. As readers will be aware, there are numerous securities which can be purchased which yield a fixed annual yield in terms of money, known as 'bonds'.[1] Good examples of

[1] Securities which do not yield a fixed and known amount of interest each year are known as 'equities'. Such, for example, are the ordinary shares of businesses.

bonds are Government securities—Consols or British Transport Stock—or the 'debentures' of ordinary businesses.

Now, since the annual yield on bonds is fixed, a change in the rate of interest will alter the prices of all bonds. For example, if a bond is issued at a time when the rate of interest is 4 per cent, the Government (or whoever issues it) will offer £4 each year to every purchaser of such a security who is prepared to pay £100 for it. If, later, the rate of interest changes to 2 per cent, the market price of this bond will rise to £200; for a new purchaser will not care whether he pays £100 for a new security giving a £2 yield (*i.e.* 2 per cent) or £200 for the old one which pays £4 per annum. He will earn 2 per cent on his money in either case. Again, if the rate of interest rises from 4 to 8 per cent, the value of the original bond will fall from £100 to £50. Changes in the rate of interest inevitably mean changes in bond prices.

It is therefore possible for individuals to make money for themselves by buying bonds when they are cheap (when the rate of interest is high) and selling them when they are dearer (when the rate of interest has fallen). Now, it is obvious that no-one knows for certain what interest rates will be in the future. Because of this uncertainty, it is possible for people to make capital gains by guessing correctly when rises and falls in bond prices are going to occur. People therefore hold money under this speculative motive in order to buy bonds (or equities for that matter) with it when the rate of interest has reached such a high level that they feel it must fall again. They make capital gains by speculating in securities, hoping to gain from knowing better than others in the market what the future holds in store.

The amount of money held under this speculative motive will therefore depend on the rate of interest. When most people expect the rate of interest to fall—when almost everyone expects prices of bonds to rise—they will buy securities hoping to sell them later when the price is higher. At such times, the amount of money held under the speculative motive is relatively small. If, however, people expect share prices to fall—if they expect a rise in the rate of interest—they will hold cash. Much more money will be held under the speculative motive. Then when the slump in share prices has run its course, they will switch into bonds at what they hope is the psychological moment, and make speculative gains as bonds become dearer once more.

These three motives, transactions, precautionary and speculative, will between them determine the demand for money. They are vital in employment theory because, as we shall discover later, changes in the demand for money are extremely important as a cause of fluctuations in employment. There is, however, one important aspect of the demand for money which we must stress. This is the essential difference between the demand for money and the demand for a commodity. When we speak of a consumer *demanding* a good, we envisage him deciding how much he can afford to buy, then giving up money to obtain it. Drawing a parallel, it might be thought that when we consider the demand for money, we can explain it by analysing the reasons for which people are prepared to give up goods in order to obtain money. There is one sense, of course, in which there is a demand for money which is constituted, in a given period of time, by the supply of all the goods offered in exchange for money during that period. But this is much more conveniently described as the *total production of the community*. The demand for money, in economic analysis, is the demand for the existing stock of money which is available to hold. The demand for money means the demand for money *to hold*. So, when one speaks of an increased demand for money, one means that the community wishes to hold a larger amount of money.

It is important always to remember that the demand for money—or 'liquidity preference' as it is often called—is always the demand for money to hold.

4. SUPPLY OF MONEY

The supply of money is defined in a similar manner. In the case of the supply of a commodity, we mean the amount which entrepreneurs sell. This supply is a flow over time. Goods are being continually produced. With money it is different. The supply of money, like the demand for money, is the supply of money *to hold*. Unless money is held by someone, it cannot exist. So the supply of money is the existing stock of money, all of which is held by someone. In other words, the supply of money at any moment is the sum of all the money holdings of all the members of the community.

There is, of course, one sense in which there is a supply of money which in a given period constitutes a demand for goods. All the money spent in a given period is a kind of demand for all the goods bought. But this is more conveniently regarded as the *total expenditure of the community*. It is not the supply of money.

The supply of money is the total stock of money. The two things
are related, but it is important to distinguish between them carefully.

We shall therefore use these terms, demand and supply of
money, to denote demand for and supply of a stock of money.
An increase in the supply of money, then, means not the sale of
money by those who possess it, but an increase in the money
stock. We shall find later that, quite apart from the convenience
of enabling us to distinguish easily between the 'supply of money'
and 'total money expenditure', this method of denoting demand
and supply of money as the demand and supply of money to hold
is especially appropriate in the case of money. There are some
very tricky problems which can only be solved if one is quite
certain about the real meaning of demand and supply of money.

It may seem rather arbitrary to define the supply of money
in this way. But the supply of any other commodity is a flow
and not a stock. Ordinary commodities are being continuously
produced, sold and consumed. There is a continuous stream of
all other goods being poured out of factories and it is this stream,
or flow, which we analyse in treating the supply of ordinary
commodities. It is realistic to regard the supply of money as a
stock because money is *not* being continually produced and consumed in the same way as goods are. Money, being a means of
exchange, is in a sense immortal. There is a stock of money
which is used over and over again for many different purposes
and in many different ways.

What, then, constitutes this supply or stock of money? We
shall concentrate our attention on bank money. In doing so we
shall ignore the *fiduciary issue* of bank notes. The fiduciary issue
was important in the past because it represented all those bank
notes which were not 'backed' by the gold which was in the
vaults of the central bank. Nowadays it is merely a pleasant
fiction suggesting that some notes are covered by gold and some
are not. In practice, the size of the fiduciary issue is decided now,
not by the amount of gold in the central bank, but automatically,
by the demand of the community for notes. The community
decides to hold so much of its money in the form of notes and the
central bank issues those notes. When, as at Christmas, people
want more notes to use for Christmas shopping, the fiduciary
issue is automatically raised. Economically the size of the
fiduciary issue is unimportant. The community decides to hold
a certain percentage of its money in the form of notes and the rest

in the form of bank balances. The central bank then issues enough notes to allow this decision to become a reality. From an economic viewpoint, the distinction between bank notes and bank accounts is unimportant.

The supply of money, then, is the total amount of money which is held. Ignoring bank notes, because, as we have seen, they bear a fairly definite ratio to bank balances, the supply of money is the supply of balances in joint-stock banks. It is therefore time to discuss the nature of bank balances—bank deposits, as they are usually called—and the way in which the amount of such deposits is determined.

5. ADVANCES CREATE DEPOSITS

A bank deposit is a liability to the bank but an asset to the customer. The banker is bound to make the deposit available to his customer in whatever form he wishes. The customer, on the other hand, can regard it with satisfaction as good, solid money. A community's supply of bank money is thus the sum-total of all the bank deposits of all members of the community. An increase or decrease in the supply of bank money will be represented by a rise or fall in the total volume of bank deposits. To understand the significance of such changes in the supply of money, we must discover how the volume of bank deposits in a country can vary.

Bank deposits, as we have seen, are supplied by joint-stock banks, but they cannot issue just as many as they wish. The volume of bank deposits in Great Britain is ultimately controlled by the Bank of England. Whether nationalised or not, the Bank of England in this country, and the various central banks of other countries, control the volume of bank deposits in their own countries. Our search for the factor determining the size of bank deposits will lead us ultimately to study the policy of the central bank. There are two stages in the analysis. First, we must discover why, given the policy of the central bank, the joint-stock banks are able to supply bank deposits at all, and to what amount. Second, we must see how the central bank can increase or decrease the volume of such deposits when it thinks it is necessary to increase or decrease the supply of money.

The first question to be asked is, How do joint-stock banks supply deposits? The answer is, in the words of the old banking maxim, that 'every advance creates a deposit'. Every time a joint-stock bank lends, or 'advances', money to a client, it creates a deposit. It is important that this principle should be fully understood.

The plain man's idea of the way in which bank deposits are created is probably roughly as follows. Somehow one gets hold of some bank notes (perhaps by stealing them). One then goes to a bank and asks to be allowed to open an account. One hands over the notes. The amount of money is entered in a ledger and the account is there. A bank deposit has been created. This, however, is not the normal way in which bank deposits are created. Bank deposits are usually created by a business man, with little or no spare cash, going to a bank, explaining what good prospects he has, and asking for a loan of, say, £10,000 to enable him to engage in business. Having proved that he is honest and reputable, and perhaps having left collateral security, the entrepreneur is given an advance of £10,000 with which he opens an account. This time a deposit really has been 'created'. Bank deposits, then, are not given *in exchange* for bank notes. They really are created by allowing business men to open accounts with money which is 'advanced' to them.

The bank deposit is created entirely by the banking system. The borrower deposits the advance in his account and is able to use it for financing his firm. By making this advance, the banker has therefore created a corresponding deposit. The two things are created simultaneously. The granting of an advance implies the creation of a deposit and *vice versa*. What is it, then, that puts a limit on the amount of credit creation which bankers undertake? This is the second problem which we set out to solve.

It might be thought that the answer lies in the credit-worthiness, or otherwise, of borrowers. This does, of course, invariably enter into bankers' decisions, but it is not of fundamental importance. There are occasions when bankers refuse to make advances even to first-class borrowers. Money is 'tight', it is said. This makes it clear that there are other limits to the ability of bankers to make advances besides the credit-worthiness of borrowers. The ultimate limiting factor is a convention of the banking profession. Bankers always keep a definite ratio between the volume of deposits which they issue and the amount of 'cash' which they possess. This 'cash ratio', as it is called, is the real limit on credit creation in the modern banking system. Nowadays joint-stock banks hold £1 in 'cash' for every £12 in deposits. Part of this 'cash' is in the form of bank notes and coin, but the rest takes the form of 'deposits' with the Bank of England. We shall discuss the importance of these deposits in the next section, but we can say now that the joint-stock banks can look on them as 'cash' because the Bank of England will always supply notes for them if required to do so. So long, therefore, as the joint-stock banks abide by the 'cash ratio', the volume of bank deposits must bear a given proportion to the amount of 'cash' which they hold. And since that part of 'cash' which is mere 'till money' will remain roughly constant, it will be on changes in deposits with the central bank that changes in the volume of bank deposits will depend.

It follows that so long as bankers maintain the 12 to 1 'cash ratio', a fall in the volume of bank deposits must be the result of a decrease in the amount of 'cash'. If we can see how such a decrease can come about, we shall have gone some way towards explaining why changes in the supply of money occur. First, however, we must notice how the change does *not* take place. A fall in the 'cash' held by a bank does not result from the fact that customers draw out cash to spend on household and personal expenditure, that firms pay wages to labour and that shops draw out till-money. This money is engaged in a circular process. It will soon be spent and will return to the bank, whence it will be withdrawn once more. Only over very long periods, or in very exceptional circumstances, for instance in time of war, will the amount of cash used under this 'transactions' motive change, assuming that the size of the national income remains roughly the same. In normal times, people will tend to draw out and pay in the same amount of cash into the bank week after week, month after month and year after year. The amount held will always average out, and the fact that money *is* drawn out provides no explanation of changes in the volume of bank deposits. Advances are created or destroyed because of changes in the amount of 'cash', and the reasons for such changes cannot be found in the actions of customers of the joint-stock banks. To find the reason for changes in the volume of deposits we must turn our attention instead to the deposits which joint-stock banks hold at the Bank of England.

6. OPEN-MARKET OPERATIONS

As we have suggested, the crucial factor controlling the volume of a community's deposits in the joint-stock banks is the size of the joint-stock banks' own deposits at the central bank. These deposits, known as 'bankers' deposits', are included in the 'cash reserve' of the joint-stock banks. If the central bank can alter the amount of these deposits, it can *ipso facto* alter the volume of bank deposits—it can control the supply of money. The central bank can, in fact, do this by means of what are known as 'open-market operations'. Here, the central bank's agent goes into the public, or 'open', market for either long- or short-term Government securities, and buys or sells securities, according to whether it is desired to create or destroy bank deposits. In this way the central bank is able to exert an ultimate control over the supply of money, with all that such control entails.

The way in which the central bank controls the volume of bank deposits can be seen most clearly if one considers first of all the case of a simplified banking system with a central bank and only one joint-stock bank. If the central bank buys £1000 worth of securities, it pays the seller with a draft on itself. This draft is paid by the seller into his account with the joint-stock bank, and the bank's deposit with the central bank increases by £1000. On this basis, the joint-stock bank is able to issue an additional £1000 of deposits by making loans to business men. There we have the essence of open-market operations. By buying securities, the central bank is able to increase the deposits of the joint-stock banks—it increases the supply of money.

But this example is too simple, and we must complicate it. It is unrealistic to think that the process of credit creation will stop where we have left it. As we have seen, the existence of the 'cash ratio' means that bankers can create £12 deposits for each £1 of 'cash'. In this case, then, the addition of £1000 to the 'cash' of the joint-stock bank will enable it to create not £1000 but £12,000 of new deposits. The effect of open-market operations is thus much greater than it would be if there were only a one-to-one cash ratio. There is a multiple effect on deposits each time the central bank buys securities. The extent to which the original purchase will be magnified in its final effect will depend on the size of the cash-deposit ratio. The smaller the proportion of cash compared with deposits, the larger the ultimate effect of a given open-market purchase of securities will be.

Here we have, in outline, the effect of open-market operations. By buying securities, the central bank increases the supply of money, provided that the banks continue to observe the cash 1 : 12 ratio. And since banks earn interest on all advances they make, it will pay them to create deposits up to the full 1 to 12 limit. Again, if the cash ratio happens to be higher or lower than

1 : 12, the total effect of a given purchase of securities on deposits will be smaller or greater as the case may be. So long as the joint-stock banks play the game and adhere strictly to the existing cash ratio, the central bank has full control over the supply of money.

We have only spoken so far of the central bank buying securities. If the central bank sells securities, the effect will be of the same kind but in precisely the opposite direction. If the central bank sells £1000 worth of securities, these will have to be paid for out of the ordinary deposits of the joint-stock bank. Whoever buys the securities will have to pay £1000 to the central bank. The result will therefore be to reduce the balance of the joint-stock bank with the central bank by £1000. Since this represents part of the joint-stock bank's 'cash', it will find it necessary to reduce the amount of its total deposits in order to maintain its 'cash ratio'. It has less cash and must therefore have fewer deposits. Since in practice the cash-deposit ratio will be about 1 to 12, the reduction of £1000 in the joint-stock bank's 'cash' will cause a reduction of £12,000 in its deposits. There will be a multiple effect of the central bank's open-market operations, this time in the direction of reducing the volume of bank credit. The exact extent of the reduction will, as we have seen for the case of an increase, depend on the size of the cash ratio.

We have so far assumed that open-market operations are taking place in a system with only one joint-stock bank. In practice there will be more than one joint-stock bank, but this makes no difference in principle to the analysis we have outlined. The central bank will still be able to control the deposits of all the joint-stock banks, provided they all abide by the cash-deposit ratio. It may happen at times that the effect of open-market operations may cause a greater effect on the deposits of one joint-stock bank than another because its own customers are buying or selling a large proportion of the securities sold or bought by the central bank. But there is no reason why this should happen except over very short periods, and in any case the total volume of deposits in joint-stock banks, as distinct from the deposits of individual joint-stock banks, will be unaffected. So long as the cash ratio is maintained at the existing level, and strictly adhered to, the central bank can carry out open-market operations just as efficiently where there are a hundred joint-stock banks as where there is only one. And in practice, even where there is no legal obligation to do so, bankers always keep closely to the cash-deposit ratio.

This leads us to an important point. We have seen that the only condition which must be fulfilled for open-market operations to be fully effective is that the cash-deposit ratio should be carefully maintained. In fact this means that the central bank is much more easily able to reduce the volume of money in the community than to increase it. For if the central bank sells securities and thus reduces the joint-stock banks' deposits with it, financial prudence will force the joint-stock banks to reduce their clients' deposits. They will not wish to give the impression that they are keeping too little 'cash' in hand. On the other hand, if the central bank buys securities, although the joint-stock banks would then be able to expand the deposits of their clients and still maintain the cash ratio, there is no guarantee that these clients would be willing to borrow. For, as we shall see later, central banks will normally only undertake the purchase of securities in times of depressed trade, in the hope of stimulating business activity by making more credit available to business men, and at such times lending is not always easy. It will therefore be found that the central bank's control over the volume of money in a country is more effective in a downward than in an upward direction.

SUGGESTED READING

Geoffrey Crowther, *An Outline of Money*, London, 1940, chapters i and ii.
R. S. Sayers, *Modern Banking*, Oxford, 1951, chapters i, ii and v.
W. S. Jevons, *Money and the Mechanism of Exchange*, London, 1875, chapter iii.
D. H. Robertson, *Money*, London, 1948, chapters i and iii.

CHAPTER XIX

THE THEORY OF EMPLOYMENT

1. A 'GENERAL THEORY OF EMPLOYMENT'

HAVING explained what money is, we can now return to the main theme of Part Two and explain the ideas put forward by J. M. Keynes in *The General Theory of Employment, Interest and Money*, published in 1936. It is interesting to note at the outset that the *General Theory* was intended to provide a more systematic and realistic explanation of the causes of unemployment than that given by the 'classical' economists, some of whose ideas we mentioned in Chapter XVII. Keynes maintained that, especially by their acceptance of Say's Law, the 'classical' economists had assumed away the problems of unemployment and had discussed a world in which unemployment did not exist.

The Keynesian theory is conceived to be 'general' in the sense that it applies equally well to economies with less than full employment, in a way that the 'classical' theory would not.

It is difficult to be sure whether Keynes' indictment of the 'classical' economists on this score is entirely fair, but they certainly discussed the problems of the general level of economic activity on so few occasions that it is reasonable to think that they did not regard them as of particular importance. As we saw in Chapter XVII, however, there do seem to be serious defects in the 'classical' theory of employment wherever this *is* explicitly stated. It will therefore be desirable to discuss some of the differences between Keynesian and 'classical' theory. It seems best to leave this discussion over until a later stage, after we have outlined Keynes' own ideas.

The essential idea put forward in the *General Theory* is quite simple and we shall begin by explaining it. In the individual firm, employment depends on the entrepreneur's ideas about how many men he must employ to maximise profits. In the economy as a whole, employment depends on the decisions of all individual employers, added together, about how many men to employ in order to maximise profits. The main factors which determine the level of employment in the economy as a whole, Keynes calls aggregate supply and aggregate demand. At any given level of employment of labour, aggregate supply price is the total amount of money which all the entrepreneurs in the economy, taken together, *must expect to receive* from the sale of the output produced by that given number of men, if it is to be just worth employing them. In other words, the aggregate supply price, when any given number of men is employed, is the total cost of producing the output made by that number of men. Unless entrepreneurs as a whole expect to cover their costs when they employ, say, X men, they will not think it worth while employing so much labour, and employment will be reduced. On the other hand, the aggregate demand price at any level of employment is the amount of money which all the entrepreneurs in the economy taken together *really do expect* that they will receive if they sell the output produced by this given number of men. It represents the expected receipts when a given volume of employment is offered to workers.

Now, there will be both an aggregate demand price and an aggregate supply price for each possible level of employment in an economy. One can therefore construct aggregate demand and supply curves (or schedules) showing aggregate demand and supply prices at all possible levels of employment. The aggregate supply curve, or function, shows how much receipts entrepreneurs *must receive* if they are to find it just worth their while to employ the various numbers of men. It therefore shows how much employment it would just pay entrepreneurs to offer (or 'supply') if they expected to receive various different amounts of money from the sale of the output made by the men they employ. The aggregate demand curve, on the other hand, will show, for these same levels of employment, how much money entrepreneurs *really do think they would receive* if they were to employ these same numbers of men.

Aggregate demand and supply curves are drawn in Figure 113. Up the y-axis are shown various amounts of proceeds (receipts) received by all entrepreneurs in the economy, taken together, from the sale of output. This is, of course, the same thing, looked at from a different angle, as expenditure by the community on the entrepreneurs' output. Along the x-axis are measured volumes of employment. The aggregate supply curve (AS) shows, for each possible volume of receipts by entrepreneurs from the sale of output, how many men it would be just worth employing. For example, if entrepreneurs expected to receive £OM′, it would just pay them to employ OP′ men. The curve AD in Figure 113 is the aggregate demand curve and shows how much money entrepreneurs really do expect to receive when they employ various numbers of men. For example, if OP′ men were employed, entrepreneurs would expect to receive £OM″ from selling the output produced.

In Figure 113 the aggregate supply curve rises slowly to begin with, implying that employment would increase fairly rapidly at

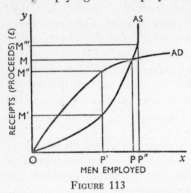

FIGURE 113

first as amounts received from selling the output of industry rose above zero. In other words, costs of production would not initially rise very sharply. If the amounts received by entrepreneurs continued to rise, employment would rise progressively less sharply until ultimately all those who wanted jobs were employed. In Figure 113 there are OP″ men wanting jobs, and once entrepreneurs' receipts had risen to £OM‴, it would be worth employing all of them. But no increase in the receipts of entrepreneurs (expenditure of the community) beyond £OM‴ would increase employment further. The elasticity of supply of labour has fallen to zero once national expenditure (income) reaches £OM‴. On the other hand, the shape of the aggregate demand curve implies that expected proceeds from offering employment rise quite steeply as employment first rises, but that the rapidity of this rise tends to slacken somewhat when employment reaches high levels. This seems likely to be the case. With income at low levels the community will be too poor to save much of its earnings.

The aggregate demand and supply curves for any community between them determine the volume of employment which actually is offered by entrepreneurs. So long as the amount of money which entrepreneurs *expect to receive* from offering a given volume of employment exceeds the amount which they *must receive* to make that volume of employment just worth while, competition between entrepreneurs will increase employment. For we shall assume throughout Part Two that there is perfect competition, unless an explicit statement to the contrary is given.

This means that so long as profitable opportunities for additional employment exist (and they will exist so long as aggregate demand price exceeds aggregate supply price) competition between entrepreneurs will force employment up. Thus, in Figure 113 so long as employment is below OP, competition between entrepreneurs will raise it. For with employment less than OP, the aggregate demand curve is always to the left of the aggregate supply curve—aggregate demand price is always greater than aggregate supply price.

On the other hand, if employment is greater than OP, the aggregate demand curve lies to the right of the aggregate supply curve. Entrepreneurs expect to receive less at each level of employment than the minimum amount of money required to make that amount of employment worth offering, and they would lose money if they were to employ more than OP men. The decisions of individual entrepreneurs will thus lower employment to OP, for they will all wish to avoid losses and will reduce

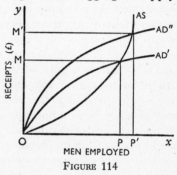

FIGURE 114

employment to do so. The level of employment in a community will thus be fixed by the intersection of the aggregate demand curve with the aggregate supply curve. Only if the amount of proceeds which entrepreneurs *expect to receive* from providing any given number of jobs is just equal to the amount which they *must receive* if the employment of those men is to be worth while, can the economy as a whole be in equilibrium. In Figure 113 this will happen when employment is OP and total receipts of £OM are expected by entrepreneurs. This is the only possible equilibrium position with the curves AD and AS, assuming that there is perfect competition.

There is an important corollary to this fact. Although with given aggregate demand and supply curves there will normally only be one position of equilibrium, this need not be at the level of full employment.

For example, in Figure 114 two different equilibrium situations are shown. With a single given aggregate supply curve AS and with the aggregate demand curve AD′ the economy is in equilibrium with the expected receipts of producers at £OM and employment at OP. But there are OP' men in the economy who want to work and there are therefore PP' men unemployed in this equilibrium position. The economy may perfectly well be in equilibrium and yet have men out of work. In this instance, only if the community is expected to spend at least £OM on the output of industry will all the available OP' men be employed. The aggregate demand curve AD" is one showing a situation where entrepreneurs do expect to receive just sufficient money to make it worth their while to give jobs to everyone who wants a job. OP' men are employed and entrepreneurs receive £OM'.

We can see, then, that there is nothing making full employment inevitable. An economy will only be one where unemployment is non-existent if aggregate demand is sufficiently large to make it worth while employing all who want jobs. This situation, where an economy is in equilibrium at the level of full employment, is in a sense an 'optimum' situation. Aggregate demand and supply are in an optimum relationship. But there is no reason for supposing that this is the *usual* relationship. The economy may just as easily be in equilibrium with some (or many) men unemployed. The 'classical theory' of employment, with its basic assumption of full employment, was over-optimistic.

One point of importance must be mentioned here. The type of unemployment we are interested in is *involuntary* unemployment. There may also be *frictional* unemployment where men are changing jobs; *structural* unemployment where one or more declining industries are suffering from severe unemployment; and *voluntary* unemployment where some workers are not willing to work at all—at least unless wages rise. Yet all these types of unemployment can be adequately dealt with on the basis of ordinary partial equilibrium theory. It is the problem of involuntary general unemployment—of men from all (or almost all) industries in the country, who are willing to work for the existing wage, or even for less, but who simply cannot find jobs—which is incapable of explanation on the basis of ordinary price theory. This is the type of unemployment whose existence was ignored, or even denied, by 'classical' economists, and we shall proceed to explain how it can occur.

2. AGGREGATE SUPPLY

We have seen that employment depends on the aggregate demand and aggregate supply schedules. It is therefore important that we should explain what these are in greater detail. The aggregate supply schedule depends, in the last resort, on physical conditions of production. As we saw in Part One, increased output of the product of any one industry is usually associated with increased employment. But this increased output and employment must be paid for. So long as marginal costs in an industry are positive, increased output is only worth producing if extra payment is made. Whether costs are increasing, decreasing or constant, extra output always means extra cost, however small. It follows that if more men are to be employed by an industry, enough extra income must be expected by that industry to make it worth while taking them on. The aggregate supply curve will therefore slope upwards to the right. More men will be employed if, but only if, entrepreneurs expect to be paid more money for the larger output produced by these men.

The aggregate supply schedule will thus slope upwards to the right. But what shape will it be ? This is a more difficult question to answer. To do so, let us make two simplifying assumptions, which we shall retain throughout our analysis of employment. Let us assume first that the money prices of all goods and factors are constant. Let us also assume that employment and output (measured at these constant prices) rise and fall in proportion with each other. That is to say, if output in money terms doubles, we assume that employment doubles also. This will make our task easier. But we must remember that this assumption is not altogether realistic.

It is not the case that every £100 spent on the products of industry has exactly the same effect on employment and output. £100 spent on, say, steel, in whose production much machinery is used but not very many men, would create less employment than £100 spent on haircuts, where little capital is used and many men. Thus, whilst it seems likely that output and employment will rise and fall together, there is no real reason why they should rise and fall exactly in step. In other words, the function relating number of men employed (N) and output (O) is likely in practice to be of the type $N = f(O)$ and not of the type $N = k(O)$, where k is a constant. Nevertheless, for the sake of simplicity we shall make the assumption that employment and income do rise and fall in exact proportion.

This is a very useful simplification because it enables us to avoid some serious difficulties. Changes in output are very difficult to measure unless only one good is being produced,

2 C

because one has no common standard by which to compare outputs of different goods. For example, if an economy produces ten more spades but ten fewer hoes, has output in general risen or fallen? One cannot say. On the other hand, changes in the volume of employment are much more easily dealt with. Different numbers of men are much easier to compare than are different combinations of wheelbarrows, refrigerators, beehives and pineapples. By concentrating on changes in employment, index number problems of this kind will be avoided.

Assuming that employment and output always change in exact proportion, what will be the shape of the aggregate supply schedule? It starts as a straight line from the origin and remains so up to the full employment level, but it becomes vertical once the level of full employment is reached. Clearly, the aggregate supply schedule must be vertical at full employment since employment can never rise above this level. The steepness of the sloping portion of the curve, however, will depend on production conditions in the economy in question.

The aggregate supply schedule, then, depends on technical conditions of production. It depends on the resources in men, machines and raw materials available to the community. Now, when one is considering the problems of unemployment, the aggregate supply schedule is not worth studying in detail. It shows how much money the community must be spending if it is to employ all resources, and this tells one how large aggregate demand price must be to maintain full employment. There is no particular need, however, to consider how the shape of the aggregate supply schedule could be altered. There is no point, for example, in trying to use resources more effectively (to produce the same output with fewer men and thereby shift the aggregate supply schedule bodily to the left) if there are men on the dole already. Keynes himself largely ignored the problems of aggregate supply because he felt that it was aggregate demand which had not received enough attention in the past.

We shall ignore supply conditions too, for we have, after all, discussed them fully in Part One. The simplest thing, as Keynes suggested, is to take aggregate supply conditions as given and to see what it is which determines the aggregate demand schedule. We can then see how it can happen that, given its resources and technology, a community can fail to keep its workers employed; and how it can remedy this failing. Nevertheless, because we shall ignore aggregate supply, this does not mean that it is unimportant. It is only when unemployment exists that communities are likely to take the view that there is no point in supplying goods more efficiently. When there is full employment —and even more when there is inflation—an improvement in productive efficiency is the only hope of economic progress. We shall therefore return to aggregate supply when we study inflation, as we shall do later on. For the moment it is aggregate demand, which the 'classical' economists resting on their comforting doctrine that 'supply creates its own demand' were able to ignore, that we must discuss.

3. AGGREGATE DEMAND

The aggregate demand schedule is the vital factor in employment theory, for only if aggregate demand is large enough will all resources be used, with any given aggregate supply schedule. But the aggregate demand schedule is more dependent on psychology than on technology. It shows how much money the community is expected to spend on the products of industry at various levels of output. Now, we have already seen that this is the same as the receipts of the entrepreneurs, looked at from a different angle. The aggregate demand schedule thus shows the aggregate receipts expected by entrepreneurs, or alternatively, the aggregate expected expenditure of purchasers, when employment is at various levels. For our present purpose, it is on the expenditure of purchasers rather than on the receipts of producers that we shall find it best to concentrate our attention.

Expenditure by purchasers is on goods, and, as we have seen, goods may be divided into two kinds, consumption goods and investment goods. The shape and position of the aggregate demand schedule at each level of employment thus depends on the expenditure of members of the community, on consumption on the one hand and on investment on the other.

4. EFFECTIVE DEMAND

We have seen that the intersection of the aggregate demand schedule with the aggregate supply schedule determines the actual level of employment in an economy, and that at this level of employment the amount of money which entrepreneurs *expect to receive* is equal to what they *must receive* if their costs at that level of employment are to be just covered. Such an equilibrium position can be looked upon as analogous to a market equilibrium where market demand and market supply are temporarily in equilibrium. Whether the equilibrium will be permanent depends largely on whether entrepreneurs' expectations have proved correct. We have seen that the aggregate demand schedule shows what entrepreneurs *expect* to receive from selling the output of varying numbers of men and that, in equilibrium, these expected receipts will be just sufficient to make that amount of employment worth offering. If entrepreneurs' expectations have been correct, this 'market' equilibrium will represent a position where all entrepreneurs will just be covering costs, and which is likely to persist for some time. It can, in fact, be looked upon also as a position of 'short-run' equilibrium.

If, on the other hand, the expectations of entrepreneurs turn out to be wrong in the 'market' equilibrium, the situation will not be one of 'short-run' equilibrium, but the aggregate demand (and perhaps also the aggregate supply) schedule will alter until such a 'short-run' equilibrium position is reached, with actual demand conditions bearing out entrepreneurs' expectations. For example, if in the 'market' equilibrium actual demand falls short of expected demand, then it is likely that the whole aggregate demand schedule will move downwards. Entrepreneurs will now expect less money to be spent on their output at each level of employment than they did before. For the current situation is the main determinant of the state of short-run expectations—the expectations on which entrepreneurs will base their output, and hence the employment they offer in the short run. As Keynes said, 'It is sensible for producers to base their expectations on the assumption that the most recently realised results will continue, except in so far as there are definite reasons for expecting a change'.[1] If the 'market' equilibrium is such that actual demand falls short of expected demand, it is therefore reasonable to assume that expected demand has been overestimated, so that producers will hold less optimistic expectations in future. In this way a short-run equilibrium position will soon be reached where expected aggregate demand and realised aggregate demand are equal. Similarly, if actual demand exceeds expectations, entrepreneurs will revise their expectations in an upward direction until again equilibrium is reached. In this 'short-run' equilibrium situation, where expectations are borne out and aggregate demand and supply are equal, the actual level of aggregate demand will determine the 'short-run' equilibrium level of employment. As we have seen, the greater aggregate

[1] *Op. cit.* p. 51.

demand is at the point where it is equal to aggregate supply, the higher employment will be.

The 'short-run' equilibrium level of aggregate demand and supply, which determines short-run employment, can be called 'effective demand'. It is that aggregate demand price which becomes 'effective' because it is equal to aggregate supply price and thus represents a position of 'short-run' equilibrium. It is distinguished in this way from all other points on the aggregate demand schedule because it represents an equilibrium position which actually *is* realised. In the next few chapters we shall explain how 'effective demand' can be deficient so that the economy can be in short-run equilibrium with less than full employment. For, as we have seen, the classical economists assumed that the aggregate demand price was always large enough to equal the aggregate supply price corresponding to full employment.

In any community, effective demand will represent the amount of money actually being spent on the products of industry. It can thus be looked upon also as the receipts of all the factors of production. For all the money which entrepreneurs receive must be paid out in the form of wages, rent, interest and profit. Effective demand thus equals the national income—the receipts of all members of the community. It also represents the value of the output of the community. For the total price of national output is just the same thing as the receipts of entrepreneurs from selling goods. And since all goods are either consumption goods or investment goods, effective demand is equal on the one hand to national expenditure on consumption goods plus national expenditure on investment goods. On the other hand, it is equal to total national receipts from the sale of consumer goods plus total receipts from the sale of investment goods.

We can therefore sum up as follows :

Effective Demand = National Income
                 = Value of National Output
  = expenditure on consumption goods
            + expenditure on investment goods
  = receipts from selling consumption goods
            + receipts from selling investment goods.

Now, since effective demand equals the volume of expenditure on consumer goods plus investment goods, we can say that employment, which depends on effective demand, also depends on the amount of consumption expenditure and the amount of investment expenditure. If consumption is constant and investment increases, employment will increase. Alternatively, if investment is constant and consumption increases, employment will increase. So, in order to discover how consumption and investment together can be kept at a high level, we shall try to find out in the next few chapters what determines consumption taken separately, what determines investment taken separately, and how they affect each other. For the fundamental idea of Keynesian economics is the very simple one that a high level of employment can only be maintained by a high level of expenditure on either consumption or investment, or both.

Before we finally embark on our outline of Keynesian theory, there is one last preliminary. It seems desirable to make a distinction between that part of effective demand which originates from private individuals and that part caused by Government spending. In the original Keynesian analysis there was little mention of Government expenditure. It was assumed (quite rightly considering the date of publication) that Government expenditure was likely to be relatively unimportant. But this is by no means so true now. The situation may therefore now be summed up as follows :

Total National Output = Effective Demand = C + I + G,

where   C = private consumption demand,
                        I = private investment demand,
                        G = Government demand for both consumption
                             and investment goods.

Broadly speaking, the size of Government expenditure is quite easy to account for. It will depend on the policies of the Government of the day and will usually be determined by political and social rather than economic factors. In the following analysis we shall for the most part ignore Government expenditure. The main exception will be when we discuss the effects of public works policies on the level of employment. Nevertheless, at a time when Government expenditure frequently constitutes a considerable proportion of effective demand in any economy, it is important to acknowledge its existence as a source of employment.

SUGGESTED READING

J. M. Keynes, *General Theory*, London, 1936, chapter iii.
Dudley Dillard, *The Economics of J. M. Keynes*, London, 1950, chapter iii.
A. H. Hansen, *Full Recovery or Stagnation*, London, 1938, chapter i.

CHAPTER XX

CONSUMPTION

1. THE PROPENSITY TO CONSUME

WE have seen how Keynes has shown that employment depends on effective demand, and that effective demand is the sum of expenditure on consumption and expenditure on investment. For the moment we shall ignore the factors determining the volume of investment and concentrate on consumption. We want to discover what it is that determines the amount of money which a community spends on consumption.

Now, the volume of consumption in a country clearly depends on the consumption decisions of individual members of the community. The sum-total of the amounts which separate individuals spend on consumption is the amount spent by the community as a whole. This may sound obvious, but it is desirable not to overlook the importance of these individual decisions. We shall therefore begin by considering what determines the consumption of an individual and proceed to discover what will determine the consumption of the community as a whole. We shall assume, as Keynes did, that consumption shows a definite and fairly stable functional dependence on income, just as in price theory amount demanded shows a functional dependence on price. There will thus be a stable functional relationship between the size of a consumer's income and the amount he spends on consumption. For example, where for any single consumer C = consumption and Y = income, then $C = f(Y)$, where f shows the functional relationship between income and consumption. f is called the 'propensity to consume'. So, if we can discover the nature of a single consumer's propensity to consume, we shall know how much he will spend on consumption out of any given income. Our first task will therefore be to explain the generalisation which Keynes made about the propensity to consume.

We want to discover some general relationship between income and consumption. It will therefore be convenient if we can ignore any other factors, apart from the size of income, which affect the propensity to consume, and which may change, concentrating our attention on changes in income. We must therefore consider what these other factors which affect consumption are, and how likely it is that they will change through time.

The propensity to consume of any individual member of a community will depend on two sets of forces. On the one hand, there will be his subjective attitude towards consumption; on the other hand will be objective data about the community in which he lives. First, let us consider which *objective* conditions will determine the shape of the schedule of the propensity to consume. Apart from money income, the main objective facts will be prices. We have seen in Part One that, so far as the consumption of an individual commodity is concerned, prices are supremely important. The outlay of a consumer on any one good can legitimately be assumed to vary solely as a result of changes in its price. When it is all goods together which one is considering, price is less important. Admittedly a substantial rise or fall in all prices will be important, since it will change real incomes considerably. It will alter the real value of money. But for our present purposes, it is much more important to see what are the effects of changes in *money* incomes than of changes in *real* incomes. We shall therefore assume that the level of prices is constant. This will enable us to construct a relatively simple theory based on the assumption of constant prices, and we can add the complications of a changing price level at a later stage.

Again, changes in consumers' tastes may alter the demand for all consumption goods, but it seems reasonable to think that in the short run such changes will not be large enough to be important. Similarly, where capital gains or losses accrue to people, their consumption may change. Once more it is difficult to be certain what the effects will be, and it is doubtful whether they are important enough to worry us here. Changes in fiscal (especially taxation) policy are likely to be rather more important, but in the main we shall overlook these also. Another possible change in objective conditions is in the size of allowances which business men set aside to cover depreciation on their factories, machines, vans, etc. This again is extremely difficult to generalise about, but is also likely to be stable in the short period.

So far, we have seen that the most important objective factor which is likely to cause fluctuations in the propensity to consume is the level of prices, and we have explicitly ruled out all possibility of such a change. One final objective factor which must be discussed is the rate of interest. In practice, as we shall see in a moment, changes in the rate of interest are not likely to have very important effects on the values of consumption. In the analysis in Chapter XIV, however, we gave an outline of the kind of analysis provided by partial equilibrium theory, and showed that if consumers were to be persuaded to consume less, the rate of interest would have to rise, assuming that the income of the community was constant. Many economists did, in fact, assume until quite recently that if the rate of interest rose, people would save more and consume less; and if it fell, they would consume more and save less. This sounds reasonable enough. But Keynes maintained that the direct effect of the rate of interest on consumption is negligible.

So far as the individual consumer is concerned, it certainly does seem to be dangerous to assume that a fall in the rate of interest will increase consumption, and *vice versa*. It is likely that this may be the normal response, but it is by no means certain. Let us suppose, for example, that a consumer with an income after tax of, say, £700 per annum is saving for his old age and invests these savings in gilt-edged Government securities. He hopes, at the end of a life of virtuous toil, to have £300 a year (ignoring tax) coming to him from his investments. Now, if the rate of interest is 3 per cent, he will know that he must buy £10,000 worth of securities. Over his lifetime he will therefore save £10,000, to have a retirement income of £300 a year. But if the rate of interest now rises to 6 per cent, what will happen ? Our investor can, of course, continue with his plans and save the £10,000. On this he will now receive £600 a year and will be able to enjoy a merry old age. But he may be quite content with £300 a year and only save £5000 instead of £10,000. In the same way, a man wishing to leave a fixed income from Government securities to his son will save less if the rate of interest rises. Thus, even if the rate of interest does have a marked effect on the savings of some people, the effect will not always be in the same direction. Some people may save more but some may save less. For the community as a whole, there is bound to be a certain amount of cancelling out, and there may not be much net effect either way.

Again, it seems likely that many people make their decisions about how much to save and how much to spend quite independently of the rate of interest. The amount of money which people put aside to prepare for whatever the future may hold in store is unlikely to depend on the rate of interest. Rainy days in the metaphorical sense are not closely connected with the rate of interest. It is therefore reasonable to argue, as Keynes did, that the rate of interest can, and should be ignored as a factor directly affecting the propensity to consume. Changes in consumption are nothing like so dependent on changes in the rate of interest as on changes in income.

We have now given the reasons for our assumption that, with the exception of changes in money income, no change in objective economic conditions will significantly affect a person's propensity to consume. We have admitted that the propensity to consume is unlikely, in fact, to remain stable over long periods, because external changes are bound to have some effect on an individual in the long run. But since we are only concerned with explaining a relatively simple theory of employment, and since we are also more concerned with the short run than the long run, we can reasonably exclude the possibility of any very great changes in objective economic conditions.

We must now consider the possibility of changes in *subjective* factors affecting the propensity to consume. Fortunately we can be much more certain here that any changes which do take place will only take place in the long run. Short-run changes are likely to be quite unimportant. In considering the subjective factors which affect the propensity to consume, Keynes was much more realistic than earlier economists. The 'classical' economists tended to over-simplify the psychological background to any decision to save. They represented it merely as a choice between present and future consumption. They stressed the virtue of thrift and made all decisions of this kind into choices between 'jam tomorrow and jam today'. Keynes brought a welcome breath of realism. He regarded decisions to consume or save as far more than choices between the present and the future. He maintained that the individual who is deciding to save is often motivated by such feelings as pride and avarice. One may well wish to have enough wealth to be able to hold one's head high, to bequeath a fortune to one's heirs, to provide a reserve for meeting such unforeseen difficulties as illness or unemployment, or merely to satisfy one's miserly instincts. Nor does Keynes think that all these subjective motives need be those which reduce consumption. They may well increase it. The desire for ostentation may lead to high expenditure. An extravagant or a careless man may waste his money. A generous man may give it away.

And there will be similar motives affecting businesses which will cause them to spend much or little. Firms with a careful or cautious owner may well put more of their funds to reserve than is really necessary and this will reduce the community's consumption. Firms will also need to set aside funds in readiness for emergencies, or to carry out investment and expansion in the future; and some firms, being more cautious or more far-sighted, will save more than others. The strength or weakness of all these motives will affect the propensity to consume of the whole community.

Fortunately short-run changes in these subjective factors influencing the propensity to consume are unlikely. As Keynes has said, these subjective consumption habits depend largely on 'those psychological characteristics of human nature and those social practices and institutions which, though not unalterable, are unlikely to undergo a material change over a short period of time except in abnormal or revolutionary circumstances'.[1] We shall therefore assume in what follows that, in the short run at any rate, the propensity to consume will remain stable.

2. THE SCHEDULE OF THE PROPENSITY TO CONSUME

Since the propensity to consume is a function of income, it follows that one can construct a schedule of the propensity to consume showing how much will be consumed at various levels of income, and it will be useful to draw this. We are assuming that it is a stable schedule over time. But that is not all we know about it. We can, in fact, realistically make several assumptions about the shape and nature of the schedule of the propensity to consume of a modern community, at least in the short run.

First, it is reasonable to suppose that as a community's income rises its consumption will rise too. But we can go further. We can assume legitimately that if income rises by a given absolute amount, say £100, consumption will rise by a *smaller absolute amount*. It is unlikely that consumption will rise by less than £1, but it is unlikely to rise by more than £99. To put it precisely, we may assume that when income increases, consumption will increase too, but not, as a rule, by so much as income has increased.

This may be put mathematically. Where δY represents a very small increase in income, and δC represents the resulting

---

[1] *General Theory*, p. 91.

increase in consumption, then $\frac{\delta C}{\delta Y}$ will be positive but less than 1.

Mathematically, $1 > \frac{\delta C}{\delta Y} > 0 . \frac{\delta C}{\delta Y}$, the proportion of an increment of income, however small, which will be consumed, is known as the 'marginal propensity to consume'.

Second, we shall take it as axiomatic that everyone must consume something. We shall also presume that people do not consume more than their total income. This can happen, for a time, though it is not normal, and, as Mr. Micawber pointed out, the result is usually disastrous. It is important to notice, however, that even this exception does not violate our first rule. If a man with an income of £300 is, at present, consuming £350, a rise of £100 in his income is unlikely to raise his expenditure to £450. Indeed his normal reaction would probably be to spend no more than £400. Of course, even here there may be exceptions. Certain people do seem able to spend more than they earn—even in the long run. But the general rule seems sound enough. Everyone consumes something and hardly anyone consumes more than he earns for very long.

Third, we shall assume that as a man's income rises his marginal propensity to consume, which we have seen is always less than 1 but greater than 0, will decline. In other words, whilst one will never consume the whole of any increase in income, when one is rich one will consume less of any given absolute increase in income than when one is poor. For example, a man with an income of £400 may be consuming £395. If his income now rises to £450, he will only consume, say, £45 of the increase. In all he will be consuming £440. Out of a further increase of £50 in his income, he may consume only £40, out of yet another £50 increment only £35, and so on. This assumption of a diminishing marginal propensity to consume is important, since it imposes a definite restriction on the shape of the curve showing the propensity to consume. We shall assume also that not only does the marginal propensity to consume fall as income rises, but that it falls smoothly, especially for the community as a whole, so that the curve showing the propensity to consume is smooth and has no kinks or wobbles in it.

On the basis of the three assumptions we have made we can now draw a curve showing the propensity to consume. We shall take the case of an imaginary community and show how much it will spend on consumption when its income is at various levels.

As we have seen, the propensity to consume of a community will depend on the propensities of all individuals and we have now seen what these will be like. The schedule of the propensity to consume for the community will be of the same general shape as those of its individual members, being obtained by adding the curves of all individuals together.

The curve TPC in Figure 115a represents the schedule of the Total Propensity to Consume for an imaginary community. It shows the total amount of consumption when income is at various

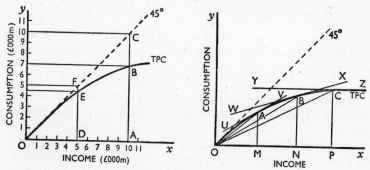

FIGURES 115A AND 115B

levels. When the income of the community is £10,000 million they consume £7000 million (AB). £3000 million (BC) is saved. When income is £5000 million (OD) they consume £4500 million (DE) and save £500 million (EF). And so on. The (dotted) 45° line shows what the total propensity to consume curve would be like if the community always consumed the whole of its income. This line represents the limiting case where nothing is ever saved. The actual position can be seen by comparison. As income rises from zero to £3000 million the whole of any increase is consumed; the curve of the total propensity to consume coincides with the 45° line. Once income rises above £3000 million, however, more and more is saved. This is shown by the fact that the curve of the total propensity to consume bends away from the 45° line. All this means is that the average and marginal propensities to consume are both falling as income rises.

This can be seen from Figure 115b. Here, the average propensity to consume at several points on the curve TPC is shown (by the slope of the straight line from these points to the origin). It will be seen that the slope of the line OA is steeper than that of OB. This means that the average propensity to consume is greater when income is OM than when it is ON. The marginal propensity to consume at any point on TPC in Figure 115b is shown by the slope of a tangent to that point on the curve. The slope of the tangent is greater (marginal propensity to consume is greater) when income is smaller (as at OM) than when it is greater (as at ON). That is to say, UV is steeper than WX. It is clear from this diagram that the marginal propensity to consume falls faster than does the average propensity to consume. For when income rises to OP, the tangent YZ, showing marginal propensity to consume, becomes horizontal, $\frac{\delta C}{\delta Y} = 0$. No-one consumes any part of an increase in income; all is being saved. But the average propensity to consume remains positive, as shown by the slope of OC. A situation where $\frac{\delta C}{\delta Y}$ has fallen to zero is unlikely to be found in practice but it is interesting to notice what the shape of the curve would be in this limiting case.

It is probably worth trying to justify the assumptions which we have made about the shape of the schedule of the propensity to consume in a modern economy, and particularly our assumption that the marginal propensity to consume declines as income increases. There are two reasons for believing that this will be so. First, if there is only a short-run rise in income, it is unlikely that the community will change its spending habits immediately so as to spend the whole of the increased income. It takes some time for most of us to get used to a higher (or lower) standard of living. Second, even if there has been a long, steady change in income, it does not seem unreasonable to think that the richer a community is, the smaller will be the proportion of any increase in its income which it will consume. For the greater is any man's income, the more of his basic human needs will have already been met, and the greater will be the tendency for him to save in order to provide for the future. But the ideas about consumption outlined above will possess greater validity in the short run than in the long run. Given time we can all become used to spending most of a larger income.

One final consequence of the fact that the marginal propensity to consume declines is worth noting. If a community includes some people who are rich and others who are poor, there will be a significant difference in their consumption habits. The marginal propensity to consume of the rich will be lower than that of the poor. Of course there will inevitably be great divergencies within each income group, but those who are miserly and those who are ostentatious, those who are careful and those who are lavish, will normally offset each other when one considers an income group as a whole. In general the poor will consume a greater proportion of their income than the rich. It follows that if, for any reason, it is desired to reduce the amount which the community is spending on consumption, it will be possible to do so by taxing the poor and giving the money to the rich. For the rich will be much less likely to spend it on consumption. Similarly, if it is felt that consumption should be encouraged, money could be taken from the rich and given to the poor. The possibility of regulating and altering consumption in this way depends ultimately on the assumption of a diminishing marginal propensity to consume.

This is about as far as one can go in assessing the probable shape of the schedule of the propensity to consume. One can, however, derive an important conclusion from our assumptions about the nature of the propensity to consume and it will be desirable to do this now. Let us assume that for some reason the income of a certain community rises. Now, if the community's propensity to consume remains unaltered (and in the short run, at least, it is likely to do so), consumption will not rise by so much as income has done. If the community wishes to maintain the increased level of income, it can do so only by spending on investment an additional amount of money equal to the difference between the increase in income and the consequent increase in consumption. Otherwise income will fall again.

For example, if a community's income has risen by £10,000 but it only consumes £6000 of the increased income, £4000 more must be spent on investment than was previously being spent if the £10,000 addition to income is to be maintained. To maintain any given level of income and employment, a community must always spend on investment an amount equal to the difference between that given income and what the community will spend on consumption when income is at that level. In Figure 115a for instance, when income is £OA the community is spending £AB on consumption. To maintain income at £OA the amount £BC must be spent on investment. It follows from Figures 115a and 115b that the richer a community is, the greater is the absolute amount of investment expenditure needed to fill the gap between the community's income and what it is spending on consumption. This may well cause difficulties, since it is not always simple for a rich community to find profitable investment opportunities.

On the other hand, if a rich community's income falls, it is likely that a larger proportion of that reduced income will be spent on consumption now that the community is poorer. As income and employment fall, therefore, a smaller and smaller absolute amount of investment expenditure will be necessary to prevent them from falling further. For example, when income in Figure 115a falls to OD only EF needs to be spent on investment to maintain income at that level. This explains why there is invariably a 'rock bottom' to a slump. In the end the community becomes so poor that it is hardly saving anything. It therefore requires only a little investment expenditure to be undertaken by private individuals or by the Government to maintain income and employment at the existing level. For example, whilst in Figure 115a an income of £10,000 million can only be maintained if investment is £3000 million, an income of £5000 million can be maintained with an investment expenditure of £500 million—a much less difficult target to achieve.

3. THE MULTIPLIER

Our discussion of the propensity to consume has shown us that a community may sometimes find it necessary to spend a large amount of money on investment if it is to prevent unemployment. We have also implied that it may not always be possible to spend this money unless the Government takes a hand and spends money on investment itself. Let us now consider a situation where there is already unemployment in a country and the Government not only wants to prevent employment falling further, but indeed wishes to raise the level of employment. The Government therefore spends, say, £1 million on building roads and the national income automatically rises by £1 million. But this is not all. As we have seen, investment and consumption stand in a complementary relationship to each other. When £1 million is spent on investment, the workers in the investment industry spend their money on consumer goods; this raises the incomes of the consumption goods workers, who in turn spend their money on more consumer goods. The initial expenditure of £1 million may thus result in a rise of several million pounds in the income of the community.

So, when there is unemployment and public works are undertaken, the total increase in national income resulting from this expenditure on public works will be greater than the amount of money spent on the public works. Similarly, the total increase in employment resulting from the public works will be greater than the number of men working on the original scheme. We can be more precise than we have been so far about the relationship between such an original increase in income (or employment) and the ultimate total increase. A precise numerical relationship is given by the 'multiplier'. The multiplier is an inherent part of Keynesian theory, but was developed earlier, in the early 1930's, by Mr. R. F. Kahn.[1] The essence of the multiplier is that it compares the relative sizes of a given initial increase in investment and the total (direct and indirect) ultimate increase in income. In other words, it shows by how many times the effect of an increment of investment has been 'multiplied' by causing repercussions on consumption and thus raising the national income.

Before we turn to a detailed discussion of the meaning and size of the multiplier, there are one or two qualifications which it will be useful to make. First, we shall calculate the size of the multiplier by assuming that there is an increase in investment over and above the recent level of investment. We shall assume, however, that this additional investment has no further indirect effects on investment, or alternatively, that any such indirect effects have been counted back into the original increase in investment. We can then confine our attention to the relationship between investment and consumption. Second, we shall continue to assume that we are dealing with a 'closed' economy where there is no international trade. If we did not assume this, and if those employed on public works could spend their money on imports, the increased consumption might take place in other countries, and some of the multiplier effects would be lost. This expenditure on imports constitutes a 'leakage' which reduces the domestic propensity to consume. Taxation will constitute a similar 'leakage' which reduces the multiplier by lowering the marginal propensity to consume. In this case, however, the fact that any money raised by taxation will presumably be spent by the Government means that there need be no detrimental effects on employment.

Third, as has been seen, the effect of an increase in investment, by working through the multiplier, is to increase both income and employment. In fact, therefore, there is both an investment

[1] 'The Relation of Home Investment to Unemployment', *Economic Journal*, June 1931, p. 173.

2 B

(or income) multiplier showing the effect of an increase in investment on income, and an employment multiplier showing the effect on employment. The latter shows the total (direct and indirect) increase in employment divided by the direct initial increase in employment. Mr. Kahn's original multiplier was an 'employment' multiplier and there is no reason why, in practice, the two multipliers should be the same. As we saw earlier, an increase in income may yield different increases in employment in different parts of the economy and at different times. We are, however, assuming for the sake of simplicity that the effects of any given absolute increase in income on employment are always identical whatever the original level of income is. This means that we can concentrate our attention on changes in income and yet that all we have to say will apply equally to changes in employment.

We turn now to the calculation of the multiplier, 'k', as it is designated in symbolic form. What determines the size of 'k'? The answer is that the size of the multiplier depends on the marginal propensity to consume. Where the marginal propensity to consume is high, the multiplier will be large, and *vice versa*. This dependence on the marginal propensity to consume is what one would expect. Where the marginal propensity to consume is low, any increase in wages paid, let us say, to roadbuilders will be mostly saved, and there will be little additional employment for bakers, shoemakers and tobacconists who would benefit from any increased spending by roadbuilders.

One limiting case will occur where the marginal propensity to consume is zero. Here none of the additional income created by employing roadmakers on public works will be spent at all. The total increase in income will be equal to the increase in the income of the roadmakers. The increase in roadmakers' income and the total increase in income directly and indirectly caused are equal. Here, then, where the marginal propensity to consume is nought, the multiplier is equal to one, k=1. The total increase in income is only as big as the increase in investment. The multiplier will therefore usually be greater than one. For it is unlikely that the marginal propensity to consume will be zero.

The other limiting case is where the marginal propensity to consume is equal to one. Here all of any increased incomes earned by roadmakers employed on public works will be spent. This will add to the incomes of shopkeepers who will in turn spend *all* their increased incomes, and so on. The multiplier will therefore be infinitely large, $k = \infty$. In such circumstances, the Government would only need to employ one roadmaker to raise income indefinitely, causing first full employment and then a limitless spiral of inflation. This case is therefore just as unlikely as the one when $k = 1$. It is certain that the real-world multiplier will be greater than one but less than infinity. Before we consider just where between these limits the multiplier will be, we must give a more precise definition.

4. CALCULATION OF THE MULTIPLIER

We have seen that the multiplier shows the ratio between an increase in income and the increase in investment which has given rise to it. If we employ the conventional notation using δI to represent a given increase in investment and δY the resultant increase in income, then the multiplier $k = \dfrac{\delta Y}{\delta I}$. Or in other words, $\delta Y = k \delta I$. But we know that the size of the multiplier depends on the size of the marginal propensity to consume (and hence on the marginal propensity to save). In fact, the simplest statement is that where k is the multiplier and s is the marginal propensity to *save*, then $k = \dfrac{1}{s}$.[1] Having defined the multiplier, we can compute its numerical size, provided we know the size of the marginal propensity to save. Let us take a hypothetical example of a community where the marginal propensity to consume is $\frac{4}{5}$ and the marginal propensity to save is thus $\frac{1}{5}$. Out of any increment in its income of £100, the community will consume £80 and save £20. Now since the multiplier

$$k = \frac{1}{\text{marginal propensity to save}}$$

and the marginal propensity to save is $\frac{1}{5}$,

$$k = \frac{1}{\frac{1}{5}}, \qquad \therefore \ k = 5.$$

[1] We saw (p. 389) that $Y = C + I$. It follows that $\delta Y = \delta C + \delta I$ (*i.e.* an increase in income is made up of an increase in consumption plus an increase in investment). Now we know that the multiplier $k = \dfrac{\delta Y}{\delta I}$. The marginal propensity to save, s ($= 1 -$ the marginal propensity to consume), $= 1 - \dfrac{\delta C}{\delta Y}$. But since $\delta C + \delta I = \delta Y$, $s = 1 - \dfrac{\delta C}{\delta Y} = \dfrac{\delta I}{\delta Y}$. So $\dfrac{1}{s} = \dfrac{\delta Y}{\delta I}$, which is the definition of the multiplier. Thus $k = \dfrac{1}{s}$ and $s = \dfrac{1}{k}$.

This means that for an investment outlay of, say, £1000 the total increase in income caused will be £5000. A given increase in investment (and in employment) will cause a five-fold increase in total income (and therefore in total employment).

The multiplier can of course also be defined directly in terms of the marginal propensity to consume. Let us call this m. It is clear that the sum of the marginal propensity to consume and the marginal propensity to save will be one. For example, where the marginal propensity to save is $\frac{1}{5}$, the marginal propensity to consume must be $\frac{4}{5}$. Thus the multiplier $(k) = \frac{1}{s} = \frac{1}{1-m}$ and the marginal propensity to consume $(m) = 1 - s = 1 - \frac{1}{k}$.

Thus, if, as in the above example, $m = \frac{4}{5}$ (i.e. $s = \frac{1}{5}$); then since $k = \frac{1}{1-m}$, $k = \frac{1}{1-\frac{4}{5}}$, $k = \frac{1}{\frac{1}{5}}$, $k = 5$. We can always obtain k provided we know either the marginal propensity to consume or the marginal propensity to save.

In these calculations, however, we have ignored one very important point. In order to simplify the arithmetic we have assumed that the marginal propensity to consume remains constant over the relevant (small) range of income. In practice, of course, this will rarely, if ever, be the case. The marginal propensity will begin to fall once the initial investment raises income, and will continue to fall as income rises further. But this in no way invalidates the result which we have obtained, though it does mean that the calculations involved become more complicated. For the multiplier will change with each change in the marginal propensity to consume, as the process works itself out. In practice one would need some measure of the 'average' marginal propensity to consume over the range of incomes in question. In our purely theoretical discussion we can ignore this.

It is also important to remember that the multiplier relates to a net increase in public investment, and that we have not considered what will be the effect of an increase in public investment on public and private investment together. We have ignored the possibility that the instituting of any particular Government investment project might lead to a rise or a fall in other investment activity. Total investment (private and public) might rise by more or less than the amount spent on public works. It might even decline if the introduction of the Government-financed investment were to discourage private investment. The net effect of any public works scheme on investment as a whole is thus not easy to predict. It depends whether private investment is discouraged or encouraged by the advent of a public works scheme, and if so, by how much. It should be noted, however, that even if private investment falls off by more than public investment has increased, this has nothing to do with the size of the multiplier itself. It merely means that the thing to be multiplied (the net increase in investment) is negative. It is much more likely, however, that increased public investment, by raising employment, will lead to greater business confidence and hence to greater private investment. But here again this has nothing to do with the multiplier as such. It merely means that the multiplicand (investment) has grown larger by the repercussions of the increased public investment on private investment.

Post-Keynesian writers have pointed out that the multiplier will be affected by time-lags—by the fact that particular pieces of investment activity will take some time to exert their full effects in raising income. Meanwhile fresh investment projects will have been undertaken and may themselves be causing multiplier effects. The calculations given above show the level of income reached when the whole multiplier process has had time to work itself out. If there are time-lags this final equilibrium position will take longer to reach than it would have done if the extra income had been spent more rapidly. The multiplier still determines the increase in income, but income rises more slowly than it would do in the absence of lags. Keynes seems to have thought that the effects of such lags would be unimportant.

Keynes' view of the size of the multiplier is that 'In actual fact, the marginal propensity to consume seems to lie somewhere between these two extremes' (*i.e.* 0 and 1), 'though much nearer to unity than to zero ; with the result that we have, in a sense, the worst of both worlds, fluctuations in employment being considerable, and at the same time, the increment of investment required to produce full employment being too great to be easily handled'.[1]

5. SAVINGS EQUAL INVESTMENT

The careful reader will have noticed that the calculation of the size of the multiplier raises the problem of the relationship

[1] *Op. cit.* p. 118.

between income, consumption, savings and investment, and, more particularly, between savings and investment. Since the analysis of this relationship between savings and investment has caused considerable trouble to many economists (including Keynes himself), we must clear it up now.

The fundamental point to remember is that savings and investment are always equal. This can be seen from the following equations. Let Y = income, O = value of output, C = consumption, S = savings and I = investment. Now we know that $Y = O = C + I$ (from the analysis of Chapter XIX). But we also know that $Y = C + S$ (*i.e.* money not spent on consumption is saved). Then $S = I$.

The concept of income can thus be looked at from two opposite directions. On the one hand, it can be regarded as what the community spends on consumption and investment—the value of output sold (total national expenditure). On the other hand, it can be looked at as what the community receives in wages, rents, interest and profits for supplying consumption and investment goods. What the community spends is not only equal to, but is identically equal to, or equal by definition with, what it receives, For although receiving income is not identical with paying income out, the amount received must equal the amount paid out, just as in price theory the amount demanded equals the amount supplied.

Now consumption appears in income whether it is calculated as receipts or as payments. The concept of consumption is not, of course, altogether unambiguous. It is not always easy to decide whether certain goods are consumption goods or not. For example, are houses durable consumer goods or capital goods ? This type of border-line difficulty is troublesome but it is not crucial from our present point of view. So long as one is consistent in maintaining one's definitions these border-line problems do not affect the result. Thus consumption in any year is expenditure on consumer goods (however defined) between 1st January and 31st December in that year. Similarly, investment expenditure in any year is what is spent on capital goods between 1st January and 31st December. Consumption appears in both the equations defining income. But it is important to realise that the basis of defining income as $C + I$ is different from that of defining it as $C + S$. As we have suggested earlier, the act of saving is not identical with the act of investing, at least in a monetary economy. It is because of this fact, because, although saving and investing

are not normally performed by the same people, they are nevertheless equal, that we must study the connection between them
with care. In particular we must discover the manner in which
savings and investment are brought into equality.

When one speaks of income as C + I, one means that money
earned by selling consumption and investment goods is income
for the people who produced them. On the other hand, when
one says that income is C + S, one is merely pointing out that one
has to decide, as an individual, whether to spend one's income on
consumption goods or to save it—and so does the economy as a
whole. The equality between savings and investment derives
from the fact that on the one hand income allocated in any year
must either be spent on consumption or saved, and on the other
hand income received in that same year is only derived either from
selling consumption goods or from selling investment goods.
Savings must equal investment.

It is investment and consumption decisions between them,
however, which are the positive or active forces in determining
the level of savings and not *vice versa*. Saving can be regarded as
a 'mere residual' which must be equal to investment. It should
be noted that our definition of saving says nothing about whether
the saver, having saved his money, decides to invest it (*i.e.* to
spend his income on building factories, etc.), to hoard it as cash,
or to lend it. All that we are concerned with is the fact that it is
not consumed. Saving is the gap between Y and C.

We have seen that investment and saving decisions are quite
separate in the modern economy. The people who decide to
build factories are very rarely the people who have saved their
money to pay for them. The decisions to consume (*i.e.* not to
save) are taken by people—consumers—who are usually quite
separate from those who decide to invest—entrepreneurs. It is
important to stress this fact because we saw that in the 'Crusoe'
type of barter economy, Crusoe decides at one and the same time
to refrain from consuming and to invest. There is no such
automatic and direct link between savings and investment in the
modern monetary economy. A study of the people who make
savings decisions can tell one nothing about the decisions which
entrepreneurs are making about investment. Nevertheless, despite
the fact that the two sets of decisions are quite separate, savings
must equal investment.

How can this happen? Let us consider, as a first approximation, a situation where consumption is fixed and investment

increases. Income will therefore rise by the same absolute amount as investment has risen. And since consumption is given, savings must increase by the same amount as investment has increased. If this did not happen, payments to entrepreneurs $(C + I)$ would differ from payments received by entrepreneurs and then paid out to factors $(C + S)$—an odd state of affairs indeed. In this simple model, where consumption remains stable and it is investment which rises, it is perfectly clear that savings must equal investment, both before and after the change in investment. But they do not do so because of any deliberate act on the part of savers. Savings are made equal to investment because income is now greater, whilst consumption is fixed. The members of the community have received larger incomes, whether they wished to or not, and, since consumption has not risen, savings must have done so. The equality of savings and investment has come about, not through deliberate decisions to save more out of a given income : it has come about through an increase in income which has made savings rise (because consumption is constant) to exactly the same extent that investment has risen. Similarly, if consumption were constant and investment fell, savings would fall by exactly the same absolute amount as investment had fallen.

The illustration we have so far used is, of course, over-simplified. It is most unlikely (as we have seen earlier) that consumption will remain constant when income rises. But this does not alter the principle, which ensures the resultant equality of savings and investment. If consumption and investment both change, then the change in income will be greater than if only investment had altered, and there will be a consequent change in both consumption *and* savings. Yet the change in expenditure on consumption will be identical with the change in that part of income which is spent on consumer goods. The new (increased) volume of investment will similarly be equal to the new (increased) volume of savings out of the higher incomes. If the whole of any increase in income is not consumed, then someone must have saved an amount of money equal to the absolute difference between the increase in income and the increase in consumption, and this will equal the new volume of investment. But as we have stressed all along, the increased investment is the dominant force, savings being brought automatically into equality with changed investment, through changes in the level of income. 'The act of investment in itself cannot help causing the residual or margin, which we call saving, to increase by a corresponding amount.'[1]

This analysis is a little more realistic, but is still over-simplified. We have assumed that changes in investment are always a result of deliberate decisions on the part of entrepreneurs. This, however, overlooks the possibility that the increased investment may be 'involuntary'—that it may result not from a deliberate decision to purchase machinery but from the piling up of producers' stocks of finished goods. These stocks are patently a part of investment, since they are not consumed but are stored for future use. They need not, however, be a result of deliberate decisions to increase stocks, but may merely result from a falling-off in demand. In other words, consumers have demanded fewer goods by saving more, and their increased savings are balanced by 'investment'. It is therefore possible to distinguish certain cases where investment and savings both diverge from what the savers and investors respectively had decided they should be. There is thus a formal parallel between investment and savings. Just as savings depend on investment—on decisions which are outside the saver's control, so investment may in a sense depend indirectly on savings—for these are affected by consumption decisions which are outside the investor's control. Not only can one have differences between intended savings and realised savings, one can also have differences between intended and realised investment.

It is important, however, not to stress this formal parallel and to remember always that it is realised saving which depends on realised investment and not *vice versa*. Investment never depends on saving, except in a roundabout way through changes in consumption and hence in income. In a 'real' or 'Crusoe' economy, where money does not exist, a decision to save always implies and necessitates a simultaneous decision to invest. Savings and investment are not only equal. They are identical. They are merely different ways of looking at the same decision. Crusoe, by deciding to pass the morning making a fishing net, has decided at the same time to 'save' his morning by refraining from 'consuming' it. He has declined the opportunity of using the morning to catch fish. He has abstained from consumption and has automatically invested. In a money economy there is no such automatic link between savings and investment. Money can be saved by one person causing another to have difficulty in selling consumer goods so that stocks pile up and 'investment' increases.

[1] Keynes, *op. cit.* p. 64.

Where there is no money, an individual who invests must make decisions to save at the same time. But in a monetary system, *an individual* can often 'save' without necessarily causing corresponding investment and can often invest even though there is no-one who is 'saving' to finance that investment.

Yet, as we have seen, *ex-post* (or 'realised' or 'actual') savings and *ex-post* investment are always equal. They become equal as a result of changes in the main independent variables in the system, like the propensity to consume, altering consumption and investment and causing changes in income. But these *ex-post* magnitudes need not be equal to what people expected them to be beforehand or *ex ante*. There is no reason why what people expect to save should equal what they are in fact able to save. *Ex-ante* (or 'planned' or 'anticipated') savings need not equal *ex-post* savings. Nor need *ex-ante* investment equal *ex-post* investment; stocks may increase or decrease more or less than was expected. We have, in fact, been talking, so far, where we have spoken of savings and investment as equal, of 'realised' savings and 'realised' investment, or, as economists often call them, *ex-post* savings and investment. When the decisions to consume and invest have been carried out, savings must equal investment. 'Anticipated', 'planned' or *ex-ante* savings and investment need not be equal. But they will always become equal *ex post* because of changes in the level of income.

The relation of *ex-ante* items to *ex-post* items is not difficult to see. If income is constant—if *ex-ante* income equals *ex-post* income—then *ex-ante* consumption must equal *ex-post* consumption, and *ex-ante* investment must equal *ex-post* investment. *Ex-ante* savings will also have equalled *ex-post* savings—and *ex-ante* savings equal *ex-ante* investment. But if *ex-ante* savings fall short of *ex-ante* investment, income will rise and savings out of the increased income will raise *ex-post* savings to equal *ex-post* investment. If, on the other hand, *ex-ante* savings are greater than *ex-ante* investment, income will fall and *ex-post* savings and investment will be equal because the community is too poor to save so much as it had hoped. This is the reason why some economists have talked in the past of inequalities between savings and investment. *Ex-ante* savings can exceed or fall short of *ex-post* investment. But *ex-post* savings and *ex-post* investment are always equal. Incomes will always change so that the community as a whole is either rich enough or poor enough to save just the same amount of money as is invested.

SUGGESTED READING

J. M. Keynes, *General Theory*, London, 1936, chapters viii, ix and x.
Dudley Dillard, *The Economics of J. M. Keynes*, London, 1950, chapter v.
R. F. Kahn, 'The Relation of Home Investment to Unemployment',
    Economic Journal, 1931, p. 173.

CHAPTER XXI

INVESTMENT

1. THE INDUCEMENT TO INVEST

WE have shown what it is that determines the volume of consumption in any economy at any time. We now turn to the second component part of effective demand and see what determines the volume of investment in such an economy. It will have been seen from the previous chapter that Keynes considered investment to be an important means of creating employment, both directly, and even more indirectly, through multiplier effects. In this chapter we shall discuss the factors which determine the volume of investment which will be undertaken at any moment by ordinary entrepreneurs in a capitalistic society. We shall not concern ourselves with Government investment, since the amount of such investment can usually be decided quite arbitrarily. Our concern will be to show how private individuals and business organisations decide upon the volume of investment which they will undertake. It is important to point out at this stage that by investment we *do not* mean the purchase of *existing* paper securities, bonds, debentures or equities, but the purchase of *new* factories, machines and the like—investment in bricks, mortar and steel. It is essential to realise that only if these assets are *newly constructed* will their purchase give employment to the men who build them. If an entrepreneur buys an asset which is already in existence, he is not providing employment for workers in the investment goods industries. We shall call this transaction by which the ownership of existing capital goods changes hands because securities are bought or sold, which is often referred to in ordinary speech as 'investment', the 'purchase (or sale) of securities'. Nevertheless new investment will normally be financed by the issue of *new* equities, or perhaps *new* debentures, by a firm.

Now, any piece of private investment will only be undertaken if it is expected that it will yield a return to the investor. Moreover, anyone who has liquid resources available for investment will usually find that there is an important alternative to investing his money in new capital equipment. It will be possible for him to earn interest by putting his money into bonds of one kind and another instead of taking the risk of buying a factory in the hope that it will be a success. It follows that if any piece of investment is to be undertaken, not only must the investor expect to earn a money return from it, but that money return itself must be somewhat greater than the return he could obtain if he were to buy existing bonds. The return must, at the very least, equal the rate of interest.

On the other hand, if the business man is not using his own money to undertake investment, it will be necessary that, at the very least, the interest on the borrowed money should be covered by expected returns. Let us therefore assume that, in the cases we shall study, entrepreneurs borrow to finance their investment by issuing commercial debentures bearing a fixed rate of interest. This means that the yield expected from a new unit of capital, the *marginal efficiency of capital*, as Keynes calls it, must never fall below the current rate of interest on debentures if that investment is to be worth while. The inducement to invest thus depends on the marginal efficiency of capital on the one hand, and the rate of interest on the other. We must now study these two factors more closely.

Let us turn first to the marginal efficiency of capital, which represents the demand for new investment goods. An entrepreneur who decides to purchase a new factory or buy a new machine first of all considers the prospective yield of the asset in question, as we saw in Chapter XIV. He buys the new asset because he thinks that he will be able to earn a series of prospective returns from the sale of the output produced by the asset during its life. Having deducted from this series of expected future returns the running costs (and the costs of co-operating factors) which he thinks he will incur in obtaining output during the life of the asset, the entrepreneur will be left with a series of 'net' returns which he expects to accrue to him over the years as the owner of the asset. It is the sum-total of this series of net returns (or 'annuities') [1] which was defined in Chapter XIV (following Keynes) as the *prospective yield* of the asset.

But, as we also saw in Chapter XIV, the prospective yield of an asset is not the only thing which an investor will have to consider when he is acquiring a new machine or factory. He will

---

[1] If the returns accrue once per annum they may be described as 'annuities'.

have to pay for the asset if it is to be produced. This price which an entrepreneur has to pay to acquire an asset is known as the *supply price* of the asset. As we saw in Chapter XIV, an entrepreneur will be more likely to buy a cheap asset than a dear one— other things being equal. It is important to realise, however, that the supply price of any kind of asset is not the price of *existing* assets of that kind. We have seen that employment is not created unless business men are buying *new* investment goods and thus enabling the investment goods industry to give employment to workers. The supply price of a particular type of asset is therefore the cost of producing a brand-new asset of that kind, not the price at which an entrepreneur can acquire one which has already been in existence for some time. This supply price of an asset is sometimes known alternatively as its *replacement cost*. In some ways this is the clearer phrase because it emphasises that the asset must be a new one.

With these two concepts, prospective yield on the one hand and supply price (or replacement cost) on the other, we can now give a precise definition of the *marginal efficiency of capital*. The marginal efficiency of a *particular kind* of capital asset, for example a type of lathe, can be calculated by relating the prospective yield of a new lathe of that kind to its supply price. The marginal efficiency of a particular type of asset shows what an entrepreneur expects to earn from one more asset of that kind compared with what he has to pay to buy it. Keynes' definition is this. 'I define the marginal efficiency of capital as being equal to that rate of discount which would make the present value of the series of annuities given by the returns expected from the capital asset during its life just equal to its supply price.' [1] In other words, the marginal efficiency of a *particular type* of capital asset is the rate at which the prospective yield expected from one additional unit of that particular asset must be discounted if it is just to equal the (replacement) cost of the asset. It shows what the rate of discount must be if some entrepreneur is to be just induced to purchase one more (marginal) unit of that type of asset. This definition explains what is meant by the marginal efficiency of a *particular type* of capital asset.

But the concept of the marginal efficiency of capital *in general* is needed also in employment theory. In any given situation this will be the marginal efficiency of that particular asset of which it is most worth the community's while to produce another unit. In

[1] *Op. cit.* p. 135.

other words, the highest of all the individual marginal efficiencies
of the various assets which could be produced but have not yet
been produced, will be the marginal efficiency of capital in general.
It will show, in any situation, what the highest return to the
community could be if one more capital asset (of the most worth-
while kind) were to be produced.

Now, since it is always possible to calculate the marginal
efficiency of any particular type of asset with any given stock of
that asset already, it is also possible to construct a schedule
showing what the marginal efficiency of such an asset would be
when the existing stock of such
assets was at all various possible
levels. The only valid generalisation one can make about the
shape of such a schedule is that
in any given period of time the
marginal efficiency of every
type of asset will always diminish as investment in the asset
increases. The reasons for
this are that, on the one hand,

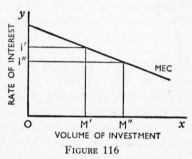

FIGURE 116

the prospective yield of any type of asset will fall as more
units of it are produced, and on the other hand, the supply price
of the asset will rise, unless some units have been unemployed in
the past. The prospective yields will fall because, as more assets
are produced, they will be able to meet the demand for the
product which they make more fully, and the need for more
similar assets will be less urgent. The supply price is likely to
rise because of rising costs in the industry making the asset. Costs
are bound to rise in the short run even if they do not in the long
run.

Since we can generalise in this way about the nature of schedules
showing the marginal efficiency of each individual type of asset,
we can do the same for the marginal efficiency of capital in general.
Having done so we can turn such a schedule into a curve, as has
been done in Figure 116.

In Figure 116 the rate of interest is measured up the y-axis
and the volume of investment undertaken in a particular period
of time along the x-axis. The curve MEC (representing the
schedule of the marginal efficiency of capital in general) shows
the volume of investment which will be undertaken in a given
period at different rates of interest. For example, if the rate of

interest is i', OM' investment will be undertaken in the period under consideration. If the rate of interest falls to i″, the volume of investment will rise to OM″. For, as we have seen in Chapter XIV, business men who wish to maximise profits will invest in new capital assets up to that point where the rate at which the prospective yields of such assets have to be discounted to make their 'net' prospective yield equal to their replacement cost is just equal to the rate of interest. In our new terminology entrepreneurs will equate the marginal efficiency of each asset with the rate of interest. We now begin to see the relationship between investment and the rate of interest. It is clear from Figure 116 that, given the schedule of the marginal efficiency of capital, the rate of interest must fall if there is to be an increase in the volume of investment undertaken. The rate of interest thus plays an important part in determining investment and hence employment.

At the moment, however, we are not very concerned with the rate of interest. We are more concerned with the demand for capital goods, so we must now see what it is that determines entrepreneurs' views on the prospective yield of assets. For production conditions are likely to be fairly stable in the short run, and the supply prices of assets, the one determinant of the marginal efficiency of capital, will thus usually be fairly stable too. Entrepreneurs' estimates of the prospective yields of assets, the other determinant of the marginal efficiency of capital, will be the important factor in the short run in determining by their stability or otherwise whether the demand for capital goods is very stable or very changeable. We shall find that in fact such expectations are often very fickle and uncertain in the real world, and that this is an important factor contributing to fluctuations in investment activity.

Before we turn to a more complete discussion of the forces which determine the prospective yield of an asset, there are one or two features of the marginal efficiency of capital which need to be emphasised. First, the marginal efficiency of any type of asset has nothing at all to do with what the actual yield of an asset has been, looked at historically, once the asset is worn out. The marginal efficiency of an asset shows the return which is *expected* from investing in a brand-new asset, not the return actually obtained from one that has already been used.

Second, it is important to stress once more that the prospective yield on which the marginal efficiency of an asset depends is composed of the total returns expected from the asset during the whole of its life (after deducting the costs incurred to maintain, man and supervise the asset). There is a danger of assuming that *all* the prospective annual returns from an asset will be equal, so that once the returns for the early years of its life are known, those in later years will be exactly the same. This is a dangerous assumption, because these later returns cannot be the same, unless the economy is a static or 'stationary' one with prices, output and population always constant.

The importance of the marginal efficiency of capital is that it emphasises the crucial place of business expectations in determining the level of employment. It is a concept which gives business expectations a central and important position in employment theory. For estimates of the prospective yields of assets depend very largely on entrepreneurs' expectations, and these estimates of prospective yields are one of the two determinants of the marginal efficiency of capital.

2. LONG-TERM EXPECTATION

It is because entrepreneurs can never be quite certain what the prospective yield of any asset will be that business expectations are so important in employment theory. We must now discuss the way in which the prospective yield of any asset is estimated. Keynes felt that expectations of prospective yields were based on 'partly existing facts which we can assume to be more or less known for certain, and partly future events which can only be forecasted with more or less confidence'.[1] Among the former facts, Keynes listed the size of the existing stock of capital assets and the strength of consumer demand for those goods which need considerable amounts of such capital for their production. This former set of facts determines the 'state of short-term expectation'. Among the latter set of facts, Keynes included expectations about future changes in the size of the stock of capital assets; in the tastes of consumers for the goods which these assets produce; and in the size of effective demand during the future life of the assets whose prospective yields are being considered. Keynes defined the state of expectations dependent on these latter considerations as the 'state of long-term expectation'.

Because investors acquiring new assets are more concerned with long-run forces than with short-run ones, and because, as can be seen from the above list, the factors upon which long-term

[1] *Op. cit.* p. 147.

expectation depends are so uncertain, it follows that investing entrepreneurs tend to put undue weight on those factors about which they feel most confident. The facts of the existing situation, and the more certain ideas about the future, enter with disproportionate weight into decisions to invest. The state of long-term expectation thus depends not only upon what entrepreneurs expect to happen, but also on how certain they are that it *will* happen—on the *confidence* which entrepreneurs have when they forecast the future. It depends in part on whether entrepreneurs think that their estimates are more likely to be right or wrong, and this will usually depend on how many certain facts there are compared with those about which entrepreneurs feel vague and unsure.

Keynes therefore held that 'the state of confidence', as practical men term it, was important. It was a factor which economists had hitherto tended either to ignore or to treat in very general terms. Keynes thought that it was important to be more explicit about this 'state of confidence' but pointed out that it would be dangerous to make arbitrary *a priori* assumptions about it. Keynes therefore spent some time in the *General Theory* explaining what he felt was the basis of business expectations and in analysing behaviour on the Stock Exchange. Let us now assume that the rate of interest on securities in general is given and show why Keynes thought that fluctuations in the expected earnings of particular types of investments, or of particular firms, could then occur. For if the general rate of interest is given, any changes in the capital values of particular investments must be due solely to changes in their prospective yields, as estimated by those dealing on the Stock Exchange.

Keynes maintained that in this context 'The outstanding fact is the extreme precariousness of the basis of knowledge on which our estimates of prospective yield have to be made. . . . If we speak frankly, we have to admit that our basis of knowledge for estimating the yield ten years hence of a railway, a copper mine, a textile factory, the goodwill of a patent medicine, an Atlantic liner, a building in the City of London, amounts to little, and sometimes to nothing; or even five years hence.' [1] This means that, since few capital assets last for less than, say, ten or twenty years before wearing out, very great risks have to be

---

[1] *Op. cit.* pp. 149-50. The whole of the chapter from which this quotation is taken, chapter xii of the *General Theory* on 'Long-Term Expectation', is well worth reading in the original.

taken when investment is carried out. It would be most surprising if the realised results of building capital assets often bore any precise relationship to the expected results.

In this context it can be argued that, in the past (say, in the nineteenth century), decisions to invest, once made, were usually made irrevocably, both by the community and by the individual entrepreneur, though no-one could make a precise calculation of prospective profits. Indeed, had such investment been based on accurate knowledge of prospective returns, it is doubtful whether much of it would have taken place at all. For it seems likely that throughout history the realised results of investment activity have, in general, been rather less favourable than those who invested thought they would be. As Keynes puts it, 'If human nature felt no temptation to take a chance, no satisfaction (profit apart) in constructing a factory, a railway, a mine or a farm, there might not be much investment merely as a result of cold calculation'.[1]

In the past, then, when the private entrepreneur invested his money, it was irretrievably sunk. But the divorce between ownership and control which is so common in modern industry, and above all the development of an organised Stock Exchange, have brought a danger of instability into the economic system. On the Stock Exchange, the prospects of many investments are reconsidered and reviewed daily—even hourly. More than this, it is now possible to 'invest' money one day and to 'disinvest' it the next. 'It is as though a farmer, having tapped his barometer after breakfast, could decide to remove his capital from the farming business between 10 and 11 in the morning and reconsider whether he should return to it later in the week.'[2]

These revaluations of investments which the Stock Exchange makes are made primarily to allow existing securities to be bought and sold, and we have seen that the exchange of such existing securities has no direct effect in creating employment. But it is inevitable that such transactions should also exert a profound indirect effect on new investment. When investment is being carried out by floating new issues, the ease with which they can be floated will depend on the Stock Exchange values of similar investments rather than on any individual's estimates of the true prospects of such investments. 'A high quotation (on the Stock Exchange) for existing equities involves an increase in the marginal efficiency of the corresponding type of capital, and therefore has

[1] *Op. cit.* p. 150. [2] *Op. cit.* p. 151.

the same effect (since investment depends on a comparison between the marginal efficiency of capital and the rate of interest) as a fall in the rate of interest.'[1]

This in itself is clearly not necessarily a bad thing. If the ease with which money can be raised depends on Stock Exchange values, and if Stock Exchange values are based on accurate forecasts of the prospects of the various companies whose shares are quoted, the effect will be beneficial. Unfortunately, in revaluing assets so frequently, the Stock Exchange has made it possible for many people to make their revaluations at the same time. And all of these people are usually as ignorant of the real values of the various assets as each other. They therefore fall back on the convention of expecting 'that the existing state of affairs will continue indefinitely, except in so far as we have specific reasons to expect a change'.[2] This is not important so long as the existing state of affairs does continue. The trouble begins when conditions change. The inevitable result of such mass valuation is that when views on the prospects of a particular investment project do change, they usually change violently, and everyone's view usually changes in the same direction. As a result it seems to be an inherent feature of the modern Stock Exchange that alternating waves of excessive optimism and excessive pessimism are almost inevitable.

But it is not only the ignorant investor who is subjected to Keynes' criticism. Even the professional dealer is not exempt. For it seems that the professional dealer is really more concerned with earning a living than with giving a correct valuation to investments, whatever the effect on his income. He therefore makes little or no attempt to find out what the real value of any asset will be in ten or twenty years' time, but merely guesses how the market will value it in a few days, or, at most, in a few weeks. He does this in order to live on the capital profits which he makes by guessing correctly. As Keynes says, 'it is not sensible to pay 25 for an investment of which you believe the prospective yield to justify a value of 30, if you also believe that the market will value it at 20 three months hence'.[3] The result is that instead of providing a mechanism for giving accurate estimates of the prospective long-term yields of various investments, the Stock Exchange provides estimates of how mass opinion will value those investments in a few days' or weeks' time.

[1] Keynes, *op. cit.* p. 151 (footnote).
[2] *Op. cit.* p. 152.   [3] *Op. cit.* p. 155.

Nor is this the only important feature of the Stock Exchange. It is likely that any valuations which are made will have scant economic basis. For mass psychology is singularly prone to overestimate the importance of non-economic factors. A fine example of this occurred early in 1946. One morning, financial newspaper headlines ran roughly as follows : 'Share prices rise as Russian troops leave Persia'. 'Severe fall later when favourite fails to win Grand National.' Now it is probable that political moves, such as the Russian withdrawal from Persia, do have important effects on the prospective yield of investments. But it is most unlikely that any real difference is made whichever horse wins an important race.

It would be wrong to suggest that members of the Stock Exchange deliberately distort the values of investments and thereby make realistic estimates of their prospective yields impossible. Since there can never be accurate foreknowledge of future events, it is only natural that any estimates of prospective yields, whoever makes them, should depend very largely on whim or sentiment or chance. But it is important to realise that in most modern economies, estimates of the value of existing investments—and therefore estimates of the prospective yields of similar projected investments—depend largely on conventional and institutional forces.

We can now see, in outline, the reason why the fact that the prospective yields—and hence the marginal efficiencies of various assets—depend on expectations of future conditions introduces an element of instability into the demand for investment goods. Investment tends to be very sensitive to changes in Stock Exchange values, and these values themselves are likely to fluctuate considerably in sympathy with succeeding waves of business optimism and pessimism.

3. THE MARGINAL EFFICIENCY OF CAPITAL

We must now sum up the argument of this chapter so far. We have seen that the volume of investment undertaken in any period depends on the rate of interest; that the schedule of the marginal efficiency of capital—the demand curve for investment goods as a function of the rate of interest—slopes downwards to the right. We have seen that the position of this demand curve for investment goods depends in a large degree on entrepreneurs' expectations of the future earnings of these goods. We have also seen that such expectations are very uncertain so that the demand for investment goods is prone to be very unstable too. It is thus desirable that we should not include expectations as an important variable in our theory of employment. We are trying to discover sufficient important determinants of the level of employment to enable us to build up an elementary theory of employment, and it is undesirable to include expectations as one of the important independent variables in our system. For one thing, expectations are very difficult to allow for, as we have seen. For another, it is possible to blame almost any event on to some peculiarity of expectations and it is difficult to check whether one is justified in doing so or not. This makes it dangerous to introduce expectations directly into a simple outline of employment theory like ours.

Fortunately this does not ruin employment theory. As we have seen, entrepreneurs tend to base their expectations largely on existing facts—hoping that everything will continue in the future as at present. And the fundamental fact of the existing situation which will influence entrepreneurs in making investment decisions will be the level of consumption. For, as we saw in Part One, the demand for investment goods is a *derived* demand which depends ultimately on current expenditure on consumption. If current consumption is high, investment will be high too, for entrepreneurs will be optimistic. If consumption is low, then investment will also be low. We shall therefore make the simplifying assumption throughout the rest of Part Two that current investment depends on current consumption. The existence of expectations will mean that in the real world the dependence is more complicated. But in our simple theory we may overlook this.

We shall assume, then, that the demand for investment goods is a function of the rate of interest on the one hand, and of the level of consumption expenditure on the other. These relationships are shown in Figures 117a and 117b.

In Figure 117a investment is measured along the *x*-axis and the rate of interest up the *y*-axis. Assuming that consumption is at a given level, say C, then the amount of investment undertaken at various rates of interest is shown on the curve C. But with different levels of consumption, investment at each rate of interest differs. When consumption is C″ (higher than C), investment is greater at each rate of interest than when consumption is C. When consumption is C′ (lower than C), investment is lower at each rate of interest than when consumption is either C or C″. So, if the rate of interest is given, investment is higher when consumption is higher, and lower when consumption is lower. For example, when the rate of interest is i′, investment is greater (at OM″) with consumption at C″ than when consumption is C. Investment is then OM. Similarly, with the rate of interest still at i′, investment is lower (OM′) when consumption is C′ than when consumption is C. For investment is then OM.

Figure 117b gives an alternative snapshot of the picture shown in Figure 117a. Here investment is still measured along

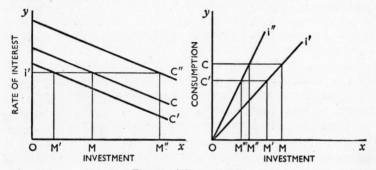

FIGURES 117A AND 117B

the x-axis, but consumption is now measured on the y-axis instead of the rate of interest. At a given rate of interest i′, the curve i′ shows the volume of investment (on the x-axis) undertaken at each level of consumption. Investment (OM) is greater when consumption is higher (at OC) and lower (OM′) when consumption is lower (at OC′). On the curve i″, the rate of interest has risen to i″. Investment at each level of consumption is now lower than it was when the rate of interest was i′, but it is still higher (being OM″) when consumption is OC than when consumption is only OC′. Then investment is OM‴. These two diagrams show, on our simplified assumptions about expectations, the dependence of investment on consumption on the one hand and on the rate of interest on the other.

There are one or two differences between consumption and investment which it is useful to bear in mind. First, whilst the demand for consumption goods is likely to be fairly stable over time, the demand for investment goods is not. Because the inducement to invest depends so largely on expectations of the future, the demand for investment goods can fluctuate violently, even when consumption remains fairly stable. By ignoring expectations, we have been able to show investment as a simple function of consumption. In fact, however, even if consumption is constant, investment can alter because of changed expectations. In Figure 117a, for example, the curve showing investment at each rate of interest for a given level of consumption (say C) may shift bodily to the left if investors become more pessimistic ; or bodily to the right if they become more confident. And the more violent the change in expectations is, the more violent the shift of the curve will be. Thus, whilst for the sake of simplicity it is convenient to ignore expectations, their importance must never be either forgotten or minimised. Second, it must always be remembered that investment depends ultimately on consumption—if no-one consumes, no-one will invest. Investment can thus be expressed as a function of income instead of as a function of consumption. For income (by definition) equals consumption plus investment, and we have seen that consumption is likely to be a fairly stable function of income.

The relationship between income, consumption and investment differs for the individual and for the whole community. The consumption of an individual depends entirely on the size of *his own* income and not at all on that of anyone else. With investment it is different. If the community's income rises, it is true that investment will rise too. But investment is likely to be carried out by different persons from those whose incomes have risen and who can therefore consume more. It is not far from the truth to say that in the modern economy most of the investment is carried out by people who consume only a small proportion of the total volume of consumer goods. As a result, if the income of the community rises, one set of people (consumers) is likely to consume more, and another separate set (entrepreneurs) to invest more. Of course, entrepreneurs do consume more when their incomes rise, but even so, they will rarely consume very much more of their own products. Investors usually invest more because *other people* have consumed more—because *other people* have larger incomes.

This is often important. For example, if consumers decide to spend less on consumption than they have done before and to save more out of a given income than they used to do, investors will tend to invest less than previously and incomes will fall. If incomes had not fallen, there would have been more savings available for entrepreneurs to invest, but entrepreneurs do not wish to invest, because they see demand falling off. So incomes fall and savings and investment are both smaller than they might have been. Again, if consumers decide to spend more on consumption and to save less, investors will invest more and incomes will rise. Although, if incomes had not risen, there would have been fewer savings to be invested, entrepreneurs feel optimistic because demand for consumption goods is rising and invest more, thus enabling incomes to rise and to supply additional savings to finance the investment.

When one considers what it is that determines the demand for investment goods in the economy as a whole, this fact that consumption and investment are carried out by different people, which we have seen to be important in some contexts, can be ignored. The fundamental fact is that, given the rate of interest, when income rises and consumption therefore rises, investment increases also. In the economy as a whole, consumption and income rise and fall together, and the fact that investment varies in the same direction as consumption, means that it also varies in the same direction as income. When income rises investment rises too, and *vice versa*. In our simplified theory we can thus say either that investment depends on consumption or that it depends on income. But it is perhaps more desirable to stress the dependence of investment on consumption because this is not only the more obvious, but also, for practical purposes, the more important fact. Investment depends directly on entrepreneurs' expectations and these depend ultimately on how much is being spent on consumer goods.

The current demand for investment goods, then, depends ultimately on estimates of current consumption expenditure modified to allow for future changes in accordance with entrepreneurs' expectations. This demand for investment goods is given by the schedule of the marginal efficiency of capital. We must soon turn to the other determinant of the inducement to invest, to the rate of interest, so that we can discover what regulates the terms on which investment can be carried out. First, however, there is one interesting, but non-Keynesian, concept which we must analyse.

4. A NOTE ON THE 'ACCELERATOR'

We have seen that the multiplier, by showing the effect of changes in investment on consumption and income, shows how a small change in investment can exert a magnified effect on income and hence on employment and consumption. But the concept of the multiplier is a relatively new idea. There is another concept which considers the relationship between consumption and investment, and which has a rather longer history. This earlier idea is known as *the principle of acceleration of derived demand*.

Quite simply, the acceleration principle (often called the 'accelerator') says this. If the demand for any consumption good increases, this will raise the demand (the 'derived' demand) for the factor of production, perhaps a machine, which makes it. But the demand for machines will rise proportionately even faster than the demand for the product has risen. The term accelerator is thus a metaphor, and in a sense it is incomplete. The accelerator in economics is not the same as the accelerator in a motor car. The idea embodied in the accelerator is not so much one of ever-increasing demand as of a functional relationship between the demand for consumption goods and the demand for the machines which make them. It makes the level of investment a function not of the level of consumption, but of the rate of change of consumption.

There is, therefore, some sort of parallel between the acceleration principle and the multiplier. The multiplier shows the effect on income (and on consumption) of a change in investment. The accelerator shows the effect of a change in consumption on investment. The two concepts could be confused, and the reader should keep the two clearly distinct in his mind. The multiplier shows the dependence of consumption on investment. The accelerator in a sense does the opposite. It shows the dependence of investment on consumption. It says, if consumption rises by X, what will be the effect on investment?

There is one rather important difference between the two concepts. The multiplier depends ultimately on a psychological fact. It depends on the propensity to consume, which is determined by consumers' tastes and habits. The accelerator, on the other hand, depends on a technical principle in the narrow sense. It depends on the durability of machines. For the strength of the accelerator is a function of the length of life of machines. The accelerator depends on the fact that machines wear out only over a period, and that the output of the industry replacing these machines will thus only represent a small fraction of the total stock of machines. It is based on technological factors.

The acceleration principle dates back to 1914 and beyond, in contrast to the multiplier, which only appeared in 1930 with the publication of Mr. Kahn's article. The idea that the dependence of investment on consumption was important—that there was an acceleration principle—was popularised mainly by J. M. Clark, with whose name the principle is usually associated.[1]

The factual basis on which the accelerator has been constructed is the knowledge that fluctuations in employment, output, etc., in the investment goods industries are greater than in the consumption goods industries. Nevertheless, the accelerator does not even pretend to be able to explain *all* fluctuations of this kind. For example, the prices of raw materials often fluctuate even more violently than the price of investment goods. The acceleration principle is unnecessary to explain this fact. The reason lies in the fact that the supply of raw materials—especially those which are agricultural commodities—is much more inelastic in response to demand changes than is the supply of manufactured goods. For the way in which an industrial economy meets falling prices is to reduce output and allow unemployment to increase. Output falls fairly sharply in response to fairly small falls in prices. In an agricultural community, however, the amount of unemployment caused by falling prices is usually small. Because competition is usually perfect, farmers tend to produce as much as they can and sell it for what it is worth. Prices have to fall very sharply when the same supply is to be disposed of but demand has decreased. An additional reason for this difference in the response of agricultural and manufactured goods to falling demand lies in the fact that combinations between producers to maintain prices by restricting output tend to be both stronger and more common in industry than in agriculture.

This problem can be solved quite simply. The problem which the accelerator seeks to solve is more difficult. It is this. Why are fluctuations in employment in the investment goods industries greater than those in consumer goods industries, and, by analogy, why are fluctuations in durable consumer goods industries more violent than those in industries making perishable consumer goods? It does not require great thought to see that the relationship between changes in the demand for house room and subsequent events in the building industry is very similar to the relationship between the demand for consumer goods and subsequent events in the industry which produces the machines which make them. The

---

[1] See especially 'Business Acceleration and the Law of Demand', *Journal of Political Economy*, March 1917, p. 217.

essential fact upon which the accelerator depends, is that machines are durable goods. The accelerator only applies in cases where the investment goods concerned are durable, and its importance is dependent on that durability.

Let us, then, outline the theory of the 'accelerator'. Let us begin by studying a situation where the demand for a particular consumer good has been stable for a considerable length of time. There will thus be a stable derived demand for the machines making these consumer goods, the size of which will depend on the rate at which the machines wear out. Let us suppose that the rate of depreciation is constant and that each machine lasts just ten years. We may therefore assume that 10 per cent of the machines are replaced each year. The annual output of the machine-making industry will be equal to just one-tenth of the stock of these particular machines. So long as the demand for the consumer good is constant, the demand for machines will be a constant 'replacement' demand. There will be no 'net' investment at all—after production to make good depreciation has been allowed for. 'Gross' investment, however, will be positive and will equal 10 per cent of the total stock of machines.

Let us assume that in a hypothetical economy there are 1000 machines making the consumer good. If the life of each machine is ten years, the output of the investment goods industry will be 100 machines per annum. If we suppose that all replacements for any year are ordered on the 1st of January of that year, we have a very simple model. Let us suppose that the demand for consumer goods now increases by 10 per cent. If the industry wants to make all these additional consumer goods, it will need another 100 machines. On the next January 1st, therefore, 100 new machines will be ordered. But the existing replacement demand of 100 machines will continue also. The demand for machines will thus rise from 100 to 200 (an increase of 100 per cent) in order to deal with an increase of only 10 per cent in the demand for consumer goods. A comparatively small rise of 10 per cent in the demand for consumer goods thus causes an enormous rise of 100 per cent in the demand for machines. Employment in the machine-making industry will double. Here, then, we seem to have a likely explanation of fluctuations in employment in the machine-making industries. This is the accelerator at work.

Whether the demand for machines is in fact likely to double as the result of a rise of 10 per cent in the demand for consumer goods depends ultimately on whether the machines last more or less than ten years. If the machines last longer then ten years, the proportionate effect on the machine-making industry will be even greater. If the machines last less than ten years, the effect will be smaller. Nevertheless the general principle remains valid. If the demand for consumption goods rises, and if producers try to satisfy this demand fully from the earliest possible moment, there will be a significant change in the demand for investment goods. But this is not the only reason for supposing that there will be very considerable changes in the investment goods industries when the demand for consumer goods remains relatively stable. Let us suppose that consumer demand, having increased by 10 per cent and having led to a demand for 200 machines in one year, now remains stable. There will be no increase in the demand for machines in the following year. The new 100 machines having been made, the demand for machines will return to the old 100 per annum for replacements. It can only exceed 100 if some of the new machines need replacing. This seems unlikely, as it will take 10 years for them to wear out. After a time, when long-run equilibrium has been reached, 110 machines a year will be demanded instead of the original 100—if no new change has intervened.

Thus, although the increased demand for consumer goods has turned out to be permanent, the effect on the machine-making industry is disappointing. Even in the long run when replacement demand has risen to 110 per annum, 90 fewer machines will be ordered than in the first year after the increase of 10 per cent in demand. The result of the working of the accelerator in our model is therefore to increase the demand for machines very greatly for one year—a relatively short time—and then to cause contraction, and presumably unemployment. If, in this simple model, one wants to avoid fluctuations in activity in the machine industry, one must ensure that the demand for consumption goods remains permanently stable. If the demand for consumer goods is stable for ever, the demand for machines will be stable for ever.

On the other hand, there could be constantly increasing employment in the machine-making industry if the demand for consumer goods were to increase from year to year. It is the falling-off in the *rate of increase* in consumption and not a decline in the *absolute level* of consumption which causes the contraction in the demand for machines. In practice, of course, one need not go quite to this extreme if one merely wants to discover a situation where employment in the machine industry would not fall, even though it might not increase. After consumption had increased for several years, the demand for 'replacements' would grow, and the rate of increase in consumption would be able to slacken off, because of the increased demand for replacements, without the expanded machine-making industry suffering any fall in demand.

To give an example, if in the first year the demand for consumer goods rises by 10 per cent, 100 new machines are ordered, raising demand from 100 to 200 machines. Once some of these machines wear out, the output of the machine industry can be maintained so long as demand continues to increase, even though it may do so at a slower and slower rate. When long-run equilibrium has been reached, say after twenty years, the replacement demand alone will be able to keep the investment industry at work. But consumption would have had to double—quite a feat. It follows, therefore, that on our assumptions in this simple model, unless there is a continual, though not necessarily constant, growth of demand, the effect of a single increase in the demand for consumer goods will be first to expand and then to contract the demand for machines.

There are, however, several points at which it is difficult to accept this extremely simplified model on which we have so far based our discussion of the accelerator. First, as we have seen, the length of the life of the machines making consumer goods is important, and it is difficult to decide whether, in practice, machines are likely to last for more or fewer years than ten. The real difficulty, however, is a rather more serious one. If anything, the explanation of the reasons for industrial fluctuations provided by the accelerator is too good to be realistic. If an increase in demand always resulted in a much more than proportionate increase in the output of machines, fluctuations in the investment goods industries would be even larger than they are. Like most economic models, our model of the accelerator at work is too simple. In particular we have assumed great inflexibility of output in the consumption goods industry and great flexibility in the investment goods industry.

In our model we have made the following assumptions. So far as the consumption goods industries were concerned, we assumed that there was no excess capacity at all. We assumed that no machines were idle and that devices such as double-shift working were out of the question. If, in fact, excess capacity did exist, then an increase in consumer demand could be met by the existing equipment and the accelerator would have no chance to work.

In the investment goods industry we assumed exactly the opposite—that there *was* surplus capacity. If, in practice, there were no excess capacity in the machine-making industry, an increase in the derived demand for machines could not call forth an increased supply of machines. The working of the accelerator depends on the ability of the machine-making industry always to produce greatly increased numbers of machines, with their existing equipment if need be. It depends on the existence of excess capacity in the investment industry. If there were no excess capacity in the investment industry, the only solution would be to put delivery dates back or, perhaps, to raise the prices of investment goods. Thus, whilst the accelerator might be able to explain the size of *price* fluctuations in the investment goods industries, it could not explain variations in output. The principle thus makes the rather severe demand that there shall be excess capacity in one industry but not in the other. This may be the case, but it looks a little improbable at first sight.

One may therefore ask whether the accelerator is not so restricted in its usefulness that it should be ignored in realistic discussions of what determines employment. The fact that it has held its own since 1914 as a useful tool of economic analysis seems to give the lie to this view. On the other hand, it is significant that Keynes entirely ignored the acceleration principle when writing the *General Theory*. He did not mention the technical principle of the accelerator, but stressed the psychological concepts of the multiplier and the marginal efficiency of capital. Keynes seems to have believed that the volatile nature of business expectations was more important in determining the volume of investment, and hence of employment, than the accelerator.

The assumptions made about expectations in the theory of the accelerator are rarely made explicit, but they are most important. The assumptions are 'static'. That is to say, it is assumed that if conditions alter, the response of consumers and entrepreneurs to these changes will be to believe that the changes will be permanent. In our example, when demand increased by 10 per cent, we assumed that entrepreneurs expected (with confidence) that the change would be permanent, that consumption would remain constant at the new and higher level, and that it would neither continue to increase nor fall back to the old level. There can be no other explanation of what happens in the situation analysed in the acceleration principle. If entrepreneurs expected that the change in demand would be only temporary, they would not buy the extra machines. If they expected further, or greater, increases, they would not content themselves with their relatively modest increases in investment. It is therefore important always to remember that every theory of employment makes some assumptions about expectations, even if they are only implicit ones.

SUGGESTED READING

J. M. Keynes, *General Theory*, London, 1936, chapters xi and xii.

Dudley Dillard, *The Economics of J. M. Keynes*, London, 1950, chapter vii.

J. M. Clark, 'Business Acceleration and the Law of Demand', *Journal of Political Economy*, March 1917, p. 217.

Gottfried Haberler, *Prosperity and Depression* Lake Success, 1946, especially pp. 85-105.

CHAPTER XXII

THE RATE OF INTEREST

1. LIQUIDITY PREFERENCE

THE rate of interest is the second important determinant, with
the marginal efficiency of capital as the first, of the volume of
investment undertaken in any period of time. The rate of
interest is the price at which loans of money are made, or to put
it another way, it is the price of money in terms of bonds. The
rate of interest equates the desirability of holding bonds with
the desirability of holding money. In this chapter, therefore, we
shall show what it is that determines the rate of interest on bonds.
We shall concern ourselves mainly with a discussion of the long-
term rate of interest on gilt-edged Government bonds. The
kind of bond we are interested in is of the type of the 'irredeemable' 2½ per cent consolidated stock known as 'Old Consols'.
As we saw earlier, the purchaser of such stock is entitled to an
annual payment of £2 10s. on every bond with a face value of
£100, whatever he has paid for the bond. Thus, if the price of a
£100 bond of this kind falls to £50, the rate of interest is 5 per cent.
If it rises to £200, the rate of interest is 1¼ per cent.

In the first part of this chapter we shall be concerned primarily
with the long-term rates of interest on irredeemable Government
stocks—on 'gilt-edged' securities. But, except in the early part
of this chapter, we are not *only* concerned with the *gilt-edged* rate.
Nor are we solely concerned with long-term rates of interest. It
seems best to take Keynes' view that, 'In general discussion, as
distinct from specific problems where the period of the debt is
expressly specified, it is convenient to mean by the rate of
interest the complex of the various rates of interest current for
different periods of time'.[1]

Since the rate of interest is the price of money loans, it is not
surprising that it should be determined by supply and demand.
In this case it is the supply and demand for money which

General Theory, p. 167 (footnote).

determines the price of money—the rate of interest. On the one hand, the rate of interest depends on the supply of money available to the community; on the other, it depends on the demand for that money—liquidity preference. What, then, determines these ? The supply of money is something which we can assume, for the moment, to be given. As we saw in Chapter XVIII, the supply of money is determined by the action of the central bank, working through the banking system. For the present, our analysis will be simplified if we can assume that this supply is fixed. The demand for money, the community's *liquidity preference*, is an independent variable in Keynes' system, just as the supply of money is. Liquidity preference depends ultimately on the psychology of the community, just as the supply of money depends on the banking system. We have seen (pp. 368-72) that liquidity preference can be split up into three parts : (*a*) money held under the transactions motive, (*b*) money held under the precautionary motive, and (*c*) money held to satisfy the speculative motive. We also saw that the amount of money held under the transactions motive and the precautionary motive depends on the level of income, whilst the amount of money held under the speculative motive depends on the rate of interest.

It is therefore possible to divide liquidity preference into two components, which we can label L^1 and L^2. L^1 is that part of liquidity preference which arises from the transactions and precautionary motives and which thus depends on the level of income. L^2 is the part of liquidity preference which arises from the speculative motive. L^2 is therefore not dependent on income but on the rate of interest. If the amount of money held under L^1 is denoted as M^1, and that held under L^2 as M^2, M^1 is a function of income (Y) and M^2 is a function of the rate of interest (i). It is important to distinguish carefully between M^1 and M^2 because this distinction is essential to Keynesian theory. Symbolically, $M = M^1 + M^2$; $M^1 = L^1$ (Y) ; $M^2 = L^2$ (i). It is also important to avoid confusion about the meaning of the demand for money to hold. As we have seen, money is created by the banking system. All this money is held by someone, so that the total supply of money, M, is equal to the total amount held. We have denoted the total supply of money by M, and the parts of that total supply of money held under L^1 and L^2 as M^1 and M^2 respectively. But whilst the amount of money actually demanded in any existing situation is always equal to the amount actually supplied, different amounts would have been demanded had conditions been different. There is therefore a schedule of the demand for money—a schedule of liquidity preference—showing the amounts which would be demanded in various different conditions. And the factors which influence the demand for money, as we have seen, are the rate of interest and the level of income. We can therefore construct schedules of liquidity preference showing how much money the community would wish to hold at various levels of income and various rates of interest. Schedules of liquidity preference are shown in Figure 118.

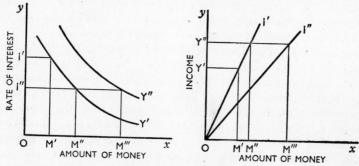

FIGURES 118A AND 118B

Figure 118 shows the relationship between three variables: the amount of money (M), the rate of interest (i), and income (Y). In Figure 118a the curve Y' shows liquidity preference when income is Y', at various rates of interest—how much money is demanded by the community at various rates of interest when income is Y'. Similarly, the curve Y" shows liquidity preference at various rates of interest when income is Y", Y" being greater than Y'. Other curves could be drawn showing liquidity preference at other levels of income. In Figure 118b, instead of drawing each curve for a given level of income, the rate of interest is taken as given instead. Thus the curve i' shows how much money will be demanded when income is at various levels, and the rate of interest is i'. Similarly, the curve i" shows liquidity preference at these same levels of income when the rate of interest is lower— at i". Figures 118a and 118b thus give two alternative versions of the liquidity preference schedule.

From Figure 118a the following conclusions can be drawn: (1) The community will hold more money at low rates of interest than at high ones, if income is constant. For example, when income is Y' and the rate of interest is i', an amount of money

OM′ is held. When the rate of interest falls to i″, the amount of money demanded rises to OM″, though income is constant at Y′. (2) At a given rate of interest, more money is held when income is higher. For example, when the rate of interest is i″ and income is Y′, OM″ of money is demanded. When income rises to Y″, the rate of interest remaining at i″, liquidity preference rises to OM‴.

From Figure 118b one can again see that : (1) If the rate of interest is given, people hold more money the larger are their incomes. When the rate of interest is i′ and income is OY′, the amount of money demanded is OM′. When income rises to OY″, the amount of money demanded rises to OM″. This diagram shows more clearly what is the relationship between the level of income and liquidity preference—that liquidity preference depends in part on the level of income. The fact that the liquidity preference schedules are here drawn as straight lines implies that the amount of money demanded rises in exact proportion as income rises. This need not be the case, but it may be. (2) Given the level of income, more money will be held if the rate of interest falls. For instance, in Figure 118b when income is OY″ and the rate of interest is i′, the amount of money held is OM″. When the rate of interest falls to i″, with income still OY″, the amount of money demanded rises to OM‴.

2. LIQUIDITY PREFERENCE AND THE RATE OF INTEREST

We have worked so far on the assumption that the demand for money under the transactions and precautionary motives depends only on the level of incomes. We have also assumed that the demand for money under the speculative motive, L^2, depends on the rate of interest alone. It is desirable that we should now justify these assumptions. In practice, of course, even the demand for money to satisfy L^1 is not likely to be completely independent of the rate of interest, for we are assuming throughout that bonds are the closest substitute for money. Therefore to hold any money under L^1 represents a sacrifice of interest. That money could easily be used to buy bonds and earn interest. It is therefore likely that, in the long run, if the rate of interest is high, people will try to hold as little money as possible under L^1. If the rate of interest is low, the sacrifice caused by holding money will be much smaller, and people will not take so much care to be economical in the amount of money they hold under L^1.

Over long periods, five, ten or twenty years, it is likely that less money will be held to satisfy L^1 if the rate of interest is high than if it is low. In the short run, however, this is much less certain to happen. Increases in the amount of money held under L^1 are likely to be much more closely connected with changes in the level of incomes than with changes in the rate of interest. To put it colloquially, the effect of a change in the rate of interest takes time to 'soak into' the system.

On the other hand, to hold money to satisfy the speculative motive (L^2)—to keep money for use in speculating on changes in bond prices—will again involve a cost. People who hold money under L^2 have to sacrifice interest which they might otherwise have earned, in order to hold this *masse de manœuvre*, and the higher the rate of interest, the greater the sacrifice. But this is not the fundamental connection between the rate of interest and the amount of money held under the speculative motive. As we have seen, the main connection is quite a different one. The demand for money to satisfy the speculative motive does not depend so much on what the current rate of interest is, as on expectations of *changes* in the rate of interest. If we study the nature of these expectations, we shall be able to see how, and to what extent, such expectations depend on the current rate of interest. This is the way in which we find a connection between the facts of the existing situation and the demand for money under L^2—a demand which is really dependent on expectations of the future. Why is it that people hold money to satisfy L^2? Why, when income is constant, do people hold more or less money in response to changes in their expectations about the rate of interest?

The economists who wrote before Keynes did recognise the dependence of the demand for money under L^2 on expectations, but they did not realise that it was expectations about changes in the rate of interest which were most important. The traditional view of economists has been that the only close substitutes for money were commodities. They thought that people were only interested in the future prices of commodities so that they could move their resources out of money and into goods when goods were expected to become dearer, and *vice versa*. If people think that the prices of commodities will rise, it will pay them to switch their money holdings into commodities in order to make profits when prices do rise. On the other hand, if people expect commodity prices to fall, it will pay to hold money and not commodities, so that the money can be used to buy up larger amounts of commodities when they are cheaper. This was the generally accepted theory of earlier economists. Keynes, however, maintained that there was not sufficient reason for accepting this theory, and challenged the traditional view.

It is clear that if people expect prices to fall, this is a good reason for refusing to hold commodities, but it is not, in itself, enough to induce people to hold money instead. There is as good a case for thinking that people will sell goods to hold bonds as for thinking that they will sell them to hold money. If people expect the money prices of goods to fall, but think that the rate of interest will remain constant, why should they shift their resources from goods to money? If people feel quite certain that the rate of interest will remain constant, then they can back their expectations just as easily by buying bonds as by acquiring cash. For they can always sell these bonds for cash, without loss, at a moment's notice. If the rate of interest is constant, people can not only store their wealth safely, but can earn interest on it at the same time. Uncertain expectations about the future of *commodity prices alone* are therefore not a sufficient explanation of the desire to hold money under the speculative motive. The desire to hold money for speculative purposes depends much more closely on changes in bond prices. It depends, that is to say, on expectations of changes in the rate of interest.

We have so far seen why it is that the amount of money held to satisfy L^1 depends on income, and that held to satisfy L^2 depends on the rate of interest. We must now see in detail how it is that we can connect expectations about the future rate of interest with the current rate of interest. For only thus can the rate of interest be made to depend on the present situation and not on future events alone.

The way in which the future rate of interest depends on the present rate of interest is as follows. If the rate of interest is high at any moment, people will naturally expect it to fall in the future. For a high rate of interest means low bond prices, and, given the psychology of the community, the lower bond prices are at present, the more likely it will seem that a future recovery is going to take place. Because bond prices are low now, compared with what most people regard as a 'normal' price, it is only natural that they should expect bond prices to rise sooner or later. It will thus seem sensible to hold bonds rather than money. A high current rate of interest will cause expectations of a fall in that rate in the future and little money will be held for speculative purposes.

If on the other hand the rate of interest is low compared with the 'normal' rate, there will be two inducements to hold fairly large amounts of money. First, the interest sacrificed by holding such money will be small since the rate of interest is low. Second, the fact that the rate of interest is low will inevitably make people expect that it will rise in the future. It will therefore be anticipated that bond prices will fall, and it would be foolish to hold bonds in such circumstances, especially as the yield is small too. It is in this way that the present level of the rate of interest is connected with expectations about the future rate of interest.

3. THE DETERMINATION OF THE RATE OF INTEREST

Having briefly shown that liquidity preference depends on the rate of interest and on income, we can use this knowledge to discuss more fully the way in which the rate of interest is determined. To begin with we shall simplify the analysis by assuming that liquidity preference depends *only* on the rate of interest and we shall assume for the moment that the level of income remains constant. It is important to bear this fundamental but temporary assumption in mind.

We may then say that liquidity preference depends on the rate of interest, in just the same way as we can say that the amount of any commodity which is demanded depends on the price of the commodity. The amount of money which is held depends on what the rate of interest is, in just the same way as the amount of a good which is actually exchanged in a market depends on what the equilibrium price of the good is. But this analysis of the dependence of the amount demanded on price tells only half the story. Price itself is not an independent variable but a dependent variable. So, just as the equilibrium price of a good is fixed by the demand and the supply of the good in question, the rate of interest is determined by liquidity preference on the one hand and by the amount of money on the other. The rate of interest, when it has thus been fixed, determines how much money will in fact be held.

In order to see the way in which the demand for money and the supply of money determine the rate of interest, let us begin with the simplest possible case. Let us assume a single change of data and see what is the effect on the rate of interest. Let us assume that the supply of money is fixed, but that a spontaneous change in 'tastes' shifts the liquidity preference schedule. This is analogous to a change in tastes altering the demand schedule and hence altering price, when the supply schedule of a good remains unchanged. We can now trace the effect of the change in liquidity preference on the rate of interest. Let us assume that the liquidity preference schedule shifts to the right. This means that at the existing price of bonds—at the current rate of interest— some people, at least, are more eager to hold money instead of bonds than they were before.

This does not necessarily mean, however, that anyone now actually buys or sells any bonds at all. We can assume, for example, that demand increases equally all over the market. Everyone's demand for money changes to the same extent. In this case there will be no buying or selling of bonds. No-one acquires more money nor does anyone hold fewer bonds. But the price of bonds will fall. In other words, people revise their views of the relative values of money and bonds. They take a less rosy view of the desirability of holding bonds and a better view of the desirability of holding money. The result is a slump in bond prices. Thus the effect of the change in the demand for money need not be to increase turnover in the market for bonds at all. There need be no change whatsoever in anyone's holdings of bonds or of money. But the rate of interest rises—bond prices fall. This can be seen from Figure 119.

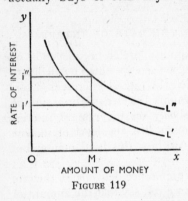

AMOUNT OF MONEY

FIGURE 119

Up the y-axis in Figure 119 are measured rates of interest. Along the x-axis are measured amounts of money. The curve L' shows how much money is demanded at each rate of interest. The rate of interest is thus i' where the (fixed) supply of money OM is all held. If everyone now wants to hold more money at each rate of interest, and the liquidity preference schedule thus moves to the right, the new equilibrium position is on the curve L". If the amount of money remains fixed at OM, the only rate of interest at which this amount of money OM will all be held is i". The rate of interest thus rises to i". The effect of the change in liquidity preference is to raise the rate of interest from i' to i".

This model, however, is too simple since it allows for no sale

or purchase of bonds at all.   There will usually be some buying
and selling of bonds going on all the time quite independently of the
rate of interest.   The real question to ask therefore is : Does a change
in views about bond prices lead to an increase in Stock Exchange
dealings in such bonds ?   A second model which we can construct
will thus be one where some one person changes his views
about bond prices, becoming, say, more anxious to hold money
and less anxious to hold bonds, but no-one else's views change at
all.   In this case there is a spontaneous change in one part of the
market but no induced change results from it.   In this situation
there must be increased exchanges of bonds.   For the person
whose views have changed will wish to sell bonds, and other
people will have to be induced to buy them, presumably by a fall
in bond prices and a rise in the rate of interest.

The real model of course will be still more complicated.
There will usually be a spontaneous change in the views of some
people about bond prices.   Associated with this there will be a
change in the views of other people.   Let us assume that a group
of people think that bond prices are about to fall and become
more anxious to hold money.   They are therefore more anxious
to sell bonds.   The views of most other people on the Stock Exchange will change too, but they need not change at the same time
or to the same extent.   They need not even all change in the same
direction.   Because of all these changes in views, some people
may become very anxious to sell bonds and hold cash, others not
quite so anxious to hold cash and so on.   Some people may even
think that bond prices are going to *rise* and not to fall, and will
become more anxious to hold bonds rather than money—they
will want to buy bonds for cash.   Whether bond prices actually
fall or rise will depend on whether those who expect a fall in
bond prices, and want to sell bonds, are trying to sell more bonds
than those who expect a rise in bond prices and want to buy.

If the former group of people is predominant, bond prices will
fall and interest rates will rise ; if the latter prevails, bond prices
will rise and interest rates will fall.   In either case an increase in
the number of Stock Exchange transactions is likely.

This seems to be a more realistic picture of what happens on
the Stock Exchange.   If it is, then the result of changed views
about bond prices will be an increase in liquidity preference if the
net effect is that those who take a more dismal view of bond
prices predominate in the market, and *vice versa*.   If the effect,
on balance, is that the liquidity preference schedule rises, the

rate of interest will rise. If the net effect is to reduce liquidity preference at each rate of interest, then the rate of interest will fall.

We have so far assumed that whether or not all views change simultaneously, and whether or not they all change to the same extent, the amount of money in existence is always constant. The result is that although, on balance, people want to hold more money, they are unable to do so because the additional money is not there to be held. They can only hold more money if more is supplied, and since more money cannot be supplied, something else in the system must give way. It is therefore bond prices and interest rates which change. Bond prices alter so that the existing amount of money and the existing supply of bonds are consistent with each other and this brings about a new rate of interest. In other words, the total supply of money is now held by people who are content to hold it at the new rate of interest, and the supply of bonds is all held by people who are content to hold them at their new prices.

Where there is a sharp and sudden change in bond prices and thus in the rate of interest, an increase in purchases and sales of bonds seems certain. For the fact that there has been a sharp movement away from the existing state of affairs means that people will take differing views about the future. Their preconceived ideas will have been suddenly shattered, and they will be even more uncertain than usual about what the future holds in store. Views will therefore almost certainly differ greatly from individual to individual. This third case is the most realistic one, but the simplest case, which does after all show the essence of the problem, will be the one where there are no changes in holdings of money or bonds when liquidity preference changes.

The rate of interest, as we have seen, depends on the amount of money as well as on liquidity preference. Changes in the amount of money will therefore cause changes in the rate of interest so long as liquidity preference does not change to the same extent. We shall now assume that the supply of money can alter, but that liquidity preference does not alter. This latter assumption is made only so that our analysis can remain simple.

We have seen that the supply of money is controlled by the central bank working on the monetary system through the mechanism of open-market operations. When the central bank buys securities worth £100, credit is expanded by about £1200, and *vice versa*. In order to simplify the analysis, let us here ignore the fact that the effect of any purchase of securities is multiplied, in its effect on the system as a whole, because of the 1 : 12 cash-deposit ratio. We also ignore the fact that there will, in practice, be a time-lag before the full effect of the original purchase of securities can work itself out in expanding bank credit. We shall assume that when the central bank buys securities worth a given amount, the deposits of the joint-stock banks increase immediately by an equal amount. We shall ignore all the other repercussions of open-market operations. If the central bank buys bonds, the simple direct effect will there-fore be to create additional money in the form of increased deposits of the customers of the joint - stock banks. And when the supply of money rises in this way, then, since liquidity preference is assumed to be given, the rate of interest will fall.

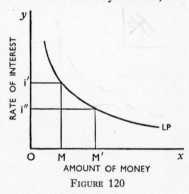

FIGURE 120

This can be seen from Fig-ure 120. The community's (given) liquidity preference schedule is there shown by the curve LP. The amount of money originally in existence is OM and the rate of interest at that stage is i'. The central bank now buys bonds and increases the supply of money from OM to OM'. As a result the rate of interest falls to i". When the central bank enters the bond market, one may say that, whilst all individuals take the same view of the relative attractiveness of money and bonds, the central bank changes its policy. It becomes more anxious to hold bonds than cash, and therefore creates money for individuals to hold. Since the liquidity preference of these individuals is given, the rate of interest falls so that the community may be induced to hold all the money which is now available.

If anyone becomes more anxious to hold bonds, the price of bonds rises. In this particular case, the price of bonds is raised by the banking authority. The price may rise by little or by much, and the extent of the rise in price will depend on whether or not people are very reluctant to disgorge bonds and hold money instead. Someone *must* be persuaded to sell bonds if the amount of money is to be increased, but the extent of the persuasion needed may differ. If bond-holders are reluctant to sell, even though

the central bank is bidding up the price of bonds considerably,
it is clear that liquidity preference is increasing very little as the
rate of interest falls. The demand for liquidity is not very
'elastic' in its response to changes in the rate of interest, and a
relatively small effort in the shape of open-market purchases of
securities by the central bank will cause a considerable fall in the
rate of interest. On the other hand, if the 'elasticity' of the
liquidity preference schedule is very great in response to changes
in the rate of interest, it will require considerable purchases of
bonds by the central bank to lower the rate of interest.[1]

4. THE RATE OF INTEREST AND INVESTMENT

We have here the essence of the theory of the rate of interest,
and there is little need for further revision. But we must introduce
one important complication. We have so far assumed that
liquidity preference depends only on the rate of interest. As we
have seen, this is a useful simplification, but it is not a very realistic
one. Liquidity preference also depends on the level of income.
A change in either liquidity preference or in the amount of money
will alter the rate of interest and thus affect the level of incomes
by altering the volume of investment activity. And this change
in income will in its turn affect liquidity preference. We must
now analyse the nature of this reaction on liquidity preference.
Its effect may be felt through the transactions motive, the precautionary motive or the speculative motive. We must therefore
try to discover which of these parts of liquidity preference is
likely to be most affected.

Let us assume that the liquidity preference schedule is given,
and trace the indirect effects of a fall in the rate of interest caused
by a rise in the quantity of money. The main secondary effect
will be on investment. The normal result of a fall in the rate of
interest, with a given schedule of the marginal efficiency of capital,
is for investment to increase, as we saw earlier. The result of this
is an increase in income, the size of the increase depending on the
size of the multiplier. But as income rises, so does the amount
of money held under L^1. The transactions motive, in particular,
will absorb a larger amount of money as income rises, so that not

---

[1] Our discussion has assumed, for simplicity, that the central bank always
increases the supply of money by buying long-term securities. In practice the
central bank may well pay as much, if not more, attention to short-term
securities, e.g. Treasury Bills. The results will be much the same in either case.

all of the increased demand for money resulting from a fall in the
rate of interest is attributable to the speculative motive. The
transactions (and perhaps also the precautionary) motive plays
its part.

It is clear that in a general equilibrium analysis of the present
kind one cannot ignore these indirect repercussions of a change in
any one variable. For the indirect results of a change in the
rate of interest may be just as important as the direct ones. The
variables in a general equilibrium system are rather like the
juggler's balls. If he is to keep them all in the air at once, he
can only neglect any one of them for more than a split second at
his peril. So, with a general equilibrium analysis, to neglect one
variable may result in giving a completely wrong answer. The
ultimate effect of a change in the amount of money in the system
is thus not only that the rate of interest falls : income and employment rise. Nevertheless, the fall in the rate of interest is an
absolutely vital link in the chain by which the increase in the
supply of money raises the level of employment. The efficacy
or otherwise of a fall in the rate of interest in creating employment
will depend on whether such a fall in the rate of interest causes
a large or small increase in investment. This depends, as has
been shown in the previous analysis, on business men's expectations. Entrepreneurs are sometimes in the mood for expanding
investment and sometimes they are not.

One can, however, legitimately expect that the effect of a fall
in the rate of interest on investment must always be in the right
direction—must always be to increase investment. A fall in the
rate of interest is unlikely to reduce investment, though this could
presumably happen. If entrepreneurs were alarmed by Govern-
mental interference with the rate of interest, they might invest
less rather than more. Their alarm at the Government's 'cheap
money' policy might lower the marginal efficiency of capital
schedule so much that the fall in the rate of interest was more
than outweighed. But it is not likely that the marginal efficiency
of capital will alter in this way. It is more likely that the demand
for investment goods may be inelastic to changes in the rate of
interest, that the marginal efficiency of capital may diminish
rapidly as investment increases, and that this is most likely to
be the weak link in the chain connecting a fall in the rate of
interest with an increase in the volume of employment.

Here, in its essentials, we have Keynes' theory of the way
to increase employment and cure slumps. The Government is

in a position to tell the central bank to indulge in open-market operations, buy securities, and lower the rate of interest. This 'cheap money' policy will make investment less expensive to finance ; and provided that the marginal efficiency of capital schedule is relatively elastic and remains relatively stable, investment and incomes will rise. If the marginal efficiency schedule shifts, however, perhaps because of changed business expectations, it may be necessary to reinforce the lowering of the rate of interest by more direct methods. If entrepreneurs refuse to invest when they can do so cheaply, then the Government itself may have to carry out a socialised investment programme. This would raise incomes directly and might well encourage private investment. Similarly, Government intervention might be necessary if the marginal efficiency schedule were inelastic to reductions in the rate of interest.

There are two other rather important points to notice. When we first mentioned the rate of interest in this chapter we explained that it was the rate at which entrepreneurs could borrow to finance investment ; that, in other words, we were mainly concerned with the rate of interest on debentures. In this analysis of the way in which open-market operations work, however, we have been concerned with the rate of interest on Government securities—the 'gilt-edged' rate of interest. For, in this country at any rate, the central bank does not buy up commercial debentures, but only deals in 'gilt-edged' securities. It is thus important to understand what is the link between the 'gilt-edged' rate of interest and the rate of interest on commercial debentures.

We may say, in the first place, that the rate of interest on debentures will always be higher than that on Government securities. The reason for this is that commercial bonds always involve a greater risk than do Government bonds. Government securities are the 'safest' possible securities, and the danger of repudiation is for all practical purposes non-existent. Commercial enterprises, however, do sometimes find it impossible to meet their liabilities. No firm, however reputable, can guarantee that changes, for example in consumers' tastes, will *never* affect its profits, and the greater risk incurred by those who invest in commercial bonds means that they will demand a greater return. The more risky the investment, the higher the return demanded.

If we call the rate of interest on 'gilt-edged' bonds the 'pure' or 'riskless' rate of interest, the rate of interest on commercial debentures will exceed this 'pure' rate by the amount of a 'risk premium'. The rationale of our analysis is thus that there will always be a relatively stable differential between the low rate of the 'gilt-edged' bond and the slightly higher rate of the commercial bond; that the rate of interest on the one will fall in step with the rate of interest on the other and *vice versa*. In other words, we are assuming implicitly that Government bonds and commercial bonds are close substitutes for each other and that central bank action in lowering 'gilt-edged' rates will lower rates on industrial debentures too.

This does not mean any serious qualification to our theory, but it is worth noting. When we discussed liquidity preference, we assumed that people could choose between holding money or one sort of bond. We assumed that there were no other close substitutes for either money or bonds, and we ignored what would happen if there were other close substitutes for money and bonds. Our admission that there are various kinds of bonds means that the demand for money is a little more complicated than we have made it appear. Nevertheless, if we assume that there is a close link between Government bonds and commercial debentures, we can see how a fall in the gilt-edged rate of interest will affect the commercial debenture rate, which is so vital a factor in influencing investment. In fact, we are quite justified in assuming that *all* interest rates will rise and fall together and that by acting on 'gilt-edged' prices the central bank can change the rate of interest at which the ordinary entrepreneur can borrow when he issues debentures.

One other point is important. We have already seen that the volume of open-market purchases which the central bank has to undertake in order to cause a given fall in the rate of interest will depend on the 'elasticity' of the liquidity preference schedule. But it is important to realise that this elasticity itself may well be different at different rates of interest. If the central bank wants to lower the rate of interest from 5 to $4\frac{1}{2}$ per cent, it is likely that it will be able to do it much more easily than if it wants to lower it from 3 to $2\frac{1}{2}$ per cent. This is partly because the proportionate change is greater, and partly because the lower the rate of interest is, the more likely people are to think that it will rise again in the near future with the consequent danger of capital losses. Thus, the lower the rate of interest is, the harder it will be to persuade those dealing on the Stock Exchange that the high bond prices are likely to persist. This is because, to keep the rate of interest at any level, the central bank has to buy up all the bonds owned by those people who think that the new price of bonds is too high to last, and the lower the rate of interest is, the more people will think that this is the case.

One can go further even than this. Keynes has maintained that there are strong forces preventing the rate of interest falling below a certain level, probably between 2 and 4 per cent. The reason for this is that once the rate of interest falls to this level, *everyone* becomes convinced that it cannot fall further, and may well rise again, and the central bank cannot bid up the price of securities further—even if it buys up *all* securities offered to it. In other words, liquidity preference has become absolute, or infinitely elastic. All the money which the bank pumps into the system will be held without inducing any fall in the rate of interest.

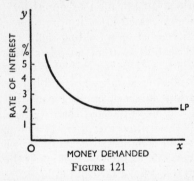

FIGURE 121

This means that the liquidity preference schedule is asymmetrical as one moves downwards along it. After a certain point it becomes horizontal — liquidity preference becomes absolute. This is shown in Figure 121.

When the rate of interest falls to 2 per cent the liquidity preference schedule becomes infinitely elastic—it becomes a horizontal line. The reason, as we have seen, is that the price of bonds is so high that, short of there being a negative rate of interest, the boom in bond prices cannot continue. The lower the rate of interest, the greater the risk of capital losses, and the smaller the likelihood of a further fall bringing capital gains. In addition, the gains for which the capital losses are risked are very small. A man may be willing to risk a capital loss of, say, £10 on a security if it brings in £10 a year, but he will not be so keen to do so if it only brings in £2. Yet when the rate is 2 per cent, the risk (and the size) of such a capital loss is much greater than when it is 10 per cent.

It may be wondered why it is that at such rates of interest everyone feels that 'rock bottom' has been reached. It is likely that no-one would be prepared to hold securities at low rates of interest, *even if they thought these rates would persist.* One reason

is that there is always some trouble and expense in turning a
security into money, whilst money can always be spent at a
moment's notice—it is perfectly liquid. It is therefore necessary
to offer everyone who buys securities some small inducement to
put his money into illiquid assets—to compensate him for their
'imperfect moneyness'.[1] It follows that the rate of interest
cannot fall to zero, since money and securities can never be
perfect substitutes.

This explanation is satisfactory in the case of gilt-edged
securities. They earn a 'pure' rate of interest partly because they
are imperfect substitutes for money but mainly because, in fact,
people are always somewhat fearful that rates may rise in the
future. But when one considers commercial bonds there is an
additional reason why rates of interest cannot fall very low. The
rate of interest on such bonds must always be high enough to
repay the lender for the risk of default by the borrower. The rate
of interest which borrowers have to pay will remain substantial,
even if the 'pure' rate of interest, where no such risk of default
exists, falls to a negligible figure.

The conclusion to be drawn from this discussion is that the
prospects of increasing investment by lowering the rate of interest
are not very bright in those situations where the rate of interest
on commercial debentures would need to fall below, say, 3 per cent
in order to increase investment. One ingenious solution to this
problem has been put forward. Certain writers have made
proposals for introducing 'stamped' money—for making the
holders of money put a postage (or other) stamp on every bank
note at intervals, thus introducing a cost for holding money.
Presumably charges would also be levied on bank deposits in
proportion to their size. This would mean that securities, which
would not be 'stamped', would be able to bear a very low rate of
interest—perhaps even a negative one—and this would clearly
stimulate investment.

5. THE FINANCIAL MOTIVE FOR HOLDING MONEY

We saw in Chapter XIV that if one analyses the rate of interest
in terms of ordinary price theory, the demand for capital goods
is determined by the (discounted) marginal productivity of capital
and the supply of capital by consumers' time preference. But

---

[1] J. R. Hicks, *Value and Capital* (2nd Edition), p. 166.

2 G

we have now seen that ordinary price theory only really applies to an economy where money acts as a numeraire and nothing more ; where there is no demand for money as such—but only a demand for money savings representing a command over real resources. We have now discovered that the rate of interest is in fact a 'monetary' rather than a 'real' phenomenon. It does not depend directly on savings decisions and investment decisions but rather on the demand for and supply of money, for money has other uses besides representing the demand for and supply of loanable funds . . . 'it equalises the advantages of holding actual cash and a deferred claim on cash '.[1] It will be useful now to clarify the differences between these two views of the rate of interest, between the 'real' theory advanced in Chapter XIV and the 'monetary' theory of this chapter.

In one sense, of course, the rate of interest is by definition a 'monetary phenomenon' because it is calculated in terms of money. In times of inflation, loans are occasionally made, and repayments contracted, in terms of commodities ; but this only happens because money has become valueless and no-one will accept it. It has ceased to be money. The rate of interest is always calculated in terms of the existing standard of deferred payments, and in all normal circumstances this will be money. To that extent the rate of interest must always be a monetary phenomenon. It is still arguable, however, that the rate of interest, whilst contracted and paid in terms of money, is determined by savings and investment decisions and not by the demand and supply of money.

So far as savings decisions are concerned, we have already given a statement (pp. 392–4) of the reasons which make it seem probable that savings are determined by the level of incomes rather than by the rate of interest. We have seen that there are strong reasons for thinking that the effects on savings of changes in the rate of interest are so insignificant that they can be ignored. But even though changes in the rate of interest may not affect savings, it would still be possible for changes in savings to alter the rate of interest. Keynes is at pains to rule out the possibility of any significant effects of this kind. 'I readily admit that the intention to save may affect the willingness to become unliquid meanwhile. This factor should certainly be included in the list of motives affecting the state of liquidity preference. . . . But it is

---

[1] J. M. Keynes, 'Alternative Theories of the Rate of Interest', *Economic Journal*, 1937, p. 245.

only one amongst many and, in practice (I should have thought), one of the least important.' [1]

Having ruled out the effects of changes in savings on the rate of interest, the next question which we must consider is whether changes in the volume of investment can alter the rate of interest, and, if so, to what extent. The idea that changes in the volume of investment activity will affect the rate of interest is, at any rate, plausible. In the *General Theory*, Keynes was attempting to popularise the notion that the rate of interest depends only on the demand and supply of money. He therefore maintained that changes in investment do not affect the rate of interest. Since this was a novel view, it is not surprising that Keynes was criticised. After several exchanges in the *Economic Journal* in 1937 and 1938 Keynes did modify the form, at least, of his theory so far as the effect of investment on the rate of interest was concerned.

Let us consider why it seems probable that the rate of interest should be affected by changes in the volume of investment. Let us suppose, to begin with, that entrepreneurs revise their ideas of the marginal efficiency of capital and therefore decide to increase their investment. In Keynes' model the entrepreneurs would finance this investment by borrowing money and the demand for money from this source would increase. In other words, as a result of the increase in the marginal efficiency of capital, the demand for loans would rise. The question which Keynes had to solve was whether or not this would raise the rate of interest. The solution which Keynes gave was as follows.

The volume of investment, as such, does not determine or help to determine the rate of interest. On the main question, Keynes maintains his position entirely. But he is prepared to admit that the increase in investment may well cause repercussions in other parts of the system which, in their turn, influence the rate of interest. In a general equilibrium system such as Keynes', a change in anything is bound to have some indirect effect, however small, on almost everything else. The important question is whether that indirect effect will be significant. In this particular case, the way in which a change in investment may affect the rate of interest is through its effect on the liquidity preference schedule, and Keynes admitted (in 1937) that this effect might often be important. If an increase in investment does raise the liquidity

[1] J. M. Keynes, 'The "Ex-Ante" Theory of the Rate of Interest', *Economic Journal*, 1937, p. 665.

preference schedule, this will raise the rate of interest. Thus an
increase in investment may raise the rate of interest indirectly,
provided of course that the amount of money remains constant.
But the result is better understood if conceived, not as a direct
result of an increase in investment itself, but as the result of an
increased demand for money—as the result of an increase in
liquidity preference.

Keynes therefore makes a distinction between the direct and
automatic effect of investment on the rate of interest which
earlier economists believed to be important and the indirect
influence of increased investment on the rate of interest through
liquidity preference, which is perfectly compatible with his own
theory. The difference may perhaps be illustrated as follows.
If the connection between a change in investment and a change
in the rate of interest is direct, then, if entrepreneurs increase
investment by 10 per cent, that will raise the rate of interest to an
extent depending on the supply schedule of savings. Given the
propensity to save, an increase in investment by 10 per cent will
always raise the rate of interest by more than it would rise if the
increase in investment were only 5 per cent. This must always
happen if the rate of interest varies directly with the volume of
investment. For if one assumes that this is the case, then one not
only assumes that entrepreneurs invest, but one also assumes that
they borrow money to do so, perhaps by issuing new commercial debentures. And one further assumes that, since the
price of bonds is related to the amount of money, increased
borrowing lowers the price of bonds and thus raises the rate of
interest.

Keynes denies that this is necessarily what happens. So far
as the impact effect of increased investment is concerned, the
assumption is that, to finance the investment, entrepreneurs will
wish to hold more out of a given stock of money, and that this
will raise the rate of interest. Keynes thus agrees that increased
investment will normally raise the rate of interest, but he asserts
that the extent of this rise will not be determined directly by the
size of the increase in investment. This is because whilst an
increase in investment means an increase in the amount of money
borrowed, there are other factors to be considered, besides the
fact of increased borrowing, if one wishes to discover the effect
on the rate of interest. Keynes maintains that this effect on the
rate of interest depends not on the increase in investment as
such but also on its effects on the liquidity preference of the

community. In particular, Keynes distinguishes between the effects (a) on the borrowing entrepreneurs, and (b) on everyone else who derives an income from the increased investment programme.

First, what will the effect on borrowers be ? This was something which Keynes did not analyse in the *General Theory*, but in the later articles in the *Economic Journal* he coined the term 'financial motive' or 'demand for finance' [1] to describe that part of liquidity preference which depends on investment activity. The active demand for money (that is, under the transactions motive) falls, according to Keynes, into two parts, 'the demand due to the time-lag between the inception and the institution of the entrepreneurs' decisions, and the part due to the time-lags between the receipt and disposal of income by the public, and also between the receipt by entrepreneurs of their sale-proceeds and the payment by them of wages, etc.' [2] The first of these demands for money represents the demand for 'finance', the last two represent the ordinary 'income' and 'business' motives for liquidity.

If an entrepreneur is planning to invest and borrows money to do so, he will find it difficult to synchronise his borrowing on the Stock Exchange with buying and paying cash for buildings and machinery. An entrepreneur who is buying machines first borrows money. Later he passes on the money to pay for the machines. During the period between borrowing the money and paying for the machines the entrepreneur holds money to satisfy the 'financial motive'—his liquidity preference rises. This would not be particularly important if there were always constant time-lags between borrowing by entrepreneurs and the spending of this money on investment. In fact, of course, different entrepreneurs are likely to hold money for different lengths of time before spending it. It is therefore not at all easy to decide how much money will be held under this part of liquidity preference. The idea that firms hold money to satisfy the financial motive is a useful one, for money held under this motive is undoubtedly important in a modern economy, though there is no simple functional relationship between the volume of investment and the amount of 'finance' held. The result of introducing the financial motive is not to deny that if investment rises the rate of interest may rise. But it explains that the rate of interest can only rise because of an associated rise in the demand for money—because entrepreneurs borrow money at one date and do not spend it

[1] *Economic Journal*, 1937, p. 247.   [2] *Economic Journal*, 1938, p. 319.

until later. The extent of the rise in the rate of interest consequent upon a given increase in investment is thus uncertain. It depends entirely on the case in question. Investment may be the same in two different cases, but if the effect on the 'financial motive' for liquidity preference is different, the effect on the rate of interest will be different too. If the 'finance' is provided by re-lending money previously used to finance a different project, there will be no effect on the rate of interest. If 'new finance' has to be found, the rate of interest will rise—unless the supply of money is increased.

This, however, is not the whole story. So far we have considered only the effect of an increase in investment on the demand for money by the investing entrepreneurs. But the money which they pay for the investment goods goes to other entrepreneurs who have produced the goods in question. We must therefore consider the effect on their liquidity preference. Their incomes have risen and they will therefore tend to hold more money under the transactions motive. We must not only consider the special and peculiar liquidity preference of the investing entrepreneurs. We must also study the ordinary liquidity preference to satisfy the transactions motive of the entrepreneurs who produce the investment goods. Nor is this necessarily the end of the story. Some of the money will have been passed on to workers in the investment goods industries and they will almost certainly hold more money under the transactions motive, for they will be better off now that investment has increased.

We have seen, then, that to consider only the direct dependence of the rate of interest on changes in investment is to look at the problem in too simple terms. A realistic analysis must always be in terms of liquidity preference. This is so in all cases. Take, for example, the extreme case where entrepreneurs exactly synchronise the receipt of loans from the Stock Exchange and their payments to suppliers. If this happens there is no change at all in the rate of interest. What happens must, however, still be analysed in terms of liquidity preference and not in terms of saving on the one hand and investment on the other.

We may therefore conclude that the 'financial motive' is an important refinement to the theory of interest. But it does not destroy the validity of Keynes' ideas. The basic fact remains unaltered. The rate of interest depends on the demand for money and the supply of money. It equates the amount of money in existence with the liquidity preference of the community.

SUGGESTED READING

J. M. Keynes, *General Theory*, London, 1936, chapters xiii and xv.

J. R. Hicks, *Value and Capital*, Oxford, 1946, chapters xi, xii, xiii and xix.

Dudley Dillard, *The Economics of J. M. Keynes*, London, 1950, chapter viii.

Bertil Ohlin, 'Some Notes on the Stockholm Theory of Savings and Investment', *Economic Journal*, 1937, I, p. 53 ; II, p. 221.

J. M. Keynes, 'Alternative Theories of the Rate of Interest', *Economic Journal*, 1937, p. 241.

'The "Ex-Ante" Theory of the Rate of Interest', *Economic Journal*, 1937, p. 663.

D. H. Robertson, 'Mr. Keynes and Finance', *Economic Journal*, 1938, p. 314.   Keynes' comments on this note, *ibid.* p. 318.

A. P. Lerner, 'Alternative Formulations of the Theory of Interest', *Economic Journal*, 1938, p. 211.

CHAPTER XXIII

KEYNESIAN EMPLOYMENT THEORY
SUMMARISED

1. THE DETERMINANTS OF EMPLOYMENT

MOVING towards a complete understanding of the Keynesian analysis of unemployment is rather like building a house. One has to learn about the meaning and importance of the various bits and pieces before one can put them together and see the whole building in its entirety. We have now reached a stage where we can start the building operation and see what kind of an explanation of the unemployment problem, and what kind of a cure for it, Keynesian theory offers. We have already been able to give a number of hints about the way in which the various parts of the theory work, but we have not yet fully shown how they fit together.

As we saw at the beginning of our analysis of employment theory, the fundamental assumption of Keynesian economics is that employment is a function of income. When a community has a large income it has high employment ; when its income is small, employment is low. But a country's income is only the sum of expenditure on consumption and on investment by individuals, by firms or by the Government. In order to explain why income (and hence employment) is high or low, the crucial factor to consider is thus the size of these three items—consumption, investment and Government expenditure—for they are the items on which income depends.

Consumption, investment and Government expenditure, as we have seen, depend themselves on various other factors, and these other factors are the ultimate determinants of the level of activity. The relationship between all these variables can be shown in Table 7.

Table 7 gives, in a rather crude form, the relationship between the important variables in the Keynesian system. The first equation shows that income (on which employment depends) is made up of consumption, investment and Government expenditure. This is the fundamental proposition of Keynesian theory which we have kept continually in the forefront of our discussion. But these component parts of income depend on other variables.

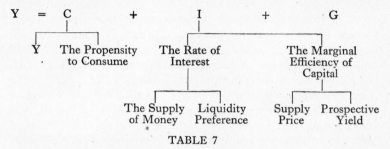

TABLE 7

Consumption depends on the level of income Y and on the propensity to consume, and, as we saw, the propensity to consume decreases as income rises. Investment depends on the marginal efficiency of capital on the one hand and the rate of interest on the other. Again, the marginal efficiency of capital depends on prospective yield and supply price, whilst the rate of interest depends on the demand for money—liquidity preference—and the supply of money. Finally, Government expenditure does not usually depend directly on economic forces but on the policy of the Government of the day, and the mood of political thinkers and pressure groups. Only at intervals, for example when economic conditions are critical, is the Government likely to have to frame its expenditure to accord very closely with economic forces.

Here in Table 7 we see in a simple form the essentials of the Keynesian scheme, and on the basis of this table we can trace the effects of a change in any one variable on the economic system. For example, let us assume that unemployment is considerable. How can it be decreased? First, we know that employment depends on income, so that an increase in employment can only come from an increase in income. From the equation $Y = C + I + G$ it is clear that an increase in income depends on an increase in C, I or G. How can this be brought about?

Consumption depends on income itself and on the propensity to consume. Since income is a dependent variable it can only be altered by altering the independent variables in the system. But it might be possible to modify the propensity to consume. If the propensity to consume can be raised, income will rise, and that will cause further rises in consumption. As we saw in Chapter XX, the propensity to consume depends on the psychology of consumers. Unless consumers can be persuaded to change their habits, consumption cannot rise. Now it is only reasonable to think that consumers' habits are difficult to alter, and that consumers will, in any case, resent interference with them. There is, however, one other possibility. As we saw earlier, the rich will tend to have a lower propensity to consume than the poor. If, therefore, one takes income away from the rich and gives it to the poor, one can increase consumption. In this way the propensity to consume for the community as a whole will be raised, and consumption and income will both rise. This may sound a somewhat drastic procedure but there is no doubt that redistribution of income from rich to poor is an effective way of raising effective demand and increasing employment, if political considerations make it desirable. One way of increasing employment, therefore, is to raise the propensity to consume.

Keynes, however, was not particularly attracted to this line of action. He thought that those who advocated an attempt to increase consumption as the real solution to the problem of unemployment [1] laid 'a little too much emphasis on increased consumption at a time when there is still much social advantage to be gained from increased investment', adding, 'I am myself impressed by the great social advantages of increasing the stock of capital until it ceases to be scarce'.[2] Nevertheless, Keynes felt that the wisest course, in the end, might be 'to advance on both fronts at once'.[3] It is not surprising therefore that Keynes should have laid more stress on ways of increasing investment than on ways of raising consumption.

As we have seen on several occasions, investment depends on the schedule of the marginal efficiency of capital which is such that the lower the rate of interest is, the greater is the volume of investment. This is because the schedule of the marginal efficiency of capital slopes downwards to the right. More investment will only be forthcoming if the money needed to carry it out can be borrowed more cheaply. The aim of any community which seeks to raise investment must therefore be either to raise the marginal efficiency of capital or to lower the rate of interest.

Now the marginal efficiency of capital can only be increased if the prospective yield of assets rises or their supply prices fall. The supply price of assets, however, is not likely to respond to

[1] *Op. cit.* p. 325.   [2] *Ibid.*   [3] *Ibid.*

deliberate attempts to lower it. It is not easy to alter physical conditions of production—especially in the short run. But the prospective yield of investment in general, whilst easier to alter, is only easier to alter in the wrong direction. A Government trying to create business pessimism could do so very easily; for example, by providing an unpopular Chancellor or by taxing investment projects. It is much harder to make business men optimistic than to alarm them. The result of any attempt to interfere with the prospective yield of assets is likely to be violent if it is hoped to reduce it, and not very successful if it is hoped to increase it. It is not easy to make business men optimistic by mere persuasion. There is little hope of increasing investment by deliberate action to alter the marginal efficiency of capital.

The rate of interest, however, provides a much more attractive target for would-be employment creators. Depending as it does on the demand and supply of money, the rate of interest may well prove responsive to judicious tampering. Liquidity preference, being another psychological phenomenon, is best left alone, for if altered at all, it is likely to alter violently and probably in the wrong direction. But the amount of money, being in the control of the banking system, seems ideally suited to deliberate alteration. We have discussed the effects of low rates of interest at length in Chapter XXII and have seen that, by increasing the amount of money, it should be possible to increase investment. Even here, though, there are some snags. We have already shown that it may not be possible to lower the rate of interest below a certain level, where liquidity preference becomes absolute, or the indirect effects of changes in the amount of money on the marginal efficiency of capital cannot be predicted. In addition investment may be inelastic to changes in the rate of interest.

Finally, though we have been able to ignore it in our analysis so far, the effect of Government expenditure must not be overlooked. The reason why we have been able to ignore Government expenditure so far is that it does not depend on independent economic variables like the rate of interest or the propensity to consume. Instead, Government expenditure is entirely under the control of politicians and is not much affected by economic forces. It is precisely for this reason that Government expenditure is likely to prove the most useful means of increasing employment. Alone of all the determinants of employment it can be controlled at will. The Government can influence the level of activity in two ways. On the one hand, by spending money on either consumption or investment it can increase effective demand and increase employment. On the other hand, Keynes regarded the true contribution of the State not as merely to spend money, but more especially to undertake any investment projects, which appeared useful, without too close calculation of their (uncertain) prospective yields. In this way, Keynes thought, the Government could offset the vagaries of the marginal efficiency of capital. The *General Theory*, however, was not a book which was concerned to any great extent with the problems of Government policy, though it certainly did not overlook its importance; and we need say no more about Government policy here.

It would be a mistake to think that the Keynesian analysis has nothing to say about inflation or full employment. Admittedly the main emphasis is on the problems of unemployment, but we shall see in the next chapter that Keynes had much to say about inflation. Meanwhile it will be useful to apply Table 7 to the explanation of how to cure inflation. The Keynesian analysis really is a 'general' theory; it can explain the problems of inflation and over-employment with ease. For in just the same way as unemployment results from a deficiency of effective demand, so inflation occurs when effective demand exceeds the aggregate supply price of the full-employment output.

This does, of course, raise one important point. We have so far ignored aggregate supply because we felt that when there was unemployment, it would be foolish to try to increase aggregate supply (with constant prices of goods), for example by raising the efficiency of labour. It would be more sensible to use all unemployed labour, before trying to make the men (and machines) who actually are at work produce more.

When the goal of full employment has been reached and passed, this objection is of no importance. The cause of inflation is that aggregate demand price exceeds aggregate supply price, so that there can only be equilibrium if aggregate supply price is raised. In conditions of unemployment this could be done by putting more men to work, increasing output, and hence raising the aggregate value of output. Once full employment is reached, however, aggregate supply cannot be raised in this way. There are no more men to employ. Aggregate supply price must still rise to equal aggregate demand price, but it does so by means of a rise in the prices of individual goods and factors of production—by inflation.

There is, however, still the possibility that increased output may come, not by taking on more men, since all are employed, but by enabling each to produce more efficiently by devising new methods or by building new machinery. In the long run, the only real escape from inflationary conditions is by increased output, in an outright shift of the aggregate supply schedule—not because prices have risen, but because more goods of all kinds are being made by the same number of men. Because he was writing in times of severe depression, Keynes could ignore ways of increasing aggregate output with a given labour force—the sort of problem which can be tackled with the kind of analysis used in Part One. Since there was not enough demand to take up the output which could already be produced if only everyone had a job, there was little point in discussing ways of increasing the potential full employment output. But in inflation it is dangerous to think that the Keynesian solution must be to reduce effective demand. In the short run, before productive efficiency can be raised, this may be so. In the long run there is no doubt that Keynes would have been as ready as anyone else to stress the need for obtaining increased output with the same labour force. In depression, a drive for industrial efficiency may well increase unemployment. In inflation it is the only hope of raising standards of living.

The conditions underlying aggregate supply have been thoroughly analysed in Part One, and we need not say more about ways of increasing aggregate supply now. In any case, since the Keynesian theory is essentially a short-run theory, it is aggregate demand which must bear the brunt of any Keynesian attack on inflation. Effective demand is the target at which the first anti-inflationary shafts must be aimed.

Effective demand can be reduced by reducing consumption, investment or Government expenditure. As we have seen, consumption, depending as it does on income and the propensity to consume, can only be reduced if the propensity to consume can be altered. People must be persuaded to save more at each level of income. In times of economic crisis, or war, it is sometimes possible to prevent or reduce inflation by persuading people to save more from patriotic motives. But it is doubtful whether much can be hoped for in this direction in normal times. It is even less likely that people will voluntarily save more. For times of inflation are times when people spend most. For one thing, since prices are rising, people have to spend more to maintain their existing standards of living. For another, the fact that prices are rising makes it desirable to buy goods now rather than in the future, when prices will have risen further. An effective way of reducing consumption would be to redistribute incomes from those who have a high propensity to consume (the poor) to those with a low propensity to consume (the rich). Such a procedure, however effective economically, is usually politically undesirable, if not impossible. It is rare, therefore, to find that inflation is checked by efforts directly to lower the propensity to consume.

The most effective method of reducing consumption is by increasing taxation on income which would otherwise have been spent on consumption. Provided there are no serious adverse effects, for example in increasing dis-saving, this will be an effective check on inflation. Investment too can be reduced by allowing the rate of interest to rise and choke off the least profitable schemes. The rate of interest will, in practice, often rise automatically in times of high employment, because the demand for money for transactions purposes will probably increase considerably. This will raise the rate of interest unless the supply of money can be increased. If the automatic rise is not sufficient, it will be possible to raise the rate of interest further by reducing the supply of money. Raising the rate of interest is likely to reduce activity much more speedily and successfully than lowering the rate will increase it. It is much easier to charge a high rate of interest and thus discourage investment than it is to persuade business men, even when the rate of interest is very low, to undertake investment if times are bad and confidence is lacking.

This leads to a most important point. The greatest danger in attacking inflation by raising the rate of interest is that the restriction of investment and the consequent multiplier effects on income will begin a deflation. Some business men are bound to lose money. They will therefore revise their estimates of the prospective yield of investment (maybe drastically), and the effect may well be to lower the marginal efficiency of capital so far that no practicable reduction in the rate of interest can bring back full employment. A rise in the rate of interest in a time of prosperity, whilst it is bound to reduce investment, may cause excessive pessimism to replace the excessive optimism of the boom and may cause serious deflation. Once again, it is the fickle and unstable nature of business expectations which is at the root of the difficulty.

Government expenditure is, on the whole, the easiest part of effective demand to reduce without causing serious political or economic repercussions. Since the amount of Government expenditure can be reduced quite quickly and easily, if there is real need, and, in particular, since the size of cuts can be decided on in advance and carried out exactly, this type of expenditure usually bears the brunt of attacks on inflation, closely supported, as a rule, by taxes on consumption expenditure and higher interest rates. A great advantage of this method of reducing effective demand is that the repercussions on private investment are not likely to be adverse, provided the cuts in Government expenditure are small. Most business men welcome a reduction in Government activity, and so long as the reductions are not very big (or the multiplier is small), there is little danger of such cuts causing a serious decline in private investment and hence in employment.

It can be seen from this brief outline that the Keynesian analysis applies equally to inflation and deflation. It is indeed a 'general' theory and is not confined to analysing either deflation or inflation. This was shown very clearly by Keynes' pronouncements on economic policy early in the war. In November 1939, Keynes wrote three articles in *The Times* showing that inflation was the result of an excess of effective demand. He suggested that, since voluntary savings were insufficient to keep down wartime consumption, a scheme of 'Compulsory Savings' was necessary. This scheme was elaborated, early in 1940, in a booklet, *How to Pay for the War*. Here Keynes expanded his original argument and, in order to stress that the 'compulsory savings' would be repaid after the war, changed the term 'compulsory savings' to 'deferred pay'. Such a policy was, of course, put into effect later in the war, though on a much smaller scale than Keynes had envisaged, in the 'post-war credits' scheme.

2. EQUATIONS AND DIAGRAMS

This summary of Keynesian theory has been carried out in the simplest possible terms; but readers will have noticed that the vital parts of the Keynesian analysis, for example liquidity preference and the propensity to consume, denote functional relationships between variables. It is therefore possible to summarise the theory in terms of equations and diagrams, and it will be useful to supplement the above summary, made in words, with a summary in such terms. It is clear that Keynes himself had such an analysis in his mind, although he rarely makes explicit use of mathematical functions. It was not long, however, once the *General Theory* was published, before other economists made their own summaries of the *General Theory*. One of the most useful, carried out in mathematical terms, was that given in an article published by Dr. Oscar Lange in 1938.[1] We shall base the following mathematical summary on this article. The advantage of a mathematical summary is that, with it, one is able to make a precise check on the verbal argument.

The whole of the general theory, says Dr. Lange, can be summed up in four fundamental equations, linking the main variables in the system. First, there is the liquidity preference function, linking the amount of money and the rate of interest :

$$M = L(i, Y). \qquad . \qquad . \qquad . \qquad (1)$$

This equation shows that the amount of money (M) which people hold depends on (is a function of) the rate of interest and the level of income. As we have seen, the amount of money which people hold under the speculative motive depends entirely on the rate of interest. Money held under the transactions and the precautionary motives similarly depends wholly on the level of income. The functional relationship between M and i is therefore such that, as i increases, M falls, and *vice versa*. On the other hand, Y and M both rise and fall together. The functional relationship L, between M and Y, is the liquidity preference function.

The second equation in Dr. Lange's summary is the consumption function. It shows the relationship between income and consumption :

$$C = \phi(Y, i). \qquad . \qquad . \qquad . \qquad (2)$$

This equation shows that consumption depends on the level of income and on the rate of interest. As we have seen, Keynes felt that the most important and certain relationship between these variables is between Y and C. As Y rises, C rises ; and as Y falls, C falls. Keynes was not so certain about the way consumption, with a given income, responded to a change in interest, and felt that any effect, in whatever direction, would be very small indeed. The functional relationship ϕ in this equation is the propensity to consume.

Third, there is the investment function showing what determines the level of investment :

$$I = F(i, C). \qquad . \qquad . \qquad . \qquad (3)$$

[1] 'The Rate of Interest and the Optimum Propensity to Consume', *Economica*, 1938, p. 12. Reprinted in *Readings in Business Cycle Theory*, The Blakiston Company (1944), p. 169.

Here we see that investment depends on the rate of interest and on consumption. Investment depends on the rate of interest because, given the marginal efficiency of capital, investment would be greater the lower the rate of interest, and less the higher the rate of interest. The marginal efficiency of capital, on the other hand, depends, in any given state of expectations, on consumption. The greater consumption is, the greater the marginal efficiency of capital will be, and, given the rate of interest, the greater investment will be. Investment depends on consumption as well as on the rate of interest.

Fourth, there is an equation showing that income is identical with consumption plus investment:

$$Y = C + I. \qquad . \qquad . \qquad . \qquad (4)$$

In these four equations there are five unknowns, M, Y, C, I and i. But since equation 4 is an identity, Y is given once we know C and I. This means that we can reduce the unknowns to four (excluding Y), and the equations to three (ignoring equation (4)). In other words, we have only three significant equations. It follows that if we are to work out the values of the unknowns from the equations we must reduce the unknowns from four to three. For in any system of simultaneous equations one must have an equal number of equations and unknowns. Since there are only three significant equations, we must have only three unknowns if we are to solve them. So, if we know the value of one of the unknowns, C, I, i or M, we can discover the values of the other three unknowns from equations 1, 2 and 3.

It is usual to take M, the amount of money, as given, since this is normally determined by the banking system, in accordance with current financial policy. This means that we now know M, L, ϕ and F, and we can thus determine the values of C, Y, I and i. Provided that the four equations are mutually consistent, the system will be in equilibrium. If the equations are not consistent, changes in the variables in the system will have to occur to bring about equilibrium of the whole system.

Readers who are not happy using simultaneous equations will probably find these four equations easier to understand if they are put in the form of four diagrams, as in Figure 122. In Figure 122a we have the liquidity preference schedule (or function) showing what the rate of interest is when various amounts of money are held. Let us assume that the economy shown in Figure 122 is originally in equilibrium with an income of Y_0

2 H

(£6000). An amount of money of M_0 (£3000) is at that time in existence. This means that the rate of interest will be i_0 (3 per cent), as can be seen in Figure 122a. Since the rate of interest is

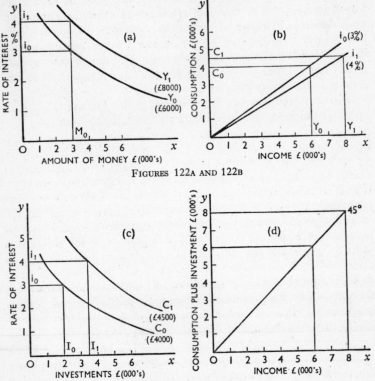

FIGURES 122A AND 122B

FIGURES 122C AND 122D

i_0 (3 per cent), Figure 122b shows that the consumption function is such that, out of the income of Y_0 (£6000), C_0 (£4000) will be spent on consumption.[1] Similarly, Figure 122c shows that with a rate of interest of i_0 and consumption of C_0 (£4000), investment will be I_0 (£2000). Finally, Figure 122d shows that when consumption plus investment is £6000 income is £6000. The 45° line shows that $C + I$ always equals Y. Since income is £6000, as in the original situation, it follows that the amount of money, M_0, and all the other variables are compatible with equilibrium

[1] The assumption here is that the average propensity to consume is constant, whatever the level of income. This enables us to draw the curves as straight lines.

at the old level of income and there will be no change in the system. It is in equilibrium.

If this were not the case, and if, for example, consumption and investment together had equalled, say, £8000, income would have to rise to £8000 and we should have had to consider equilibrium with different values of the variables; for this would mean that the system was not in equilibrium. Income would have risen and that would have changed the position of the liquidity preference schedule; this would have affected the rate of interest, and so on. The effect of these various changes would thus have to be traced through the complete system.

Still using Figure 122, we can trace what would happen if income did in fact rise to £8000 with £3000 of money still in existence. The liquidity preference schedule would now rise to Y_I; for the demand for money under the transactions motive would have risen now that income had risen from Y_0 to Y_I—from £6000 to £8000. Assuming M to be fixed at £3000, the rate of interest would rise to i_I (4 per cent) (as shown in Figure 122a). With i_I at 4 per cent and with an income of £8000, consumption rises to £4500 (C_I in Figure 122b). The consumption function moves slightly to the right as the rate of interest rises—people save slightly more. Investment with i_I at 4 per cent and C_I at £4500 is £3500 (Figure 122c). From Figure 122d we can see that income which is equal to C + I (£4500 + £3500) is now £8000. Since this is equal to the new and higher income of £8000, the system is in equilibrium at this new level of income.

The set of diagrams is thus able to show whether or not the system is in equilibrium, just as the equations did. Provided one knows the shape of the four functions and the value of any one of the dependent variables M, C, I and i, one can work out the changes in the whole system which will follow on a change in any one variable. These two methods of summarising Keynesian theory mathematically are thus a useful supplement to the verbal statement given earlier in the chapter.

3. THE DEFINITION OF INCOME

We have said a great deal about income in these last few chapters on Keynesian theory, and have tried deliberately to give the impression that income is an unambiguous concept; for there were difficulties enough without creating difficulties of definition. But income can be defined in a great many different ways. There is no single comprehensive definition and some definitions are more useful than others. Two definitions of income are extremely important in Keynesian employment theory. It will pay us, therefore, to look at these two definitions of income carefully, showing just where each fits into the Keynesian scheme of analysis.

We have already seen that in any community the national income is equal to the value of the national output. We can therefore take as our starting-point the fact that in any period, say one year, 'gross' national income, the total amount of money received by all factors of production (by everybody in the community), is equal to the 'gross' national product—the value of the total output of the community. In Keynesian theory this concept of 'gross' national income is not particularly useful as it stands. Keynes defines 'income' for any given year by subtracting from the gross national income the costs which entrepreneurs have incurred during that year by using their capital assets and not leaving them idle. There is no difficulty in dealing with that part of the national income received by the hired factors. This is unambiguously the income of those members of the community who receive it. We can call this part of 'gross' national income *factor cost*. It is the cost of all the hired factors to all the entrepreneurs in the country. The rest of 'gross' national income is more difficult to deal with.

Let us for the moment ignore the part of entrepreneurs' receipts which they pay out to other factors of production in rent, wages and interest. Let us, that is to say, ignore factor cost since its amount is easy to calculate. The remainder of entrepreneurs' earnings are their profits and it is these which they try to maximise. But in making decisions about how much employment they should offer in order to maximise profits, the profits or 'income' which entrepreneurs consider is not 'gross' in the way that 'gross' national income is. An entrepreneur who is calculating the size of his 'income' has to take into account changes in the value of his capital assets. In the case of entrepreneurs, the main consideration of this kind will be the extent to which their machines, buildings and the like have suffered depreciation or obsolescence during the year.

In calculating how big an output to produce, however, an entrepreneur will be able to ignore that depreciation or obsolescence which would have happened *whether he had produced any output or not*. These depreciation costs are 'fixed' costs in the sense that they play no part in determining which is the most profitable output to produce. The 'income' which entrepreneurs expect to earn, which determines the shape of the aggregate demand schedule and hence helps to determine effective demand, must therefore exclude only those depreciation costs which entrepreneurs *deliberately incur* by using their capital assets instead of leaving them idle. For such costs of using machinery *are* under the entrepreneur's own control. The entrepreneur himself decides how big an expense in the form of depreciation and maintenance he will incur merely by deciding that he will produce a given output. This expense represents what Keynes calls the *user cost* of producing the given output. It is the cost of using the machinery rather than leaving it idle.

Let us assume, for example, that an entrepreneur has a machine worth £100 and that at the end of a year, having been used to produce output, it is worth only £90. The user cost of the machine is then £10, provided that the machine would have remained worth £100 had it not been used at all. In practice, however, the machine would probably have automatically suffered some depreciation even if it had not been used. It might be, for example, that had the entrepreneur not used the machine, the most worth-while—the 'optimum'—procedure would have been to spend £1 during the year on keeping it in running order. This might have maintained its value at £95 instead of £90.

In this instance, user cost for the year in question is £4. It is the difference between the decline in the value of the machine when it is used (£10) and the depreciation which would have occurred in any case (£5) plus the 'optimum' amount of money spent on its upkeep (£1). This equals £6—made up of £5 loss in value and £1 maintenance cost. User cost is £95 – £1 – £90 = £4. In words, it is the 'optimum' value which could have been preserved from one year to the next, minus the cost of preserving that optimum value, minus the actual value of the machine at the end of the year. By adding together user costs for all entrepreneurs in an economy, we obtain aggregate user cost for the economy. And by subtracting this aggregate user cost from the 'gross' profits of all entrepreneurs, we obtain entrepreneurs' 'income' or 'profit' in Keynes' sense. It is these 'incomes' which entrepreneurs will attempt to maximise.

Now since the remainder of entrepreneurs' receipts (that is those not going in profits or in user cost) will be paid out in wages, rents and interest (*i.e.* factor cost), the 'income' of the community is equal to the sum of all entrepreneurs' receipts from selling output (gross national income, which Keynes denotes as A) minus total user costs (which Keynes calls U). 'Income' in Keynes' sense is A – U. The importance of 'income' defined in this way is that 'since it is the entrepreneur's expectation of the excess of this quantity over his outgoings to the other factors of production which he endeavours to maximise when he decides how much employment to give to the other factors of production, it is the quantity which is causally significant for employment'.[1] 'Income' to Keynes is therefore a kind of 'gross' income but differs from the normal definition of gross national income by excluding user cost.

This definition of 'income' is the one used in most of Keynes' analysis. However, Keynes feels that when the community is deciding how much to spend on consumption it is 'net income' and not 'income' upon which its decisions will depend. The reason why we have so far considered 'income' (*i.e.* A – U) is, as we have seen, that entrepreneurs who are fixing output to maximise profits will only take into account that change in the value of their capital assets which is under their own control—user cost. But in deciding how much of their income they will *consume*, people will need to take account of *involuntary or uncontrollable* changes in the value of their assets. For business men, the main changes in this category will be the result of their assets becoming outdated by new inventions, or becoming less effective because of the passage of time.

This will mean that when deciding how much of their profits they dare spend on consumption, entrepreneurs will have to allow for the fact that their assets have lost value as a result of the passage of time and irrespective of whether they have been used or not. Entrepreneurs who do not allow fully for depreciation before spending their incomes will be reducing the value of their assets—they will be consuming their capital. Consumption would then take place at the expense of the capital assets of the community and, rightly, most people are anxious to 'maintain their capital intact'. On the other hand, it is possible that entrepreneurs may act too cautiously, and that 'financial conservatism' may lead entrepreneurs to set aside more money than is necessary to maintain their capital intact. If this occurs, consumption may be unnecessarily restricted and employment thereby reduced.[2]

[1] Keynes, *op. cit.* p. 54.
[2] Keynes' comments on this problem will be found in the *General Theory*, pp. 98-104.

What Keynes calls 'net profits', on which entrepreneurs' consumption depends, therefore exclude not only user cost but also an allowance for ordinary depreciation and obsolescence. This second deduction Keynes calls *supplementary cost* and he denotes it as V. For the community as a whole, therefore, 'net income' is $A - (U + V)$. It is gross national income minus *both* user cost *and* supplementary cost. It is this 'net income', and not 'income' as defined above, which determines the consumption of the community.

We have so far ignored the possibility that there may be a rise in the value of capital assets which will *increase* consumption in the same way as supplementary cost reduces it. User cost can scarcely be negative, nor is it likely that, when we are considering industrial assets as a whole, supplementary cost can be negative—that the value of assets will rise and not fall during the year. But for those members of the community who own assets of other kinds, increases in the values of these assets are quite possible. For some people, net income might exceed gross income. It is not likely, however, that net income will exceed gross income *for the community as a whole*. Industrial user cost and supplementary cost together will invariably be greater than increases in the value of non-industrial assets. To sum up, then, in Keynesian economics 'income', which helps to determine employment by determining the most profitable outputs for entrepreneurs, is $A - U$. 'Net income', which helps to determine consumption, is $A - (U + V)$.

Keynes also defines savings and investment in two ways. 'Savings' in Keynesian economics excludes user cost and is equal to current investment or simply 'investment'. For 'savings' equals 'income' minus consumption, whilst current investment in any period equals 'output' minus consumption. So, since 'income' equals 'output', saving equals current investment. Similarly 'net savings', which is equal to 'income' minus supplementary costs minus consumption, is equal to 'net investment', which equals 'investment' minus supplementary costs. It is important to bear these definitions in mind when reading Keynes' *General Theory*.

SUGGESTED READING

J. M. Keynes, *General Theory*, London, 1936, chapter iii, section 2, pp. 27-8 ; chapters vii and xviii.

Gottfried Haberler, *Prosperity and Depression*, Lake Success, 1946, chapter viii.

Dudley Dillard, *The Economics of J. M. Keynes*, London, 1950, chapters i and iii.

Oscar Lange, 'The Rate of Interest and the Optimum Propensity to Consume', *Economica*, 1938, p. 12 (reprinted in *Readings in Business Cycle Theory*, Blakiston Press, Philadelphia, 1944, p. 169).

CHAPTER XXIV

KEYNES AND THE CLASSICAL ECONOMICS

1. THE EQUATION OF EXCHANGE

IT is now time to fulfil a promise made earlier and to compare some of Keynes' views with those of earlier economists on the same topics. The first three sections of this chapter will summarise the ideas of earlier economists about output and prices, and show how Keynes' views differed from them. The last section of the chapter will show the differences between Keynes' views and those of earlier economists about the way in which changes in the level of money wages influence the level of employment.

The 'classical' economists' ideas about changes in the general level of prices are to be found in what is known as the 'Quantity Theory of Money'. Attention is there focused on the connection between the price level and the amount of money. There is no single 'Quantity Theory of Money' which can be accepted as authoritative. Almost all economists writing before Keynes laid stress on the relationship between the amount of money and the level of prices, but they made their propositions with differing degrees of emphasis and precision. For the sake of clarity let us distinguish three main versions of the 'Quantity Theory of Money'.

First, there is the *equation of exchange* or the 'Fisher Equation', so called because it was formulated by the American economist Professor Irving Fisher. The equation of exchange states that if M is the amount of money; if V is the velocity of circulation (or the number of times that each unit of money is used during a given period); if P is the price level; and if T is the volume of trade (or the quantity of goods exchanged against money during the period), then $MV = PT$. In other words, the quantity of money multiplied by the number of times that each unit of this money is used during any period of time, equals the price level of goods multiplied by the volume of such goods bought during that same period.

Second, there is what can be called the 'rigid' version of the quantity theory of money. This states that prices always change *in exact proportion* to changes in the quantity of money. If the amount of money is doubled, prices double. If the amount of money is halved, prices fall to half their original level. So, if M represents the amount of money and P represents the price level, this version of the quantity theory of money can be expressed as $M = kP$, where k is a constant. In other words, the amount of money always bears a given and constant relationship to the price level.

Third, some economists hold to a 'less rigid' version of the quantity theory, abandoning the idea that prices bear any definite proportional relationship to the quantity of money. This version of the quantity theory states that if the amount of money (M) increases, prices will rise ; and if M decreases, prices will fall. But there is no attempt to say *by how much* prices will alter as M alters. This is the 'unrigorous' version of the quantity theory.

Since the 'classical' theory of prices takes different forms in the writings of different economists, it will be useful to discuss these three different statements of the quantity theory in some detail. Before this is done, however, there is an important point to be discussed. It is fashionable nowadays to describe the quantity theory of money as a 'truism'—as self-evident. Keynes himself says that 'the quantity theory is a truism which holds in all circumstances, though without significance'.[1] There is much to be learned from discussing the differences between the 'equation of exchange' and the two other versions of the quantity theory of money given above in the light of this description of the 'classical' theory of money. So far as the equation of exchange is concerned, one can go even further than to call it a truism. One may say that the equation of exchange, $MV = PT$, is a tautology. It is true by definition and asserts nothing about causal relationships in the real world. It cannot say what is the cause of any change and what the effect. In other words, it cannot show which is the independent variable and which the dependent variable. This can be seen more clearly from a study of the meaning of the word 'truism'.

The word 'truism' has two distinct meanings. On the one hand, it describes statements which point out an identity between two objects and are therefore true by definition. If someone says 'a cow is a cow', he is saying something which is not only self-

[1] *General Theory*, p. 209.

evident but which must be true by definition. If a cow is defined in a given way, then both cows in the sentence will answer to the same definition. The statement tells us nothing at all about cows but merely repeats a definition. This type of statement is a tautology. It is incapable of adding to knowledge, since it tells us something which is both self-evident and inevitably true.

On the other hand, a truism may tell us something which is trivial and self-evident, but which is not necessarily true. If someone says 'that cow is brown', this is a truism but not a tautology. A cow could be white or black. Now the fact that the cow is brown will be quite obvious to anyone who looks at it, but will not be self-evident to a blind man or to a man a hundred miles away. To say that the cow is brown will be a triviality, a banality, to a man who can see the cow. But if you write to a man living miles away and explain that you have seen a cow which is brown, he will have learned something. You have added to knowledge by writing to him.

A truism may therefore be either a tautology and self-evident, or it may be trivial and obvious but nevertheless not true by definition. In the latter case it would be a truism but not a tautology. One must be careful, in speaking of a truism, to be clear whether one means a tautology or merely a platitude. This applies to the description of the quantity theory as a 'truism'. Some versions of the theory are truisms and can add to our knowledge. Others are mere tautologies and tell us nothing. This is the basis of our distinction between the equation of exchange and the quantity theory proper.

The equation of exchange is a real tautology. It makes no assertion about happenings in the real world. It is simply true by definition. It is not a theory showing the effect of, say, a change in the amount of money on prices in the real world. Thus if we denote the expenditure of the community in a given period by E, the equation of exchange can be written as $E = E$. This is true by definition. For the equation $MV = PT$ merely splits up expenditure in two different ways. From the point of view of the community as consumers, total spending is equal to the money they hold (M) multiplied by the number of times (V) which each unit of it is used during a period. From the point of view of the community as producers the expenditure of the community in the given period is the volume of trade (T) (the number of goods and services exchanged) multiplied by the price (P) at which these transactions take place.

Writing the equation $E = E$ as $MV = PT$ merely means that from the point of view of a set of individuals as consumers, their expenditure can be summed up as $M \times V$. For the same people as producers, expenditure on their output is $P \times T$. The equation $MV = PT$ is true by definition. It is therefore desirable to use the term quantity theory only when one is referring to statements which describe the effect of a given change in the amount of money on prices. The equation $MV = PT$ is not a theory about the behaviour of P in response to changes in M. It merely states an identity.

Nevertheless, whilst it is desirable to make this distinction between the Fisher equation and the 'quantity theory' proper, the equation of exchange is useful. It does split up the expenditure of the community from the point of view of consumers on the one hand, and of producers on the other. It also distinguishes the significant parts of expenditure looked at from these viewpoints. This is important, since by singling out the variables for separate study as a preliminary to considering the effects of changes in M, the equation of exchange shows what are the variables which can be affected when M alters. Indeed, one cannot fully analyse the 'rigid' and 'less rigid' versions of the quantity theory without separating the relevant variables in the way that the 'Fisher Equation' does.

2. THE QUANTITY THEORY OF MONEY

We turn now to the two other examples of 'classical' ideas about the relationship between prices and the amount of money. First we shall consider the 'rigid' quantity theory which states that if the amount of money changes by X per cent, prices will also change by X per cent—and in the same direction. This is not a tautology. It is not true in all circumstances, and exceptions can be thought of quite easily. The theory can therefore be tested, and perhaps refuted. This is important. For even though the theory may not be universally true, it does at least provide a useful basis for a discussion of changes in the general level of prices.

When, then, is the theory likely to be true? The simplest way to show this will be to consider the likely effects of an increase in the supply of money on prices and output in various conditions. Let us assume that there is an increase in the quantity of money in a hypothetical economy, brought about by open-market operations. What will be the effects ? As we have seen earlier, the rate of interest is likely to fall and (given the schedule of the marginal efficiency of capital) investment will rise. Income will therefore rise and this is unlikely to leave output and prices unaffected. If the economy is initially suffering from unemployment, the result of the increase in the supply of money is likely to be a rise of output. Prices, on the other hand, will not rise, so long as the increase in M is accompanied by a sufficient fall in V, or a sufficient rise in T, or both. The 'rigid' quantity theory assumes either that neither V nor T ever alters, or that any change in one is always cancelled out by a change in the other. It is thus invalid where V and T do change. For if V and T do alter, this is clearly not without effect on P. One important function of the equation of exchange is therefore that it does show which factors have to be assumed constant (V and T) if the 'rigid' quantity theory is to hold good.

Where there is unemployment it is likely that the volume of trade will rise as M is increased and the 'rigid' quantity theory is unlikely to hold. Once full employment is reached, however, the rigid theory will come into its own again. T cannot now alter because all resources are employed, and all changes in M must exert their full effect on P. Of course, we here assume that V remains constant after full employment has been reached—that changes in M do not increase V, or, what comes to the same thing, do not reduce liquidity preference. So long as the increase in M and the consequent increases in prices are not serious, V may indeed be constant, and the 'rigid' quantity theory may hold. But if inflation becomes serious, and money becomes progressively more and more valueless, people will spend it more and more quickly in order to avoid being left holding money which is depreciating rapidly. V will therefore rise. If V does rise, the strict version of the quantity theory again fails to explain the situation. For since T must be constant, prices will rise more than in proportion to the increased supply of money.

This type of situation is, however, explained by the 'less rigid' version of the quantity theory. This says that as M rises, prices are likely to rise too, but makes no statement about the extent of such price increases. This 'less rigid' theory holds wherever M and V together are rising more rapidly than T. In conditions of full employment T will be constant and this version of the quantity theory holds whenever M is increased, so long as V does not fall. It will also hold when there is unemployment provided that T does not rise faster than M and V together. Since these conditions are not necessarily compatible with the rigid theory, where M and P must change in exactly the same proportions, we need the less rigorous theory to explain them.

The only possible exception to the quantity theory, whichever the version, would be where prices fell (or remained constant) as the amount of money rose. This might happen where unemployment is great if, when M rises, T rises faster or V falls. Now V is unlikely to fall substantially when T rises. If business activity is increasing it seems improbable that money will change hands less frequently. On the other hand, it is conceivable that in a recovery from a slump, the rise in T may outrun the rise in M and V. But it is unlikely that this will happen very often since industry will usually be subject to diminishing returns, as output rises. The general claim of the quantity theory that an increase in M will not lower P seems likely to hold in most circumstances.

One final point must be made. It is important to distinguish between autonomous changes in V and T and changes induced by alterations in M and P. In the short run, independent (autonomous) changes in V and T are unlikely, whereas in the long run economic progress and changed habits may alter both of them. In the short run, however, changes in the quantity of money can easily induce great changes in T, and more especially in V. Such changes must not be ruled out. Short-run rises in the velocity of circulation in booms and falls in slumps are the cause of serious and damaging fluctuations in activity, employment and prices.

We have now seen in outline what the 'classical' Quantity Theory of Money says. Let us contrast this theory with Keynesian ideas and show what differences there are between the two.

3. INFLATION, OUTPUT AND PRICES IN KEYNESIAN THEORY

As was seen in the previous chapter, Keynesian theory is not simply a theory which explains the causes of unemployment. It is just as relevant (if not more relevant) to the problems of full and over-full employment as the 'classical' Quantity Theory of Money is. There is, however, one rather serious analytical difficulty for Keynesian theory. It is difficult to provide a satisfactory formal definition of inflation. The 'classical' theorists, as we have seen, assumed that full employment always existed, so that any increase in the amount of money would always raise prices. *Any* increase in the supply of money was inflationary. When the supply of money is increased in conditions of large-scale unemployment, however (the usual Keynesian hypothesis), its main effect will be to raise output, not prices. The increase in the amount of money can then scarcely be called inflationary. Yet prices may rise slightly, perhaps because industry is producing under conditions of diminishing returns. Is this slight price rise inflationary? These problems of definition—When is full employment reached? and Where does inflation start?—will be more easily settled, in so far as they can be settled, after we have discussed the behaviour of output and prices in conditions both of unemployment and of full employment.

Let us assume, then, that the amount of money (M) in a hypothetical economy is increased by open-market operations, and that the economy is one where it is always possible for such an increase in the amount of money to increase employment by lowering the rate of interest and hence increasing investment so long as full employment has not been reached. We shall also assume, as a first approximation, that all factors of production are in infinitely elastic supply so long as there is any unemployment and that they are homogeneous and perfectly divisible.

Finally, we assume that effective demand and the amount of money always increase and decrease together in exactly the same proportions. On these assumptions, so long as there is any unemployment, a sufficient increase in M can always bring about full employment. Industry will be producing under constant returns, so that prices will neither rise nor fall as output increases, and output will rise in exact proportion with effective demand whenever effective demand increases. Every increase in M will lower the rate of interest just far enough to cause a sufficient rise in investment to ensure, through multiplier effects, a proportionate rise in effective demand.

Once full employment is reached in this model, output will cease to respond *at all* to changes in the supply of money and in effective demand. The elasticity of supply of output in response to changes in the supply of money, which was infinite as long as there was unemployment, falls to zero. The entire effect of changes in the supply of money is exerted on prices, which rise in exact proportion with the increase in effective demand. On the very simplified assumptions so far made we may conclude, with Keynes, that 'So long as there is unemployment, *employment* will change in the same proportion as the quantity of money;

and when there is full employment *prices* will change in the same proportion as the quantity of money'.[1]

This situation is shown diagrammatically in Figures 123a and 123b. Figure 123a shows the relationship between changes in the supply of money and changes in output. As the amount of money rises from zero to £OQ, physical output rises in proportion and the 'output curve', showing output as a function of the amount of money, is a rising straight line passing through the origin. The slope will depend on production conditions and on

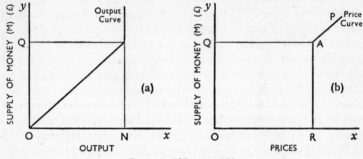

FIGURES 123A AND 123B

the scales on the two axes. Once the amount of money rises to £OQ the full employment output ON is being produced. Any further rise in M can cause no rise in output above ON and the 'output curve' becomes vertical. Figure 123b shows the relationship between prices and the supply of money. So long as the supply of money is less than that amount which causes full employment (*i.e.* £OQ), prices are constant at the level OR. Once the money supply exceeds £OQ, any further rise in M increases prices in exact proportion with the rise in M and the 'price curve' RP becomes a rising straight line. This happens here beyond point A. AP produced would pass through the origin. In this model, then, inflation begins as soon as the amount of money exceeds £OQ. But so long as M is less than £OQ no price rise occurs when M is increased.

The assumptions made so far are of course much too simple to provide more than a very rough approximation to reality. We must now complicate the picture by making the assumptions more realistic. The least realistic assumption is that effective demand always changes in exactly the same proportion as the amount of

[1] *Op. cit.* p. 296.

money. This becomes apparent if one considers the mechanism
by which employment and effective demand are increased as M
rises.

The link between a rise in M and a consequent increase in
effective demand will be the rise in investment, caused by the fall
in the rate of interest brought about now that the increase in M
enables members of the community to satisfy their greater demand
for liquidity at the lower rate of interest. In order for there to be
a fall in the rate of interest, the amount of money held under L^2
must rise, but there is no reason why the fall in the rate of interest
necessary to induce a given absolute increase in output (employment) should always require the same absolute increase in M,
whether effective demand is high or low. Moreover, if the fall
in the rate of interest stimulates investment and, through the
multiplier, causes a rise in effective demand, it is likely that
demand for money under L^1 will rise also because buyers need
more money for current transactions. This may well move the
whole liquidity preference schedule to the right and mean that
the increase in the supply of money is unable to exert its full
influence on the rate of interest and hence on effective demand.
Again, the way in which the increased income resulting from the
new effective demand is shared between rich and poor will affect
the size of the multiplier, and the effect of increased investment on
income. The connection between a change in the supply of money
and the resulting change in output will be nothing like so simple
as we have so far assumed.

The only generalisation one can make with certainty is that an
increase in M is very unlikely to cause a *fall* in effective demand
(or income). Changes in M and in Y are likely to be in the same
direction. But one can make no useful predictions about the
nature of the relationship between them. For this will depend,
among other things, on the effects of a change in M on the conditions determining liquidity preference (*e.g.* business transactions'
demand); on the size of the multiplier; and on the marginal
efficiency of capital schedule—none of which effects can be
predicted with accuracy. To suggest that the relationship
between changes in M and induced changes in effective demand is
not very complex would be misleading.

We must also abandon the assumption of homogeneous
factors of production. This again is not realistic. In the real
world there will be both increasing and decreasing returns. It
seems probable that, over those ranges of output which are

2 I

important in practice, returns are more likely to diminish than to increase, though this need not happen. One can, however, reasonably assume that costs, and hence prices, will begin to rise some time before full employment is reached. One reason why prices may rise, especially during the early stages of recovery from a serious depression, is that prices will probably have been abnormally low, and profits extremely small during the depression. The first stages of recovery may thus raise prices to their pre-depression level, even though no further rise takes place until expansion has gone much further.

We come now to two of the most important practical unrealities of the assumptions we have used so far. We have discussed the possibility of diminishing returns over the whole of the economy causing prices to rise continuously as employment increases. We have seen that such price rises are likely but not inevitable, since there may well be decreasing costs in some industries. But it is very likely in practice that many prices will rise when employment reaches high levels, because certain factors of production are in inelastic supply. Some specialised factors may be in short supply whilst other factors, which are unfortunately not interchangeable with them, are still unemployed. This will cause 'bottlenecks' and will lead to price rises in some sectors of the economy, whilst there are still unemployed resources elsewhere. Thus some factor (and commodity) prices may rise quite sharply long before full employment has been reached.

The other serious practical difficulty is that, apart from these physical 'bottlenecks', Trade Unions are likely to press for higher wages, at least in the more prosperous parts of industry, long before all unemployment has disappeared. This is not a question about which one can ever be dogmatic, but it is reasonable to think that during a slump even the most ardent Trade Union is unlikely to press for higher money wages, concentrating its efforts on maintaining employment. As employment and output rise, however, increases in money wages will probably be obtained, and these will reduce the effect on output of a given rise in M and lead to some price increases. Once full employment is reached, any further rises in money wages will bring a 'spiral' of inflation with wages, prices and the supply of money chasing each other upwards.

To sum up, then, the simplified assumptions with which we set out in our efforts to contrast the behaviour of output, prices and the supply of money in conditions of unemployment and full employment need complicating in four ways. If this is done we shall have a more realistic theoretical framework, and also a more satisfactory basis for discussing the nature of inflation. The four complications are : (1) that changes in effective demand will not normally be in exact proportion to changes in the supply of money ; (2) that returns will usually diminish (or perhaps increase) and will not normally be constant as employment and output rise ; (3) that 'bottlenecks' will often occur before all resources are

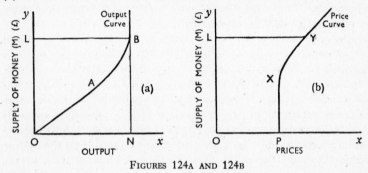

FIGURES 124A AND 124B

employed ; (4) that money wages will usually rise before full employment is reached.

If one imposes these restrictions on the assumptions used so far, the shapes of the curves showing changes in output and prices as a function of changes in the amount of money will not be as shown in Figure 123, but will more probably take the shapes shown in Figure 124.

In Figure 124a as the quantity of money supplied rises above zero, output at first rises proportionately. Once returns begin to diminish, however, and once more and more of the additional money is absorbed by increased liquidity preference as the rate of interest falls lower and lower, output will rise more slowly. When the full employment output ON is neared, bottlenecks will occur and money wages will rise so that the rate of growth of output slackens off considerably. When £OL of money has been pumped into the economy, full employment is reached and output ceases to increase at all as M rises further. The whole effect of the increasing money supply is spent in raising factor and commodity prices. In Figure 124b prices remain constant to begin with as output increases but soon start to rise under the influence of diminishing returns. Towards the level of full employment prices rise more quickly and, once full employment is reached (where $M = £OL$), elasticity of supply of output is zero and prices rise in proportion with the supply of money.

We may now return to the conundrums stated at the beginning of this section. When does inflation begin ? Is it when prices begin to rise ? Or is it when elasticity of supply of output in response to changes in the supply of money is zero? And when is full employment reached ?

In the simple model used earlier, the answers are simple. So long as any factors are unemployed, elasticity of supply of output in response to changes in M (which we shall denote as e_o) equals one.[1] A given proportionate change in M calls forth the same proportionate change in output. When all factors are in use, e_o equals 0. Employment is full. Again, when there is unemployment the elasticity of prices in response to a change in M (which we can denote e_p) is zero. Once employment is full, $e_p = 1$. Prices begin to rise in proportion with M and inflation has begun.

In the case portrayed in Figure 124, however, the problem is more complicated. In Figure 124a, below point A on the output curve (showing the effect of changes in M on output), $e_o = 1$. Above point B, $e_o = 0$. It therefore seems reasonable to call B the point where full employment is reached. Employment is full at every point beyond B, that is when M is greater than $£OL$. *We may therefore define full employment, theoretically, as occurring when the elasticity of supply of output in response to increases in the supply of money (or alternatively in effective demand) is zero.* One difficulty, however, is that in practice it rarely proves possible for an economy to reach the point where $e_o = 0$. There is always frictional unemployment ; some men are always changing jobs. There may well be structural or voluntary unemployment too. The idea that full employment only occurs when 100 per cent of the labour force is employed, and $e_o = 0$, is useless in practice. Nevertheless it seems desirable to have an unambiguous theoretical definition of full employment. And even in practice everyone would agree that (to refer again to Figure 124a) full employment would occur much nearer to B than to A.

Just as it is difficult to define full employment, there is a similar difficulty in defining inflation. Nevertheless, when there is full employment a rise in the supply of money is always accompanied by a rise in prices. If there is full employment, one may

---

[1] Keynes uses the same symbols in the *General Theory*, especially in chapters xx and xxi. But he uses them to show the response of output and prices to changes in *effective demand* and not, as we have, to changes in the supply of money.

therefore justifiably call a situation inflationary when either prices or the supply of money are rising, because in practice both will normally rise together. Referring again to Figure 124b, it is clear that, in the situation there shown, no-one could ever describe the increase in M as inflationary below point X on the 'price curve'. Nor could there be doubt that the situation is inflationary above point Y. It is the range between X and Y which causes trouble. As we have seen, the existence of 'bottlenecks' and the fact that money wages will begin to rise before full employment is reached means that there is here a modified inflation—what may aptly be called a 'cost inflation' because costs are rising. 'True inflation', as Keynes calls it, only begins when the elasticity of supply of output in response to changes in $M(e_o)$ falls to zero.

We see, then, that in practice there is no complete dichotomy between conditions of stability and of inflation, as there is in the simplified model used above. It is clear that conditions are unambiguously inflationary when output is completely unresponsive to changes in the money supply. But below this level even if prices are rising one cannot regard such rising prices as being entirely harmful, though they would be if they were not accompanied by *any* increase in output. Rising prices are the penalty paid by society for the increase in output and prices must rise if extra output is to be obtained.

So much, then, for the problem of defining conditions at, above and below the critical point of full employment. If there is full employment and/or inflation, the doctrines of the classical economists, of the kind outlined earlier, come back into their own. In particular the quantity theory of money is able to explain what is happening. But when increases in the supply of money have no effect on prices and merely increase output, the quantity theory of money has nothing to say. Nor can it tell us very much about what is happening when prices and output are both rising. It is only when employment is full, when output ceases to rise, and T in the 'Fisher Equation' is therefore constant so that an increase in the supply of money can only affect prices, that Keynes accepts the quantity theory as agreeing with his own ideas.

But even with full employment the agreement between Keynesian and 'classical' ideas is only an agreement about effects and not about causes. There is still a fundamental difference between the two schools in their views about the link between rising prices on the one hand, and increasing money supply on the other. In 'classical' theory, the increased money supply is regarded as raising prices directly. For Keynes, on the other hand, the crucial factor is the effect of the increased supply of money in lowering the rate of interest *below* the level at which (in conjunction with the marginal efficiency of capital) it will stimulate sufficient investment to create full employment. Once full employment is reached, any further fall in the rate of interest cannot increase the volume of *real* investment and *real* consumption. It merely raises the money prices of goods.

In conditions of full employment, then, the quantity theory in its strict form does apply. T is constant, for the elasticity of output in response to increasing M is now zero. So long as there is no serious inflation, V in the 'Fisher Equation' can be taken as constant also. If inflation does become serious, however, the strict quantity theory ceases to apply. V tends to rise and it is only the 'unrigorous' version of the quantity theory which has anything to say about the relationship between prices and the supply of money. Extreme inflation has never occurred recently in Britain or the U.S.A., but has not been uncommon in Central European countries during the 1920's and the 1940's. Keynes deals with cases of such *hyperinflation* very briefly.

The main feature of hyperinflation is that money loses almost all its value. Prices rise to fantastic levels, and the velocity of circulation becomes enormous. Money is losing value so rapidly that people are unwilling to hold it for more than a few moments. One of the chief dangers of such inflation lies in a failure to appreciate its power. For the strict quantity theory overlooks the vital part which changes in V can exert when the increase in the supply of money is considerable. If the amount of money doubles, it is possible that prices will only double—that V will remain constant and that it is only the direct effect of M on P which need be considered. But a much larger increase in M, such as occurs in hyperinflation, will certainly raise V. This in turn will raise prices more than in proportion to the initial rise in M. If the supply of money is increased to ten times its original amount, prices are not likely to become only ten times as high. They may rise to a thousand or even a hundred thousand times the old level because the velocity of circulation will become very large.

Put into Keynesian language, what has happened is this. The velocity of circulation is really the obverse of liquidity preference. If the demand for money is high, then money circulates slowly, V is low, and *vice versa*. Changes in V are, so to speak, the external manifestation of changes in liquidity preference. It is therefore possible to explain the fall in liquidity preference, induced by a large increase in M, in terms of ordinary Keynesian analysis. The explanation is familiar. When prices rise beyond a certain point, people begin to speculate on the likelihood of a continuing price rise. This is not important in normal times, for liquidity preference is then unresponsive to changes in commodity prices. If commodity prices rise sharply and at an increasing rate, however, people realise that the only possible result will be that money will become quite valueless. Liquidity preference therefore falls off sharply.

Depending on how quickly they see the signs of this runaway inflation, people make a serious attempt to spend as much cash as they possibly can and buy goods instead. Instead of holding bank notes and deposits, they buy grand pianos and art treasures. Explaining this in terms of the conventional motives for liquidity, we may say that there has now been a large change of data. Formerly bonds were a close substitute for money. Now bonds are just as useless as money is. Since they bear interest fixed in terms of money, and since they are only redeemable in terms of money, bonds and money become equally valueless. As a result, no-one bothers to hold money for speculation on the Stock Exchange. Everyone buys 'real' assets of kinds which they think will best retain their value after the inflation is over. Since to hold either money or bonds is to risk loss, the speculative and precautionary motives for holding money vanish. Everyone holds goods.

The transactions motive is likely to survive rather longer in hyperinflation. Even though it is foolish to use money as a store of value, it can be used as a medium of exchange. The inconvenience of barter makes people use money for this purpose for as long as possible. Nevertheless, even though money is still used as the medium of exchange, the amount held under the transactions motive will increase much less than in proportion to rises in prices. Workers paid weekly will spend all their earnings immediately they receive them. If they keep money for a day, or even an hour, prices will have risen. The effect may even be that workers demand to be paid daily instead of weekly. So even the demand for money to satisfy the transactions motive falls off sharply.

The concept of liquidity preference is therefore able to explain hyperinflation as satisfactorily as it explains normal monetary conditions. The change of data has, however, been substantial.

In these conditions, unless there is a sharp reversal of monetary policy and liquidity preference is increased considerably, it is certain that the existing type of money will be unable to maintain its position as money for much longer.

These, then, are Keynes' main ideas about inflation. There are one or two further questions which remain open. First, there is one very important question about full employment. If an economy recovers from a slump by increasing the supply of money and raising effective demand, is it possible for the economy to stop the expansionary process at, or just before, full employment is reached ? Many people think that the economy will overshoot the full employment level, enjoy a temporary boom, and then relapse into depression once monetary support is taken away. Alternatively, it is sometimes argued that if the expansion in the supply of money is halted before full employment is reached, a slump may ensue without a preceding inflationary boom. Yet other people think that if the increase in the money supply is gradually tapered off as full employment is approached (and perhaps a slight rise in the rate of interest is allowed), it may be possible for an economy to settle at a high-level equilibrium with full employment. There is no certain answer to this question. Yet it is obviously an important one from the point of view of economic policy.

Second, it is often argued that prices must rise slowly but continuously if full employment is to be maintained. Many people feel that unless there is slight inflationary pressure all the time, deflation will develop. As a corollary to this, it is argued that it would be rash, in such an inflation, to raise the rate of interest in order to discourage investment, as this might begin a deflation. It is often maintained that direct control of investment is essential—that it is better to keep the interest rate low enough to encourage a large number of entrepreneurs to invest, and then make them queue to avoid causing inflation by attempting too much investment, rather than to raise the rate of interest in an attempt to ensure that the queue is of just the right length. For once the rate of interest is allowed to rise from the low level of the 'cheap money' era which caused full employment, there is a danger that it may be difficult to lower again. Liquidity preference may alter, if people lose faith in the Government's ability to maintain 'cheap money' permanently and begin to fear capital losses as successive Chancellors of the Exchequer retreat from and return to a low interest rate policy.

One final point about liquidity preference in such conditions is worth mentioning. Perhaps if the Government, having succeeded in its drive for a low rate of interest, continues to increase the supply of money in order to maintain this low rate, liquidity preference may change in such a way as to absorb all the extra cash. But it is quite conceivable that some of the extra money may spill over into the purchase of securities representing new investment. If full employment is reached, however, and if there is direct control of investment, this may not be possible. The effect of the increasing money supply may be merely to cause other new vents for money to be opened. Keynes always assumed that the only real substitute for holding money was buying bonds. But where a 'cheap money' policy is being pursued, a further alternative to holding money or bonds may develop. Money may be transferred to the purchase of consumer goods. This possibility was not discussed by Keynes. But if it does happen, and it may if a cheap money policy is pursued for any length of time and causes significant price rises, it may modify the rigid Keynesian doctrine that people must either hold money in cash or use it to buy bonds. They may decide to buy durable goods and hold them in order to sell again when prices of such goods have risen. People may have more faith in the continuance of inflation than in the continuance of low rates of interest.

4. MONEY WAGES AND EMPLOYMENT

The final problem which we must consider in this discussion of the theory of employment is the relationship between changes in money wages and in employment. We saw in Chapter XVII that one of the main points at issue between Keynes and the 'classical' economists was whether a cut in money wages would increase employment. We saw there that workers are usually much less willing to accept a cut in money wages than to accept a cut in real wages. In practice, therefore, cuts in money wages are resisted strongly and, as we saw, often justifiably. But it is desirable that we should show whether those economists who maintain that a cut in money wages will increase employment are *theoretically* right. The suggestion that wages should be cut may be so objectionable that a wage cut cannot be put into practice— perhaps because of the money illusion. But it is nevertheless interesting to discover whether there is any *theoretical* justification for the view that wage cuts could increase employment. The reason why we have had to postpone a discussion of this 'classical' idea that a reduction in money wages will increase employment is that the analysis of the effects of such a cut in money wages is much more complicated than one might suppose. For the indirect effects, which classical theory ignored, are very important.

The 'classical' explanation of the effect of wages cuts is a relatively simple one. If wages fall, the prices of the products made by labour fall too. This will increase output, to an extent depending on the rate at which the marginal revenue productivity of labour is diminishing—on the elasticity of demand for labour. It is possible to interpret such a statement as meaning that when money wages are cut, the demand for the products of labour as a whole is unaffected. But whilst this view is correct for a single industry, it is unrealistic for industry as a whole. Fortunately it is not necessary to make such unlikely assumptions to support the claim that a fall in money wages may increase employment. If money wages fall, prices will fall somewhat, and this will increase the demand *in real terms* of those people who derive their income from profits, rent and interest. Again, although money wages have fallen, the amount of money earned by labour as a whole can rise provided only that the elasticity of demand for labour is greater than unity.

Nevertheless, economists who believe that a cut in money wages will increase employment probably ignore the effects of such wage cuts on effective demand. As we have just seen, it is possible to interpret the idea of the 'classical' economists in such a way as to show that effective demand will in fact increase, in real terms, provided the fall in wages reduces prices. But, in general, the 'classical' economists tended to ignore the problem of whether aggregate effective demand would or would not be stimulated by falling money wages.

Arguing from the fact that a cut in money wages in a single industry will increase employment, some economists hence argued that a cut in wages in *all* industries would increase employment in *all* industries. But whilst in particular equilibrium analysis one is justified in taking the demand for the product of an individual industry as given, there is no such justification when one considers all industries. The demand for the product of any one industry ultimately depends on the wages paid to, and amounts of money spent by, workers in other industries. A general equilibrium analysis of wage cuts is futile unless it pays great attention to the problem of whether aggregate demand will rise or fall as wages are reduced. The question we must answer is, Will aggregate effective demand in terms of money remain constant, or if it comes to the worst, will it fall less than in proportion to the cut in money wages? If the answer is yes, employment will rise when wages are cut; but if it is no, employment will fall. We must therefore pass now to an analysis of the way in which effective demand will respond to a cut in money wages.

The 'classical' economists, by neglecting the role of effective demand in their analysis of changes in money wages, seemed to assume that there was some direct link between falling wages and rising employment. We have seen, however, that in Keynesian analysis one always considers the effect on employment of any change in the economy, by seeing what happens to the three main determinants of employment—the propensity to consume; the rate of interest; and the marginal efficiency of capital. If we can discover the way in which a change in money wages will affect these three variables, we shall have solved the problem.

Keynes thought that the main repercussions would be as follows. First, a reduction in money wages will presumably reduce prices, the extent of the reduction depending on the nature of supply conditions, and especially on the proportion of wages to total production costs. This will mean a certain amount of redistribution of real income from wage earners to those members of the community whose money incomes have not been reduced. Keynes guessed that the net effect would probably be to reduce the propensity to consume. For wage earners are likely to consume more of their income than other (probably richer) sections of the community.

Second, if entrepreneurs believe that although money wages have fallen now they will rise in the future, this will be favourable to employment. For if entrepreneurs believe that this will happen, they will feel more optimistic about future prospects and the marginal efficiency of capital will rise. Again, the fact that money wages and therefore prices are expected to rise in the future will make it desirable to buy consumer goods now rather than later, and this may temporarily raise the propensity to consume. If, on the other hand, the fact that wages have fallen is taken as an indication that they will fall even further in the near future, this will tend to reduce employment; for the marginal efficiency of capital will probably be depressed. Entrepreneurs will regard future prospects for selling consumption goods as less rosy. This will also encourage consumers to postpone consumption until further wage reductions have reduced prices.

Third, the fact that the wage bill has fallen and that prices, and perhaps some other incomes, have fallen, will mean a reduction in liquidity preference. The demand for money under the income and business motives will probably fall. This will lower the rate of interest, if the supply of money is not reduced. Thus investment will be stimulated. If it is expected that wages and prices will continue to fall, this may lead to expectations of further similar falls in the rate of interest and will tend to reduce the demand for money for speculative purposes also. If, however, it is thought that wages are likely to rise again, the reduction in the rate of interest will be less marked, especially on long-term bonds.[1]

Fourth, there is the possibility that a reduction in money wages may make entrepreneurs optimistic (perhaps irrationally) and this may raise the marginal efficiency of capital and increase investment. On the other hand, if workers become despondent about their position, an outbreak of labour troubles may well offset this favourable reaction.

Fifth, the effect of falling prices on the burden of debt may be unfavourable. If prices fall far enough, entrepreneurs may be unable to pay debenture holders their statutory dues, and firms may fall into the hands of the receivers. Again, the burden of the National Debt—largely made up of fixed interest-bearing securities—will become important. High taxation will sap business confidence. The effect of both these factors will be to reduce investment. Finally, we must point out that we are concerned in this book with a 'closed system'. In practice, the main favourable effects of a reduction in money wages are likely to come from the effect on the exporting industries, which can now sell their goods more cheaply as compared with foreigners.

If we confine our attention to a 'closed economy', we see that the main hope of increased investment lies either in a rise in the marginal efficiency of capital or in a fall in the rate of interest. Let us consider these possibilities more carefully. There is a hope that if wages are thought to have fallen to 'rock bottom', the effect may be to raise the marginal efficiency of capital—since entrepreneurs look forward to a time of rising prices and activity, and since current consumption is stimulated by people who hope to forestall expected price rises by buying now. The worst

[1] See Keynes, *op. cit.* p. 263.

possible situation is one where wages and prices are expected to continue a slow but steady slide downwards. In practice this might well happen. It would be unreasonable to expect Trade Unions to agree to meet each slump by a substantial all-round reduction in money wages. Trade Unionists (rightly) believe that the incomes of rentiers and entrepreneurs would not undergo an equal fall, and the desire for social justice remains a real force in the Trade Union movement. What is more likely to happen is a slow downward movement of wages as one section of workers after another allows the forces of depression to break down its resistance to wage reductions. Since a once-and-for-all wage reduction is out of the question, it seems likely, so far as effects on the marginal efficiency of capital are concerned, that a policy of keeping money wages rigid is the best one.

There remains the rate of interest. What can one hope for here? If the amount of money falls as money wages fall, one can hope for little. But if the quantity of money can be kept stable when the level of wages falls, the fact that the demand for money under the transactions motive also falls will reduce the rate of interest. Keynes therefore concludes that it should be possible to exert a beneficial influence on the rate of interest by lowering money wages but keeping the supply of money constant—though here again the adverse effects of falling wages on the marginal efficiency of capital, and the difficulty of lowering the rate of interest below the point where liquidity preference becomes infinite, are important. As Keynes says, 'a moderate reduction in money wages may prove inadequate, whilst an immoderate reduction might shatter confidence even if it were practicable'.[1] Thus the really crucial point is that there is no reason to hope for any greater success in lowering the rate of interest, and hence increasing investment by reducing the level of money wages, than by increasing the supply of money. In fact, there are three substantial practical objections to a 'flexible wage policy' as an alternative to the open-market 'flexible money policy'. These objections are as follows.

First, as we have suggested, it is quite unreasonable to expect that Trade Unions will (or should) accept all-round reductions in money wages of equal size for every class of labour. In democratic states, the accepted system of collective bargaining between individual unions and employers' associations means that any wage reductions would be piecemeal—the workers in the worst bargain-

[1] *Op. cit.* p. 267.

ing position suffering most seriously and most quickly. The institutions of democratic societies are such that it is much easier to affect interest rates by open-market operations than by cuts in money wages. A dictatorship might succeed, a democracy never would. One can imagine such a policy succeeding in Russia but not in Britain or the United States.

Second, for reasons of social justice also it is unreasonable to expect workers alone to accept cuts in money wages. Such cuts must inevitably increase the relative standard of living of other sections of the community. So far as social justice is concerned it seems desirable that, since some classes in the community have their income fixed in terms of money, all classes should have incomes fixed in such a way. A policy of increasing the supply of money in time of depression would probably be preferable to cutting wages, since, assuming that money wages remained constant, it would mean that members of all classes would suffer much the same change in real incomes as prices rose.

A final practical objection to a policy of flexible money wages is that it would increase the real burden of debt, whilst a policy of increasing the supply of money would reduce that burden. And there can be no doubt that an increased burden of debt in most communities would place an intolerable burden on debtors.

So far as a closed system is concerned it is certain that the best short-run policy is to keep money wages as stable as possible. For, apart from the serious practical objections listed above, the effect on the marginal efficiency of capital of steadily sagging wage and price levels is likely to be so bad that employment will be seriously affected. Stable wages and prices, however, will prevent the expectations of entrepreneurs becoming unduly pessimistic. The effect of stable money wages will be to reduce the extent of fluctuations in employment even though they cannot be prevented entirely. In the long run, when production is likely to rise steadily, one can choose between constant wage levels and slowly-falling prices or constant prices and slowly-rising money wages. But in practice, long-run problems tend to be less important than those of the short run.

How, then, can one sum up the debate between Keynes and the classical economists on the problem of whether money wages should be allowed to fall? The 'classical' theory, as one would expect, applies in the case of an individual industry. The partial equilibrium analysis holds so long as other things are equal. And the most important 'other thing' is the demand for the industry's product. When one is considering a single industry, it is reasonable to assume that demand is unaffected when wages in that industry are cut. When one turns to the question of all industries, however, the problem of what happens to aggregate effective demand is a crucial one.

Keynes shows that his quarrel with the earlier economists about the effects of cuts in wages was not so much over conclusions as over methods of analysis. In certain circumstances it is theoretically possible for reductions in money wages to increase employment, though in fact such reductions may be impracticable. But a complete answer can only be given if attention is paid to *all* repercussions, and especially to repercussions on the Keynesian determinants of employment—the propensity to consume, the marginal efficiency of capital and the rate of interest. It was in failing to realise how these vital determinants of employment interact that pre-Keynesian employment theory showed its real weakness.

SUGGESTED READING

Geoffrey Crowther, *Outline of Money*, London, 1940, chapter iv.

D. H. Robertson, *Money*, London, 1948, chapter ii.

J. M. Keynes, *General Theory*, London, 1936, chapters xix, xx and xxi.

Dudley Dillard, *The Economics of J. M. Keynes*, London, 1950, chapters ix and x.

A. P. Lerner, *The Economics of Control*, New York, 1946, chapters xxii and xxiii.

J. M. Keynes, 'Relative Movements of Real Wages and Output', *Economic Journal*, 1939, p. 34.

Ralph Turvey, 'Some Aspects of Inflation in a Closed Economy', *Economic Journal*, 1951, p. 531.

CONCLUSION

WE can now make some general comments on what we have tried to do in this book. One way of summing up the difference between the analysis of Part One and that of Part Two is to say that the former was concerned with the Economics of Scarcity, the latter with the Economics of Waste. In Part One we assumed that all resources in the community were fully employed, and that to set more resources to producing one commodity must inevitably mean that less of another commodity was being made. In Part Two we were concerned with what can be described as the Economics of Waste. We showed that an economy can have many unemployed resources—men and machines—which could have been usefully employed producing goods for the community but are left idle because the level of activity is not high enough to keep them all fully at work. This distinction is clearly an over-simplification ; but to describe Part One as studying scarcity and Part Two as studying waste is quite useful.

In the price theory of Part One we spent most of our time discussing particular equilibrium analysis and our theory was, therefore, Marshallian in the sense of being partial equilibrium analysis. We usually confined our attention to one market at a time and did not trouble to try to connect these particular markets up in a general equilibrium system. The reason why we spent so much time discussing this kind of economics, which pervades Marshall's *Principles of Economics*, is that the *Principles* is the only book from Marshall's generation which has remained a true standard work. We have, of course, said a great deal about ideas to be found in more recent writings, especially those of Mrs. Robinson and Professor Chamberlin, but all this kind of analysis is Marshallian in a broad sense. It is all particular equilibrium analysis. That is not to say, of course, that nothing has been written on general equilibrium analysis. In Marshall's own day Walras [1] and Pareto [2] were particularly interested in general equilibrium analysis, and at the moment Hicks' *Value and Capital*

---

[1] See his *Éléments d'économie politique*, Lausanne, 1874.
[2] See his *Manuel d'économie politique pure*, Paris, 1909.

gives a good standard treatment of general equilibrium. But in English (and American) economics particular equilibrium analysis has always held pride of place.

Part Two was concerned with employment theory and we therefore spent most of our time in a discussion of Keynes' *General Theory of Employment, Interest and Money*. Our action in spending almost the whole of Part Two in discussing the analysis in this one book is probably rather more contentious than that of discussing 'Marshallian economics' in Part One, and probably needs more justification. Nevertheless it is fair to say that Keynes' book was revolutionary in the sense that it caused great consternation in economic circles. We have not been primarily interested in what Keynes' predecessors may or may not have said about the likelihood of full employment. Our main concern has been to show what the Keynesian analysis is about, and to explain the many concepts which Keynes used. The reason for this is that if one is to understand contemporary discussions of employment theory, it is essential first of all to master the essential parts of Keynes' terminology.

For this reason we have avoided some of the more obscure parts of the Keynesian terminology. In particular, we have avoided any discussion of Keynesian *wage units* which he used as a simplifying device. Nor have we discussed *user cost* in anything like the detail in which Keynes considered it. Readers who are interested in these concepts should consult the *General Theory* itself.

But the real reason why we did not spend time in Part Two summarising other recent works on employment theory is that there is no post-Keynesian orthodoxy. There is no single work, and no single author, whose views on employment theory one can summarise instead of Keynes' own ideas as they appear in the *General Theory*. It should also be realised that Keynes' influence on practical affairs was (and still is) far greater than that of any other twentieth-century economist. The importance of Keynes' analysis for the history of economic doctrines lies especially in the fact that his theory was so readily applicable to contemporary problems. In particular, the analysis put forward in the *General Theory*—an analysis which had been intended to provide an explanation of the mass unemployment of the 1930's—was destined to play a vital part in enabling Great Britain to overcome the inflationary stresses of the Second World War. To a smaller degree it has underlain post-war fiscal policy. Readers who are

2 K

interested in Keynes' influence on practical affairs are referred to
the relevant chapter in Professor Dillard's book *The Economics of
J. M. Keynes*,[1] and also to Mr. R. F. Harrod's exhaustive biography
The Life of John Maynard Keynes.[2]

We pointed out in the Introduction that the value of economic
theory lies in providing a framework of analysis which can be
used by applied economists in interpreting facts about the real
world. It will probably be best to say something now about the
usefulness of economic theory, of the kind which we have outlined
in helping to analyse such practical problems. It will be remembered that our main underlying assumption has been that of
'rationality'. We have assumed in particular that consumers
always strive to obtain the greatest possible satisfaction from
spending their incomes, and that business men always try to
make as much money as possible. Some economists have criticised this concept of rationality and have suggested that it is not
a useful hypothesis about the real world. So far as consumers are
concerned, one's views naturally depend to some extent on one's
beliefs about human psychology. But there must be few people
who would claim that the great majority of consumers attempt to
derive as little satisfaction as they can from spending their limited
incomes. Admittedly some consumers may not know what is
best for themselves, and spend their money on goods which
actually harm them, whilst others may buy goods which they expect
will give them satisfaction, but which in fact do not. But, in
general, the assumption we have made seems a sensible one.

The assumption of rationality in the theory of the firm has
been much more severely criticised. It has been suggested that
to claim that all business men want to maximise profits is ridiculous.[3] Critics of the marginal analysis seem to make their attacks
on two main lines. On the one hand, it is suggested that entrepreneurs do not wish to make as much money as possible—that
business men are not greedy calculating machines. On the other
hand, it has been suggested that since business men can never be
quite sure about the demand conditions for their product, even
if they know what cost conditions are, they will only be producing
an output which they *think* maximises profits and this need not
be an output which actually *does* maximise profits.

The first criticism is quite justifiable. It is perfectly possible

[1] Chapter xii.   [2] London, 1951.
[3] See, for example, P. W. S. Andrews, *Manufacturing Business*, London,
1949.

that many business men do not wish to maximise profits, but the assumption of 'rationality' amongst business men seems a most reasonable one to make until empirical research provides a better hypothesis ; and so far it has failed to provide one. The second criticism is rather more difficult to deal with. If business men are not sure what the demand and cost conditions for their product really are, they may well go on for a considerable length of time producing outputs which do not maximise profits. Yet since they are not certain what line of action really would maximise profits there is very little they can do to improve matters. This kind of situation is especially likely to occur wherever there is oligopoly. It probably accounts for the belief current among economists that in such situations entrepreneurs are content to go on charging existing prices for their product, so long as they make reasonable profits. Entrepreneurs may well fear that any change will be for the worse.[1]

A further type of hypothesis about the real world which applied economists would have to test before making confident generalisations would be, for example, Keynes' view that in the main a community's liquidity preference depends on the demand for money for the speculative motive. Such an assumption may well be wrong and it is the job of the applied economist to put this kind of hypothesis to the test by comparing it with real-world experience.

Whatever they think about the actual assumptions made in current economic theory, however, applied economists will generally find it useful to discuss their problems by using the so-called 'tools of analysis' which we have used. For example, in discussing problems concerning the prices of such things as basic raw materials and foodstuffs, it is impossible to produce really sensible generalisations without analysing the problem in terms of demand and supply, and elasticity of demand and supply. Similarly, economists considering the effects of changes in Government expenditure on investment projects will find it necessary to make use of the concept of the multiplier. In particular, it would be necessary to provide some fairly precise measurement of the size of the multiplier in practice.

We may, lastly, consider the usefulness of economic theory in

[1] Readers who are anxious to see what has been written about this subject in economic periodicals should consult the list of articles given in D. C. Hague, 'Economic Theory and Business Behaviour', *Review of Economic Studies*, 1949-1950, vol. xvi, p. 144 (footnote).

helping in the formulation of economic policy. It might be thought that, since in the post-war world market conditions have been abnormal, with inflation existing throughout the world in greater or smaller degree, price theory of the kind outlined in Part One would be useless. It is true, of course, that post-war conditions have been very different from conditions before 1939, but it remains true that ordinary price theory (suitably handled) can deal with all the important price problems of the present day. Similarly, it might be thought that Keynesian unemployment theory is of little value in the post-war world. At the time when this book goes to press the problem of waste, in the sense of general unemployment, is almost completely absent. Employment is full, or more than full, in nearly every country. But we have seen that Keynesian theory is quite capable of analysing the problems of inflation. It is also quite possible that the full employment existing today may itself be partly the result of the fact that Keynes' influence on practical affairs was so very strong, and that some (at least) of his theories are being put into practice.

We have shown in this book, then, that in order to analyse economic problems one must first build up models of economic systems which approximate to reality, without being unnecessarily complicated. One must attempt to make general assumptions which lay bare the essentials of the system. The models which we have used here are not necessarily those which are most appropriate to any particular economic system. It is perfectly possible that our assumptions, even though they are generally used, do not apply to the real world of the present day. But this does not mean that a study of the models themselves is not useful. What we have tried to do is to give readers a general picture of the way in which economic models can be built up, and the kind of assumptions which have to underlie them. The reader who has mastered the analysis of this book will have seen how such models can be constructed and handled. He will therefore be able to construct his own hypothetical economies for himself and to use his own models to solve the problems in which he is most interested, making those assumptions which in his view come closest to reality.

FURTHER READING

Readers who wish to continue their study of economic theory might well read the following books, most of them recently published. Parts of some of these books have already been recommended in reading lists to individual chapters.

R. G. D. Allen, *Mathematical Analysis for Economists*, London, 1937.

J. S. Duesenberry, *Income, Saving and the Theory of Consumer Behaviour*, Cambridge, Mass., 1949.

William Fellner, *Competition among the Few*, New York, 1949.

A. H. Hansen, *Business Cycles and National Income*, New York, 1951.

Bent Hansen, *A Study in the Theory of Inflation*, London, 1951.

J. R. Hicks, *Value and Capital* (2nd Edition), Oxford, 1946.

J. R. Hicks, *A Contribution to the Theory of the Trade Cycle*, Oxford, 1950.

Oscar Lange, *Price Flexibility and Employment*, Bloomington, Ind., 1944.

A. P. Lerner, *The Economics of Control*, New York, 1946.

P. A. Samuelson, *The Foundations of Economic Analysis*, Cambridge, Mass., 1947.

J. A. Schumpeter, *Capitalism, Socialism and Democracy*, New York, 1947.

J. A. Schumpeter, *The Theory of Economic Development*, New York, 1934.

INDEX